Lyn,

Your review thanks
for the ...
of the ... journey.

All the best

...

Successive Journeys:
A family in four continents

Nicholas Herbert

(Lord Hemingford)

Bright Pen

Visit us online at www.authorsonline.co.uk

ISBN 978-07552-0432-8

Authors OnLine Ltd
19 The Cinques
Gamlingay, Sandy
Bedfordshire SG19 3NU
England

This book is also available in e-book format, details of which are available at
www.authorsonline.co.uk

For Jenny,

who bravely married into this tribe

*The family tree at Hemingford
Abbots.*

Great families of yesterday we show,
And Lords whose parents were the Lord knows who.
[Daniel Defoe: *The True-born Englishman.*]

CONTENTS

Prologue   1

Part I – The Herberts

1.   From Egleton to Camberwell   5

2.   On the Lincoln circuit   10

3.   From Oxford to the Marshalsea   16

4.   From King's Lynn to Biggleswade   20

5.   From Bermondsey to Bedford & Exeter   29

6.   Cambridge, Cadiz, Buenos Aires & Asuncion   37

7.   From the Welsh Marches to Cambridge   48

8.   From Ramsholt to Wallstown   55

9.   From Stockland Bristol to Tiverton & Reading   59

10. From Portugal, via Leghorn, to Dorking   75

11. Via Capetown to Hemingford Abbots   84

12. Siam, Paardeberg, Egypt, Salonika & Manea   99

13. From Watford to Westminster   117

14. Calcutta, Ceylon & Wales   142

Part II – The Bells

15. A Dawn Raid   155

16. From London to Nagpore & Shanghai   166

17. From Edinburgh to Bloomsbury   182

18. From the Alps to Cadiz & Spanish Town   186

19. From Galway to the Rio Cobre, Hamburg to Haiti
& Bombay to the Seychelles.   196

20. From Inverness to Darien & Farenough   204

21. From South Shields to New York & Chateau Pen   207

CONTENTS (Continued)

22.From Wexford to Nova Scotia & Jamaica   212

23.From Bristol to Antigua & Rhode Island   215

24.From Kingston to Watford & Hemingford Abbots   219

Part III – TheClarks

25.From the Merse to Featherstone   229

26.From Bellister to Ashcroft   240

27.From Haltwhistle to all four continents   250

Part IV – The Jacksons

28.From Carmunnock to Hexham   270

29.From Hexham to Haltwhistle   280

Part V – Dennis & Elizabeth

30.From Ardmore to Bramston   287

31.From the Nursery to the Altar   294

32.From Watford to the Gold Coast   306

33.From London to Beirut, Djibouti & Budo   323

34.From Reform to Revolution   330

35.From Uganda to Ghana   346

36.From Africa to Huntingdonshire   359

Acknowledgements   376

Sources   377

Index   379

PROLOGUE

The thought of a family history causes the stoutest literary heart to sink. Will it be snobbish? Why ask: of course it will. In everybody's pedigree there is a Mary Ann Snooks from the cottage under the hill, from whom we draw exactly the same number of genes as we do from the patrician head of the house; but Mary Ann Snooks does not keep journals or write letters and history must be drawn from those who do.- Priscilla Napier: The Sword Dance.

My two grandfathers, both respectable, upwardly mobile Victorians, were as different in temperament as could be. Dennis Henry Herbert, for example, chewed every mouthful thirty-three times and very often pre-conditioned any meat with which he was faced by making little indentations in it with his knife before committing it to mouth. John McClare Clark, on the other hand, rarely seemed to chew his food at all and frequently found himself, in the interests of politeness, chasing a lone green pea round his plate for ten minutes at the end of the course. He was famous for having covered his porridge with a layer of cream and then, having been diverted by some conversation, loading eggs and bacon on top of it, assuming that the plate was empty.

Faced with a joint, their techniques were equally different. Dennis would proceed, after some preliminary sharpenings, to cut very slowly and precisely, slices of the utmost delicacy, so paper-thin that, if they had been held up to the light, I am sure they would have been translucent. John Clark's more robust approach produced portions that were less elegant, but retained some of the warmth of the cooking, which was lost in Dennis's technique.

Dennis, when I knew him, had a rather sedate Morris 10 with blue upholstery, which he drove with what my mother later described as "bloodcurdling caution". This was exemplified in his reaction to a vehicle coming up behind. As soon as he detected it in the rear view mirror, he would pull into the side of the road and wait for it to pass. This was not so bad on many a rolling English road, but if he happened to catch a glimpse of something one or two hills away, it made progress agonisingly slow. John Clark, long before I knew him, acquired a Singer which, when he first drove it, collided with a tree. He thereupon gave up driving forever and employed a chauffeur named Sutherland instead.

1

John McClare, I suspect always preferred horseback. There is a story about him going out collecting rents with a needle, left by a careless seamstress, in his breeches. This, allegedly, worked its way into his posterior so far that it could only be retrieved at the end of the day by his brother-in-law pulling it out by the thread! On the other hand, there is no evidence that Dennis was ever on a horse - certainly no photograph survives showing him in the saddle. The two men were also physically opposites. John Clark was of average height, thickset and a little florid of countenance. Dennis Herbert was tall, thin and, if not exactly sallow, was inclined to be pale.

My grandmothers I find much more difficult to compare. One of them, Mary Graeme Bell, who married Dennis Herbert, I knew very well; the other, Marion Jackson, died 17 years before I was born, a death which was so traumatic for the Clark family that she was rarely spoken about. They differed, of course, in longevity. Mary, or May as she was known, lived to be 83; Marion died at 39. May's marriage lasted 42 years, Marion's only 16. May had only two siblings, Marion had 15. May was already much travelled when she married a husband 14 years her senior; Marion, when she married John Clark in 1899, had made an enterprising teenage visit to a German family and toured the Western Isles of Scotland; she was 23 years younger than her husband, and rather less than half his age when they married. He was 45 and she 22. Nevertheless, the two women appear to have had some things in common. Both devoted much time and energy to charitable works and the war effort and both were much-loved. These words from Marion's obituary in the *Haltwhistle Echo* could equally well apply to May: "There were few institutions of a philanthropic character but found her a whole-hearted generous supporter." Both women were strong-minded and energetic, though in the manner of their time subservient in many things to their husbands.

I have long been interested in how the characteristics of these four people have been reflected in their descendants - and in the influences which they themselves inherited from their forebears. What follows is an attempt to throw some light mainly on the second question, since I have thought it prudent not to characterise the living. All these people made their own journeys through their own eras and in their own worlds. Is it possible to distil from their histories some common essence? I am not sure, but it is worth a try.

The book is divided into five parts. The first four, named after my four grandparents, deal with each of them in turn and with their forebears; the fifth covers my parents, Dennis Herbert and Elizabeth Clark, whose romance began almost literally in the nursery and lasted for some 60 years. Priscilla

Napier's admonition about the inevitability of snobbery in family history (quoted above) is certainly a hazard, but I can at least plead that the female line figures here as strongly as the male – otherwise many of the most remarkable people, and the best stories, would have had to be excluded. However, the exponential increase in numbers of forebears which this approach produces and the need to avoid the "Methusalah begat" problem of biblical genealogy, mean that some lines have to be drawn. In general I have excluded peripheral individuals about whom no more is known than that they existed, but who ought to appear on a full family tree. Priscilla Napier and my wife, Jenny, must jointly take the credit for my reluctant conversion to this necessity. Nevertheless I have thought it right to do justice to the phenomenal child-bearing capacities of Ann Okes (18 children), Isabella Jackson (16) and Elizabeth Bell (14), to name only the more prolific.

Anne Vernon, who wrote a delightful history of the Morrells and was a friend of my Uncle William Clark, noted her good fortune in that her subjects prospered from one generation to another, lived for generations in the same area of Yorkshire and *never threw anything away*. My subjects have not invariably prospered – the Francos declined from supreme wealth in a few generations – and have been more peripatetic than the Morrells, but I come proudly from generations of hoarders, particularly of family history and my wife has been unable to wean me of bulging files, boxes of photographs and endless repetition of oral history. However, she has persuaded me that Bishop Butler was right in one sense when he said "The fact that something may be the truth does not lay on one the duty to utter it," and that not *all* the material lovingly preserved by my forebears can be included. I may have been less exclusive than she would have wished.

The work of a number of my relations and of other expert people who have taken an interest from time to time in the genealogy of our family deserves a special mention. Dennis Henry Herbert and May Bell both became interested in family history at a young age. May left copious notes, dictated to her by her aunts in Jamaica when she was a young teenager. Dennis got the bug when he was an undergraduate at Oxford - a very unusual time of life for that to happen. But it meant that the information which *his* aunts could contribute was not lost and aunts, though they may not always tell the full story, can be a very useful source of colourful detail.

My cousin, Francis Clark-Lowes, produced a monumental volume on the Clark family history at an equally young age, capturing a great deal of first hand material which would otherwise have disappeared. My mother, when we lived in Uganda in World War II and were short of books, regaled me with much oral family history, expressed in characteristically vivid terms. Edward Powley, of Kimbolton, contributed to the Herbert pedigree and Richard Butterfield, a friend and neighbour first of my father and then of mine, took the large amount of material available on the Herberts in hand and by expert detective work, carried it forward to the point of establishing without peradventure that we are not Herberts at all - at least not through the male line, but we will not go into that yet. Donald Montague has made the study of the Bell family his own, having amassed a notable compilation of their details on his website, and Charles Backhouse, the husband of my distant cousin Pamela (a Jackson descendant) has catalogued with admirable precision details and photographs of the descendants of Marion Jackson's father and mother, Daniel and Isabella. The help of many others is acknowledged elsewhere.

I record my great thanks to all these people without wishing, of course, to lay at their door any conclusions, or errors, that may emerge in the following pages.

September, 2008

Two Grandfathers. L to R: Dennis Herbert, Mrs. Dows, John Clark & William Clark

Part I

-------------Chapter 1 -------------

FROM EGLETON TO CAMBERWELL

┌─ **Ralph Harbottle,** b. 1614, m. circa 1636, d. 1655
┌─ **Dennis (I) Herbert,** chr. 1643, m. 1668, d. 1724
└─ **Elisabeth (--?--)**
Dennis (II) Herbert, chr. 1673, d. before 1709
　m. Anna Vincent
　└─ **Jane Biggs,** d. 1722

> People will not look forward to posterity who never look backward
> to their ancestors.- *Edmund Burke, Reflections.*

On October 23rd, 1614, when James I had been on the throne for 11 years, Zachary and Martha Harbottle christened their fourth son, Ralph, at the little parish church of Egleton near Oakham in Rutland. The times were turbulent - it was less than a decade since Guy Fawkes had tried to blow up the Houses of Parliament. King James had recently dissolved the so-called Addled Parliament, which failed to pass a single act; and he was giving Fawkes's Roman Catholic heirs a hard time, but not hard enough for the Puritans who wanted severer measures. The notorious Duke of Buckingham was coming to power and war on the continent was looming. Nevertheless it must have been a happy occasion in the small church at Egleton: the little boy's grandparents, Edward and Joan Harbottle, and Clement and Elizabeth Smith from nearby Hambleton, will have been part of the family gathering. The Harbottles had been well-known in the area for several generations and in the village since about 1540 and would feature prominently in the Heralds' Visitation of Rutland in 1618/19. They sprang from an aristocratic background in Northumberland, one of whose members was reputed to have been slain in hand-to-hand combat with James IV of Scotland at the Battle of Flodden a century before the Egleton christening.

Martha may perhaps have been hoping for a daughter, a sister for Robert, aged 6, and Christopher, aged two (their brother Henry had died when he was only six months old in 1610), but she was destined to have a wholly male family with Ralph being followed by Valentine (1616), Edward (1619) and Zachary (1621). Unaccountably none of these sons were to grow up to live in Egleton. We do not know why, but the family seems to have fallen on hard times and when the Heralds revisited Rutland in 1680 the Harbottles did not figure at all.

****

At St Olave's Church, in Tooley Street, Southwark on November 26th, 1643, Ralph and Elizabeth Harbottle baptised *their* fourth son, Dennis. By now life was considerably grimmer - the Civil War was a year old; at the Battle of Newbury two months earlier the Royalists had suffered heavily and afterwards Charles had withdrawn towards Oxford. Not far from St. Olave's the Globe theatre, like other theatres, had been closed by law and the Westminster Assembly of Divines, summoned by the Long Parliament, had just begun its 10-year attempt to reform the English church. All was uncertainty. Within a year Ralph and Elizabeth's eldest son, Ralph and their two eldest daughters, Bridget and Mary, would be dead - victims no doubt of the plague which was to engulf the area in the next several years. The parents will have tried to make the christening a joyous occasion, but we have no idea whether any of Dennis's grandparents were present because we do not know for certain that the proud father was the same Ralph who had been baptised 29 years earlier in Rutland. There is strong circumstantial evidence to suggest that he was, but it is not conclusive.

Richard Butterfield, who knows more than anyone about this problem, has tracked down several Harbottles with a similar pattern of Christian names who were married in the 1680's and 90's at St. James, Duke Place, a church in London notorious for offering marriages without licence or banns. None of these has yielded a clue to our problem, which, as Richard explains, is compounded by one regrettable problem:

> Turning to Ralph Harbottle, who brought up his family in the parish of St. Olave's , Southwark, we face one unfortunate fact. A twelve-year period from 1627 to 1639 is missing from the surviving parish registers. It was during that period that Ralph must have married, although we cannot be certain that the wedding took place in that parish. The marriage entries at St. Olave's were simple and gave no

6

clue to origin or parentage and the only certain piece we would have learnt would have been his wife Elizabeth's maiden surname. The baptismal entries for their children are variously spelt variations of Harbottle and Herbert. It is highly probable that the first syllable of Herbert was pronounced 'HAR' (c.f. Derby, Berkeley and clerk) and the family may have preferred a shorter name. However, it is also possible that the wife's maiden name was Herbert and that that was the name they chose to use.

Southwark and Blackfriars were the centre of the hatmaking trade and Ralph Harbottle was a Feltmaker, or a maker of hats, a member of the Worshipful Company of Feltmakers, which in 1604 had secured its independence from the Haberdashers and was now a fully-fledged Guild in its own right. Its members were known colloquially as "The Gentlemen" because of an incident in 1588 when Queen Elizabeth I was passing down Holborn Hill on her way to Tilbury and was greeted by a crowd of well-dressed men wearing polished beaver hats celebrating the defeat of the Spanish Armada. When she asked who they were she was told they were journeymen hatters, at which she exclaimed "Then these journeymen must be gentlemen."

Despite the ravages of the plague and the usual prevalence of infant mortality, Ralph and Elizabeth raised four of their eight sons to adulthood, each of them apprenticed to a different trade, but all their three daughters died young. John, the heir, followed his father as a Feltmaker, after an apprenticeship in the Haberdashers' Company, William (1641-1709) was a Bricklayer and Cornelius (1645-1710), the youngest and perhaps the most successful, was a Clockmaker. He was apprenticed to one William Grout, who later became the second husband of Cornelius's mother. His son became Master of the Clockmakers' Company and, as a Common Councilman of the City of London, exhibited Jacobite sympathies. Clocks and watches made by him or his eponymous father still occasionally come up for sale in the showrooms.

Ralph's fourth son, Dennis (Dennis I in our story), whose christening we have noted, also achieved the Mastership of his chosen company, the Cordwainers' - the Guild of shoemakers whose name derived originally from Cordoba in Spain where some of the finest shoemaking leather was obtained - but it must have been hard going. He was bound apprentice for eight years at the age of 13 to Arthur Mountayne in 1656, a year after the Cordwainers had introduced a series of severe austerity measures. The Company had been impoverished in the early years of the century by James I's demands on the City for "loans" to supply the finance which Parliament would not grant him -

a practice, which has an oddly modern resonance. By the time of the Civil War the City was having to find £10,000 a week so that, by 1642 the Cordwainers had begun to sell the Company silver. Things went from bad to disastrous in 1666, the year Dennis became a freeman both of the Company and of the City of London. Cordwainers' Hall was utterly destroyed in the Great Fire of London and the company lost most of its other properties as well. The brave Clerk salvaged some valuables but these had to be sold to defray expenses.

It was during the lifetime of these four boys that the family surname began to evolve. At birth they were all Harbottles, but later began to describe themselves as Harbert or Herbert. Dennis's apprentice binding in 1656, for example, was in the name of Harbottle, as was his appointment to the Livery in 1680. He continued to be so listed until 1688 when, in July, he was listed as Harbottle, but at the next meeting of the Court in October the name occurs as Herbert. There is no question of the two entries referring to different people as Liverymen were listed in order of precedence and on both occasions the name is flanked by John Wayte and Lambert Tree. Other variations on the surname in parish registers are Harbert and Harbett. By an odd coincidence a family of Harbottles in Wales made a similar change at about the same time. We have no explanation for the change, beyond the assumption that it was an exercise in abbreviation. The timing has given rise to a theory that the name change was somehow connected with the advent of William and Mary from Holland and the Glorious Revolution and the dates are indeed intriguing. The invitation to William was carried over to Holland by Admiral Herbert in July (when Dennis was still Harbottle), and the Admiral was then in the van when the Dutch party sailed for England in November (by which time Dennis was Herbert). If you could shorten your name to produce Herbert, this was possibly a good time to do it, but it is pure speculation to suggest that this was Dennis I's motivation.

At this stage Dennis I had been married for 20 years (to Jane Biggs) and had a 15-year-old son, Dennis II, whom he took on for a seven-year apprenticeship the following year - on May 14, 1689. Dennis I was then still a Liveryman and it was not until 1697 that he began 23 years' service on the Court of Assistants; in 1701 he was Warden and in 1702 Master. Dennis II meanwhile had married Anna Vincent, the daughter of a tempestuous dissenting Divine, Rev Nathaniel Vincent, and produced a son, Dennis III in 1695. Not long after this, however, Dennis II died - years before the old man, who lived on with Jane at their home in Peckham until she died in 1722 and he two years later. They lie buried in the churchyard of St. Giles, Camberwell.

8

In his will, made two years before he died, Dennis I described himself as "ancient and infirm but of sound disposing mind" and he proceeded to demonstrate that, not only had he plenty of which to dispose, but he had very definite ideas on how and to whom it should be disposed. He listed 11 messuages or tenements in Little George Street, Stepney, four in Peckham, a leasehold messuage or tenement on London Bridge, and unspecified numbers in Whitechapel and Southwark. These, or the proceeds of their sale, were nearly all to pass to his great grandson, Dennis IV, but emphatically not to his grandson, Dennis III. This is how he instructed his Executors:

> [They] shall pay and apply all and singular the rents issues and profits of the said premises and every part thereof to and for the Sole and separate use of my Grand Daughter-in-law Elizabeth Herbert, wife of my Grandson Dennis Herbert without the intermeddling or Controul of her said Husband for and during the present Couverture for the maintenance of herself and her son Dennis Herbert and in case she shall survive her said husband then upon Trust that they shall assign the said Premises to her and my said Great Grandson Dennis Herbert, her son, share and share alike....

This formula for excluding his grandson was repeated again and finally, just in case the Executors had not got the point, he added that the proceeds of sale should be paid out "only as my said Granddaughter-in-law shall solely and without her Husband order and appoint so that her now Husband Dennis Herbert shall have no power over, intermeddle with or control the same". Clearly the young man, now 20, had severely displeased his Grandfather. Still he was not completely cut out of the Will. The properties in Whitechapel were originally left to two of Dennis I's nephews on condition that they pay Dennis III eight shillings a week. Then, in a codicil to the Will signed in June, 1723, that legacy was revoked and the premises left to Dennis III and his heirs forever.

Chapter 2

ON THE LINCOLN CIRCUIT

┌── **Dennis (II) Herbert**, chr.. 1673, m. 1695, d. bef.1709
┌── **"Dr."Dennis (III) Herbert**, b. circa 1695, m. 1723, d. 1770
└── **Anna Vincent**, b. circa 1673
Dennis (IV) Herbert, b. circa 1730, d. 1803
m. Anne Pateman
└── **Mary Fisher**, b. 1704, d. 1800

> To assist the country stage my fav'rite scheme
> To prove that rural troops have real merit,
> When manag'd as they ought with proper spirit. - *George Alexander Stevens*

What had happened to ignite this spectacular family row between the Cordwainer and his grandson? Young Dennis III had been bound apprentice in 1712 for eight years to Henry Lukin, Citizen & Apothecary of London, but it is very unlikely that he completed his indenture. By the early 1720's he had become an itinerant actor and was treading the boards all over the north of England, which was not what a Master of the Cordwainers' Company expected of his grandson. We have no details of Dennis III's early Thespian efforts, nor of his marriage to Elizabeth or the birth of his son, Dennis. Indeed the only knowledge we have of those two individuals is the references to them in Dennis the Cordwainer's 1722 Will. But they did not survive for long because Dennis III married again in Lincolnshire on February 7, 1722/23. It is even possible that, if the rift was complete, they may already have been dead by the time Dennis I named them as beneficiaries. The new bride was Mary Fisher, who may well have come from a well-known acting family of that name. The marriage took place at Withcall, four miles south-west of Louth in the Lincolnshire Wolds. Their first child, Nathaniel, was baptised at St Peter's Droitwich in 1726, their second, Elizabeth in Carlisle in 1728 but their peripatetic lifestyle makes it difficult to trace details. However, by 1728 Dennis was running his own company. In April of that year he was in Newcastle-on-Tyne and, as the following description makes clear, was in hot competition for audiences.

In 1728, another company under Mr. Herbert secured the Moot-hall in April, as we learn by the following announcement: - "Mr. Herbert with his Company of Comedians (by letters of recommendation) is come to Newcastle-upon-Tyne, to attend the quality and gentry, and shall stay the races."

Mr Keregan's company also arrived at their usual time, and advertised their performances to commence in race-week. The great attraction of both houses was the "celebrated dramatic entertainment called the Beggar's Opera, as it was performed at the Theatre Royal in Lincoln's Inn Fields". Mr Keregan had secured Mr. Hullet, the original Macheath from London, whilst the same part was performed in Mr. Herbert's theatre by Mr. Woodward "who lately performed it at York, in Mr. Keregan's Company."

"Doctor" Herbert, as he was invariably known in view of his Barber-Surgeon origins, was the kind of character anyone would be proud to add to a family's history - provided that he had lived long enough ago - and some highly entertaining accounts of his activities can be found in the theatrical reminiscences of the time. It is true that when he died in July, 1770, the *Norwich Mercury's* obituary was, for the time, a long one and gave no hint of any eccentricity:

> On Thursday the 5th instant died Mr Dennis Herbert, aged 75 years. He was the oldest Manager in England, having been Master of a Company upwards of forty years in Norfolk and Lincolnshire, of whom it may with strict justice be declared, that no person in any station could be more respected than he was by all who were acquainted with him; and to his Memory, with the utmost Propriety, that seldom deserved Character may be applied. That he is dead, of whom not anyone knew ill.

As a family historian I wish the *Mercury* had put in rather more fact, but as a journalist, I know that it is much easier to lay on the adjectives. The temptation to eulogise the dead is normal, but you cannot racket around in the acting profession for upwards of 40 years without attracting some attention and there are many anecdotes about Dennis the Actor which indicate that he was far from conventional. There is no evidence that he went into practice as a surgeon, which is perhaps just as well, given that he took to consuming no fewer than 93 half-pints of ale between 5.00 am., when he rose, and nine at night when he took supper. This meant that he frequently forgot not only his lines but even on one occasion when playing Douglas in the fifth act of Henry

IV Part 1, whether it was he or Sir Walter (played by his eldest son, Nathaniel) who was supposed to die in their vigorous on-stage duel. When he chose the wrong option, he was stridently reminded by his wife, Mary, from the wings, "Curse your old soul, it's the child that's to die, not you!" So he got up, re-fought the duel and emerged the victor to the ironic cheers of the audience. Ale, of course, was both cheap and weak in those days and was much safer than water, but consumption on Dennis Herbert's heroic scale required financing. Charles Lee Lewes, who spent two years as a member of Dennis's company, gave the following hilarious account of one particular incident:

> This extraordinary gentleman was blessed with a provident wife; she gave him a daily allowance of half a crown for pocket-money, a plentiful supply you must allow, but thirsty Dennis Herbert frequently found it too little. Shame would not suffer him to apply to his wife for any additional allowance; but as he wisely foresaw that the half-crown would be insufficient for the expenditure of a whole day in such a town as Lynn, he made use of an ingenious stratagem to enlarge his stock. The necessary attention required at the theatre caused Mrs. Herbert to sleep soundly during the morning, which put a scheme into old Dennis's head of supplying himself liberally, without being detected, or accused to being more extravagant than there was a necessity for. I said before he was an early riser; a thirsty spark that must be quenched was his sole motive for it..... His spouse's pockets were always carefully tied up together, and deposited under her head. Dennis, taking advantage of her whilst she was under the dominion of the drowsy god, would artfully draw away the depositary of her cash, and purloin from thence such sums as he thought proper, carefully restoring the bags to the place from whence he took them. This trade of filching from himself he followed for a great while, and chuckled with the thoughts of having such a safe resource, without casting one thought on the ruinous consequences which might ensue to his family by such an extraordinary procedure. But the time drew nigh for a fatal stop to be put to this unnatural fraud.
>
> Mrs. Herbert was most punctual in the payment of all the tradespeople's bills any way connected with what concerned the theatre, as the tallow-chandler, carpenter, painter, & etc.; their demands she made a rule to discharge every morning after play-night; but the sensible deficiency she often found, on examining the contents of her pockets, surprised and shocked her. She could not possibly account for it but by her pockets being picked, and who could do that? None but her old chamber-mate, Dennis. She therefore resolved to detect him; for which purpose, on the next play-

day, she took a comfortable nap, to qualify her for the intended vigil.
Her plot succeeded. About five next morning, just at the glimmering
of daylight, Dennis stole softly out of bed, and ere he drew on his
small-clothes, he fell to rifling the never-failing budget. But as soon
as he began, the watchful wife cries out

"Oh, curse upon you, you old fumbling rascal: have I found you
out?"

"What's the matter, Moll? Damn it, I believe my breeches are
bewitched. I can't get my feet thro' 'em; have you been sewing them
up at the knees for fun, Moll?

Here he kept grunting and tugging to get on the pockets, or
money bags, which he pretended to mistake for his breeches. But his
spouse was not to be imposed upon thus: she told the whole of this
iniquitous transaction to the highly-diverted company at next
rehearsal.

Lewes said he thoroughly enjoyed his time with the Herberts. He
described it as a happy and respectable company in which the sharing of
profits was superior to any other. Mary was clearly a formidable character, a
trait which she demonstrated when, after Dennis's death, Nathaniel came
hastening back from touring the West Indies to claim what he assumed would
be his inheritance – managership of the Company. When he found that his
mother had already given the job to her son-in-law, George Alexander
Stevens, Nathaniel was furious and set up a rival company to try and do his
mother down. He was said to be a good country actor unsurpassed in the role
of coarse comic characters, whom he resembled in real life, being "a man of
not very polished manners, fond of society who loved a cheerful glass". He
seems to have put his heart and soul into the job. At Sheffield in a pantomime
in which a wooden head was poked up through a trap door to be whacked by
the clown, he stuck his own head up when the wooden one got lost and was
knocked insensible. There was alarm in the theatre, greatly relieved when,
from below stage, came the cry: "My Jesus, I'm a dead man. He's killed me.
He's killed me." He then reappeared and went through the remainder of the
show as if nothing had happened. Despite this resilience, however, he proved
no match for Mary Herbert and his venture failed. It took a deputation of his
friends – and the fact that the son-in-law had found a more profitable line of
work – to mollify her. Even then she insisted on his buying the company and
providing her with a yearly income. Nathaniel, of course, had no money so he
had to offer a partnership to James Whitely, a well-known theatrical manager
who in turn installed James Shaftoe Robertson as his deputy. When Robertson

died a few years later, Nathaniel began to get into difficulties again and eventually, "being a little encumbered in his private affairs and tired of a falling house, by the advice of his brother Dennis he sold his share for £300 and by the aid of his brother Dennis he took the White Horse Inn, Baldock, where he died."

George Alexander Stevens was also intermittently a member of Herbert's Company, though his merit as an actor was woundingly described as "less than mediocre" and "contemptible". However, he had been able to charm another member, the boss's daughter, Elizabeth, whom he married in about 1750. He had a good knowledge of the classics and a ready wit and produced an extensive *oeuvre,* consisting of verse, plays, novels and skits, but his lifestyle was rackety and he belonged to a large number of drinking clubs. It can have been no surprise to Elizabeth when, in 1761, he did a spell in Nottingham gaol for debt. Writing of the episode, he said:

> As a hunted deer is always shunned by the happier herd, so am I deserted by the Company, my share taken off, and no support left me, save what my wife can spare me out of hers.

He managed to persuade an organist friend to raise enough to get him out of prison and thereafter things went rather better for a while. The great actor, David Garrick counted him as one of his friends, describing him as "a very honest liberal-minded man", and he gave both George and Elizabeth parts at Drury Lane, while George was also given a benefit. By 1770 when Dennis III died and his widow, Mary, wanted George Alexander Stevens to take on the Company, he had developed a one-man show called *A Lecture upon Heads*, which was a runaway success and amassed him a fortune (which he later squandered). It went through 40 published editions, became a staple in the English-speaking theatres of the world and was much pirated to Stevens's fury. His biographer, Gerald Kahan, has described the show as follows:

> Standing behind a long table covered with a green baize cloth and dozens of papier-mâché busts and wig blocks he began his two-hour long monologue satirizing one type after another: an Indian Chief, Alexander the Great, a London Blood, a Billingsgate Fishwife, a Horse Jockey, a Conjuror, a Frenchman, a Spaniard, a Dutchman and finally a Methodist Parson.

This formula had the great advantage of not being classified as a play, which meant that performances did not have to be licensed. Moreover, no elaborate scenery or costumes were required and the busts were fairly easily transportable. It was no wonder that it flourished even across the Atlantic. It is to be hoped that Elizabeth's loyalty to her husband was well rewarded during this brief period of prosperity.

We know that Stevens was acquainted with Oliver Goldsmith because he wrote him a letter soon after the première of *She Stoops to Conquer* in 1773 asking for seats for two of his nieces, and there is a possibility of a more interesting connection. Richard Butterfield explains:

> In the Consistory Court of Lincoln the will of Mary Harbottle, described as of St. Botolph in the City of Lincoln, widow, was granted probate on March 27th, 1695. The will had been drawn up on May 2, 1693, and in it she mentioned rents and arrears due to herself from her son (clearly from a first marriage) Antony Lumpkin and her grandson John Lumpkin. The similarity in names to the characters in Oliver Goldsmith's play *She Stoops to Conquer*, where the mother of the oafish Tony Lumpkin had married, as her second husband, a Mr. Hardcastle, is striking. There has been a certain amount of literary speculation about the origin of the story behind Goldsmith's play. At the time of his death, it was believed that the story and possibly the names, came from his native Ireland, but apparently his sister discounted this. There is, however, evidence that Goldsmith stayed at the Lumpkin's place in the Isle of Ely, where he may have sketched out the idea for a play. It would be intriguing to know whether he met Dennis Herbert, the Actor-Manager, on the Lincoln Circuit.
>
> Also intriguing would be the idea that one of the Egleton Harbottles was the second husband in question. Mary Harbottle's first marriage was to Antony Lumpkin, senior, in 1633.

Some time in the decade George Alexander Stevens, his faculties now declining with age, sold for a moderate sum his original *Lecture upon Heads* to Charles Lee Lewes, his former colleague in Dennis III's company. Eventually he completely lost his senses and, in the words of his obituary in the *Gentleman's Magazine*, "exhibited a miserable spectacle of idiotism and fatuity", while retaining his bodily faculties. In this pitiable state he seems to have lived for several years with his brother-in-law, Dennis Herbert of Biggleswade, nursed no doubt by the faithful Elizabeth, who survived him by many years until she died, aged 83, in 1813 at the home of her nephew, Cornelius Pateman Herbert at Setch in Norfolk.

Chapter 3

FROM OXFORD TO THE MARSHALSEA

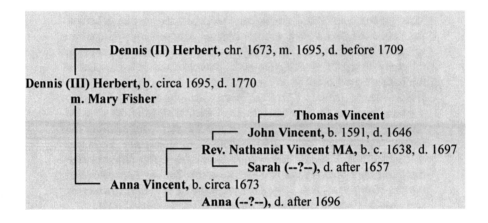

Dennis (II) Herbert, chr. 1673, m. 1695, d. before 1709

Dennis (III) Herbert, b. circa 1695, d. 1770
   m. Mary Fisher

Thomas Vincent

John Vincent, b. 1591, d. 1646

Rev. Nathaniel Vincent MA, b. c. 1638, d. 1697

Sarah (--?--), d. after 1657

Anna Vincent, b. circa 1673

Anna (--?--), d. after 1696

Do not think that I came to bring peace on earth. I did not come to bring peace but a sword. - *Jesus Christ, quoted by St. Matthew.*

His pen was going when his tongue could not – *D.N.B.*

One day in August, 1670 the Actor-Manager's grandmother, Anna Vincent, learned by chance that her new husband, whom she supposed to be in the Marshalsea gaol in Southwark, had been spirited away secretly to Westminster. There he was being kept incommunicado in the Gatehouse prison so that his many supporters should not know where to find him. Fortunately a friend had seen the authorities putting Rev. Nathaniel Vincent into a boat in Southwark and had followed in his own skiff to see where they were taking him. Nathaniel was a turbulent Dissenter, who had refused to sign the oaths of allegiance and non-resistance to the crown which recognised the King as head of the church. He had consequently been ejected from his parish at Langley Marsh, in Buckinghamshire, on St. Bartholomew's Day, 1662. He spent three years as chaplain to the Blount family at Tyttenhanger in

Hertfordshire, but about the time of the Great Fire of London he had set up a flourishing non-conformist meeting-place in Farthing Alley, Southwark, where despite being regularly harassed by the authorities, he defiantly preached to gatherings of several thousand devoted followers. When ordered to stop preaching, his customary reply was that he was speaking with the authority of the King of Kings. On one occasion soldiers had trained four muskets on his pulpit and dragged him out of it by the hair, but their attempt to take him away was frustrated by the congregation who overpowered the troops and released him.

Some time later, however, the soldiers managed to capture him. He was fined £20 and taken to the debtors' prison, but the authorities were embarrassed by the number of his supporters who were visiting him there. Hence the attempt to smuggle him away to Westminster. Anna, however, was made of stern stuff. She mustered enough money to secure a brief meeting with Nathaniel and set about getting all their friends and acquaintances to petition the king and council for his release. She managed to get him out of close confinement in seven weeks and procured him writing materials, but he still had to remain in prison for six months for infringing the Five Mile Act, which prohibited clergy from living within five miles of a parish from which they had been ejected, unless they would swear never to resist the king or attempt to alter the government of Church or State.

To agree would have been totally out of character and untypical of the family for Nathaniel's father, John Vincent (1591-1646) had also been persecuted for nonconformity. He had inherited the family estate at Northill on the eastern edge of Bodmin Moor from his father, Thomas, and after matriculating from Oxford, he became a student at Lincoln's Inn in 1612. He then took Holy Orders and had a parish in Cornwall, but the bishop drove him out and he began a peripatetic journey from parish to parish so that, it was said, his many children were all born in different counties. Finally he obtained the rich living of Sedgefield in County Durham, but enjoyed it for only two years, leaving his widow, Sarah, to try and recover a £60 loan that John had made to parliament. John's eponymous heir settled at Northill, but the second son, Thomas, was also an active nonconformist, who distinguished himself by preaching in London throughout the Great Plague and moreover fearlessly insisting on visiting the victims. Miraculously he survived and enjoys, with Nathaniel, a prominent position in the pantheon of Dissenting Ministers. Both boys followed their father to Oxford, Thomas to Christchurch and Nathaniel to Corpus Christi, where he became a chorister at the age of ten. Both also had phenomenal memories. Thomas had the whole of the New Testament and the

Psalms by heart and Nathaniel, at the age of seven, used to repeat from memory, for the benefit of the family, the sermon which his father had preached earlier in the day.

When Nathaniel eventually emerged from the Gatehouse prison, he and Anna were able to settle down to married life and over the next dozen years they produced six children. Then the harassment resumed and officers frequently came to break up Nathaniel's services. When Judge Pierce turned up in 1682 and commanded him in the king's name to step down from the pulpit, he got the standard King of Kings reply and, after that the congregation posted watchmen to signal the approach of officers of the law. Then Nathaniel would disappear and the congregation would sing psalms until it was safe for him to resume his oration. Eventually, however, the authorities trapped him and he was summoned to appear at Dorking assizes where he was sentenced to three years' imprisonment, after which he was to be banished from the country.

However, he and Anna, who was unwell following the birth two months earlier of her sixth child, took the best legal advice they could get and a flaw was found in the indictment so that a plea of *Habeas Corpus* could be brought before the King's Bench. With his expensive four or five counsel Nathaniel turned up on six successive days without being able to get a hearing. Anna kept pestering the court with pleas for bail, but had little luck, until one day she managed to get the attention of one judge, who noticed that Nathaniel had been kept waiting for so long. He asked the court if there were any reason why bail might not be taken for his appearance and Nathaniel was released. It cost him £200 but he was able to resume his preaching. Somehow, though the spark had gone and he could no longer command such large attendance until the accession of James II when restrictions were removed. The greatest sadness of his life, which pained him far more than all the tribulations which his nonconformity had brought down upon him, was that a schism occurred in his congregation in 1692, when 60 of his communicants deserted and went over to a rival.

Nathaniel was a prolific author, at least one of his books, *A Covert in the Storm,* being produced in prison so that "his pen was going when his tongue could not". Other titles include: *The Conversion of a Sinner,* and *The Day of Grace; Heaven or Hell upon Earth: a discourse on Conscience; The Conversion of the Soul; The True Touchstone* and *The Love of the World Cured.* He also edited *Morning Exercise against Popery,* a collection of 25 sermons preached by eminent divines in his pulpit at Southwark. If the message of his literary output was stern, he was nevertheless adjudged to be rather more human than many of his nonconformist brethren:

> He was of smarter, more brisk, and florid parts than most of his dull and sluggish fraternity can reasonably pretend to; of a facetious and jolly humour, and a considerable scholar.

Several of his tracts were reprinted in the late 20th century by evangelicals, but it was as a preacher that he really shone. His sermons were said to have commanded attention, raised affection, and struck awe into the consciences of his hearers, but he was also compassionate and, according to Edmund Calamy, who wrote a definitive account of the dissenting clergy:

> As a Christian, he was ready on all occasions to start some serious discourse, and whatever company he came into, like an open box of precious ointment, would leave some sweet perfume behind him. His compassion to the poor was great, and he was liberal in doing good at once both to body and soul.

He suffered severely from "a quartan ague", a condition like malaria which was apt to recur at four-day intervals and was particularly difficult when he was in prison, but he accepted the pain and affliction with patience and, when the end came, which it did quite suddenly on June 22, 1697, he had all the certainty of his ilk. "Why weep you for me, who am going to the eternal inheritance?" he asked. His final thought, however, was for his people: "I find I am dying; Lord, Lord, have mercy on my family and congregation."

Little is known of Anna and Nathaniel's six children except that one of them, Anna, married Dennis Herbert, son of the Master of the Cordwainers' Company, and was therefore the mother of Dennis III, the Actor-Manager. The Cordwainer's disapproval of his grandson is recorded. Had he lived to witness the goings-on on the Lincoln Circuit, Nathaniel, author of *A Warning to Secure Sinners to prepare for Judgement,* would surely have been equally censorious – and yet might it not have been his maternal grandfather's "smarter, more brisk and florid parts" which showed up in his errant grandson?

Chapter 4

FROM KING'S LYNN TO BIGGLESWADE

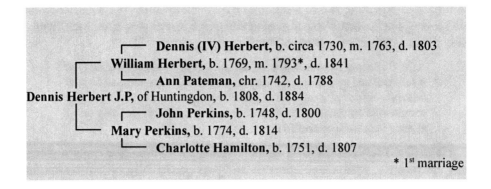

Dennis (IV) Herbert, b. circa 1730, m. 1763, d. 1803
William Herbert, b. 1769, m. 1793*, d. 1841
Ann Pateman, chr. 1742, d. 1788
Dennis Herbert J.P, of Huntingdon, b. 1808, d. 1884
John Perkins, b. 1748, d. 1800
Mary Perkins, b. 1774, d. 1814
Charlotte Hamilton, b. 1751, d. 1807

* 1st marriage

All the Herberts had good hearts. - *Sarah Hicks*

Every man is trying either to live up to his father's expectations or make up for his father's mistakes – *Barack Obama.*

A key date in the history of the Herbert family is May 17th, 1757 when Parliament granted an Act to make eight miles of the River Ivel navigable between Tempsford and Biggleswade. This meant that, for the first time, coal and other heavy goods could be carried all the way from King's Lynn on the Wash to Biggleswade in Hertfordshire. Four years earlier, the Actor-Manager's second son, Dennis IV, who had been apprenticed in King's Lynn in 1746 to a merchant and brewer, had received the Freedom of the town and begun building up his business interests. According to his gravestone he was a merchant in Biggleswade for 45 years, which means that he must have moved there in 1758, the year the new canal was opened. So he and his master were quick to spot an opportunity and, before long, boats plying his trade were carrying a great variety of goods such as coal, iron, timber, tiles, peas and beans, wheat, barley, oats, rye and flour all the way to Biggleswade. In the River Ivel Toll Book, showing tolls paid on upriver traffic for the decade 1767-1777, Dennis's boats have the greatest number of entries. Meanwhile in 1763 he had married Anne Pateman, a girl from Langford, a few miles south of Biggleswade, where he rapidly became a leading citizen, so that, for example, when Biggleswade was devastated by a dreadful fire in 1785 it was Dennis Herbert who took upon himself to write an appeal for help to Lord Hardwicke, then the owner of Wimpole Hall.

In addition to his shipping activities Dennis had become involved in brewing. The Setch Brewery outside King's Lynn was started by him in 1767 and after the Biggleswade fire he and his partner, Samuel Wells, acquired three inns there. In 1796 he acquired 10 pubs in the villages round King's Lynn but a more significant acquisition was the Red Lyon (later the Rose & Crown) in Godmanchester which he bought in 1793, giving the original documents to his son, William to hold. And in 1794 William, with a £5,500 mortgage from his father, acquired the Huntingdon Brewery, which stood on the High Street. William was thus established, at the age of 25 at a strategic point halfway between King's Lynn and Biggleswade - a decision well in line with his father's acumen, especially as William had, in December 1793, married Mary Perkins, daughter of John Perkins, three times Mayor of Huntingdon.

Over the next decades the Herberts established themselves in Huntingdon. William himself became Mayor in 1804, although he suffered a bit of a setback the following year when he was fined £200 for illegally sprinkling the malt on the floor of his malthouse in Fenstanton. He mounted an energetic appeal, but only succeeded in getting the fine reduced to £50. He was active in Godmanchester in the acquisition and disposal of property and this little difficulty with the law did not prevent him from becoming Mayor of Huntingdon for a second time in 1811, in which year, incidentally, it was formally recorded by the Minister and Churchwardens of All Saints, Huntingdon, that "he did receive the sacrament of the Lord's supper". This was not some kind of atonement, but a requirement under the Test Act of 1672 which was designed to prevent Roman Catholics or extreme Protestant non-conformists from taking public office.

That was also the year in which Mary (née Perkins) produced the last of her 11 children - in 17 years she bore William five sons (none of whom married) and six daughters. But three years later she was dead and lies buried in the churchyard of St Mary's, Huntingdon. *The Cambridge Independent Press and Chronicle* recorded rather charmingly: "With real concern we announce the death of Mary the wife of Wm. Herbert, Esq., of Huntingdon, on Saturday, the 30th ult.. By this melancholy and unexpected event her dearest connections have sustained an irreparable loss, her acquaintances are deprived of an invaluable friend and the poor of a kind and constant benefactress." Two years later, in 1816, William married another Mary, the daughter of Thomas Verney Okes, a noted Cambridge doctor. She was almost 20 years his junior and was to outlive him by nearly 30 years, dying in 1870. She and William had four unmarried daughters and, finally, in 1824 a son, Henry Herbert, who was to become the Rector of Hemingford Abbots.

One of William Herbert's sons by his first marriage - inevitably called Dennis - outdid his father in public service, becoming Mayor of Huntingdon in 1843, 1850, 1854, 1859 and 1861, and succeeded him at the Brewery. He also seems to have inherited from his grandfather a penchant for acquiring public houses. In March 1859 this Dennis Herbert, was described by a radical MP in the House of Commons as "a common brewer at Huntingdon, who had a public house in every village and every place in the county." This description produced a chorus of "Hear, hear" and a ministerial retort to the effect that if it were true that he had so many pubs at least it showed that he must be a man of substance. These entertaining exchanges took place in the course of a complaint by Mr. T. Duncombe that too many Tories were being elevated to the magistracy in Huntingdon, which he described as a pocket borough of the Master of the Queen's Buckhounds, Lord Sandwich, who was also the Lord Lieutenant. Mr. Duncombe asserted that Huntingdon had more magistrates than policemen and, with a population of only 64,000, the county was smaller than several metropolitan boroughs which were not so favoured. He complained that six Tories had recently been appointed while three Liberals whose names had been put forward for the bench had been passed over. People in Huntingdon who did not happen to belong to the Tory party, he claimed, said that Mr Herbert was rather an awkward man to sit upon the bench on a licensing day.

The Tories, of course, were robust in defence. Mr Sotheron Estcourt, for the Home Office, reminded the House that one of the most eminent men in the history of the county had himself been a brewer of Huntingdon who, though he might not have aspired to the office of Justice of the Peace, had nevertheless reached the position of chief magistrate of the state. Besides, the law provided that brewers were disqualified from sitting on the bench when the interests of their own trade were at stake; this was perfectly normal. General Peel, brother of Sir Robert, as M.P. for Huntingdon, was strong in support of Herbert, who had already been several times mayor and Mr Fellowes, member for the county, referred to the respectability of the appointees and their qualifications to act as magistrates. Mr Duncombe later disavowed any offence, pointing out that the words "Common Brewer" were posted over all the doors of publicans and, in truth, the description did not bear then today's rather pejorative nuance.

It was particularly important to Dennis Herbert, of Huntingdon, to have his respectability reaffirmed by these great men. Admittedly his father, as we have seen, had also been Mayor of Huntingdon, and his grandfather, had amassed a considerable fortune as a general merchant and trader across much of Bedfordshire, Huntingdonshire, Norfolk and beyond. But, as we know, there lurked a little further back in the family tree some much less reassuring history. At a safe 250 years' distance a man who rifled his wife's pockets for beer-money may be acceptable, but Dennis of Huntingdon will not particularly have relished him at less than 100 years' distance. An aspirant to the magistracy, even in a place that could be described as a pocket borough, could not afford too exotic an ancestry and there were doubtless a number of spiteful individuals in the area who were not above airing any dirty linen that might be available. Intriguingly, for example, just three months before the debate in the House of Commons, there appeared in the well-respected magazine, *Notes and Queries,* the following item:

> In the early part of the last century there were three brothers of the name of Herbert, respectively christened Dennis, Nathaniel and (I believe) Vincent. They were in some way related to the Earls of Pembroke whose arms they bore........ Dennis & Nathaniel took to the stage: in consequence of which their other brother, Vincent (?) would not acknowledge them and they were lost sight of by the family. They were afterwards discovered acting at the theatre at Lynn, co. Norfolk by Lord Herbert, who happened to be in the boxes and who shook his cane at them, saying "You young dogs, we never knew where you were." This Lord Herbert was said to be their cousin.
>
> Can any of your readers tell me:
>
> 1. What Lord Herbert is here spoken of?
>
> 2. From which earl of Pembroke were the two brothers Dennis & Nathaniel descended?
>
> If none can answer the above questions perhaps somebody will be able to tell me how I should be most likely to obtain information on this subject. I can find no mention of their names in the Parish Register at Lynn.
>
> Three Mullets.

The identity of Three Mullets remains a mystery, but his questions must have seemed to Dennis Herbert of Huntingdon a bit near the bone. Nor can he have relished the reply from Mr. A.H.Swatman, a solicitor in King's Lynn, which appeared about four weeks before the parliamentary debate. Swatman began well, thus:

> Dennis, Nathaniel and Vincent Herbert are names familiar to many elderly Lynn people, but your correspondent Three Mullets mistakes the date of their existence. It was at the end of the last century that the first of the name settled at Setchey or Wormegay, near Lynn, where they became partners in a large brewery, still existing. The family came from Biggleswade, where they traded as merchants. Subsequently some of them settled at Baldock, and others at Huntingdon where, I believe, they still exist. The anecdote about Lord Herbert discovering his cousins on the stage of a theatre at Lynn must be a fiction. Lynn possessed no theatre until 1760, or thereabouts, and I can find no trace of a Lord Herbert ever visiting the town.

But then, Oh dear!, he went on:

> The Biggleswade Herberts may possibly bear the Pembroke arms, and yet have no descent from that house; for this they may have to thank their seal engraver. It is well known that since the creation of the first Baron Carington every ambitious Smith uses his Lordship's arms, and the custom of adoption is very prevalent amongst parvenus.

A.H.SWATMAN, Lynn

Like many modern lawyers, Mr. Swatman, was selective in his facts, which so far as they went were mostly accurate. But he managed to airbrush Dennis the Actor out of the picture with suspicious ease. Three Mullets's anecdote may be a fiction, but Dennis the Actor was alive and acting for 10 years after Swatman says King's Lynn first had a theatre and he was most certainly in the area long before the end of the 18th century. As early as 1746, as we have seen, he had apprenticed his son there and his fame - or notoriety - was considerable.

Were it not for Swatman's waspish reference to parvenus adopting the arms of their employers, one might wonder whether he had been put up by Dennis of Huntingdon to obscure the existence of Dennis the Actor. But Swatman seems to have had a point. Much of the family silver which I have inherited is adorned with the crest of the Pembroke Herberts, which Rev. Henry also had embossed on the Rectory writing paper and my grandfather, when he was elevated to the peerage in 1943, declined to register arms because the College of Heralds would not permit him to indicate descent from the Pembrokes in the design. In the 1970s, when Richard Butterfield established beyond a peradventure that we were not descended in the male line from the main Herbert family, my father at once discarded the Herbert signet ring which he had worn for most of his adult life. There is no doubt that towards the end of the 18th century, the Herberts began to suffer from collective amnesia about the Harbottles and Dennis the Actor and, in pursuit of respectability, adopted (if that is not too polite a description) the Herbert crest to which they were absolutely unentitled. In this connection it is not relevant that Rev Henry Herbert of Hemingford Abbots was actually descended from the Welsh Herberts in the female line.

I am inclined to acquit Dennis of Biggleswade of this deceit. By the time his father died he was already 40 and he had to cope thereafter with his sister, Elizabeth, and her husband, George Alexander Stevens, who by then had lost his money and his wits and had joined Dennis of Biggleswade's household. Stevens died in 1784. I doubt whether, having lived with the reality of the theatrical connection for half a century, Dennis of Biggleswade would have begun to write it out of the script at that late stage. His sons, however, are another matter. George (1766-1806), who worked with his father but died unmarried at a relatively early age, can probably be discounted, but William (1769-1841), Dennis (1771-1861), Cornelius Pateman (1772-1834) and Nathaniel Vincent (1780-1844) were all making their way towards respectability.

Dennis purchased into the 40th (2nd Somerset) Regiment of Foot and, by dint of further purchases, had a distinguished military career in the course of which he served with the forces under the Duke of York and Lord Moira, in the Carib War in St. Vincent, in St. Domingo and at the action against Copenhagen in 1807. He was inspecting Field Officer of Militia in Nova Scotia as a Lieutenant Colonel (1808) and a Colonel (1814). He was promoted Major-General in 1825 and Lieutenant General in 1838 on the occasion of Queen Victoria's Coronation. When he died, leaving a large family, he was a full General, the fifth in order of seniority in that rank. His wife Jane (née Anstruther), whom he married in Guernsey in 1801, came from a well-connected Scottish family and one of his sons, Frederick Anstruther (1827-1911) became an Admiral and sported the Herbert crest on his writing paper. General Dennis would not have relished the Thespians, but he was far enough away, perhaps, not to worry about them too much.

Cornelius Pateman was another brewer and co-owner with his father of a number of hostelries in the King's Lynn area and Nathaniel Vincent, having proved to be unsuited to business, became a schoolmaster in Biggleswade and later moved to London. Both of these two had families and would probably not have been averse to masquerading as members of the aristocratic Herberts. None of these brothers would have any memory of their grandfather, except George, who was four when Dennis III died, and of the others only William might have met him as an infant. In the absence of any certitude, these brothers must stand accused of a remarkable cover-up, which was so effective that for over a century their descent from the Actor-Manager was concealed and an alternative scenario was foist upon their descendants. Which of them may have been the moving spirit we cannot know, but William is the most likely. He was the oldest of the surviving four sons and perhaps had the most to lose by being unmasked. You would have expected his marriage to Mary Perkins to take place in Huntingdon, to which he was the first of the family to move and where he was destined to be Mayor, but in fact it took place in the rather grander surroundings of St Bartholomew the Great in London. William looks like a man with the social pretensions which were current in the Victorian era and other evidence points in the same direction. A signet ring which I inherited came from the last male heir of General Dennis Herbert; it was not made before 1822 and some of the tableware which bears the Pembroke crest dates from the mid-19th Century. This puts them clearly in the time of William, his siblings and his son, Dennis of Huntingdon, who is actually recorded as subscribing to the idea of descent from the Pembrokes.

When Dennis Henry Herbert began his investigations in the late nineteenth century the picture was already obscure. His Aunt Caroline was a believer on the grounds that she used to stay with the Herberts at Muckross Abbey in Killarney and "they treated her as kin", but there was a fallacy in this as the Muckross Herberts were Clives in the male line who had adopted the name of Herbert from a female. There was some vague talk of an ancestor who was a bookseller on Old London Bridge, but the following description sent to him by his second cousin, Sarah Hicks, in 1891 is significant:

> I remember your uncle Dennis (Dennis of Huntingdon) naming his
> idea of the Pembroke descent to my grandmother, when she rather
> discouraged his views.....My grandmother never spoke of pedigree,
> but always ended her remarks upon the family by saying 'All the
> Herberts had good hearts'.

Sarah's grandmother was Ann, wife of Cornelius Pateman Herbert, the King's Lynn brother. She clearly knew the score, but was prepared to be discreet about it and, as we have seen, Dennis Henry never found out the whole truth. My father, Dennis George Ruddock Herbert, who was Dennis Henry's son, spent a good deal of time discussing the issue with his father both as a boy and as an adult. In retirement, and before he knew the answer, he wrote a paper entitled *Who were the parents of Dennis Herbert of Biggleswade?* In it he traced various people to whom Dennis Henry had access and their relationship with Dennis of Biggleswade. His conclusions were:

> It was a subject likely to interest such people in an age when social standing was highly regarded. Their menfolk were brewers, parsons, solicitors, army officers and they lived in rectories and other substantial houses typical of the upper middle class. And many, if not all of them held a belief that they were descended from the noble Herbert family, whose crest they had no scruple in inscribing on their silver and their writing paper.
>
> I am not here concerned to discuss whether this belief may nor may not prove true. The only reason I have stressed it is astonishment that those who held it could not trace their male ancestry for more than two or three generations. There must, one concludes, have been something in the origins of the merchant of Biggleswade of which he, and perhaps his children, were ashamed. My father thought it was a connection with the stage.

We now know how tantalisingly close Dennis Henry was to the truth, but it would not have pleased him.

In fairness to William and his son Dennis, despite their desire for social advancement, they did have a sense of propriety. For example, when, in 1834, the Earl of Sandwich proposed to Dennis of Huntingdon that he should let his name go forward for election as an Alderman, he declined because, he said, he knew that his father, William, had strong objections to the sons of existing Aldermen being elected. They did much in the public service and were pillars of the community - solid citizens - but they were not at all dashing or romantic. William's other son, however, did have a bit more dash about him. This was Henry, destined later in life for Hemingford Abbots, who seems to have inherited from his mother some of the devil-may-care attributes of his mother's family, the Okes's.

Mary Okes (1783-1870), 2nd wife of William Herbert of Huntingdon

Dennis Herbert (1808-1884), of Huntingdon, the "Common Brewer"

Chapter 5

FROM BERMONDSEY TO BEDFORD & EXETER

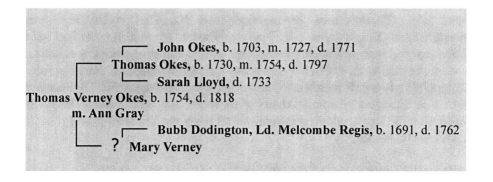

John Okes, b. 1703, m. 1727, d. 1771
Thomas Okes, b. 1730, m. 1754, d. 1797
Sarah Lloyd, d. 1733
Thomas Verney Okes, b. 1754, d. 1818
m. Ann Gray
Bubb Dodington, Ld. Melcombe Regis, b. 1691, d. 1762
? Mary Verney

"Having put his hand to the plough, he did not look back.- *Thomas Okes's Memorial*.

On November 17,1730, the same year as Dennis Herbert of Biggleswade, Thomas Okes was born in Grange Walk, Bermondsey, Southwark. He was the son of John Okes, a Jerquer in the London Custom House, and Sarah, née Lloyd, who, however he was scarcely to know because she died when he was only three. She was only 38 and it was only six years since she had married John Okes at Finchley in 1727. She was buried in Camberwell Churchyard

A Jerquer was a customs officer and John must have done well at it because he was able to send his son to Eton. Thomas went on to King's College, Cambridge, in 1749 as a scholar, and took his BA in 1754, MA in 1758, ML in 1761 and MD in 1769. At Cambridge he struck up a friendship with Charles Darwin's grandfather, Erasmus, a respected physician and a well known poet, philosopher, botanist and naturalist. When Erasmus Darwin's father died in 1754 it was to Thomas Okes that he wrote a long account of his feelings. Thomas took part in the Seven Years War (1756-1763) as an Army Surgeon in the 83rd Regiment of Foot, which was founded in Ireland in

October, 1757. In 1762 the Regiment embarked for Portugal and took part in the campaign there, in particular the action at Marvao, a village near the Spanish border in the Serra Sao Mamede mountains north of Badajoz. These proceedings rank among the most obscure ever undertaken by the British army and the 83rd's role in it was minor but, as its most recent historian points out, it achieved its objectives of deterring a Spanish invasion with minimal casualties and as such deserves some consideration. It certainly involved a great deal of marching about in rugged conditions with inadequate footwear and there was a good deal of sickness, so we can assume that Surgeon Okes was kept busy. When the Regiment was disbanded in Ireland in June, 1763, Thomas took up practice as a Physician in Bedford, later transferring to King's Lynn and finally to Exeter. By this time he had been thrice married and produced six children, which for so uxorious a character and by the standards of later members of the family, must be put down as a disappointingly small number. When he died, in 1797 aged 67, Thomas was buried in Exeter Cathedral, where a stone on the wall nearby bears an inscription in Greek, which translates as "Having put his hand to the plough, he did not look back."

We shall meet some of his children by his second wife, Rebecca Lydia Butcher, in South Africa in a later chapter. Robert John (1767-1840), who was saved from drowning when he was six, was a member of the Royal College of Surgeons, and accompanied his younger brother Holt to Capetown on the ship *Gambia* after a relatively short career as a surgeon in the Cambridge militia. He died in 1840 unmarried. The Okes family established themselves in Capetown, where Holt opened a Classical Academy for boys in 1831 and his wife, Patricia a school for girls later in the same year. Holt would ride over to Wynberg either on horseback or in a smart chaise to take services. A passing Indian army officer, who was critical of the Church of England's lack of energy or organisation in South Africa in general, nevertheless noted that "It would be ungenerous not to mention the obligation the village is under to Dr Okes who, from disinterested and praiseworthy solicitude for its welfare, attends every Sabbath morning and performs divine service. For the trouble and expense of coming from Cape Town I have not heard that he receives any remuneration." However, there is evidence that Holt did begin to receive a Government salary for his clerical duties in 1840 and a note in his own handwriting, which records the dates of his long service to the churches at Wynberg and Rondebosch, confirms that it was for the two years 1832-33 before the church was built, that he was unpaid. It was not until 1836 that he moved to Plumstead House at Wynberg. A learned man (he was a Doctor of

Divinity at Cambridge) Holt continued to produce works with titles like *Verses on the Celestial Sphere, Catechism relating to the Six Days' Creation* and *A Sermon preached at Wynberg on account of the Irruption of Kaffirs into the Colony.* He also, at some length, calculated the date of the Crucifixion, which he reckoned took place on Friday, April 7, A.D.30. When he and Patricia died they were buried at The Hermitage, to which they had moved some years earlier, but their tombstones were destroyed when a road was made through the property.

Holt had a twin brother William, another academic who was a Fellow of Caius College, Cambridge, and 14th Wrangler. In 1825 he became Rector of Lavenham, Suffolk, and wrote a guide to the church, which is in the British Library. After his marriage to Augusta Butcher in 1833, he became Rector of Wheatacre, Norfolk, and Vicar of Mutford and Barnby in Suffolk. He had no children. There was another brother, William Samuel, who died young. John Thomas, the only child of Thomas Okes's third marriage to Ann Otto Bayer [9 Feb, 1789 at St Thomas the Apostle, Exeter] also died young.

Holt and Patricia took two sons and three daughters with them to South Africa. The two boys both married. Thomas Holt Edward (and his wife, Elizabeth Scott, had five children before Thomas was burnt alive in a grass fire in 1861 in Natal, and Robert Frederick, who married Ellen Short in 1843, produced a son and furthered an Okes affinity with Australia by going to live at Brighton, near Adelaide. Pamela Holt (1802-1881), Holt and Patricia's eldest child, married twice - first Captain Caithness, a sailor and merchant, to whom she bore a daughter Eliza and secondly in April, 1852, Samuel Smart, an Australian lawyer who had previously been married to her sister, Mary Ann (1804-1851), who had died in Australia twelve months earlier. Holt Okes did not approve of this marriage, which was, however, legal in South Africa at the time. Ellen (1811-1860) became engaged to young William Herbert, a brother of Dennis of Huntingdon, who stayed with the Okes's in Capetown soon after they arrived there, but William died on his way back to England in 1833 and Ellen later married Captain Horace Clarke Beevor, of the Indian Civil Service, had a family of five children and also emigrated to Australia. Margaret (1806-1854) as we have seen, looked after her parents and survived her father by less than three weeks. The girls in England were:

Frances Alicia (1809--1874) who married Major Henry George Hart, of the 49th Regiment, whose sister was the Elizabeth Scott who married Frances's brother Thomas. They had nine children - a family touched by tragedy and triumph. The eldest son lived only five years and the second and third were drowned at Blackwater, near Fermoy, when the 12-year-old tried unsuccessfully to save his nine-year-old brother from drowning. The next three sons became senior soldiers, one of them, Sir Reginald Clare Hart, winning the Victoria Cross in Afghanistan and becoming a keen family historian.

Isabella Clara (1813-1858) married an A.D.C. to Queen Victoria, Col W Pattle, C.B. but had no offspring.

Despite the substantial exodus to Australia, the Okes's continued to flourish in South Africa and remained in touch with their Herbert relatives, but it was not always easy to keep track. In July 1905, for example, Dennis Henry Herbert received a reply to his enquiries in the following terms:

> I received your letter three mails since but I am sorry I could not reply to it sooner. My mother Portia Victoria Pamela who died at Ladysmith July 1863, had two brothers who survived her, Holt and Henry Matson Robert. The latter died some time back, unmarried, the former I have never seen but indirectly I have heard that his wife was the daughter of a Dutch colonist named Sterk and that they have two sons and three daughters. These again have married into Dutch families - the lines of demarcation run deep and I am afraid that it will not be possible to give you further particulars of them.

This uncompromising verdict came from John M. Bell, of Johannesburg, who added that he planned to come to England and was always ready to answer Dennis's questions. Whether they ever met is not known. Nevertheless contact was made and has been maintained. In 1973 Miss Sterk's grandson, Holt, and his wife Nancy, who evinced distinct lack of sympathy for the white Nationalist government, visited Hemingford Abbots and, at Exeter, had Thomas Okes's Greek epitaph translated for them by five clergymen. Almost 20 years after that their son, Holt, stayed at Hemingford Abbots and 10 years later still their daughter-in-law pored over family trees on the living room floor there.

Although Thomas Okes's two later marriages produced a good crop of descendants, it was his first marriage, on February 23, 1754, at St. George's, Mayfair, which was to prove the most productive in the long run. The bride was Mary Verney, of Wantage, who is reputed to have been the natural daughter of George Bubb Dodington, Lord Melcombe Regis, an exotic late Augustan politician of a venality remarkable even for those unsavoury times.

However, in private life he was less unattractive, was a more than passable poet, and became a fast friend of Voltaire, whom he entertained at his appallingly vulgar seat, Eastbury, in Dorset. For the first 29 years of his life he was plain George Bubb, son of Jeremiah, whom Horace Walpole snobbishly dismissed as an apothecary, and Mary (née Dodington), whose father had married into the Temple family from Stowe and whose brother George had made a fortune as a founder of the Bank of England. Uncle George had no children so our George inherited a substantial fortune. The evidence for Mary Verney's paternity comes not only from a Memorandum on the Okes Family compiled by the aforementioned holder of the Victoria Cross, Major General Sir Reginald Hart, but from records left by her grandchildren. Neither give a source for it and neither seem to have known her surname, but Dennis Henry Herbert, who was a cautious man, accepted it as true and it has descended in the family ever since. It is strengthened to something near certainty by the fact, hitherto unrecorded by the family, that Dodington left her £500 in his Will. She died in Bedford in September, 1764, causing Thomas to remove to King's Lynn.

Dodington's marital affairs were complicated. He kept his marriage to Mary Beaghan a secret for 17 years. This was said to be because he had given "a dark lady named Mrs Strawbridge" a contractual promise to marry none but her on pain of a £10,000 forfeit. A more prosaic reason may be that his important Temple relatives stood to inherit his large estates if he had no heir and he did not want to alienate them. When he finally told Lord Chobham about the marriage, Dodington was able to add the welcome news that it was childless. However, there was talk of a natural son and it is thought possible that a long correspondence in Dodington's papers with a certain Mrs. Anne East and her son relate to an illegitimate issue but his biographers make no mention of a natural daughter. There is, though, an enigmatic entry in his diary for June 20, 1754, saying "This day put a cruel end to a long and tender friendship." On the day of Mary Verney's marriage to Thomas Okes, Dodington gave no inkling in his published dairy that anything exceptional was happening.

Thomas Okes and Mary had only one child, Thomas Verney Okes, born five months after the wedding, on 23 July, 1754 in Aldersgate St., London. Of his education and early life nothing is known, but he became chief surgeon at Addenbrooke's Hospital in Cambridge, and is said to have been in demand all over East Anglia. He achieved something like fame in 1799 when he treated Elizabeth Woodcock, who survived after lying under the snow for eight days at Impington near Cambridge. Mrs Woodcock, the mother of several children by an earlier marriage and of a two-year-old whom she was still breastfeeding, was on her way back from Cambridge late at night when her horse shied during a snow storm and, after she had dismounted, ran off. She pursued and caught it but was too exhausted to remount and the snow built up around her. After eight days, during which she remained at least semi-conscious, she was discovered still alive by passing neighbours who called in Dr. Okes to attend to her. He ordered that she be put to bed, given small quantities of weak broth occasionally (but not so much as to overload the stomach), denied any strong drink and not brought near to any fire. For the next 45 days Thomas Verney and his pupil supervised Mrs Woodcock's recovery, which in the early stages was impeded by the number of visitors drawn by the extraordinary circumstances of her case. Later Thomas Verney wrote a blow-by-blow account of the treatment, which consisted of an alarming sequence of clysters (enemas) of mutton broth, doses of saline mixture with antimonial wine, opium, strong decoctions of Peruvian bark, a mixture of oil and manna and eventually, and surely to her delight, port wine brought by her local clergyman. Meanwhile the Doctor was concerned with the mortification of her feet, which began to smell offensively. For this he prescribed very hot poultices of stale beer and oatmeal three times a day - and more opium. On Sunday, February 10th, for example, a week after she had been discovered, Thomas Verney reported:

> *Sunday 17th* - The mortified parts were extremely offensive, and I removed a large quantity of integuments which hung loose at the bottoms of her feet; she requested that the cataplasms (poultices) might be renewed *as often as possible,* and applied *very warm,* which was done three times in the day. She continued very weak and low (that is, as to bodily strength,) but her mind was very calm, and she endured her pain and illness with most wonderful fortitude."

By Thursday she had overcome an attack of violent diarrhoea but "several toes were so loose that I easily removed them with the scissors" and the following day she got out of bed for the first time. By now her bowels were in a good state, but she had little relish for meat, preferring strong broth in large quantities and milk porridge, washed down with some wine and ale. During March the remainder of her toes came off, her feet were exquisitely painful and she began to be so sleepy that her attendants were very worried, but she held on until on

April 17th - The sores are now free from sloughs, and become evidently less every day; her appetite is tolerably good, and her general health has begun to amend; but with all these circumstances in her favour, she feels herself to be very uncomfortable, and in fact her prospect is most miserable. True it is that her life is saved; but the mutilated state in which she is left, without even a chance of ever being able to attend to the duties of her family, is almost worse than death itself; for from the exposure of the Os Calcis, in all probability it will not be till after some months that the bottoms of her feet can be covered with new skin; and after all, whenever this event takes place, they will be so tender as not to bear any pressure; the loss too of all her toes must make it impossible for her to move herself, but with the assistance of crutches.

Summing up, Thomas Verney concluded that Mrs. Woodcock's survival had been in large part due to her managing to stay awake for the first five days of her ordeal because she felt no cold except in her feet. Having no evacuation from the bowels and making very little urine had also contributed since in the torpid state in which she remained, there was no exertion of the body which could waste the frame. Finally her remarkably calm state of mind throughout had powerfully contributed to her survival.

His conclusion was that the directions of the Humane Society for the treatment of persons suffering from extreme cold or long abstinence from food should be enforced. They turn out to be familiar to anyone who suffered from chilblains in youth - to avoid direct heat and instead rub the affected parts with snow or immerse them in cold water and afterwards chafe them with flannel. To diminish fever (which had nearly been fatal for Mrs Woodcock) "let the party be restrained most cautiously from taking too much or too nutritious food; spirits likewise, or wine, should on no pretence whatever be administered, till they have first been copiously diluted with water." Then it is back to the clysters of meat broth and doses of opium and camphor and, in cases of mortification, Peruvian Bark, though not until suppuration has come on.

This cordial endorsement of Humane Society recommendations was reciprocated and Thomas Verney Okes was awarded in the following June the Silver Medal of the Royal Humane Society for the successful application of its principles. As for Mrs Woodcock, she did not long survive, but became a legend in the area. A memorial, now in the Folk Museum at Cambridge, was erected on the spot where she was found and poems, songs, pictures and drawings celebrating her case were in circulation - but someone at least tried to blacken her reputation. Beneath the record of her death, on July 11, 1799, in the Impington parish register is written, in another hand: "She was in a state of intoxication when she was lost. N.B. Her death was accelerated (to say the least) by spirituous liquors afterwards taken - procured by the donations of numerous visitors." If this is true and not an opportunistic initiative by the Temperance movement, celebrity status seems to have been just as hazardous at the end of the eighteenth century as it is in the twenty first.

At any rate the whole affair clearly did Thomas Verney Okes no harm. With a team of assistants and pupils he undertook a great deal of University work which, "enabled him to make many influential friends who were of great assistance to him in getting his large family started in life". Large his family certainly was for he had, depending on which pedigree you follow, anything between 18 and 23 children.

Chapter 6

CAMBRIDGE, CADIZ, BUENOS AIRES & ASUNCION

```
                          ┌──  Thomas Okes, b. 1730, m. 1754, d. 1797
              ┌── Thomas Verney Okes, b. 1754, m. 1777, d. 1818
              │            └──  Mary Verney
Mary Okes, b. 1783, d. 1870 (+ 17 siblings)
   m.  William Herbert
              │            ┌──  Joseph Gray, d. 1807
              └── Ann Gray, b. 1756, d. 1837
                           └──  Anne Cock, b. 1729, d. 1819
```

Who shall find a valiant woman,
Her children rose up and called her blessed.- *Proverbs 32*

All Thomas Verney Okes's numerous children were borne by his long-suffering wife, Ann Gray, daughter of another Cambridge surgeon, Joseph Gray. It is worth recording the names and dates of birth of this remarkable family:

1. Mary Anne b. Feb 7, 1778
2. Jane b. Sep. 25, 1779 m. Rev Francis Creswell, Rector of Waldingfield, Suffolk d.s.p. 1870
3. George b. Sep. 2, 1780 d.
4. Thomas b. Jun. 17, 1781 d.
5. Thomas b. Aug. 15, 1782 d.
6. Mary b. Jul. 12, 1783 m. William Herbert, of Huntingdon
7. Ann b. Aug 8, 1784 m. Rev Jos. Hopkins, Vicar of Hartford, Huntingdon
8. Elizabeth b. Jul. 9, 1785 d. 1787
9. Francis b. Jul. 4, 1786 Curate of West Wratting, Cambs. d. Nov. 6, 1825
10.Charles b. Sep. 2, 1787 Lieut., R.N., Governor, Naval Knights of Windsor.
11.Henry b.Mar. 8,1789 d. Apr. 8, 1821 at Buenos Aires.
12.William b. Feb. 13, 1790 Lieut., R.N. d. Sep. 2, 1810 at Antigua.
13. Sarah b. Mar. 25, 1791 d. 1793

14.Peter Thomas Walter b. May, 1792 d. 1793
15.John b. May 22, 1793 m. Mary Elizabeth Collin Martin, of Epping
16.Persis b. Jul. 23, 1795
17.Richard b. Dec. 15, 1797 Provost of King's College, Cambridge. m. Mary Elizabeth Sibthorpe
18.Caroline b. May 23, 1799

So in the 23 years between her marriage on May 5, 1777 and the end of the century, when she was 44, Ann bore a child every year except 1788, 1794. 1796 and 1798. Perhaps it was in the expectation of no further progeny that the proud parents decided to give Peter three Christian names, but it seems to have been this which caused some of the confusion over the number of children, though unless he were assumed to be triplets the mistake is elementary. A note in the family bible claims that, besides the 18 children listed above, five more who died young were baptised at St. Michael's, Cambridge. The registers of that parish, however, do not bear that out. In the end it must have been either Ann's body clock or a New Year resolution for a new century that prevented the birth of any younger sibling for Caroline.

Charles Okes, the second oldest boy to grow to manhood, narrowly missed the Battle of Trafalgar. He was a Midshipman on H.M.S. Seahorse in the Mediterranean from May 23rd 1803 to December 1806, but Seahorse was not at the battle in October, 1805. During his 14-year career he saw only minor actions but served on the North American and West Indian stations, at Cadiz during the Siege by the French and in the Channel. When the war with the French ended, he left the service at the age of 27 and went to live with his elder brother Francis, a clergyman, and eventually with his younger brother, Richard, at Eton. In 1830, at the age of 43, he was appointed to be a Naval Knight of Windsor, a sinecure providing accommodation in Travers College within the precincts of Windsor Castle. The Knights were established under the will of Samuel Travers who decreed that they be "superannuated or disabled lieutenants of English men-of-war", single, with no children, inclined to lead a virtuous, studious and devout life, who could be removed if they gave occasion for scandal. They were established in 1795 and disbanded in 1892. One day in 1832 William IV, arriving at morning service in St. George's Chapel, observed one of the Knights dressed in an old plain blue coat with a common red handkerchief round his neck. The King, who had himself been a serving officer, at once sent a message instructing the Knights, Charles Okes among them, to parade after the service when he gave them a right royal dressing down for not appearing, especially on a Sunday, in proper dress. He decreed that in future on Sundays and Feast days they were to wear full dress uniform and on weekdays un-dress uniform. "You all of you know it is done on board a ship," he said, "and what is the reason you don't do it here?" He required the Provost of Eton to summon another parade, consulted his son Captain Lord Adolphus Fitz-Clarence, R.N. as to the propriety of their turn-out and, on being told that it was correct, announced that he was sending them venison for their Mess table. Charles Okes, in a memorandum on the incident, recorded that the Provost told him later the King had said:

> "Well, I gave them a good blowing up on Sunday last, I will now set that all right again. Bring them up to me at noon on Saturday next that I may see how they look in their Full dress. I will then tell them about the venison myself. They will like that better."

Charles himself rose to become Governor of the Naval Knights. His younger brother, Henry, was more entrepreneurial. He was engaged in July, 1818, in Liverpool at £300 for one year with expenses paid, to go to Buenos Aires, via Brazil on behalf of one John Parish Robertson, who though he was only 25 had already served 11 years in South America. What the new recruit was to do when he got there was studiously vague - the job offer simply said he was to promote "certain objects to be hereafter discussed" and place himself under the direction of Robertson's company for a year from the date of the appointment with a possible second year in prospect. Within weeks of arriving in Buenos Aires, and with only six months of his firm contract to go, Henry was planning for the future after Robertson.

> My object in going to Brazil was to gain all the information necessary to plant & dress cotton. My employers have it in contemplation to form an establishment of this kind on the confluence of the Parany and Paraguay rivers at a place called Corrientes. Cotton is one of the riches of that province which has never been cultivated & it is calculated that the growing & cleaning this article for the Brit. market gives 140 p.c. profit in 12 months. Now I cannot say whether Messrs ---- will have any desire to keep me in their service nor have I of course any idea on what footing - but it is high time for me to think of doing something for myself on a more solid footing than that of a stipulated income.

His only handicap, he thought, would be a lack of capital so his idea was to get his brother Francis, to persuade their brother-in-law, Rev. W. Cresswell, Vicar of Great Waldingfield, Suffolk, to put up a loan of £1,000. "I know of many who would readily enter into my plan," he wrote, "but it is desirable with me not to give unnecessary publicity to what I have in contemplation, and therefore I particularly request that it may not go beyond yourselves whether it do or do not meet with his approbation." Mr Cresswell was unable to resist this conspiratorial approach and must have been further stimulated when Henry suggested that they should communicate through Francis, with whom he had adopted a form of shorthand for confidential matters. Henry was soon writing to say that he might call upon the money at any time, but then matters took a very different turn.

Whether the cotton idea was merely a blind or not, it was soon abandoned as unlikely to pay and Henry was enrolled into a much more dubious undertaking dreamt up by William Parish Robertson, who claimed that it cropped up by chance because a consignment of mathematical instruments, telescopes and theodolites, microscopes and electrical machines which was supposed to go to India, was delivered to Buenos Aires by mistake. Henry was a keen mathematician so Robertson said to him. "Now, Okes, here is a brilliant opening for you. Make a selection of these, and go up with the instruments to Dr. Francia." Henry may have been a greenhorn, but even he knew enough to doubt whether this idea could be a serious one – Dr. José Francia was the enigmatic Dictator of Paraguay, who pursued with the utmost severity a policy of isolating Paraguayans from the world outside and subjecting them to his absolute power within. According to the Robertsons, he ran a torture facility, known as the Chamber of Truth, which dealt with some 400 political suspects a year. Moreover he particularly hated British merchants, whom he described as "downright swindlers" and he had form with the Robertson brothers, whom he had expelled from his country only four years before.

William Robertson, in memoirs written a dozen years later, asks us to believe that Henry was converted to this crazy idea by the argument that he would not be meddling in politics and that, with his mathematical skills not only would he have nothing to fear from El Supremo Dictador, but could "hope for everything which you could possibly desire in the way of commercial advantage". The profit motive was strong in Henry, but it was not going to be fed by a consignment of microscopes. When he agreed to go he must have known that there was more to it than that. At any rate he quickly sent off to Francis a sealed letter "which you will only open <u>in case you should hear of any thing fatal occurring to me</u>". He then launched, presumably by way of explanation, into a lengthy passage of shorthand, which has so far proved frustratingly indecipherable despite the best efforts of experts in both Cambridge and Oxford. The letter was later accepted as Henry's will; it left to Francis and Charles Okes all decisions about what should happen to his property in the event of his death.

The journey was so dangerous - because of civil war in Argentina - that Henry had to travel the whole way to Asuncion by boat, a "commodious vessel" fitted out for him by the Robertsons in which he set sail from Las Conchas on January 17th, 1820. On the eve of his departure he told Francis he was dreading the journey:

> My navigation is by the Parana and will be a very trying undertaking at this season of the year. Heats insufferable, Mosquitos innumerable, Fleas, Flies etc. incalculable and accommodation (if any) most d-----ble. Of course I am <u>much</u> occupied with my "preparativos", for independent of what is to be prepared for such a journey, and that with a considerable property under my charge, I have many accounts to terminate here and a great variety of "documental" labour to accomplish.

According to Robertson's account, this "considerable property" included "two or three pair of pistols, and a couple of fowling-pieces," which were not listed in the manifest and not intended for military purposes. This concealment was done not because there was any need to smuggle arms on board (he used italics to suggest how ridiculous such a thought would be!) but to avoid the cupidity of chiefs along the river and it was believed that only Henry and the captain knew about them. However, this was a very considerable euphemism. In a letter to William Robertson's brother, John Parish Robertson in Liverpool, Henry made clear what was really afoot. A three-way deal had been struck between Henry, the Robertsons and a mysterious pair of Paraguayans, Aguirré and Grassis, who had "friends" in Asuncion. This involved false bills of sale, which enabled a cargo vessel, loaded with "a cargo of Flour and a variety of articles of furniture for the Dictator as asked for by himself", to obtain a British pass.

> She will also take 200 Stand of Arms – the safe conduct of which, you must be aware, forms almost the corner stone of our hopes from Paraguay. But I feel sound confidence in the success of this part of the operation. The measures we have taken to evince this are these: Aguirré, who I suspect can do anything he pleases at the Fort, has procured permission to embark these arms, under the form of an order to convey them, on account of the Government, to St. Nicholas, where the Army acting against Montomera has its depot! By an understanding with his friend General Rodriguez, acting there, the cargo will be received, and the Government Order for ye conveyance and delivery of ye Arms signed, as if accomplished, so that should it be averred on any part of ye voyage that the vessel was

41

known to have embarked arms, she can justify it by having been
ordered to do so by ye Government as represented on ye documented
forms for that purpose; and remove the suspicion , if any, of ye Arms
being still on board, by ye document testifying their discharge at St.
Nicholas.

The problem was that when he set out Henry was not sure how the civil
wars were going or under whose control various strategic ports were going to
be when he got there. Though he evidently kept a journal of his journey, it has
not descended with his other papers, so we are are reliant on the unreliable
Robertson for what actually happened. He says that the expedition was
delayed for a month at San Nicholas because the authorities resented the
vessel's British pass. However, they were eventually allowed to proceed to the
Bajada, capital of Entre Rios province, where things took an awkward turn.
Information leaked out that arms for Paraguay were on board.

> The vessel was suddenly filled with troops and poor Okes was
> thrown into great consternation. "I heard," he said, "after I had
> returned to the cabin, the order given to open the hatches, and to
> discharge the cargo. The work of search began. For three hours the
> *tipones* of flour, cases of merchandise, and bales of goods were
> tumbling over my head. The unfortunate Charles, who constantly
> heard from his bed-room the noise of the workman's hammer fitting
> up the scaffolding in Whitehall, was, I dare say, less disturbed than I
> was by the business now going forward."

However, Henry had told John Robertson that "the place appointed for the
secretion of the Arms, I think will protect them against even a suspicious
search," and his confidence proved justified. Nothing was found and the ship
was allowed to proceed to Corrientes on the Paraguayan border. At Asuncion
Henry was hauled at once before Francia, who, when shown the scientific
instruments, proved as amenable as Robertson had expected. He allowed
Henry to conduct his business, which he did over the next four months, before
embarking on the return journey having done so well that, once the boat was
fully loaded, he still had a large surplus of goods and cash which he left in the
hands of his agent. If this was risky, what Henry brought back to Buenos Aires
sold, in Robertson's words "to so enormous a profit, that it paid off the whole
of the original investment he took with him, and left him besides several
thousand pounds as his own share of profits". No wonder he was able to write
to Mr. Cresswell in Suffolk thanking him for his willingness to lend £1,000
and adding "it would have been of ye greatest moment to me had not our
Paraguay operation been planned upon a scale of such perfect generosity &
confidence towards me as to render all other assistance unnecessary". Being a

cautious man, however, he added the hope that, if things went wrong, Cresswell would again support him.

Henry invested much of his dubiously-gotten gains, in partnership with Messrs Fair, Eastman and McKenzie, in ventures in Peru and Chile, much merchandise travelling in the ship *Jane Gordon*. Then, when staying with John Fairs in the country outside Buenos Aires, he fell from the rooftop and was killed. John Parish Robertson gave the following account in a letter to Francis:

> On the fatal day of the accident (the day before yesterday) your Brother dined at home & in the evening with Mr. Fair & a Mr. Ludlam went to the House top, which, in the style of all Houses here is made flat & to walk on. Here they all continued till about dusk when Mr. Fair & Mr Ludlum came down. In what words, my dear Sir, shall I say the rest – Your Brother we presume sat down on the parapet, or , probably, to observe something, had stood upon it, and losing his balance he fell from it to the ground. Hearing the fall Mr. Fair instantly hurried down stairs & medical aid was procured. It was all in vain, for he expired almost immediately after the fall.

He was buried next day in a newly-acquired British burial ground, the first Englishman, it was believed, to be buried in British consecrated ground in South America. No clergyman was in the area so the service was read by the Commander on the station, Capt. O'Brien, and "every respectable Englishman in the place assisted in discharging for him the last sad office which, in our turn, we shall surely all require."

The Government acted quickly – but not so quickly as John Robertson, who at once packed up all Henry's private papers in a sealed writing desk and had it shipped out on the *Lavinia* to London just before the authorities demanded that they be impounded. Since there was no will in the country, the Court for Adjudging Foreign Property demanded that all of Henry's assets that were in the country should be paid over to it. Fortunately it was all either in, or on its way to, Chile or left in Paraguay and Robertson's legal advice was that the Government would have to give way, but in his long summary Robertson added the caution that those running things in Argentina were arbitrary in their proceedings and "have no moral restraint and a very slight political one over their actions". For the next five years matters hung fire. Francis, who we must presume knew the whole story from Henry's shorthand communications and diary, while expressing consistent gratitude to Robertson and Fairs for their efforts on his behalf, did begin to wonder when he heard nothing for a year at a time. He seemed to have no priestly scruples about

Henry's "speculation" but, when he died in 1826 things were still unresolved and his brother Charles took over the mantle. In Asuncion the good Dr. Francia was as quick off the mark as the Argentinians – and more successful. He seized all Henry's assets and did away with his partner. Whether the Okes family ever received a penny I have not been able to ascertain.

The youngest of Thomas Verney Okes's sons, Rev. Richard Okes, D.D. (1797-1888) was the most eminent. Educated on the foundation at Eton, his contemporaries included William Mackworth Praed, Lord Derby (the future Prime Minister), Pusey and the poet Shelley. He won the Browne medal for the best Latin Ode in 1819 and 1820 and became an assistant master in 1821, rising to Lower Master in 1838 and being appointed in 1850 Provost of King's College, Cambridge. When he heard the bells being rung to mark Richard Okes's inauguration as Provost, a witty Fellow penned the following verse:

> How Kings have slept in Oaks of old,
> Our English Chronicles have told:
> But Fortune now the changes rings,
> For Okes tonight shall sleep in King's.

Richard Okes's entry in the *Dictionary of National Biography*, which was based on personal information from old pupils and colleagues, paints an affectionate picture:

> He was a conspicuous figure in the school and college world and innumerable anecdotes grew up round his marked and vivid personality. Many school generations of Etonians carried away a lively recollection of his dry and caustic wit, his shrewd remarks, his slow and deliberate speech, his inimitable Latin quotations, drawn chiefly from familiar sources, such as Horace or the Eton Latin grammar, his curious punctiliousness about minutiae of school discipline, usages and phraseology. He was a successful tutor, having at times as many as ninety pupils, and impressed his colleagues as well as the boys, with a strong sense of his painstaking accuracy.

At King's one of his first acts was to abandon, in 1850, the privilege which entitled members of the College to take the B.A. degree without examination, and he was justified when it turned out that they could do well without such outrageous privilege. He had to contend with the introduction of great changes in the university, the result of two successive university commissions, and, though conservative by inclination, he loyally carried out their reforms, and presided over the college with much dignity and kindliness for thirty-eight years. He was Vice-Chancellor in 1851, but University politics did not attract him and he thereafter refused to serve again. As editor of a new series of '*Musae Etonenses*', he wrote witty Latin sketches of the contributors, and as a member of the Governing Body he presented, with Dr Hawtrey, a heraldic window in the school museum.

A portrait of him by Sir Hubert von Herkomer, described by his nephew as "remarkably successful and charming" hangs in the Great Hall in King's, showing a slightly hunched figure, balding but bewhiskered, with eyes full of humour. Richard married, in 1826, Mary, daughter of Allen Sibthorpe, Esq., of Guildford, Surrey, and they had three daughters, only one of whom was married, but she gave him eight grandchildren. The daughters were friends of Dennis Henry Herbert and supplied him with information about the family, much of it from the Okes family Bible, which had been given to one of them by a Professor Hughes, who found it on a Cambridge bookstall.

According to John Saltmarsh, a Fellow of King's, Dr Okes was the last provost to use the Provost's Coach, a great lumbering vehicle drawn by four horses, in which provosts used to travel to Eton or tour the college's extensive estates round the country. "It was painted a bright yellow and picked out in black, and the college arms were on the panels. The inside held four, or even six; a footman sat beside the coachman on the box and there was a dickey behind. It was very high, and the Provost climbed in and out by means of a pair of folding steps." Dennis Henry Herbert remembered it well for Richard used to travel in it when he came, with his two unmarried daughters, for his usual visit to his nephew, the Rector of Hemingford Abbots, during the Long Vacation. Dennis Henry recalled:

> As a small boy it was my joy on those occasions to sit in the coach while it was driven from the front door to the stable yard, and then to see the coachman release the two carrier pigeons who were to carry back to King's the news of the Provost's safe arrival.

How astonished Dennis Henry would have been to know that his son would one day live in those stables, now converted into a very comfortable house. Much of this featured in correspondence in *The Times* in 1937 when Sir Ian Malcolm challenged the paper and "the great confraternity of Old Etonians" to recover the ancient chariot so that it could be used at the Coronation of King George VI. He said he could not believe that it, and its sister vehicle at Eton, could have been sawn up for firewood or sold to travelling showmen. But Mr. Saltmarsh tracked down a former employee of Mr. Hunnybun, the Cambridge coach builder to whom the coach was sold, at

Richard Okes's behest, in 1887. He said that it had indeed been broken up and the wheels bought by the landlord of "The Jolly Waterman", who used them for furniture removals.

Richard Okes died at Cambridge on 25 Nov, 1888, and was buried in the crypt of King's College Chapel, where, having been ice cold for many years, it is now unendurably warmed by the heating system nearby.

Of Thomas Verney Okes's several daughters, we shall notice only one, Mary, who was an artist of some merit, winning several awards from the Royal Society for the Arts for pen and ink drawings. It ws she who, as we have seen, became the second wife of William Herbert of Huntingdon.

Mary Okes's prizewinning 1808 drawing, (Courtesy Royal Society for the Arts, London)

Henry Okes's private shorthand, so far indecipherable.

FROM THE WELSH MARCHES TO CAMBRIDGE

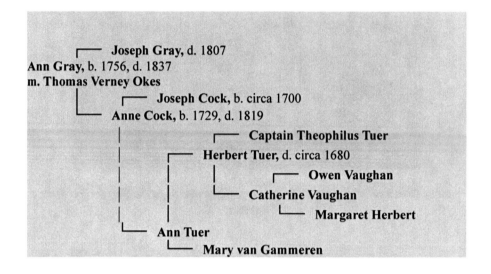

Joseph Gray, d. 1807
Ann Gray, b. 1756, d. 1837
m. Thomas Verney Okes
Joseph Cock, b. circa 1700
Anne Cock, b. 1729, d. 1819
Captain Theophilus Tuer
Herbert Tuer, d. circa 1680
Owen Vaughan
Catherine Vaughan
Margaret Herbert
Ann Tuer
Mary van Gammeren

If transitory things, which soone decay,
Age must be lovelyest at the latest day – *John Donne.*

For all Ann Okes's prodigious feats of childbearing, it is an extraordinary fact that, as Dennis Henry Herbert recorded, in 1905 there was only one living male Okes descendent of Thomas Verney Okes and he had no children. But, if Anne's contribution to the descending family tree in the male line was less than might be expected, she transmitted much of the Okes's academic quality and spirit of adventure into subsequent generations. She also brought much in from the past, allowing the erstwhile Harbottles to claim genuine Herbert descent from the family of "the most noble and incomparable paire of bretheren," William Herbert and Philip Herbert, the third and fourth earls of Pembroke, to whom was dedicated the first Folio of Shakespeare. The descent was through various female lines, from Margaret, a sister of the poet George Herbert and his dashing diplomatic brother, Lord Herbert of Chirbury, and therefore from their mother, Magdalen Herbert, who inspired some of John Donne's greatest poetry - in particular:

The Autumnall.

No *Spring*, nor *Summer* Beauty hath such grace,
As I have seen in one *Autumnall* face.
Yong *Beauties* force our love, and that's a *Rape*,
This doth but *counsaile*, yet you cannot scape.
If t'were a *shame* to love, here t'were no *shame*,
Affection here takes *Reverences* name.
Were her first yeares the *Golden Age*; That's true,
But now shee's *gold* oft tried, and ever new.
That was her torrid and inflaming time,
This is her tolerable *Tropique clyme*.
Faire eyes, who askes more heate then comes from hence,
He in a fever wishes pestilence.
Call not these wrinkles *graves*; If *graves* they were,
They were *Love's graves*; for else he is no where......

Literary critics invariably describe Magdalen as "pious" or "grave", but to be able to appreciate, at the age of 44, a poem hymning the wrinkles on her face and comparing her to an enormous plane tree she must have had a sense of humour. The poem epitomises the difficulty which later generations had with the metaphysicals like Donne and George Herbert, in whose work wit often supersedes emotion, but Magdalen probably had no such problem. The relationship between them - what Izaak Walton calls "amity" - was evidently platonic, but one critic, noting that despite the many 'sacred Indearments' between them Magdalen becomes, after a few lines a mere topic for wit, feels bound to add: "But I rather suspect that, strange as it may appear to us, such wit was expected and appreciated even by the grave Mrs. Herbert." Magdalen was carrying her tenth child when her husband, Richard Herbert, died in 1596, but she raised the whole family for 12 years on her own before, in 1608, she married a man half her age. This was Sir John Danvers, whose complexion was so perfect that when he was on the Grand Tour Italians gathered in the streets to admire it. The marriage was happy, despite the disparity in age, because as John Donne said "she had a cheerfulness agreeable to his youth and he a sober staidness comfortable to her more years".

Magdalen was not only stern and virtuous, but a fascinating woman, who had learned the art of graceful living and had a gift for making people happy. She also loved music and gardens and the company of lively intelligent minds. According to Marchette Chute, whose delightful book, *Two Gentle Men,* contains a humorous and sensitive account of the Herberts, it was just as well that Magdalen had so many sons because "With her vigorous intelligence and her vitality, she would have been insupportable if she had been left to concentrate on only one." She certainly took her maternal duties so seriously that when her sons entered Oxford she went with them, keeping them in Walton's words so much under her own eye, as to see and converse with them daily without any rigid sourness as might make her company a torment to her child. That must have taken some doing, because several of her sons, as befitted the great great grandchildren of "that incomparable hero" and master of the pole-axe, Sir Richard Herbert, of Colebrook, were feisty individuals prone to duelling and fighting. Edward claimed in his Autobiography that he never drew his sword on his own behalf, but he seemed to draw it quite frequently on behalf of others. Richard bore the scars of 24 duels, William broke his sword in combat in Denmark but managed to prevail using only the hilt, and Thomas performed various acts of derring do in the Navy. Henry, as Master of the King's Revels, was the scourge of the acting trade as he was a control freak and wanted the power to licence every form of performance himself.

The others were more peaceable, but even the saintly George was reputed to have kicked over the traces in Cambridge, where however Magdalen did not follow him. He later became Public Orator at Cambridge, a public relations job which required him to pen flattering letters to the king, and then Rector of Fugglestone and Bemerton and one of Britain's best-loved poets and hymn-writers. He also spent a substantial amount of money repairing the church at Leighton Bromswold, Huntingdonshire, only a few miles from where his sister's descendants settled 200 years later. When Magdalen died in 1627 at the beautiful home in Chelsea which she shared with her second husband, John Donne preached one of his noblest sermons about her. He spoke of her as the best wife, the best mother, the best neighbour, the best friend and the best example. He mentioned her holy cheerfulness and religious alacrity (the best evidence of a good conscience) and said that, though in her last days she had suffered some melancholy that put a half damper on these qualities, yet she never disputed God's proceedings or doubted his goodness and mercy to her. Dealing with her family, he said:

> In that ground, her Father's family, she grew not many years. Transplanted young from thence, by marriage, into another family of honour, as a flower that doubles and multiplies by transplantation,

she multiplied into ten children: Job's number and Job's distribution, (as she herself would very often remember) seven sons and three daughters. And in this ground she grew not many years more than were necessary for the producing of so many plants.

Some of the tact which enabled her mother to remain on terms with her sons must have rubbed off on her daughter, Margaret, whose marriage on November 3, 1606 to Owen Vaughan of Llwydiart brought to an end a feud between the two families. They had three daughters, one of whom, Catherine, married Theophilus Tuer, a coal merchant of Bridge Street, in Cambridge, who came from a long line of clergymen and was a Captain in the Royalist forces during the Civil War. Their son, Herbert Tuer, was a painter, four of whose seven known paintings remain in the family and are of his parents, his wife and himself. Another, of Sir Leoline Jenkins, is in the National Portrait Gallery and a sixth, of a man in full armour standing by a pillar, was sold in New York in October, 1988. The Rijksmuseum in Holland has two further paintings believed by some to be the work of Herbert Tuer, but others disagree. So not much is known about Herbert Tuer, but he did rate the following mention in Horace Walpole's *Anecdotes of Painting in England*:

> Herbert, who received his name from his maternal uncle, withdrew, with his youngest brother, Theophilus, into Holland, after the death of Charles I. The latter followed arms; Herbert applied to painting, and made good progress in portraits, as appears by some small ones of himself and family, now in England, where however they are little known.

He married twice, first Mary van Gammeren, from Utrecht, by whom he had a daughter, Anne, and secondly Elizabeth van Heymenbergh. His death is not recorded but is believed to have ocurred at Utrecht in about 1686. Herbert Tuer's sister, Catherine, married (as his third wife) William Cole, a farmer at Babraham, near Cambridge. It was her second marrriage. Her children by William Cole were three daughters, Mary, Catherine and Jane and a son, Rev. William Cole, a delightful diarist and antiquary, whose manuscript is a mine of genealogical information. Rev William was, therefore, a first cousin of the painter's daughter, Anne Tuer, who married Joseph Cock, another Cambridge character, whose standing in the social scale became a matter of mild dispute among historians of the period. One described him as "an honest man who got a handsome fortune as a carrier at Cambridge". To this William Cole, took exception. In his diary he wrote: "It would have been kinder to have styled Dr Cock's father a merchant, which was his real profession, though he kept several waggons to convey the Suffolk and Cambridgeshire butter to Messrs.

Mawdsley & Daking, the greatest cheesemongers, I suppose, in the world."

According to Cole, the Cocks' daughter, Anne (1729-1819) fell in love with and married Joseph Gray, a Surgeon and apothecary of Cambridge, "a very pretty Person of a Man, a Native of Norwich,....a very good Sort of Man & in great Business," but he was disapproved of by the bride's mother and brother, who were never reconciled to her thereafter. When her husband died, of a violent fever in 1766, the *Cambridge Chronicle* recorded that "he was a gentleman eminent in his profession, generally respected and esteemed, and has left a numerous young family and an afflicted widow to lament the loss of a tender parent and affectionate husband." Anne must have been a decisive woman. Only a day after her husband's death she decided that the apothecary business was so strong that she could carry it on. It would serve, after all, to help feed the numerous young family. A notice appeared in the paper declaring that with the help of her late husband's assistant, Mr. Jackson "who has been some time in the shop and acquainted with the patients, and hath given general satisfaction," and the advice of an eminent Cambridge apothecary, Mr Arbuthnot, Mrs Gray begged the continuance of the favours of her Friends.

It was the daughter of Anne and Joseph Gray, another Ann (1756-1837), who became the prolific wife of Thomas Verney Okes and was the mother of Mary Okes, who married William Herbert of Huntingdon.

Captain Theophilus Tuer in 1856

Catherine Tuer (née Vaughan)

Herbert Tuer, the artist in 1856

Mary Tuer (née van Gammeren)

Magdalen Herbert (née Newport), "a fascinating woman".

FROM RAMSHOLT TO WALLSTOWN

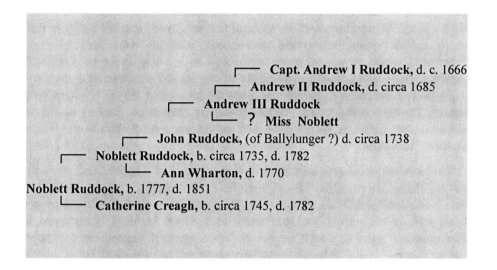

```
                                  ┌── Capt. Andrew I Ruddock, d. c. 1666
                          ┌── Andrew II Ruddock, d. circa 1685
              ┌── Andrew III Ruddock
              └── ? Miss Noblett
          ┌── John Ruddock, (of Ballylunger ?) d. circa 1738
   ┌── Noblett Ruddock, b. circa 1735, d. 1782
          └── Ann Wharton, d. 1770
Noblett Ruddock, b. 1777, d. 1851
   └── Catherine Creagh, b. circa 1745, d. 1782
```

Old man, you're like to meet one traveller still,
A journeyman well famed for courtesy
To all that walk at odds with life and limb;
If this be he now riding up the hill
Maybe he'll stop and take you up with him.-*Ralph Hodgson: The Moor*

Ramsholt, on the Suffolk coast near Sutton Hoo, is now so small a place that it hardly even merits the description of hamlet. It has a most attractive church with an unusual oval-shaped tower, and the *Ramsholt Arms* caters to a flourishing boating trade, but there is little sign of other dwellings. However, it was once a thriving port and it is even possible that Captain Andrew Ruddock, who came from Ramsholt, sailed from there for Ireland in 1649. The local squires were the Wallers and General Waller, as one of Cromwell's generals, very likely recruited young Ruddock. At any rate Andrew landed at Youghal, Co Cork, as part of Oliver Cromwell's invading force in November of 1849.

Nothing is known of the young man's martial career - by most accounts he was a mild man - but he evidently gave satisfaction to his commanding officer, the formidable General Henry Ireton because at the end of the campaign he was granted a substantial property on the edge of the small town of Doneraile. The Castle of Wallstown had been the scene of a brief but violent episode during the war when the Roman Catholic inhabitants, the Wall family, declined to swear allegiance to the Commonwealth or to surrender the castle. The Cromwellians planted a cannon on high ground to the south and, with one devastating round, created such a breach in the defences that the Walls fled. The building and its associated lands were occupied by another family called Nagle for the rest of the war, but they were then given to Captain Ruddock. However, there was a curious episode in which Ruddock, knowing Nagle to be penniless, jokingly offered to sell him back the property. Nagle on the advice of a lawyer, accepted the terms and lodged a guinea as a deposit. He then waited until Ruddock was at Church on Sunday and took possession of the place, which he would not release until he had been given a grant of £50 a year.

This kind of naivety seems to have been typical of Captain Andrew, who was regularly defrauded by his neighbours. For example, he kept a number of shire horses with bald faces and long tails and his neighbours used to get them, without his permission, to do their work. Once Ruddock is supposed to have observed a horse, which he thought he recognised, being used to plough another farmer's land. When he was seen approaching, the ploughman tucked one of the horse's ears under the poll strap of the blinkers. Captain Andrew came up and remarked that he would have taken the animal to be one of his except that his had two ears. Another unauthorised borrower simply knotted the tail of the horse which Ruddock failed to recognise since his horses all had long tails. The Captain liked to feed the rooks in snowy weather and he instructed his workers that all stones picked up on his land were to be carried, sometimes as much as a mile, and deposited on a pile near the castle. The heap remained until 1837 when the stones were used in the making of a new road.

When Captain Ruddock died in about 1666 his son, Andrew, was confirmed in his lands. This Andrew is believed, on the evidence of a note from Miss Gertrude Ruddock to her nephew Dennis Henry Herbert at the beginning of the twentieth century, to have married a Miss Noblett, but no confirmation of this has been found, there being a dearth of records in Ireland because so many were destroyed in the 1916 uprising. The next Andrew, who succeeded in 1685, was clearly made of sterner stuff than his grandfather as he had to defend his ownership against a determined effort by the Wall family to get it back. When James II was on the throne the Irish Parliament was minded to reverse the grants of land made under the earlier regime and the King reluctantly signed a new Act which allowed the landholders of 1641 or their heirs to take steps to recover their land. However, all activity on this front was suspended during the war lest "some may neglect the public safety of the kingdom upon pretence of attending their private concerns". In a chancery bill filed at Dublin on May 28 1690, Andrew Ruddock of Wallstown stated that having for three years past been "in quiet and peaceable possession of the lands of Wallstown and Tullagh by virtue of a title yet in being and undetermined", he and his wife and children had been turned out by Cahir Callaghan, James Wall and several others, who came and committed "several outrageous and cruel actions". A second simultaneous action involved an accusation that Callaghan and Wall had threatened to run Robert Wall of Dunevally off the lands he held and to drive off his cattle. In this case Sir Richard Nagle was the landowner under the Act of Settlement and, in a highly unusual action he proposed to restore the land to Robert Wall. But the whole scene was changed by the outcome of the Battle of the Boyne, which was fought five weeks after these court actions, and which meant that King William's forces were in possession of County Cork. If James Wall had managed to seize anything, he did not have long to enjoy it.

So Andrew Ruddock had reasonable security in his lands when, four years later, he married Abigail Barry. They had three children, yet another Andrew, who married Catherine Stawell in 1718, Rachel, who married Edward Croker and John, described as "of Ballylunger", who was alive in 1729.

In Bristol, where the Ruddocks had long had connections, John Ruddock married Ann Wharton in the early 1730s and they had a son, Noblett. It is very probable - but has yet to be proved - that this John Ruddock was the same man as John Ruddock of Ballylunger. He must have died fairly soon after Noblett was born because Ann made a second marriage, to William Basil, on May 6, 1739 at St. Nicholas, Bristol. Noblett, who married Catherine Creagh, began recording the family's births, deaths and marriages in his Holy Bible. We know from this that his father was called John and that his mother was Ann Basil or Bassel, née Wharton and we know from other evidence that the family owned land in Doneraile. In the family bible Noblett recorded that "my cousin, Catherine Creagh, daughter of Dr. John Creagh of Donerail" was godmother to his daughter Hannah Wall Ruddock, born in

1768. Moreover the godparents to his son Andrew were Edward Croker, of Rawleighstown, Co. Limerick, and his wife, who was Rachel Ruddock, John Ruddock of Ballylunger's sister. All this confirms the connection, but the evidence for equating the two Johns still remains circumstantial.

There had been Ruddocks in Bristol for years, several of them in the shipping business, which in those days in Bristol was usually a euphemism for the slave trade, but they are difficult to pin down exactly. More work is required, and it is difficult to know whether to be reassured or dismayed by the entry in the parish register which records the baptism of Noblett Ruddock, the son of Noblett and Catherine. The entry reads:

> June 25, 1777 Noblett, son of Noblett & Anne Ruddock.
>
> (It appears from other parts of the register-book – See Aug 18, 1775 & May 6, 1778 – that the mother's name is here by mistake written Anne instead of Catherine which is confirmed by the testimony of the said Noblett, son of Noblett & Catherine Ruddock. Thos. J. Biddulph, April 19, 1800)

Anyone who has tried to navigate among the numerous Nobletts, Annes, Johns and Catherines within the Ruddock family must have sympathy with Mr. Biddulph's predecessor, but it makes one wonder how often such mistakes may go uncorrected in parish registers. At any rate Noblett and Catherine had a numerous family, though a predictably large number died young. As an example, their son John who was born on January 14th, 1773, was baptised by the curate at their house the following day, formally received into the church on February 18th and

> on Sunday morning ye 23rd of May 1773 he, my son, died suddenly in a Convulsion Fitt as we suppose (being found dead by his mother's side when she awoke in bed), aged 4 months & 8 days.

Life was indeed a lottery, but the Ruddocks' son, Andrew, was more fortunate; he survived both the small pox, which he took from his mother "in the Naturall way" when he was not quite two years old and the measles, which his mother also had, when he was four in 1770. We do not know the exact date of the latter illness, but a daughter Ann was born in May and died in December that same year. Mothers had to be strong in the eighteenth century. These young children who died and their grandmother Anne Bassell were all buried in the Wharton family vault at St. Stephen's, Bristol, which Noblett had had refurbished as a "burial place for my family whilst in England" and where he said he intended to bury his father, John Ruddock., suggesting a continued connection with Ireland.

-------------Chapter 9 -------------

FROM STOCKLAND BRISTOL TO TIVERTON & READING

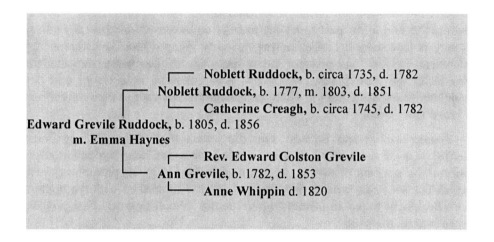

```
                        ┌──── Noblett Ruddock, b. circa 1735, d. 1782
           ┌──── Noblett Ruddock, b. 1777, m. 1803, d. 1851
           │            └──── Catherine Creagh, b. circa 1745, d. 1782
Edward Grevile Ruddock, b. 1805, d. 1856
    m. Emma Haynes
           │            ┌──── Rev. Edward Colston Grevile
           └──── Ann Grevile, b. 1782, d. 1853
                        └──── Anne Whippin d. 1820
```

I wish you to write smaller and put your lines closer together, so as to have room to say a great deal more. - *Anne Ruddock*

Noblett and Anne Ruddock decided in 1819 to send their two eldest sons to school at Tiverton in Devon. Their good friend Mr. Barter recommended it and Noblett was keen that his boys should become fluent in Latin. So at the end of August the parents set off with Noblett aged 15 and Edward, 14, on the 45-mile journey from their home at Stockland Bristol on the coast of Somerset close to where the Hinkley Point nuclear power station now stands. Nowadays it would take about half an hour on the motorway, but then it was a day's journey. On the way home the parents stopped off at Noblett's sister's house at Hope Corner near Taunton and finally after almost a week away they got home to the Vicarage to find letters from the boys.

The Vicarage was a new two-storey building, three bays long and two rooms deep, recently built with assistance from Bristol Corporation which held the patronage. It replaced a building which in 1815 was described as "small and ruinous, a mere cottage, very old and thatched with unceiled rooms and in bad repair." Noblett, who graduated from Trinity College, Oxford in 1799 (MA 1802), was instituted as Vicar at about this time (October, 1814), but he and Anne will not have lived in this unpromising dwelling. Noblett became a Curate of St. Stephen's, Bristol in 1804, having the previous year married the daughter of the Rector, Rev. Edward Colston Grevile. The Greviles and the Ruddocks were old friends - Edward Colston Grevile's parents were godparents to one of Noblett's sisters - so the marriage must have been particularly pleasing for the two families. In March, 1814, Noblett was licensed to two additional stipendiary curacies near Bristol, at Weston-in-Gordano and Easton-in-Gordano, in which latter place he was required to live in the parish. By the time he collected yet another stipendiary curacy, at Dodington in 1816, he was "already Vicar of Stockland Gaunts als. Stockland Bristol" and resident in the benefice. So the chances are that the Ruddocks and their family, which by now consisted of six sons and one daughter, Mary Anne born in 1815, had an auspicious start to their new life in a brand new home.

Young Noblett and Edward kept the letters they received from home during the next two and a half years so we have a one-sided but nevertheless informative account of events. Anne was delighted with the promptness with which her sons had written, but she was not too impressed with the content and she sought to put an instant stop to the old schoolboy ruse of spacing the words out on the page:

Stockland Vicarage

Septbr. 1st 1819

My dear Boys Noblett and Edward

I was very much pleased with you for writing to me so soon and very glad to see you were both well. I dare say by this time you are quite settled and find yourselves very comfortable. We hope in your next letter you will give us some particulars respecting the school, such as the plan of your lessons, how many boys there are, how your time is divided and your Papa begs particularly you will tell him what books you are on and whether you think any of those we have here would be of any use to you. If they will they shall be sent to you. Has Miss Richards said any thing to you about your clothes? Have you enough of every sort? I dare say Mr. Barter told you, as he told us, that Tiverton School was the making of him, and may be of you if you are good boys. I hope and believe you will consider what you are about and attend well to your lessons and endeavour to get to the Head of the School as soon as possible, which will be a great credit to your Papa as well as to yourselves. Your Papa wishes to know if you have done any Homer and Verses and what the subjects were. The next time you write I wish you to write smaller and put your lines closer together, so as to have room to say a great deal more: it would be a good plan if you have any place to keep it in, to begin a letter as soon as you receive one and then write a few lines at a time as any thing occurs to you, or you have time.........

On Saturday we returned home and found your brothers and sisters all well. We called at Mr. Porter at Enmore on our way and Miss P. gave me some cuttings of flowers and I brought a quantity from your Aunt Oliver. Is there anything in those two garden pots that are by the geranium cuttings under the garden wall? The hen that was sitting on the roof of the house has only hatched five chicks. We have had some very tremendous hail storms, indeed the weather has been so bad both yesterday and today that it prevented your Papa going to Bath as he intended, he means to go next Monday. I had a letter on Saturday from your Aunt Oliver. Your Uncle Edward is better though not quite well. Let us know when you write next how Mrs Barlow is. The Races were very well attended and the Ball excellent. Mrs & the Miss Grounds all enquired for you on Sunday. Mind not to go into the water when you are hot. If you buy any fruit do not eat too many plums. All here unite in best love to you both with, my dearest boys, your very affectionate mother A.R.

This splendid letter set the pattern of exhortation, homely solicitude, accounts of Papa's journeyings, bulletins on the family's health, relentless demands for information, enquiries as to academic progress and chips of news and gossip which was to flow from Stockland to Tiverton for the next two and a half years. But not only from Stockland. Anne's sister, Elizabeth Grevile, who lived with her parents Rev Edward Colston Grevile and Anne (née Whippin) at Clevedon, near Bristol, weighed in every now and then too. Her first letter on September 7th, 1819 was a catalogue of the family, listing Uncle Edward Grevile (b 1793) "who writes to us that he is much the same", Grandpapa and Grandmama, who are gone to Whitchurch for a fortnight, Aunts Mary and Sally, who are at home, Aunt Charles (wife of Charles Grevile b 1848), who has just given birth to another little girl - "I have to wish you joy of a new cousin" and Cousin Sally, who is beginning to talk.

Aunt Elizabeth too is remorseless in her demand for details. "Tell us the rules of the school, how much time you give to work and how much to play, how many boys there are altogether, and how many in the house with you. You both can write to us on one sheet of paper and direct to Clevedon near Bristol. As you have left Stockland so lately, you can tell us what state your garden is in. Do your marigolds flourish? Have you got a good collection of flowers? "

Soon Rev. Noblett joins the correspondence, showing by example how to fit 74 tightly written lines and the address, "Master Ruddock, Revd. M.P. Richards's School House Tiverton, Devon," on a single sheet of paper correctly folded for the post. In an era when schools could be cruel and violent places, he is delighted with what he hears.

> I am satisfied from what I have been able to ascertain that you have much more indulgence in many respects than ever I had when at school. You will, I am persuaded, not abuse it: if you behave yourselves with kindness & condescension towards your Masters, you will find this the most effectual method of making them your friends, & securing their goodwill & assistance when you stand in need of them."

There follows a catalogue of detailed questions about what Mr Richards had examined them in, what he had said about their verses, from what authors did they choose their quotations, how many classes were there above them, are they taking care to go up with their lessons tolerably perfect as they are finding them easy? This is the way to get up to a higher class, where they might be taught by Mr. Richards himself. After all this Rev. Noblett allows himself to dwell on the benefits of warm sea bathing which Uncle John Ruddock has gone to Weymouth to seek, though he is still not gaining strength as fast as he would wish. He also promises to send newspapers regularly for the boys to read and, perhaps, pass on to Mr. Richards. Then back to business. "Edward is a very lazy fellow - we have had no letter from him since he has been gone." The mare is going to be put out to grass, leaving him the pony to ride. Then a final injunction to be good boys and a postscript. "N.B. This will be put into the Bridgwater Post this Thursday morning & we suppose it will reach you about Midday, Friday. Yours was brought us by Mr. Mason Thursday evening."

This produced the desired response from Edward, whose letter "entirely relieved us from our apprehensions about him, as we did not know whether he had forgotten us, or his lessons were so hard that he was obliged to devote all his time to the study of them". On the contrary apparently. Noblett is thrilled to hear that the boys may be moved up a class where he is sure they will find

Homer relatively easy once they have got used to the idiom and dialect.

> I shall expect to see you very much improved as poets when you
> come home. Let me know whether the boys in doing their lessons
> take places in their classes according to their merit. I am inclined to
> think they do & that one day a boy is at the head & the next at the
> bottom. Are there any medals or prizes given for proficiency in any
> particular study?

Naturally he wants details, if so, and if there are examinations this quarter
he would like to be furnished with particulars and with the names of boys who
distinguished themselves. He thinks they must have had a good time when
Mrs Rockett was kind enough to invite them to dinner and he hopes they
behaved themselves accordingly. Sadly the bathing at Weymouth has done
little for Uncle John who continues very unwell indeed but Noblett thinks he
must persist with it as this (October) is the most salutary season for bathing.
He is sending with the letter two Homers, Edward's Roman History and a
Grecian History "together with a <u>little</u> cake, which we hope you & your
colleagues will be able to dispose of.". We learn too a little of the boys'
younger brothers. Johnny, the next in age, is shockingly idle and has been
taken off the Greek Grammar. Andrew (aged 9) has been put on it instead and
Charles (aged 7) has started Latin. They will be ready to be examined by the
schoolboys when they come home. John grew up to be a Solicitor in
Bridgwater, so he turned out all right in the end, but he was certainly outshone
in the correspondence by Andrew who made a number of telling, though
frequently unpunctual, interventions. Here is one dated November 8, 1819:

> My dear Edward , M.D.E.

> I received your letter on Saturday the 30th and we were all very glad
> to find you were well. My Uncle Edward is much the same. Charles
> gets on very stupid with his Latin. Moses and Aron (dogs? cats?) are
> both very well. Tell Noblett Mr Jeffrey is at home; he is pretty well
> but does not yet serve his Church. Papa went to Westbury to hold his
> Tithe Dinner on Monday the 1st of November. My Uncle John is so
> ill that his servant wrote to My Uncle Oliver's to tell him of it and he
> sent Joseph over Wednesday the 3rd to ask Papa to go with Uncle
> Oliver to Weymouth the next morning in a Chaise but Papa not being
> at home, Mama sent William on the poney to Cross the same evening
> to ask if Papa was there and if not to sleep there and to get next
> morning to Westbury before Papa set out to come home for Papa to
> go from Westbury to Weymouth but William found Papa at Cross
> and slept there and Papa took a Chaise and went to Hope Corner to
> go to Weymouth with my Uncle Oliver the next morning. Mama has

since received a letter from Papa in which he says that my Uncle John had a fit and that he is quite recovered from the effects of it, looks a great deal fatter in the face and that he is now going on very well. Charles has fallen against the bar of the grate in the Nursery and has burnt his wrist so that he cannot write and he has therefore postponed it to another letter. Papa means to stay at Weymouth till sometime next week. Papa has had a clock made and it stands by his room door. My Mama my Brothers et Sorores desire their love to you.

Believe me

My dear brothers

Your's very affect

Andrew Nelson Ruddock.

P.S. Write as soon as ever you can.

Was there a hint here of Andrew's future course in life? With that mastery of, and interest in, the details of his father's journey you might postulate journalism or, perhaps, travel agency; in fact Andrew became a surgeon, as did the "stupid" Charles. Clearly the family's consuming interest in the health of various uncles rubbed off on the children. Beneath the weight of the relentless demand for facts and with so many correspondents to keep happy the boys in Tiverton began to struggle. On December 1st Anne wrote saying she was pleased to get a recent letter as it was a long time since they had heard, but of course if letter-writing in any way interfered with their studies their parents would not want them to do it and would conclude that no news was good news. She congratulated them for asking for the newspapers not to be sent, assuming that this was because they had plenty to do and were disposed to make the best of their time. Meanwhile they had done well to write to Grandpapa on his birthday.

On the day George III was buried, February 15, 1820, Noblett preached at St. Stephen's in Bristol. There were no services in the surrounding churches but the bells tolled all day. Anne, who seems to have been ignoring the boys' pleas to stop the flow of newspapers, noted that in the latest ones they could read about the "horrid conspiracy" which was going on in London - presumably George IV's ultimately successful attempt to prevent prayers being said for "Queen Caroline" and to bar her from the coronation. The new cow house is finished and most of the cattle, bar the yearlings, go in quietly. Papa gives a sad report on Uncle Edward. Anne promises gingerbread, asks for details of the election in Devon and reports that the bladder has been removed from the football which will be oiled and put away for the summer. Young Dick (born 1813) has caught up with his Latin grammar and is making a start on cyphering and Catherine (b. 1817), though she talked about them for a few days after they went back to school, now seems to have forgotten about her senior siblings.

The "chairing" of successful members in the election proved to be a great day out for the young Ruddocks, who went in to Bridgwater to watch and were thrilled with their excursion, not least because a kind neighbour gave them a lift. Noblett, of course, relayed every detail to Tiverton with a sarcastic reference to "the radical gentlemen" who had contested the election in Bristol and been roundly defeated. Another great event was the funeral in Bristol of a Mr. Goldwyer, who was buried with full masonic honours, the members walking four abreast, sporting their aprons, collars and cuffs, white edged with blue or purple with gold trimmings, and all carrying nosegays. Anne said that if she could have rid herself of the memory that it was a funeral she would have called it a very pretty sight. There were trumpeters and drummers followed by six clergymen carrying a large open Bible on a purple cushion trimmed with gold and then the corpse covered with a superb pall ornamented with 10 large escutcheons and on the top the apron collar and cuffs of the deceased. The whole ceremony took over four hours and seems to have been thoroughly enjoyed by one and all.

In this letter, dated March 31, 1820, we get the first mention of the illness of the children's maternal grandmother, Anne Grevile, which was soon to prove fatal. The boys' sisters had been farmed out to their Aunts and their mother was in Bristol helping with the nursing. "Your poor Grandmama has been so unwell that we have all been fully employed." But she was now rather better. Then a few days later came this from Noblett:

> Queen's Square
>
> Tuesday evg.
>
> April 4th, 1820

My dear Boys,

I am grieved to have to perform the painful office of communicating to you the melancholy news of your poor dear Grandmama. She continued to mend till Tuesday morning, when unfortunately her complaint took a turn for the worse, & the medical men said there was then no hope of her recovery. From this time she continued gradually to decline, evidently getting weaker, till about three o'clock today, when nature became quite exhausted, &, I lament to say, breathed her last, very placid & composed, & in the full possession of all her faculties. We are all of course very much distressed, particularly your dear Grandpapa, who must feel the loss very severely, but yet bears his affliction quite as well as could be expected. Will one of you write a few lines to Mr. Barlow to acquaint him with this melancholy event? Will you mention it to Mr. Richards, & tell him we shall feel ourselves much obliged to him, if he will please to order a pair of black trousers for each of you to wear for your best. Thank Edward for his letter to me, which I will answer as soon as I can spare time. I left home yesterday morning & arrived here about three o'clock. Your brothers at home were very well. I suppose you will hear from some of them soon after our return, which will not be before the latter end of next week.

Will you excuse my writing any more at present - another time I hope to be better able to correspond with you. Your Mama, Grandpapa, & Aunts desire their best love to you both, together with,

> my dears,

> your's very affectionately,

> N. Ruddock

Mama thanks you for her letter just received, & wishes you to have some new crape put on your best hats three parts of the way up.

Oddly no account exists of the funeral. Perhaps it was too painful to chronicle, but the boys were evidently not present. They must have been at a loss to know how to respond and on April 21 Noblett was forced to enquire whether they had received his letter bearing the melancholy news. He did not wish to break in upon their studies on his own account but he begged them to lose no time in writing to their Grandpapa "as I am persuaded he will esteem it kind; & it is nothing more than is due to the memory of your Grandmama, & the regard you have for all your relatives who are so good to you". Then it is back to the relentless quest for information. What line does Sir Thos. Acland take on the Catholic Question? Noblett is told he supports it, which would lessen him very much in his estimation. What is the price of cider in the Tiverton area? He sends a pudding left over from the Tithe Dinner and some gingerbread and a silk handkerchief each to wear round their necks instead of a black ribbon. He says their mother would like to write "but is not in spirits." Finally he tells them that their youngest brother, Little Willy, was christened at St. Stephen's on Thursday, 13th. inst.

In the autumn of 1820, with the boys back at Dr Richards's school, there is ominous news of young Noblett being ill, but meanwhile it is Edward who is giving cause for concern, though he *did* remember to take his vitriol. Aunt Oliver has reported that he ate his food very fast indeed, giving rise to this maternal rebuke:

> If this is your usual practice it is the cause of your being so thin, and of all the sickness you feel, as it is impossible the food you take in can afford you the proper nourishment if you swallow it large; I therefore beg my dear boy that you will eat slow and be sure to masticate your food properly before you swallow it. If you attend to this advice, I have no doubt you will soon find the benefit of it. (Shades of Anne's great grandson, Dennis Henry Herbert, who chewed each mouthful 33 times!).

Three weeks later, though, Noblett has been ill after a smallpox vaccination, and his mother begs him to take care:

> You will recollect that the mornings and evenings are now getting cool and that after the complaint that you have had a cold caught at the beginning of the winter may not easily be got rid of. I am glad to find you are not of the cricket party. I am sure the exercise would be too violent and I hope Noblett will be careful not to overheat himself or expose himself to cool air after playing."

What would Anne have thought if she had known that nearly 50 years later her granddaughter, Mary, would marry a "dashing cricketer", Henry Herbert?

If Edward was still feeling at all under the weather when he received brother John's letter of October 11, he must have been considerably buoyed up by its tone.

> I went to Miss Evered's Cottage yesterday evening to tea and supper. There were about 26 of us at Supper. I did not come home till past 12 o'clock. We supped in the great room up stairs. Miss Harriet Sweeting is staying at Mr. Evered's; she has not been there a fortnight, she is very unwell. The Miss Evereds had laurel boughs trained round the walls of the supper room at the cottage. Mr John Evered and Mr. John Knight of Cannington let off some fireworks, which were very beautiful indeed. Papa took his great mare in the gig, and William the manservant rode the little mare to Cross, because Papa did not know whether she (his mare) would go as steady as he could wish. Papa is having the shutes made for the old house against the garden and they are to be put up next week.

The Olivers were clearly important figures in the family. William Oliver had married Anne Ruddock (Noblett Senior's older sister) at All Saints, Bristol in 1804 and they now lived at Hope Corner near Taunton. Andrew, in his next letter, was full of his visit to them. He had been into Taunton three or four times and gone out coursing with his uncle and his huntsman, John Fudge, when they coursed a hare across three or four open fields and eventually achieved a kill.

Then on December 1 Anne has some sensational news from Queen's Square, Bristol:

> I must now tell you what a terrible fright we were put in last Monday evening just after tea. Jane came running to the Parlour and said her master's room was all on fire; we immediately ran up stairs and saw the bed in a blaze and the room so filled with smoke that it was impossible to stay there a minute; your Aunt Eliza took up Mary Ann who was in the adjoining room, Thomas called out fire and three men who were papering came in and the gentlemen from Mr. Brickley's; by their assistance the fire was soon put out, tho' not till the furniture of the Bed was destroyed and the whole of the bedding and carpet nearly so. The room is now being put in order and we are nearly as composed as usual. I am happy to say your Grandpapa and the rest of us are all pretty well except that your Aunt Eliza, Sally and myself have colds which were certainly increased by the fire as the house was very damp and cold after the fire in consequence of the great quantity of water carried up; and your Aunt Sally and myself sat up all night to watch the room.

After Christmas John went away to school in Bridgwater and, when he had settled in, gave just the kind of detailed account of proceedings which the family would require.

> Mr. Danvers sees the letters which we write but we can sneak a letter every evening if we like it. We have half holidays every Wednesday & Saturday evenings. We get up at 7 o'clock and do our grammars and learn our lessons till 9 when we go to breakfast and walk till 10 when we go in and ought to come out at 1 but we seldom come out till after dinner. We go in at 3 and come out at 5 but then we got to write out exercises and learn our grammars for the next day by the time we have done it it is past 7 when we go to supper & then to bed. There are 7 boys with myself in our class I am at the head of it and W.H. Evered is the 2nd. There are three classes above us, in the two first there are two boys one in each, in the third 3 boys. I do greek Testament and Gk dialectics with them. We have hot cakes for breakfast. There are about 5 and 20, about 10 of which are dayboys. Our Class does Ovid, Caesar Dilectus. Saturdays we read and spell. I

am at the head of the spelling class. After breakfast Sunday Morning
we translate the collect into Latin for Monday's exercise. I can put a
letter into the post any evening when it is dark. We generally go to
play in the field where Matthew's Fair is held and jump over the
brooks. Some one generally jumps into the water every time we
jump. I have only jumped in once up to my knees. The boys only
play marbles. I remain etc. John Ruddock

This is an archetypal Ruddock letter, giving plenty of detail, evidence of
competitiveness in the writer, a degree of independence and an interest in the
classics. If Noblett and Anne read it, they will have been delighted with it. By
now Noblett is on the look out for scholarships at Oxford for his eldest son
but finds that the Gloucestershire scholarship had virtually been promised to
someone at the last election. However, he is undaunted, urging young Noblett
to be diligent with his studies.

> The examination at John's is a very severe one, as much so I believe
> as at any college; the only chance of succeeding there or elsewhere is
> by endeavouring to qualify yourself in the best way you can. I am
> inclined to think the candidates are examined in Horace & Homer,
> Livy, Demosthenes, Herodotus. Xenophon, & the Greek plays of
> Sophocles, Aeschylus etc. Any of these books, I should think you
> would do well to read as you find you have time, but perhaps the
> better plan would be to ask Mr. Richards to put you upon a course of
> study, which you may pursue from time to time, without breaking in
> upon your regular school occupations. It has just occurred to me that
> you would do well to pay particular attention to your compositions,
> as I know they have always great weight in determining the merits of
> the candidates.

> I should have written to you before in answer to yours of the 5th inst.
> which we duly received but we have been in a shocking state here
> for some days past. Nancy went downstairs leaving Catherine &
> Willy in the nursery, when unfortunately poor Willy's clothes caught
> fire, & he was very nearly burnt to death. Mr Toogood at first said
> there was no chance of his living, but I rejoice to say, our
> apprehensions have now subsided, & the poor little fellow has, we
> hope, past the worst. We have sent to Clevedon for one of your
> Aunts, whom we hope to see the beginning of next week........Your
> Mama has been almost worn out by her constant assiduities to Willy,
> as he will not suffer any one else to do any thing for him.

Aunt Sally duly came from Bristol and must have been a great help with
the nursing as Anne, who was six months' pregnant, soon wore herself out.
Sally stayed for several weeks and the next bulletin, almost a month later

pronounced Willy to be improving steadily with the doctor dressing his burns every other day and Anne or Sally managing the interim days. Noblett, however, reported that they had had to cope with a great amount of proud flesh which had retarded Willy's recovery. He urged the boys to take care not to catch anything so that they would not bring any infections when they came home for the holidays. By mid-June Andrew, the future surgeon, reported that Willy was going on well but "there is a bit on the back of the ear and the arm which is not healed".

After the holidays, in September, Noblett reported the birth of his latest child, who "in compliment to the family" was named Grevile and was their eleventh. After a difficult start and, though very little in size, he was reported as going on better and appearing healthy. Finally in October Aunt Sally was able to return to Clevedon, where the first signs of its ascent as a fashionable watering place were reported by Aunt Eliza. Park farm, she wrote, was sold and was being extensively built over and bathing machines were being established. "Dont you think Clevedon will be a fine place?"

Young Noblett's 18th birthday, on February 24, 1822, passed unnoticed. Perhaps he was at home for it, but in March the correspondence resumed briefly. First, Andrew contributes the following entertaining account of a sale at a nearby farm:

> On Monday the 18th he sold all the live stock, on Tuesday the waggon carts drags chains etc. with some hay; the third day, Wednesday, ladders, bird nets and farming implements. They then about five o'clock sold dairy utensils and brewing do. they then went into the house and sold the beds, furniture etc. till about half after ten. It then closed for the evening; if he had sold two hours longer he would have finished for the people were all as drunk as the devil and in the spirit to bid for every thing which was put up.

The correspondence ends with Noblett's letter to his eldest son on March 22, 1822, in which he gives some grim news:

> Nineteen or twenty children have died in Bridgwater lately of a complaint somewhat resembling the croup. Mr Dawes had two children ill with it, but by taking it in time they were soon restored & are now about as usual. It shows itself by a difficulty of breathing, & the method of treatment found most effectual is repeated emetics. Tell Edward there is an epidemic at Weston Zoyland, of what is I believe this Typhus fever, occasioned by the long continuance of the floods, together with the distress & poverty of the inhabitants. I cannot say how many have been buried there, but a great many.

After this we have no more correspondence because disaster overtook the family. Young Noblett, the apple of his parents' eye from whom his father expected so much, died at school two months after his 18th birthday and was buried in the churchyard at Tiverton on April 26. Whether he was a victim of the croup-like disease (probably diphtheria) or typhus, about which his father had recently written to him, we do not know. The records, in the manner of genealogists, simply say "died young", and the family bible contains only a brief sentence recording his death and burial.

It must have been a particularly awful experience for his younger brother Edward, so recently commended by his parents for writing to say that Noblett had been unwell, to have to communicate the terrible news. One hopes that Dr Richards may have done it for him. If only the family had continued to keep letters, we should know the full story. As it is we only know that Edward followed in his father's footsteps, going on to Trinity College, Oxford, where he matriculated on April 20, 1823, aged 18. To his father's undoubted delight he was an exhibitioner from 1825-1828, obtained a BA in 1827 and an MA in 1830. He then went into the church and became curate of Westbury-cum-Priddy, where his father was the Vicar. Westbury lies at the foot of the Mendip Hills between Wells and Cheddar; and Priddy is in the hills above. On appointment on October 8, 1832, Edward was to be paid a relatively generous £120 a year and, in the words of the Bishop of Bath & Wells, "we allot the Vicarage House, Offices and Garden and require you to reside therein as soon as same are completed; in the meantime we require you to reside within the Parish."

"To them that hath shall be given." Edward had, a few days earlier married Emma Haynes, who was descended from one of the richest families in the land and must have brought with her a substantial "dowry". The marriage took place on September 21, 1832, at Millbrook, near Southampton, where the bride's brother, David Haynes, was the curate. They were soon blessed with children - Arthur Edward Vyvyan (b. 1833), Mary, the future wife of Henry Herbert (1834), Lucy Mary (1837), Montague Grevile (1839), Emma Mary (1840), Mary Emily (1842), Fanny Mary (1843), Elizabeth Mary Gertrude (1844), Edward Noblett (1847), Reginald Colston Grevile (1848), Charles Edward (1850) and Edward Stanley Colston Grevile (1852). After his father died on April 27, 1851, Edward did not retain his curacy and the family moved a few miles away to Wrington, near Congresbury. In 1856 Edward Grevile Ruddock died there of a liver complaint leaving Emma with 12 children, eight of whom were under 15.

71

Little is known of the character of Edward Grevile Ruddock and his early demise at the age of 50 meant that most of his daughters did not know him very well. Since it was they who provided a great deal of information about the family to Dennis Henry Herbert when he began his researches in the early twentieth century, Edward was destined to remain inevitably a shadowy figure. His photograph suggests a rather melancholy person, perhaps a little weak and liver disease raises the spectre of the demon drink. However, his choice of bride entitles him to a degree of fame as we shall see in a later chapter. The couple were clearly fixated on the names Edward, for obvious dynastic reasons, and Mary, perhaps just because they liked it, but it is pleasantly eccentric to give all your six daughters the same name, though fortunately leavened in five cases by another name as well.

Of their dozen children no fewer than nine died without issue. Montague Grevile worked in the Inland Revenue Secret Department, married Sarah Amy Hay and lost three of his four sons in the First World War. The eldest, Edgar Herbert Montagu, had three children, the first of whom, Rev. Reginald Ruddock, retained his great great great grandfather's family bible, from which his wife Evelyne generously transcribed the family details for her near-namesake, Evelyn Ruddock, of Belfast. The fourth son, Arthur Percy Grevile, went to South Africa, married Hester "Hettie" Yeld and gave rise to a flourishing Ruddock clan in that country. In 1938 he brought his wife to Hemingford Abbots to renew his acquaintance with the village which he remembered visiting when he was six years old in 1886. When he came to England again after the war, in 1954, Hettie was too unwell to accompany him and she died in 1959. In old age he married Dorothy Hardwick and he died in 1964. During the second world war, the eldest of Arthur and Hettie's six sons, Montague Alleyne Grevile, came to Europe where he met and married his cousin, Kathleen Gertrude Fry. When he returned to South Africa she was supposed to follow him a few months later, but she never did. They were eventually divorced and he married Mary Ruddock (née Barrett), the widow of his younger brother, Arthur Edward, who had died in 1945. The other brothers, Harold Anson, Sebert George, Edgar Douglas and Reginald Noel all married and all but the youngest had children in South Africa. Their journeys continue.

Rev. Noblett Ruddock (1777-1851)   *Anne Ruddock (née Grevile)*

Stockland Bristol Old Church, now demolished

Emma Ruddock (née Haynes), 1810-1892   *Rev. Edward G. Ruddock (1805-1856)*

The Ruddock family. Back L to R: Fanny, Montagu, Emma, Edward. Middle: Stanley, Mary, Emily. Front: Arthur, Emma (née Haynes), Gertrude, Charles, Lucy, Reginald.

Chapter 10

FROM PORTUGAL, VIA LEGHORN, TO DORKING

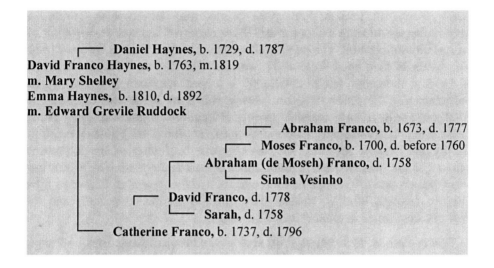

Daniel Haynes, b. 1729, d. 1787
David Franco Haynes, b. 1763, m.1819
m. Mary Shelley
Emma Haynes, b. 1810, d. 1892
m. Edward Grevile Ruddock

Abraham Franco, b. 1673, d. 1777
Moses Franco, b. 1700, d. before 1760
Abraham (de Moseh) Franco, d. 1758
Simha Vesinho
David Franco, d. 1778
Sarah, d. 1758
Catherine Franco, b. 1737, d. 1796

"Under Peace Plenty" - *Motto of the Franco family*

In the mid-eighteenth century Benjamin Disraeli's great grandfather, Isaac Siprut de Gabay, was a small-time jeweller in London. He would buy uncut diamonds in India on his own account or obtain them on credit from the dominant diamond importers, Abraham and Jacob Franco. Then he would cut and polish them himself and make them up into jewellery. The Francos were Sephardic jews who had come to England almost a century earlier and were immensely powerful, having in some recent years cornered no less 60% of the market for diamond imports.

It was therefore foolhardy of de Gabay to decamp to Holland with a quantity of diamonds, which he had obtained from the Francos but not paid for, and a large sum of money he had obtained from selling other unpaid-for diamonds. The Francos sent a description of the fugitive to their agents in Germany, France, Italy and the Netherlands, listed the details of the bills of exchange he was carrying and asked them to publicise the matter in the newspapers. With no outlet for his diamonds and no takers for his money, de Gabay was forced to come back to Britain, where at the behest of the Francos, he was immediately arrested.

The tale is told by Gedalia Yogev in *Diamonds and Coral: Anglo-Dutch Jews and Eighteenth Century Trade,* an analysis of Jewish involvement and dominance in a trade which at the time was centred on London, Amsterdam and Leghorn. It is of interest here because it introduces us to the Franco family, Sephardic jews of Portuguese origin, who had come to Britain via Italy in the seventeenth century after Oliver Cromwell relaxed the prohibition on Jewish immigration. The paterfamilias was Abraham Franco, born in 1681, who when he died aged 96 in 1777, was described by the London Magazine as "a Jew merchant worth £900,000" - a vast sum which would equate nowadays to £72 million. His son, Moses, was born in Richmond, Surrey, in 1700, but seems to have operated mainly in Leghorn, which was a key centre in the triangular coral and diamond business at which the Francos excelled. During the War of Spanish Succession at the beginning of the eighteenth century, silver was in short supply and the East India Company would not allow the exports of it which had hitherto fuelled the import of diamonds from Fort St. George, Madras. Instead they threw open the coral trade and the Francos were quick to exploit their advantage.

Moses Franco died before 1760 and it was his two eldest sons, Abraham and Jacob, based in London, who were de Gabay's nemesis in 1756. They deployed their younger brothers to strategic posts - Raphael and Joseph to Leghorn and Solomon to India. Solomon went first to Bombay in 1743 under an agreement with the East India Company as a "free merchant" and later in 1749 to Madras. When he died in 1763 he was described as "an eminent Hebrew merchant of Madras". Jacob, of Fenchurch Street, married his niece, Simha, daughter of Abraham, and played a prominent part in the London Sephardic community, being a pillar of the Bevis Marks Synagogue and becoming a member of the original Board of Deputies of British Jews in 1760, the same year that he was granted arms by the College of Heralds. The arms incorporated the family badge from the Leghorn synagogue, showing a palm tree growing out of a fountain and bearing the family motto, Sub Pace Copia, or Under Peace Plenty.

With a member of the family in each of the key centres of the trade, the Francos were well placed and their dominance was extraordinary. Jewish firms were strong in the diamond trade, but they dominated the coral trade to an even greater extent. Of the £1.6 million worth of licences granted between

1750 and 1774, for example, no less than £1.2 million worth, or 75%, were issued to Jews and the Francos in particular, who in the 1740s also imported over 50% of the annual value of diamonds. Although they concentrated on coral and diamonds, the Francos, whose Portuguese forebears were not above a bit of piracy, particularly in Portugal's Brazilian colonies, also dealt in precious metals, cereals and slaves. In 1767, for example, they chartered a ship to carry a cargo to West Africa, and barter it for slaves to be shipped to Puerto Rico. A contract with the shipowner obliged the Francos to supply him with four six-pounder guns. Much of this trade, passing through Spain and Portugal (where Jews could not operate openly since the Inquisition) was on the fringes of legality, but Jamaica, having been British since 1655, offered a useful channel for South American precious metals to reach Europe. Knowledge of foreign languages and contacts with relations across the West Indies gave the Jews advantages which others lacked in the world of contraband. The Francos did not neglect this opportunity and two of Raphael Franco's sons were posted there at the end of the eighteenth century.

Raphael was the son of Jacob, who remained the senior member of the family after the death of his brother Abraham in 1758. Jacob did not die until 1777, by which time Abraham's son, David, had been enjoying his enormous legacy for two decades, but there was plenty of money to go round and the cousins (who were also uncle and nephew) lived accordingly. In June 1780 Horace Walpole attended "an exceedingly pretty firework" put on by Raphael in honour of the King's birthday at his home at Little Marble Hill in fashionable Twickenham. His portrait was painted in the same year by Gainsborough and was so well-regarded that, when it was sold at Christies, 130 years after he died in 1781, it fetched 6,200 guineas, a record for a man's portrait by Gainsborough. Raphael married, in 1761 Leah d'Aguilar, daughter of an eccentric Baron of the Holy Roman Empire and had several sons some of whom who, as we have seen, represented the Franco enterprise for a time in Jamaica. One of their descendants, Ralph Franco, inherited a baronetcy from an uncle, Sir Massey Lopes, whose surname he adopted. The present Lord Roborough is descended from him.

David Franco lived just as prosperously but less ostentatiously than his cousin. In addition to his London house in Fenchurch Street, where the family's original base seems to have been, and the tenancy of a substantial house in London Road, Twickenham, David bought in 1767 a splendid country mansion romantically named Lonesome Lodge. He must have been attracted by the prospectus, whose author could have held his own with the most gushing of twenty-first century estate agents:

From the Delightfulness of the Situation every comfortable Indulgence may be expected: instead of that dull Solitude which the Name of it may seem to imply, there is the noblest Employment for the Mind; the highest Entertainment for the Eye; it is a Retirement denied to Care; it is a Spot where Pleasure ever awaits you: it is as Milton says, a happy rural Seat of various 'Views' for, turn every Way, and tread every Path, it will be found that all the Ways are Ways of Pleasantness; and all the Paths are Peace."

The house had been built 27 years earlier on the outcrop of sandy land below Leith Hill near Dorking by a Dutch merchant, Theodore Jacobsen, who was attracted to the area by the availability of a sort of fish stew called Water Souchy, a Dutch delicacy consisting of perch boiled and served in its own liquid. He set about acquiring parcels of contiguous land over a period of about 20 years. Jacobsen, who was connected with the Thomas Coram Foundation for the care of destitute children in London, designed the house himself and diverted the Tillingbourne, a little stream running down towards Wootton Hatch, a pub on the A25 between Dorking and Guildford, so as to form elaborate ornamental waterworks. His efforts evoked differing reactions. One later critic dismissed the house as "a small edifice, of slight architectural pretensions," but by then it was in a dilapidated state. In its heyday it inspired more enthusiasm:

The residence, a neat structure, is charmingly situated at an agreeable distance from the public thoroughfare; and the hills in the background, by filling up the scene, give a peculiarly fine effect to the whole. In the front of the house are two small neat pedestals, supporting ornamental urns; and a small *jet d'eau* is constantly throwing forth a limpid stream, which, returning to its destined basin, breaks the silence that prevails all around. Contiguous to the road is a curious cascade, overhung with trees, the water falling nearly sixty feet from the supereminent rock, over the several graduated ledges or descents, into a small stone basin:

With woods o'erhung, and shagged with mossy rocks,
Whence on each hand the gushing waters play,
And down the rough cascade white-dashing fall,
Or gleam in lengthen'd vista thro' the trees.

Some of the statuary was by Rysbrack and there was a notable carving by Grinling Gibbons depicting musical instruments. This elegant establishment was presided over by the Housekeeper, Jane Romsey, and the Steward, John Roach, both of whom were remembered by name in David's enormous 17-

page Will, along with numerous other of his servants in Twickenham and the City. His wife, whose name we do not know, must have died young. They had a single daughter, Catherine, born in 1737, who married a London wine merchant, Daniel Haynes. David approved of the match because he made Daniel one of his three executors and left him £10,000 in his own right besides the £30,000 left in trust for Catherine, who also inherited Lonesome Lodge. Catherine's first-born, a son named William Richard, was born in 1758 and was followed, five years later by another son, Daniel Franco. A sister Elizabeth, who died in infancy and twin brothers, who lived for only a few weeks in 1771, completed the family. The Haynes parents were clearly considerable figures in the community, though they also spent time in Fenchurch Street and in Twickenham. They established a charity for the benefit of the poor of the parish of Wotton - £50 being given by Daniel when he died in 1787 and another £100 by Catherine a decade later. New Southsea annuities were purchased on each occasion and by 1888 these were converted into Consolidated Stock to the tune of £287.7s 0d. The dividends were used to buy flannel for the poor in Upper Wotton and flour in the chapelry of Oakwood nearby. The Haynes's were buried in a splendid tomb at the west end of Wotton Church, which is better known for housing magnificent marble memorials to the family of the diarist, John Evelyn, who lived at Wotton House. The Haynes tomb could not rival the Evelyns but its iron railings seem to have evoked some interest. They were reputed, at the end of World War II to have been removed to the Victoria & Albert Museum, but no trace of them can be found there. On a visit to the churchyard in the 1980s we found, under a tree, some lozenge-shaped stone cartouches and nearby a large flat stone recording the deaths of three generations of the Haynes family. The cartouches have now been returned to the site of the tomb, whose ruinous state has been partially remedied, but they are scarcely legible now.

Nor is there much to be seen of Lonesome Lodge, which was inherited respectively by William Richard (d. 1804), his brother, David Franco Haynes (d. 1811), and David's son, Daniel Franco Haynes (1793-1852), who sold it in 1821. The site is now covered with rhododendrons, but deep within there is a pillar of stonework, which looks as though it may have formed part of a balustrade, and some remains of the brick cellars. The rest was sold for building material in about 1850 by the Duke of Norfolk, who acquired it, apparently as a staging post on his journey from Arundel to London, but found it in inconveniently poor condition.

The sale in June, 1821, however, was a fine affair. Prospective purchasers were invited to view, by ticket only, the elegant villa, erected with superior taste, and "offices, appendages, Pleasure Grounds, Plantations and Shrubberies, Excellent Garden with Forcing Houses and Green House" All of this together with a beautiful estate of over 500 acres would, the sale particulars said, form "a complete residence for a family of the first respectability".

The vendor, Daniel Franco Haynes, certainly seemed to meet that description at the time. He should have been very comfortably off and had been married two years earlier in June, 1819 to Mary Shelley, daughter of Sir Timothy Shelley, Bart., of Castle Goring, Sussex. Why, then, was he selling? The Francos had taken considerable pains to ensure that the estate remained in the family, specifying in their wills a strict order of succession and it was 10 years since he had inherited Lonesome on the death of his father in 1811. One might have expected that the newly-married couple would settle down happily there in luxury and respectability.

We have very little evidence upon which to go. Daniel Franco Haynes was a wine merchant, with interests in Isleworth, but how successful we do not know. Was he, in the manner of rich young scions, a spendthrift? Had he gambled or frittered away what must have been a very comfortable inheritance? Or did he, or perhaps Mary, simply not like the place? The couple had moved out some time before to Ashtead, eight miles away, where their children, Mary, Edward and Flora were baptised on July 20, 1820, October 22, 1821 and September 23, 1825 respectively.

All this was eminently respectable, but it was not to last. Mary, of course, was the sister of the poet, Percy Bysshe Shelley, who had already begun to outrage conventional opinion both by his writing and his sexual behaviour. Shelley's first wife, Harriet, had drowned herself and the poet had decamped to Italy with his second wife, Mary Wollstonecraft. Now, in May 1827, Mary suddenly eloped with 35-year-old James O'Hara Trevor, who came from Millbrook, near Southampton, where Daniel's younger brother, David, was the Curate. For over a year Daniel was unable to locate the runaways; then in late August, 1828, he found them living near Dover and at once began legal proceedings against James Trevor in the Court of Common Pleas. He obtained judgement by default and damages were assessed at £2,000, plus costs, before the Sheriff of the County of Surrey. But after this Mary and Trevor disappeared again and Daniel was unable to collect. Against Mary in the Court of Arches at Canterbury Daniel obtained "a definitive sentence of Divorce from bed and board and mutual cohabitation", but this ecclesiastical verdict did not dissolve the bands of matrimony. That could only be done by the expensive means of a private Act of Parliament, but Daniel was still rich enough to pursue this option. The Act takes the form of a petition by Daniel in which he complains that since the elopement Mary has "cohabited with and carried on an unlawful and adulterous intercourse and criminal conversation" with Trevor, that Mary has dissolved the bond of marriage, deprived Daniel of the comforts of matrimony and (and this is perhaps the real rub) he, Daniel "is liable to have a spurious issue imposed upon him to succeed to his estates and fortune unless the said marriage be declared void and annulled by the authority of parliament."

The petition goes on:

> May it therefore please your Most Excellent Majesty (out of your princely goodness and compassion to your said subject's misfortune and calamity) that it may be enacted and be it enacted by the King's most excellent Majesty by and with the advice and consent of the Lords Spiritual and Temporal and Commons in this present parliament assembled and by the authority of the same that the Bond of Matrimony between the said Daniel Ffranco Haynes and the said Mary his wife being violated and broken by the manifest and open adultery of the said Mary the same is hereby from henceforth dissolved annulled vacated and made void to all intents constructions and purposes whatsoever and that it shall and may be lawful to and for the said Daniel Ffranco Haynes at any time or times hereafter to contract matrimony and to marry as well in the lifetime of the said Mary as after her decease with any woman or women whom he might lawfully marry in case the said Mary were actually dead........."
>
> .....and so on, ensuring in addition that all courts would recognise such marriages, all children from them should be deemed legitimate, and could inherit land and buildings from their father and other ancestors, that all this should obtain in His Majesty's dominions as well, that Daniel should have the same rights over any future wife's property as any other husband, that Mary be barred and excluded from any rights she may have had in property arising from her marriage to Daniel, and that Daniel should have no responsibility for any possessions which Mary might acquire in future.

All this expensive legal language, running to seven pages and addressed to George IV, by comparison with whose scandalous morals James O'Hara Trevor's conduct pales into insignificance, is unlikely to have detained either the King or Parliament for long, pricey though it must have been. The act is endorsed "Soit fait comme il est desirė."

So far as is known Daniel did not avail himself of the matrimonial freedom granted him. By 1841 he was living, evidently unattached, back in Ashtead and in 1851 he was living alone, with a housekeeper and a groom, at Leatherhead. The following year he died and was buried at Wotton, being erroneously described on his tombstone as "of Lonesome in this parish" though he had not lived there for over 30 years. His children, meanwhile, had been brought up by their grandmother, Elizabeth Haynes (née Marshall) in Millbrook with the assistance of their unmarried Aunt Betsey. When Elizabeth died in 1847 at the age of 75 she too was buried at Wotton - with her late husband, and they were joined by Rev. David Haynes, the former curate, two years later. Mary continued to live with her James as man and wife (presumably they married after the divorce) and had several daughters; in 1851, for example, they were living in Worthing with an unmarried daughter, Margaret, and a married daughter, Florence Blake.

By the mid-19th Century the enormous fortune which the Franco family had built up was considerably diminished, reduced by a combination of large families, indulgence, indolence and the divorce, so when Daniel Franco Haynes's younger sister, Emma, went to the altar with Rev. Edward Grevile Ruddock, she brought with her a dowry which, though ample was certainly not spectacular. Their marriage settlement was made on September 1, 1832, and when it was wound up 60 years later it was worth £10,230 3s 1d. Since there were no fewer than 15 beneficiaries, Emma's executors, were not dispensing vast sums to individual members of the family. Some of the £602 15s 11d received by Mary Herbert may well have formed part of the capital into which Henry had to dip in order to send his son to Oxford. Now, ten generations on from Abraham Franco and his £72m fortune, there is one diamond ring, valued at £4,000 in 2000, which is believed to have come down from that branch of the family and even that was always euphemistically said to have belonged to an ancestor who was an "Italian princess".

Lonesome Lodge, Wotton, Surrey, country house of the Franco and Haynes Families.

Wotton Church, Surrey, showing the Haynes family tomb with railings.

Chapter 11

VIA CAPETOWN TO HEMINGFORD ABBOTS

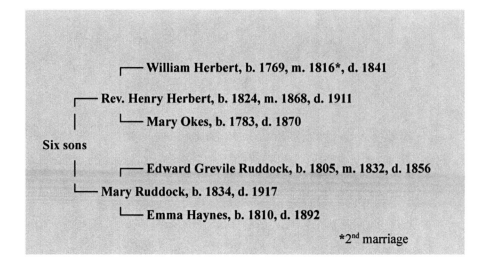

William Herbert, b. 1769, m. 1816*, d. 1841

Rev. Henry Herbert, b. 1824, m. 1868, d. 1911

Mary Okes, b. 1783, d. 1870

Six sons

Edward Grevile Ruddock, b. 1805, m. 1832, d. 1856

Mary Ruddock, b. 1834, d. 1917

Emma Haynes, b. 1810, d. 1892

*2nd marriage

If God has willed that, though one in heart, you should remain separate in this life, He has not so willed it of the future. Nothing in His grace can divide you there, if only you follow after righteousness here. -Anonymous letter-writer.

In January, 1888, Rev. Henry Herbert was 63; his 20th wedding anniversary was imminent and he was in the 21st year as Rector of Hemingford Abbots. His eldest son, Dennis Henry, was rising 19 and desperate to go on to Oxford from the King's School, Ely, where he had won two scholarships. But the agricultural depression had hit Henry hard. If Dennis was to make it to Oxford, help was going to be needed. Henry sat down and wrote the following letter:

Hemingford Abbots Rectory
St. Ives.

Dear Sir,

I find some statement is required to show need of aid in getting my son up to the University should he pass a creditable examination. I shall be happy to reply to any questions as to income & etc.

The income of this living is derived from Glebe Farms which, after being on my hands some time, was were let last month at from last Michaelmas at 9/- per acre instead of 28/- and 30/- as in previous years.[430 acres].

I have six boys to provide for & my private income does not amount to £200 per ann: and am therefore obliged to draw from capital. Two scholarships which my boy obtained at the King's School Ely were of course a great help to me.

I am dear Sir,

Your's faithfully,

Henry Herbert.

We do not know to whom this epistle was addressed (It survives probably only because Henry made the mistakes in the second paragraph and wanted to send a fair copy.), but it shows that his income was reduced at a stroke from about £625 a year to £193.10s 0d. These were not inconsiderable sums at the time. They would equate to £50,000 and £15,480 respectively but whereas bringing up six sons on £50,000 a year may well have seemed comfortable, such a sharp reduction in income would make things extremely difficult. Besides there had been a period of some years when the farms were vacant and produced no income. No wonder Henry often used his birthday letters to exhort his son to greater efforts. "Exhibitions & Scholarships are what you must especially look out for - and you will I am afraid have to give up many a work (accomplishments !!!) as well as pleasures so as to compete for them. But the next three years will be the decisive ones - don't lose time - above all do not waste time."

Repeated emphasis on the importance of scholarships and exhibitions, though not the sole content of the letters, which also contain snippets of local gossip and news, was believed by my father to have had a regrettable effect on Dennis Henry, putting him under stress which he then replicated when he himself became a parent. Anyway it became a central tenet of my father's thinking that children should not be put under such stress. Nevertheless Dennis Henry did his duty and obtained an exhibition to Wadham College, Oxford, chosen in the belief that it was one of the best of the smaller colleges suitable for a poor man. He seems to have been happy there and used to speak reverentially of Wadham years later, so Henry's soundings among his friends were worthwhile. Henry had himself been at Oxford - at Worcester College - but he had gone down in 1845, forty-three years earlier, so his knowledge was out of date. Of his own years at Oxford little is known, but he left after three years without taking a degree.

This must have been a disappointment to Henry's father, William, none of whose other 13 children from two marriages went to university. Perhaps it was fortunate that he had died four years earlier when Henry was still at Eton. William, as we have seen, had been a pillar of Huntingdon society and his son Dennis had already completed the first of his five terms as Mayor. They were steady people, determinedly making their way up the social ladder, but Henry was not quite like that and what he did next - he sailed for South Africa to do tutorial work - must have worried the family, especially as his older half-brother William had perished at Malta on his way back from Cape Town in 1833. (Henry's move resonates particularly because when, two generations later, his grandson, my father, decided on a teaching career in Africa, he was widely assumed to have committed some dreadful *faux pas* and to have been sent into decent obscurity!)

Henry's reasons may have been connected in some emotional way with his failure to take a degree. Or was it the prospect of taking up residence with two elder unmarried sisters and a widowed mother which influenced his choice? He was a handsome young man, to judge by an engraving in my possession, and he must have wanted to see the world. Moreover, his mother's uncle, Rev Holt Okes, D.D. was already in South Africa, where he had opened a Classical Academy for boys in January 1831. We shall never know what caused his nephew to follow him, but Henry had inherited from his mother's family a spirit of adventure. The Okes's were not only more academic than the Herberts, but, as we have seen, they were even more numerous, had a habit of dying in interesting circumstances and are buried all over the world.

But, if the Okes's had an indirect influence upon Henry's character, they also had a direct effect on his education. When he was only eight he was sent as a Colleger to Eton, where his uncle, Richard Okes, was Lower Master. As early as 1832 he was reporting favourably on Henry's progress to the boy's grandmother, Ann Okes (née Gray) and she, in turn, hurried round to William Herbert's house in Huntingdon to pass on the report. "I knew it would be a great comfort to them, " she wrote " to hear so good an account of Henry, indeed it is highly gratifying to us all. He is a dear little boy, and I hope and trust he will reward his dear mother for all the time she has given up to him and for the good principles she has instilled into his little mind." Richard Okes remained a friend and counsellor of Henry for many years and must have given his approval for the South African venture.

And so in the second half of 1845 Henry arrived in Cape Town, where he lodged with Holt Okes and his wife, Patricia (née Busby) who had herself kicked over the traces in youth, escaping from a Roman Catholic convent to marry a man five years her junior. Holt, a small, dapper man, was the younger of twins, whose mother, Rebecca Lydia (née Butcher) did not survive their birth. He was a Doctor of Divinity, published learned works in Latin, English and Greek and mastered Hebrew so that he could better interpret the *Holy Bible*. He had kept boys' schools at Linton, near Cambridge, and at Woodford, Essex, but the family were inclined to be extravagant, which may account for the fact that, at the age of 53, he embarked with his wife, two sons, three daughters and his elder brother, Robert, on the four-month journey to the Cape. Patricia, a noted beauty in youth, was possessed of a very cheerful and sanguine temperament, which must have stood her in good stead in South Africa where at the time English women were a rarity and life was extraordinarily tough. *Hints for Emigrants' Wives*, published much later in 1859, for example, noted that there was very little room for drawing room graces. A wife, besides supporting her husband and instructing their children should know how to cook and bake, how to iron and get up linen, clean and put in order the sleeping and dwelling-rooms and be well-skilled in the use of the needle. "Besides all this she should have the temperament and bodily strength which will enable her to find pleasure in these household engagements." The Okes family seem to have been equal to the task. Patricia, who was five years older than her husband, pre-deceased him, dying in 1848, when she was 76. Holt's death in 1854 when he was 77, was seen as a merciful release however, he by then being described as a sad man weary of life. They were already in the evening of their lives when young Henry arrived from England and it must have been a comfort to have direct news from home after 15 years' exile.

Life in the colony suited Henry. He was a man of action - thoroughly at home with horse and gun, as his obituarist put it - and evidently revelled in his two expeditions up country against the natives, once nearly losing his life because he was determined to obtain a specimen of a rare South African bird from a wood occupied by the enemy. His cool courage and presence of mind enabled him to escape with both his life and the bird - now, alas, unidentified. Henry's arrival in the colony had coincided almost exactly with the outbreak of another of the frequent Kaffir Wars fought against Xhosa tribesmen who had been dispossessed of land and responded with cattle raids across the frontier. The so-called "War of the Axe", or seventh Kaffir War, began in March 1846, sparked by an incident in which a Kaffir was apprehended for stealing an axe, but later freed by a force of his compatriots while being taken to appear before the magistrate. What gave the incident the little extra *frisson* which the Victorians loved was that the prisoner was handcuffed to another man and the rescuers, unable to undo the handcuffs, simply lopped off the hand. No doubt the story did the rounds in Cape Town and was a powerful recruiting agent for bodies like the Cape Mounted Rifles, the Wynberg & Simon's Town Volunteers or the other volunteer corps which joined the regular army units in the campaigns. The war has been described as little more than the seizing of cattle or the destruction of crops, though significant as marking a major step on the road from black independence to white control. However, contemporary accounts by participants make it clear that it was, for them at least, rather more exciting than this deadpan assessment. The Xhosa carried out a classic campaign of the kind which we now know as guerilla warfare and the campaigning conditions were rugged.

Back in Cape Town Henry fell under the spell of Robert Grey, the first English Bishop in South Africa, who arrived in 1848 to find his diocese "in a most forlorn condition". Conditions, as described by Gray's biographer, were certainly daunting:

> The diocese stretched for six hundred miles from west to east; it was necessary to organize the whole work from one corner of the vast area. There was then, and for fifteen years afterwards, not a mile of railway track in the Colony; the roads were mere tracks, passable only to horses and slowly moving ox-waggons. Over the 277,000 square miles of territory were dotted isolated families and little groups of Church people, whom the Church had almost wholly neglected. Many of them had clung to the tradition of Churchmanship in spite of every discouragement; no sooner had the Bishop arrived than he began to receive piteous appeals for priests, and promises to build little churches and schools if only they could be served. The Bishop reckoned that fifty priests would be none too many to meet the most pressing needs; he had but seventeen, few of them his own choice, some unsatisfactory.

Holt Okes had for the past 14 years been officiating chaplain at Wynberg, a village some miles from his home, and was to continue for a further six years in partnership with another clergyman. The new bishop does not seem to have been impressed, commenting: "I have made some important changes. Mr -- goes to Wynberg, an important parish utterly neglected and overrun by East India visitors who with long purses and pious purposes, are the pest of the place. I caught one of them praying extempore in the church here last Sunday."

Poor Holt! It seems scant thanks for so much largely unrequited service, but new brooms are unrelenting, and the Bishop was trying to make up for lost time. He was on the look out for likely recruits to be sent out from England, but there was one already on hand, about whom he may even have known something before he came, for his brother lived in Godmanchester, just over the river from Huntingdon where Henry Herbert was born. Anyway Henry seems to have impressed the new man and, despite the lack of a degree, he was soon under training for Holy Orders beneath the Bishop's own roof. Gray ordained Henry as a Deacon in December, 1849. Finding that education did not top the local agenda, (As one critic put it, "These people don't understand art; all they understand is hunting and drinking.") Gray founded the Collegiate School of the Diocese of Cape Town at Protea and Henry became Assistant Master under its first principal, Rev. H.M. White, himself a recent arrival from England. The school was modelled on Radley, and was designed "to fit pupils for secular employment and professions as well as for the church." The Bishop's Chaplain was Vice-Principal, but he was busy with other things, so the burden of the teaching fell on White and Herbert, though as they began with only six pupils, the burden was not excessive. However, numbers increased and in 1850, for lack of space, the school removed to Woodlands at Rondebosch. Here the Principal and his assistant, whom he described as "an excellent helper", cleared a space in the dense woodland for playing fields and incidentally let in a view of Table Mountain. Henry, who was said to be a dashing cricketer, was also responsible for supervising games. One contemporary account describes him "pegging out a fairly good cricket field in spite of the troublesome moles". He was popular but very strict in school and you could not take liberties with him out of school without coming to grief, according to the school's official history, which also notes that he was a "munificent donor" to the school library. The Bishop and his wife did not approve of church music so there was none at the school, which was perhaps fortunate since neither Mr. White nor Mr. Herbert had any music in them. Now known as Bishops, the school, which opened its doors to all races in 1978, is still flourishing.

The first prize-giving was not until 1857, by which time Holt Okes had been in his grave for three years and Henry had departed for home. The school's historian noted that Henry was ordained priest on the fourth Sunday in Advent in 1855 and left shortly afterwards " to follow his priestly calling." Altogether Henry spent 11 years in the colony with only one brief return to England in 1853, when he met Mary Ruddock, the 18-year-old daughter of a clergyman, and plighted her his troth. No doubt he would have liked to take her back with him to Cape Town, but the Ruddocks were made of more cautious stuff and, besides Mary was the eldest girl in a family of 12, the youngest of whom had been born only the year before. She could hardly be spared for a madcap venture in South Africa. So she would have to wait - and a long wait it turned out to be.

To the great regret, we are told, of the Cape Town Diocese, Henry decided in 1856 to return to England permanently. He had watched the decline and death of Holt and Patricia Okes and must have been shaken by the death, only 18 days after her father, of Margaret Okes, who in the manner of Victorian womanhood, had devoted herself to the care of her parents. He was aware of his own mother's advancing age - she was now 73 and living in the small village of Westbury-on-Trym on the edge of Bristol with two of her daughters, who were now clearly not going to marry. His half-brother, Dennis, was still going strong in Huntingdon, where he had recently concluded the third of his multiple terms as Mayor, but he could hardly be expected to take responsibility for his father's second wife, who was no relation. Henry must have concluded that it was his duty to provide a home for his mother and, besides, there was the lure of Mary Ruddock.

And so, not without some regret, Henry turned his face away from Gray's great enterprise and sailed for home. He landed at Swansea in September, hastened to his mother's house and read the prayers at evensong. "I think, " his mother wrote to her brother Richard Okes, "there was many an eye glistened for us amongst the poor as well as the rich on the following day at Church, when the Minister read aloud that 'Henry Herbert desired to return thanks to Almighty God for his safe and prosperous voyage' and then followed it on in the thanksgiving." Such gratitude was not uttered lightly in those days for it was an arduous voyage from the Cape, lasting up to four months. Nor did news travel any faster. The letter announcing his return arrived just after Henry did, having come by the same ship. Henry's next job was to be Curate of Harkstead and Erwarton, two tiny villages on the flat Shotley peninsula between the Rivers Stour and Orwell south of Ipswich. For a man of 32 with Henry's experience of the wider world it must have been difficult to settle into a curacy in so small a community - or even, a year later, into the perpetual curacy of Seer Green in Buckinghamshire, though that had the distinct advantage of being within striking distance of the Ruddock household in Reading. At Seer Green he was able to accommodate his mother and his sisters, Emma and Caroline, but perpetual curates were paid directly by the diocese, enjoying no income from Glebe lands and the pay - £100 per annum (the equivalent of £8,000 nowadays) - certainly did not enable Henry to contemplate marriage. For five more years he toiled away in Seer Green and Mary Ruddock continued to wait for him. What strains this put on the relationship we can only imagine, but there is a fragment of a letter which suggests that they may have despaired of ever being united. The author is unknown as only the first part survives. It is addressed to Mary from London, dated February 18, 1861, and says:

> You know how very glad I must be for anything which can give you comfort, as I feel assured Mr. Herbert's letter must have done. If God has willed that, though one in heart, you should remain separate in this life, He has not so willed it of the future. Nothing in His grace can divide you there, if only you follow after righteousness here, from each other and from Christ. I hope, dear Mary, you have the comfort of Mr. Romanis' visits again. I should be very glad to hear you saw him as often as you could wish. Whether it may please God that your time here be longer or shorter this new tie, if I may so call it, will be no hindrance to you, but rather make you desire more earnestly that blessed time, when sorrows and partings shall have for ever an end. I sometimes almost feel inclined to think such a parting, dearest Mary, well nigh too"......

There the surviving letter ends, leaving us tantalised as to its significance and meaning. What had Mr Herbert said in his letter? Was Mary afraid that she was dying? Was Mr. Romanis a suitor? He is revealed by the 1861 Census to have been a curate at St Mary's, Reading, aged 36, a widower living with two daughters and two older sisters quite near the Ruddocks. Was he alienating Mary's affections? It would have been a tough task for her, at 27, to move into the Romanis household. We can only speculate, but at any rate it was cold comfort for Mary to be told that she might have to wait for eternity before her love for Henry could be consummated. In the event good fortune, in the shape of Dennis Herbert of Huntingdon, came to the rescue. Three years earlier Dennis had sold the brewery in Huntingdon to James Marshall, severing the family's links with the licensed trade, and not long afterwards he purchased the advowson of Hemingford Abbots from Lady Olivia Sparrow. He now presented his half-brother, Henry, to what was a relatively prosperous living. On January 25, 1868, Henry was "inducted into the real, actual, and corporal possession of the Rectory of Hemingford Abbots in the County and Archdeaconry of Huntingdon". This was the start of the Herbert family's association with the village, which was to play an important role in their affairs for the next century and a half. The association began auspiciously because Henry could now afford to marry Mary Ruddock. He lost no time; the wedding took place just five days after the induction. She was 33 and Henry 43.

Over the next decade Henry and Mary produced six sons, which considering Mary's age was no mean achievement, and established themselves in the hearts of the parishioners. A close friend, Rev. R. Bruce Dickson wrote:

> Mr Herbert and his capable wife, by their earnest and devoted work and kindly attention to the bodily as well as spiritual needs of the parishioners endeared themselves to a circle of friends of all classes. It is probably not too much to say that while their work was not hampered by the disabilities, age and ill-health, which came upon them in the latter years of Mr. Herbert's life, every inhabitant of the parish felt that the Rector and his wife were about the best and truest friends he or she had in the world, and were the first persons to resort to in trouble or difficulty of any kind.

When he had been Rector for 21 years - the same year that he was grappling with paying for Dennis Henry to go up to Oxford - the parishioners clubbed together and bought him a silver jug suitably inscribed.

As we have seen, the agricultural depression in the 1870s and 1880s hit the clergy hard. From 1874 to 1894, when he was Rural Dean of Huntingdon, Henry bore a double burden, in that while suffering himself he had also to console many other country parsons similarly afflicted. In dealing with these difficulties, Henry was said to have shown the "patient tact, forbearance and courage which were characteristic of him," gaining the respect even of those who differed from him. There was a hint in Mr. Dickson's eulogy that Henry hung on as Rector longer than his health warranted, but he had little option. Without substantial private means he could not survive otherwise. He and Mary were also praised as parents. A headmaster said that the boys had more cause to be thankful to God for their parents than any children he knew. Their few surviving letters to Dennis Henry tend to support the view that they were a close-knit family and that the community at Hemingford, St. Ives and Godmanchester meant much to them. Mary, in her spiky handwriting, makes frequent references to letters from her other sons, shows the usual motherly concern about his health, mentions friends and neighbours and usually adds a short homily. Here is her 1888 birthday letter - rather more businesslike than usual:

Hemingford Rectory

Feb 24th

My darling Dennis,
Many happy returns of tomorrow, I wish you most sincerely, and pray God it may be the beginning of a successful, and happy year to

you. If you are doing your very best, and striving to do what is right for God sake, it must be in one sense a happy one, come what will. If you live and all goes well, it will be an eventful year in your life, dear, and making quite a fresh start. I am glad you are feeling stronger. I think you should certainly go on with Cod liver oil whilst this cold weather lasts. Tell me when you write if you think the pills suit you and I shall send you some more. I have enclosed 3/-, 2/- for Richard and 1/- for George. R. wants one for himself and the other is for Trevellyan. He asked for 1/6 and G asked for 2/6 but we think 1/- each will be enough for them - our expenses are very heavy now and we cannot very well send more. If you think it needful, will you give it to them & I will send it to you. I don't think G. wants any for himself. I hope to write to Willie in a few days & will tell him about shorthand. I have no coffee in the house. I shall be sending soon. Your loving Mother, M. Herbert.

Given that between the age of 35 and 45 she had produced six hale and hearty sons, - the birth of Dennis Henry in 1869, was soon followed by Edward Grevile (Teddie), Louis William (Willie), Richard Charles, George and Francis Falkner - Mary decided that she was entitled to take things a little easier, so though perfectly well, she took to a Bath chair and was never afterwards seen in public without it - and no doubt the sons had to push. She kept in regular touch with her six brothers and five sisters, several of whom supplied much of the information about the family which has passed down the generations. Mary was said to be a very inquisitive lady - some said "nosey" - and, when doors opened unexpectedly, as they frequently did in the Old Rectory, later generations used to say that it was Great Granny come to see what was going on.

The house was then much bigger than it is now, with a large central hall and extensive rooms on the west side, since demolished, and the six acres of garden and paddock incorporated what later became the village school playing field. The 120 yards of garden between the house and the river were divided by paths into three equal sections of 40 yards each traversed by a double herbaceous border. The cows in the cowshed had their names painted above the doors of their stalls and there were also pigs, goats and chickens, extensive orchards and Peter's field, where the donkey who pulled the donkey cart lived a peaceful existence. At the front of the house a Wellingtonia tree, planted by one of Henry's predecessors to mark the death of the Duke of Wellington, was beginning to loom large and Henry had it moved further from the house, earning the gratitude of his descendants as it grew to over 120 feet and was said to be extraordinarily large for the conditions. Round the whole property ran a wide driveway bordered by trees. The Herberts habitually kept several servants. In 1881, for instance, when the youngest boy was two, they had a cook, a nurse, a housemaid and a gardener's boy resident in the house. I believe two other gardeners were also employed. There is a picture of one with the donkey which, with its hooves suitably shod in leather boots, also pulled the mower across the extensive lawns - a far cry from the 21st Century battery-powered robots which now keep the grass in order.

Whether it is apocryphal or not, I like the story that Henry, who once hunted Kaffirs on the South African veldt, used to fire from an upper window at suitors who came in pursuit of the servants, dodging among the stones in the next-door graveyard for shelter. It is also said that he was responsible for the absence of a non-conformist chapel in Hemingford Abbots. When one was in the offing, he bought up the land on which they were proposing to build it, and it later became the site of the Village Hall. Dennis Henry Herbert, was born in 1869 and has left a description of the village in about 1875. It is a picture of a small, intensely rural, agricultural community in which the average wage was 12/- per week, people made their own entertainment and were clearly delineated between the gentry and the rest, but nevertheless knew, and understood, each other well. One of Dennis's favourite characters was "Old Haynes", who busied himself keeping the birds off the cherries and whittling sticks with a sharp knife in the churchyard. He left the knife to Dennis in his will and it was a prized possession.

In 1908 Henry suffered a serious stroke and was effectively disabled from further work. His third son, Willie, came home to help. Years later his daughter-in-law, Madeline, recalled this difficult period when Henry had to be lifted in and out of bed by Willie and two nurses. "I used to plan him tasty dishes as the nurses gave him bread and milk for each meal until he called out in revolt! That is ancient history but I'm happy to have known him from 1907 to 1909 & his charm & courtesy were something to remember." Eventually, on July 27, 1911, Henry died. His body was taken into the church on Friday night and the five of his six sons who were in England (Teddie was still in the Far East) took turns watching over it through the night before the funeral on Saturday. There was a large turnout of family, of clergy from surrounding parishes and of Hemingford parishioners. The *Hunts Post* recorded that Mr Brown of Huntingdon was at the organ and the singing of the well-trained village choir was remarkably good, especially in the beautiful hymn "Peace, Perfect Peace", which was sung at the graveside.

> The coffin of plain unpolished oak, was made in the village by Mr.
> James Smith and was borne to the grave by eight lifelong residents

of the village in Hemingford. On the coffin and extending its whole length was a cross of white flowers from the widow, with two wreaths, one from the deceased's six sons and his daughters-in-law, and the other from his five grandsons. About the grave, which was lined with moss and edged with white flowers were upwards of fifty floral crosses and wreaths."

All this seemed fittingly to emphasise the strong links Henry had forged within the county in general and Hemingford Abbots in particular and the newspaper concluded by saying that they recognised his good work with pride as coming from a member of a Huntingdonshire family, born and living the greater part of his long life in Huntingdonshire. A more lasting tribute was embodied in a new east window in the church, commissioned by the family in memory of Henry. A contemporary critic gave this description of the window, which remains an important feature of the church:

> The subject is a symbolical representation of the Crucifixion, worked out in the following manner: The design is based upon the words "Ego sum Vitis Vera." (I am the True Vine), which words are placed upon a scroll at the foot of the cross. The window consists of three lights of equal size. The centre light consists of the Christ upon the cross, with the Blessed Virgin and St John at the foot, and at the top two angels placing a crown, emblematic of victory, on our Lord's head. The cross is the main stem of the vine, and from the base of it there extend two branches, which run up into the side lights, and with their ramifications form the background. The "Fruit of the Vine" consists of four groups of Saints - the lower ones composed of three and the upper ones of two - amid the curves of the branches.

Henry's widow, Mary, lived on for six more years until in February, 1917, she died peacefully in the early hours of Ash Wednesday morning and was buried with her husband. By this time the Great War was already two and a half years into its catastrophic progress, and her five younger sons were either serving or destined to serve, as recorded on the Roll of Honour in the church, in the Royal Flying Corps, the South Lancashire Regiment, the Rifle Brigade, the Egyptian Coastguard Service and as Chaplain to the Forces. Teddie, who had been wounded in an air accident some weeks before, and Richard, who was with the Rifle Brigade in Salonika, were unable to attend her funeral. The *Hunts Post* recalled how much she had valued the handsome tray with which parishioners had presented her at her silver wedding in recognition of her kindness to the sick during her 25-years' residence. "The older generation will well remember her ceaseless energy in the parish and her goodness to the poor and the sick throughout the many years of her long married life."

*Henry Herbert in youth. Mary
Ruddock's fiancé*

*Rev. Romanis. Was he a rival for Mary
Ruddock's hand?*

The Rectory, Hemingford Abbots, when Henry Herbert was Rector

Mary Herbert (née Ruddock) with her daughter-in-law, May (née Bell), in the Drawing Room at The Rectory, circa 1902

The Pony cart at The Rectory

Caroline Herbert, Patron of the living

Rev. Henry Herbert (1824-1911)

Mary Herbert (née Ruddock) 1834-1917

Chapter 12

SIAM, BURMA, PAARDEBERG, EGYPT, SALONIKA & MANEA

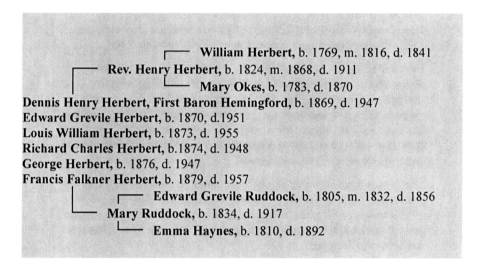

William Herbert, b. 1769, m. 1816, d. 1841
Rev. Henry Herbert, b. 1824, m. 1868, d. 1911
Mary Okes, b. 1783, d. 1870
Dennis Henry Herbert, First Baron Hemingford, b. 1869, d. 1947
Edward Grevile Herbert, b. 1870, d.1951
Louis William Herbert, b. 1873, d. 1955
Richard Charles Herbert, b.1874, d. 1948
George Herbert, b. 1876, d. 1947
Francis Falkner Herbert, b. 1879, d. 1957
Edward Grevile Ruddock, b. 1805, m. 1832, d. 1856
Mary Ruddock, b. 1834, d. 1917
Emma Haynes, b. 1810, d. 1892

How very nice it is to see
Our kind relations come to tea,
But better far it is to know
That when they've had their tea, they'll go.- J.B. Morrell

Between them all Henry and Mary's sons exhibited many of the characteristics of their Herbert, Ruddock and Okes forebears – academic ability, an uncomfortable mixture of conventionality and eccentricity coupled with a regrettable tendency, in one or two cases, to drink and a reluctance to come to grips with financial reality. All of them followed their eldest sibling to King's School Ely, but it appears that further financial stringency forced Henry and Mary to curtail the careers there of the younger boys.

Edward Grevile (1870-1951)

Teddie became a mechanical engineer and was employed by Teak Forest & Saw Mills in Siam (now Thailand) and Burma. In 1901 he married Olive Una, daughter of Rev. George Linton, whose father lived at Hemingford Park, but she died in August 1904, six weeks after giving birth to a baby son, Charles. When the news reached Hemingford, Henry sat down and wrote out a tribute for the Sunday service:

> On August 12th there came by cable the news that one well know in our parish had passed away. Olive Una Herbert, the wife of Mr Edward Grevile Herbert, our Rector's second son, was intimately associated with Hemingford, being the granddaughter of the late Rev. James Linton of Hemingford House and a niece of Colonel Linton from whose house she was married on Nov. 6th, 1901,

> For some time previous to her marriage she was much at Hemingford, and endeared herself to us all by her universally kind and happy disposition. Her short but happy married life was spent far away in Bangkok and Rangoon, and we who knew both her and her husband so well must feel a specially deep measure of sympathy with him on whom such a heavy blow has fallen while far distant from his home relations and friends.

> She leaves a son Charles Henry, born on June 30th last & while we thank God that He has been pleased to deliver her from the troubles of this world & give her peace, let us pray that He will give support to her husband in his trouble and spare the little son to be a comfort and a joy to his father.

Teddie carried on in the Far East until 1916 when he joined the Royal Flying Corps and served in the Scout Squadron in France, where he suffered a slight head wound in a flying accident in January, 1917. Later employed by Burmah Oil, he seems to have made a small fortune. Certainly he was known as the member of the family with money, but, like many others, he suffered grievously in the Stock Exchange slump of the late 1920s. Teddie took a great interest in Hemingford Abbots. He built and let four houses on the east side of the Village Hall and gave land for both a playing field and a Hall. He was similarly generous to the wider family. He gave his younger brother Francis substantial gifts of money in the 1920s and spent a great deal of time trying to get Francis to run his life more efficiently. Two letters give the flavour of these exchanges:

March 4th, '24

(Tuesday)

My dear Francis,

Many thanks for yours of 29th, with post mark of 1st inst., which reached Reading yesterday.

I was too busy to acknowledge it last evening & this is my first opportunity. I am very pleased to hear that you appreciate the changed outlook, & that you are determined to take advantage of it. I trust you will, for it is the turning point - & I am unable to make another. Still, it will have to be very stiff work, & you will have to watch most carefully. I shall hope to get some details on Saturday next at Warminster (Wilts). Please thank Madeline for her letter which I shall no doubt find at Warminster.

Thanks for D's balance sheet dated 30/1/22, which I recd. with your letter.

Your affect. brother, E.G. Herbert

Ryatts Hotel

Cheltenham, Glos.

July 21st (late)

My dear Francis,

I have your letter of the 17th inst, which arrived on Friday afternoon, but I went away on Friday & returned to Cheltenham this morning & only brought in my luggage & collected my letters this evening. I never come in for lunch, as I am out from breakfast to dinner.

I don't feel it necessary to make any apology to you for delay in writing, as I have repeatedly warned you against these "eleventh hour" calls for assistance, & I am feeling exceedingly annoyed with you. You know that one of the chief reasons for making you keep accounts is that you can then see in advance when you will need assistance, yet months have gone by without you sending an account, & only futile promises have come in since Whitsuntide. After all that I have written & said to you, I feel it is too bad of you.

I am sending you herewith a cheque for £20, & I trust that you will send me your accounts without any further delay.

I finish work at H.Q. the end of this week, & I shall be out in my district again by the 1st August, so unless you know of any certain address, send to the Sports Club, St. James' Square, S.W.1, who will forward to me when I send an address once a week.

I am very tired so will not write more.

101

Your affectionate brother

E.G. Herbert

Teddie himself was living a peripatetic life, moving from hotel to hotel, and he was hard-pressed financially as his commission from the company fell short of his expenses, so his assistance for Francis was coming out of capital. Towards the end of his life, in 1950, Teddie gave his great nephew and nieces tennis posts and a net for the court on the Old Rectory lawn - a most generous gift. I remember him as an upright, stiff old gentleman, who must have had a love of children for he was able to converse freely and interestingly with a schoolboy of 15. By that time he had long sold his retirement house in Sheringham, parted with his beloved collection of bird books and his carefully-catalogued egg collection and given up golf, which had been a favourite pastime. His nephew Myles remembered years later the pleasure of visiting Teddie in Norfolk, tempered by the pain of having to leave the beach early to dress for dinner followed by bridge. The boys called him "Yes, well, but" because that was his initial response in conversation. Teddie went to live in London, where he survived the war as a Fire Watcher in the ARP, though he evidently had some close shaves, particularly from the "doodle-bugs". He used to make light of these after the war, but in November 1944 the Premier Hotel, where he was living, was rendered unfit for habitation and the Bedford, to which he moved was not much better. He told his brother Francis: "This place is not too good, as the top floor was burnt out and water did much damage - this was incendiaries - and the doodle-bugs did quite a bit of blast damage even here." Francis's comment on this was "Personally I think I would seek safer quarters unless I had good reason for not doing so, but 'every man to his taste'."

In 1951 Teddie died at the age of 81. His son, Charles grew up to become a senior civil servant in Canada, where he married Henrietta Dorothea Begg in 1934 and had two daughters. His wife, who was known as Nettie, suffered from a mental illness which confined her to hospital for many years, and in 1955 Charles himself was killed in a car crash near Camden, New Jersey. The girls, Mary Macdonald and Caroline, who were also involved, were badly injured but recovered. Mary married Dieter Doktor in Toronto in 1961.

Louis William (1873-1955)

The next of Henry Herbert's sons, Willie, was an Army Officer. He fought in the Boer War in the Welch Regiment, notably at the Battle of Paardeberg, where he distinguished himself. A frontal attack on the Boer position, ordered by Lord Kitchener, was a disaster and Willie's unit of 300 suffered 60 casualties. When darkness fell they had still not taken the Boers' Laager and had become separated from the rest of the force. Willie volunteered to swim the river with a message from his Brigadier General explaining the situation and asking for help, but he could find only two other companies, who were equally lost. He swam back and told the general. At midnight he was asked by the general to go again with another officer, Captain Fausset, of the Essex Regiment. "We crossed and hunted everywhere within a radius of 2 miles," he wrote to his parents. "It was pitch dark. About 2.30 we were surprised by a party of 10 Boers & taken prisoners to the Laager." In the event they were kept captive by General Cronje for only a couple of days and were released in time to take part in what Willie said was even fiercer fighting at Driefontain and to be present at the Relief of Kimberley. There were two strange consequences of the Paardeberg incident. Newspapers in England printed what purported to be a letter from Willie to a relation describing bad treatment allegedly suffered at the hands of the Boers. Willie was outraged and authorised his brother Dennis to deny the story. The papers carried a lengthy retraction, quoting Willie as saying it was absolutely untrue that they had been denied food and water for two days. They had suffered no indignities and the Boers were particularly civil. "They fed us as well as we could expect considering most of the laager containing food was burnt the first day of Paardeberg and at the end of the siege they practically had no food left."

Legend had it that Willie was told he was to be nominated for a gallantry medal, possibly even the Victoria Cross, and was so disappointed when nothing materialised that he resigned his commission. The reality may be a bit more prosaic, but there is a grain of truth in the story. Two senior officers wrote to Willie, who was by now embarkation officer at Cape Town, expressing their disappointment at his lack of recognition. This is how Willie summarised the situation for his brother Dennis:

> I was not mentioned in despatches & didn't deserve it. Others had done very much better than I did & have been through it all & had a much harder time, while I've been down at the Base. Col. Banfield wrote me a very nice letter but I don't think it was necessary. He says "I was very sorry to see that your name did not appear among those mentioned. When I found that your name was not among those mentioned in the first list published by Lord Roberts I wrote to Gen. Stephenson & to the then O.C. Welch mentioning what you had done in swimming the river at Paardeberg, the full account of which I am sorry to say I did not hear till long after it occurred. I suggested that

O.C. Welch should get a full account of it & send it in. I have since heard that you had already been mentioned in the list of those sent in from the Battalion. And Gen. Stephenson wrote saying that he had also mentioned your action; so I cannot understand it. I am writing again to Gen. Stephenson about you as it seems very hard that you should have been omitted when it seems to me that you should have been one of the first mentioned...... I won't let it drop until I have found some one to act."

Very particularly nice and kind of Col. Banfield but I think he has rather made a mountain out of a molehill as my services were practically nil & the expedition on which I set out failed. Col. Ball also wrote saying "I am sorry not to see your name amongst the list. I made enquiries when I got up here & heard it had been sent in, but like one or two others it appears to have been removed in London."

However there it is & I think it had better remain as it is.

Willie did resign from the regiment rather impulsively (to the distress of his C.O. who wrote expressing his concern), but that was not until 1905 so if it was in a fit of pique at his treatment, it was not done without time for reflection. Anyway it was a bad mistake. Though he tried, for example, for the Chief Constableship of Suffolk and the command of the Hertfordshire territorials, Willie never managed to get employment in civilian life, living on his retired pay and spending much time managing his (rather small) investments. However in 1914 he quickly rejoined the Army, crossed to France with the South Lancashire Regiment and was present at all actions from Mons to the First Battle of Ypres inclusive, rising to command the battalion for 14 days at Ypres. He then became a casualty and spent several weeks at Osborne in the Isle of Wight, which was a military hospital. He returned to France, but served behind the lines as a Staff Officer in the Casualty Branch, and was awarded the D.S.O. It was gazetted in the Queen's Birthday Honours List in June 1916 and was evidently given for general services rather than a specific act of gallantry. From 1917 to 1919 he commanded the 3rd South Lancashire Regiment in Crosby, Barrow and Dublin.

As a young man Willie was much in demand with the ladies, but spurned them all. When eventually he married Amy Jarvis, he told his brother ungallantly "Beggars can't be choosers". However, Amy was a good sort and an excellent companion. They had no children, but were always on hand to help other members of the family out if they were in difficulty. In the second World War they had to abandon their house on the exposed East Anglian coast, just boarding up the windows and locking the doors, and they moved to

Dorset for the duration. My father was particularly fond of them, contributed to the purchase of their house and used to visit them regularly in Gorleston-on-Sea, Norfolk, where Amy kept a fish shop.

Richard Charles (1874-1948)

Richard went to King's School, Ely, and in September, 1891, his parents came up with the idea that he should go into the church if he could get a degree. His brother, Dennis, was despatched to Ely to enquire as to his prospects, but received a rather equivocal reply. However, he regarded the form master as unconvincing and a promise was extracted from the head that Richard would be given private lessons in Greek and Latin and a report made to his father. Richard himself was quite taken with the idea and Dennis recorded in his diary the view that he had common sense "and so I think he could get a degree if he made up his mind to it and worked." Unfortunately Richard did not live up to Dennis's optimism and, although he was admitted to Selwyn College, Cambridge, he did not take a degree. In 1901 he was living with his parents and was described as a Nurseryman and employer. He served in the Rifle Brigade in the First World War, and was, for a time, posted to Cyprus, Salonika and the Middle East. His father seems to have had some doubt about Richard's reliability as he was the only one of the sons for whom it was felt necessary to set up a trust fund so that he could not get his hands on the capital which he inherited. Latterly he lived near Southampton, having married Kathleen Emily Reeves, who according to family legend was Lord Swaythling's coachman's daughter. They had a daughter, Mary Ruddock Herbert, who married John Kent, and had two daughters. Richard died in 1948, the third of the six brothers to go within a few months.

George (1876-1947)

George took to the sea at the age of 14 on the School Ship, *H.M.S. Conway*, under the aegis of the Mercantile Marine Service Association. His father took him to Liverpool by train on Monday, September 8, 1890 and soon afterwards he signed a pledge:

> I, G. Herbert, do most solemnly and sincerely declare that, during such time as I belong to the *Conway*, I will with God's help, abstain from all Drinking, Smoking, Swearing, or Impurity, and, as much as in me lies, endeavour to persuade my comrades to do the same.

This was standard practice on *Conway*, which was moored off Rock Ferry pier in Liverpool, and was a fee-paying school designed to prepare boys for service in the Merchant Marine. The fees were about £40 per year. George served for several years on merchant ships - in 1900 when he was about to take his Second Mate's exam, his ship was chartered for Shanghai and his mother was expecting him to be away for a long time. Later he joined the Egyptian Coastguard, becoming a *Bimbashi*, or Major. In due course he returned to Hemingford Abbots, living originally at Cherry Orchard, and became a county Alderman. He married Muriel, widow of Ernest Ebsworth, of Harcourt, Hemingford Grey. They had no children but doted on their dog, Nigger. Muriel died in 1937. In later life George built The Tall House in Royal Oak Lane, which he rudely named The Erection. When the author was playing cricket round Huntingdonshire in the mid-1950s, elderly gentlemen used regularly to come up and, with a nod and a wink, describe some of George's more outrageous peccadilloes, apocryphal or otherwise. He spent a lot of time in his garage trying to perfect, unsuccessfully, a non-dazzling headlight for motor cars. When he died unexpectedly at Christmas, 1947, (the hospital had reported only a few days before that he was likely to make a good recovery from a bladder problem.) he left, characteristically, two wills and a degree of confusion. Lawyers were proceeding on the basis of the first 1939 Will, in favour of a Miss Ellaby, who was actually assisting them going through papers when they came across another Will, made not long before his death, in favour of Miss Sybil Watts. She was at the time living in St. Ives and it was said that George and she were planning to marry. There is plenty of evidence that he was lonely and was looking for a wife.

Miss Ellaby behaved with admirable dignity, but the drama caused consternation among George's surviving brothers and Francis was despatched to vet Miss Watts and discover whether she would release items of family interest. He reported that he was agreeably surprised by her. "She did not strike me as being in any way eccentric or excitable, but very common-sense and rational, and made me very welcome and appears anxious to be fair to both the Herbert and Ebsworth families." By this time there had been another development. A former neighbour of George's reported that he had made a secret drawer in his desk, where he kept valuables. Following her detailed instructions, the lawyers duly came up with three strings of pearls. Miss Watts was assured that, since they had been found in the house, they were hers.

Francis Falkner (1879-1957)

Francis, it is said, wanted to become a gold miner in South America, but was required by his father to become his curate. This, if true, belies Henry's reputation as a good father. He, of all people, should have understood the benefit of adventure and travel in early manhood. Francis was popular, handsome and charming, and a keen sportsman. At Emmanuel College, Cambridge, he obtained an M.A.. and after a time at theological college in Wells, he became Curate in Marlow, Bucks in the autumn of 1904 and was ordained by the Bishop of Oxford at Cuddesdon on September 23, 1906. It was not long before he was required at Hemingford, however, and he was already resident there when, on June 2, 1909, at Bisham, near Marlow, he married Madeline King, a sprightly, petite, attractive woman three years his junior, who was also a native of Huntingdonshire, born at Catworth, 15 miles from Hemingford.

It must have seemed an auspicious occasion - two strikingly handsome, attractive people setting out together with a degree of security behind them because Francis knew that, when his father died, his Aunt Caroline, who by now owned the patronage, would offer him the living. Soon they were following the Herbert family tradition of producing sons - no daughters had been born since Caroline herself in 1822. Kenneth Falkner Herbert was born on February 7, 1910 to be followed on April 29, 1915 by another son, Henry Myles. The family lived at Thorpe Cottage until Francis did indeed become Rector on the death of Henry in 1911 when they moved into The Rectory. By then they were thoroughly immersed in village events. For example, in 1909 both Francis and Willie were referees at the annual Hemingfords' Regatta. In the following year, only six months after Kenneth's birth, Madeline became the first member of the family to win an event, taking the Ladies Punting trophy, quite an achievement for one so slight. By 1913 she was so thoroughly accepted as to be invited to distribute the prizes, for which she received a hearty vote of thanks. Francis was President that year, the last before the outbreak of war, when it was recorded that "The whole day was marked by a spirit of simple enjoyment and harmony of feeling."

In 1917, after the death of his mother, Francis became an Army Chaplain, serving with the 69th East Anglian Division, and was posted to the East Midlands. After the war things began to go wrong. Francis was ill in 1919 and afterwards claimed that it was as a result of this that his financial affairs got into a muddle. Be that as it may in January, 1921 his brother Dennis was writing to him: "Your letter reached me this morning. I am very sorry to hear of your trouble, and of course I will do all I can to help you - though I am afraid that is not much. I think borrowing £500 (or indeed any substantial amount) is out of the question. As far as I know you have no security to borrow on....." and then, 10 months later:

> I am too sorry & distressed about the whole business to blame you: but there is no getting away from the fact that since you first wrote to me nearly a year ago you have never given me the chance to help you so far as I could: the result is things merely get worse & worse, & I cannot see how I can get you out of the mess.
>
> But I repeat again several things I have said before: - (1) It is no use resigning the Living without first looking out for something else (2) You must let Madeline know the whole position exactly (3) I cannot advise you without full details: these I have never had in any complete form, & the old list of debts of last spring must now be out of date & incomplete. You have never given me any proper statement of your income, nor do I know what help you have had otherwise than through me or what you have been living on during the last three months.
>
> I am still anxious to help you as far as I can, but I fear that I cannot do much more than advise, & this is impossible until you face things properly & give me full information. If you will do this you had better come & see me in about a week or 10 days <u>after</u> you have got out in writing full particulars of everything: I can at least then see if it is possible or not to save your furniture etc. from creditors: but unless you do something quickly you will find all your things seized & sold & yourself in the Bankruptcy Court.

His brother Teddie came to the rescue with a loan of £1,000 secured, inadequately, on Francis's furniture and and house contents. Dennis seems also to have assembled others who were prepared to help, but for the next decade or more either Dennis or Teddie was cajoling, bullying and beseeching Francis to get his affairs in order and to level with them as to the state of his indebtedness. They regularly sent him £10 or £20 to tide him over. In February 1924 a crisis arose over a County Court summons requiring payment of £37.17s.7d within eight days. Francis told Madeline that he had to find the money at once and was going to a close friend to stand security but did not add that he had been told that, if the money were not found, the bailiffs would come and take possession at any time. To Teddie he wrote "If it got to the Bishop's ears that I had had a County Court summons issued against me, or that the bailiffs had taken possession I might be asked to resign the living, or at any rate would never stand a chance of preferment in the future in any shape or form." What was happening in part, as his son Myles later recorded, was that Francis, brought up pre-war, was ill prepared for a sudden social change. After the war the tenant farmers were near-bankrupt and could not pay the rents due, let alone any higher rent to match inflation and it was, of course, unthinkable that a man of the cloth should deal harshly with his tenants.

Poignantly on May 31, 1924, Francis was appointed Rural Dean of Huntingdon, one of whose duties was to inform the Bishop of all matters concerning the Clergy and other officers of the church "which he may deem it necessary or useful that the Bishop should know." He was also to inspect the Churches and Chapels in the Deanery and their books, ornaments and utensils and report any alterations. Within weeks the Ely Diocesan Board of Finance were writing to say they had not received the figures of the apportionment made upon the parishes of the Deanery. "I must further remind you that nearly half the year is gone," wrote Canon Evans, the Hon. Secretary, reprovingly. It seems a little hard since Francis had only just begun the job and, on enquiring of the Bishop before he accepted the post what was involved, had been told that there was nothing to it except to provide a shoulder for his fellow clergy to cry on. There was the additional worry that Myles's health was giving serious cause for alarm. The boy suffered from colitis and was so delicate that he had to be taught at home by a governess. Various eminent physicians were consulted in vain but it was not until he was 10, and someone suggested that he be put onto goat's milk, that the trouble cleared up and Myles was able to go to school. He never looked back and became a sprightly nonagenarian.

It was about this time that Teddie took on primary responsibility for pressing Francis to sort his finances out. Francis wrote to him on February 29, 1924, promising a budget drawn up on Teddie's instructions. He added:

> I cannot thank you for all you have done. You will never realize the burden which you have lifted from me, and which I have been literally groaning under for years. It has given me an entirely changed look on life, and I feel that I can really start afresh, and am determined to show that what you have done for us has not been altogether in vain."

Alas it was a false dawn. A year later, on March 5, 1925, Francis was writing

> I can assure you that it is my last wish to irritate or to obstruct you. Please don't think that I do not appreciate all you have done for us: in fact it is because I do appreciate the extent of your help that the position is galling and humiliating to me. I hate writing to you, and I hate even more writing to ask for more and more money. If it were not for the fact that I have a wife and family I would have left here long ago.

To this *crie de coeur* he received the following stern admonition:

> With regard to the first para of your letter, may I repeat what I have
> told you before, that you should make your personal feelings come
> second to what is your duty. You say you hate writing to me - which
> is quite apparent, & even now you have not answered my questions.

By this time it was clear that Francis needed to move from Hemingford
Abbots. The Rectory was expensive to run and the Bishop and Archdeacon
were trying to find him another living, but most of those offered an income of
between £300 and £400, providing no solution. At last it was agreed that he
should go to Manea, a remote Fenland town near March, which, as one
anxious friend remarked, was the absolute antithesis of Hemingford Abbots.
Teddie was still offering help to tide them over the move, but the parishioners
at Hemingford made a presentation to Francis of an album, two pictures and,
crucially, £82 in cash. Difficulties arose over a proposed sale of surplus
garden equipment, which however formed part of the security on Teddie's
loan. Finally in October, 1925, the move took place.

There is a gap in correspondence of almost three years at this point,
but when it resumes in August 1928, things had not much improved. Francis
told Teddie on August 4 that Madeline was "quite ready to undertake all
management of money affairs." To this Teddie responded by demanding, by
return of post, a clear and definite promise from Francis that he would hand
over to Madeline all money he obtained from whatever source. Francis was by
now supplementing his income by journalism, writing nature notes for
national newspapers and magazines under the pseudonym Marsh Harrier, and
Teddie made it clear that he expected this revenue to be handed to Madeline
too. Whether this happened or not we do not know, but seven years later in
August, 1935 Teddie was still making Francis a loan of £50 for August, with
strict instructions on how it was to be spent. He accompanied this letter with
an extraordinary homily:

> The first question is, Why are you finding all these difficulties? Do
> you honestly believe that we can find a solution for all our
> difficulties in God & in the Gospel? I know very well what a big
> question that is - & the difficulty of giving an unqualified yes, but it
> can be done, & there are plenty of men today who can do so, & who
> will discuss the whole matter frankly & fully with others in order to
> help them. I no longer hesitate to affirm the truth of the statement
> that we can find a solution of <u>all</u> our problems through God & the
> Gospel - by my own experience, quite apart from the mass of
> experience of others. That does not mean that I assert my will & my

way, or I should be a spoilt child, but as "<u>my</u> way" becomes "<u>our</u> way" it so becomes my own wish because I find it the better way.

The more we yield to God's way, the less we worry, the less we fear, & the greater our peace of mind - but there must be the yielding, the whole-hearted surrender of selfish motives. And the more we find "that we are given more than we asked or thought."

It is, as you very well know, far too big a matter to be dealt with in a few pages - but I do not hesitate in the statements I have made, & each day provides new experiences in the same direction.

If we try to hammer away in our own way, & in our own strength, we must expect trouble. But if we will face life, as it is, step by step, seeking light from above, we shall lose our worries & our fears, & steadily rise up to a more peaceful & happier life.

This may be summed up into many different heads - personally I should say the best word is Prayer - I hope you will give it your most earnest thought, & you know that I am only too willing to do anything at any time that can be a help.

Francis's reply, if any, to this extraordinary appeal is not recorded, but it seems to have led to some kind of breach. A year later Francis was writing to Dennis declining an offer of further help on the grounds that it might result in matters going from worse to worst, as past help undoubtedly resulted in matters going from bad to worse. "If I had continued to carry on with Teddie's well-intentioned help I believe it would have sent Madeline out of her mind." Whatever arrangements may have been put in place as a result of this proved sadly ineffective and in 1941 Madeline left Manea forever, after which contact between them was minimal. Life at Manea had been extremely difficult, but years later Madeline could still conjure up good memories of the people there. Writing in 1977 to her nephew who had just been there, she said: "How thrilled the people would be to have you & hear about Francis. They were so good to us all - such kind-hearted people - if they liked you." They obviously liked *her*. On her 96th birthday in 1978 she had a galaxy of cards and several letters from Manea, including one from the 80-year-old retired Road Man, who, she said, wrote wonderfully.

Their son, Ken, had married Kathleen Robertson and it was Kathleen who came to take her mother-in-law away. Madeline went back to Huntingdonshire with the boys, living at Hartford, across the river from Hemingford. From now on the breach was more or less complete. In November, 1944, Francis told his brother Willie that he had sent Madeline and

Kathleen some game, which they had not acknowledged. When he enquired whether it had arrived, he was told it had but had been given away. He was now doing a little shooting, though without a dog he did not get very good bags. He had also joined the Observer Corps at the beginning of the war and was continuing to do his stint on frosty November nights despite a feeling that it would be a better occupation for a younger man. Meanwhile financial affairs at Manea were still pressing. In October, 1943, the Manager of Lloyds Bank at March wrote complaining that Francis was depending on loans from colleagues; he wanted him to take his overdraft elsewhere, but after a lengthy correspondence he relented with obvious reluctance.

When the war ended in 1945, Francis had been at Manea for 20 years. He was 66 and broke, but still in possession of a sharp mind and tongue. He was still a member of the Education Committee of the Isle of Ely County Council, a member of the Management Committee of Doddington Hospital, a member of the Nene & Welland Fisheries Board and Chairman of the Isle of Ely Society for the Blind. He served on the County Council Small Holdings and Diseases of Animals Sub-committee and was, for a time, Vice Chairman of the North Witchford Rural District Council and a trustee of Homerton College, Cambridge. He was also Vice President of the Cambridgeshire Committee of the British Legion. He had enemies, but many friends. Nowadays he would have been able to retire from Manea. In the event he carried on for a further eight years, by which time the situation was disastrous. In the spring of 1953 Francis made the Bishop of Ely aware that he could not go on any longer and intended to resign, but added that he had nowhere to go. The Bishop accepted the resignation but only after a period of bureaucratic nonsense could it take effect. The Bishop told Francis's nephew, Dennis:

> He says he has no money: but so long as he is Rector he is responsible for duties - the clergy are helping out but that cannot go on indefinitely........Have you any idea what is happening? If he is really 'on the rocks' I can help to a very small extent from a fund at my disposal. The position at Manea is very sad: the house in a terrible state of dirt, and I am afraid there are many debts.

The position was indeed difficult. Francis had allowed people to "squat" in the house and they were refusing to move out. Francis was moving from pillar to post and ended up in what would formerly have been dubbed the workhouse. Two particular consequences flowed. At Dennis's suggestion, the Bishop got in touch with Francis's son, Ken, which prompted a resumption of contact between them. Negotiations were afoot for Francis to go into a home in Sussex which required a signed guarantee that, if they could no longer accommodate him, the signatory would do so. Ken's unwillingness to sign such an undertaking did not matter in the end because the home, having had Francis for a trial period, decided that he would be too disruptive and might foment rebellion among the other inmates. The second outcome of the Bishop's letter was that Dennis went over to Manea, accompanied by the author (then an undergraduate on vacation) to recover what little there was left of Francis's possessions. The Vicarage was empty of furniture but cluttered with empty half-bottles of whisky. The squatters were no longer in evidence and we brought away a motley collection of clothing and papers, which included a number of photographs and letters - much of the source material for this account.

At about this time, taking stock of his finances and reckoning that his pension of £74 per annum and superannuation of £250 p.a. gave him an annual income of £324, Francis proposed himself as a paying guest at The Old Rectory at £3 per week, a proposition which he was soon having to acknowledge was "impossible in the circumstances". Just how impossible was revealed when he did come to stay for a week in the following December and upset his hostess by going to bed with his boots on. After this Francis decided to take Dennis's advice and he went to a British Legion ex-officers' home at Englefield Green, Surrey. He and Willie decided to transfer the advowson of Hemingford Abbots to Dennis in January 1954 and this was eventually done.

On September 21, 1957 Francis died, the last of a line of extraordinary brothers, and his remains were interred at Hemingford Abbots next to those of his father and mother. Their sons, Ken and Myles, were brought up in Hemingford Abbots and had many friends there, with some of whom Ken remembered stealing apples. Ken was himself remembered for having climbed half way up the Wellingtonia on the Rectory lawn in order to fix an aerial for the family's crystal radio set. Myles gave a sprightly address to a large gathering of the family at his own 90th birthday party in 2005.

But it was Dennis, the eldest of Henry and Mary's sons, who was eventually to cement the family's links with Hemingford Abbots by choosing the name for his title.

Herbert family in front of the family tree at Hemingford. L to R: Back: Richard, Willie, George. Seated: Dennis, Rev. Henry, Mary, Teddie. Front: Francis

Dennis & Teddie

Back: Dennis & Teddie. Middle: Willie, Dick, George. Front: Francis

Edward Grevile Herbert (1870-1951)

Captain L.W. Herbert (1873-1955)

George Herbert (1876-1947)

Francis Falkner Herbert (1879-1957)

George Herbert's ship. Painted by him on a pillowcase.

George's pledge

Bimbashi Herbert

------------Chapter 13 ------------

FROM WATFORD TO WESTMINSTER

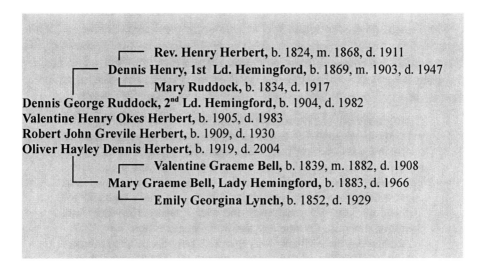

Rev. Henry Herbert, b. 1824, m. 1868, d. 1911
Dennis Henry, 1st Ld. Hemingford, b. 1869, m. 1903, d. 1947
Mary Ruddock, b. 1834, d. 1917
Dennis George Ruddock, 2nd Ld. Hemingford, b. 1904, d. 1982
Valentine Henry Okes Herbert, b. 1905, d. 1983
Robert John Grevile Herbert, b. 1909, d. 1930
Oliver Hayley Dennis Herbert, b. 1919, d. 2004
Valentine Graeme Bell, b. 1839, m. 1882, d. 1908
Mary Graeme Bell, Lady Hemingford, b. 1883, d. 1966
Emily Georgina Lynch, b. 1852, d. 1929

I would sooner be rude than dishonest – *Dennis Herbert, M.P.*

On Monday, September 21, 1931, Dennis Henry Herbert was in charge of a debate in the House of Commons which would give effect to the National Government's decision to go off the Gold Standard. He had been elected a few days earlier to the post of Chairman of Ways and Means, so he took the chair when the House was discussing financial matters and when it was in committee. With the world price at double the rate at which the British Government was legally compelled to sell gold Ramsey Macdonald and his Chancellor of the Exchequer, Philip Snowden, had decided that they must act quickly or the nation's reserves would disappear.

The timing was tight. The Government announced its decision on the Sunday and the Bill was to be passed through all its stages by both houses on the Monday. Confident of support, or careless (it was not clear which) the Government had failed to suspend the parliamentary rule which says that business must be completed by 11.00 pm. But delays occurred, a member called Eyres-Monsell was raising objections and soon after 10.00 pm Dennis was handed by a government Whip a piece of paper from the Treasury with the following message, written in pencil:

> We learn with alarm that there is a possibility of the House not finishing this Bill to-night. If the Bill does not become law before business hours to-morrow, the Bank of England will lose the whole of its gold before 10.30 am.

The message was not addressed to anyone in particular, but when Dennis suggested it should be given to the Prime Minister or the Chancellor, the Whip replied that they could not be contacted and the Chief Whip had decided it should be given to him. He had to do some quick, but careful thinking. Dennis recorded later in his memoirs, *Back-Bencher and Chairman*:

> Clearly the third reading could probably not be obtained before 11.00 pm without my goodwill. But my course was clear. It was my duty to facilitate the business of the House, and while seeing that all parties got a proper hearing, to prevent unreasonable obstruction and delay. The whole House, with the possible exception of not more than about a dozen members, wanted the Bill to pass, those who did not had said all they had to say over and over again, and my duty was therefore obvious. Closure on any further discussion was clearly justifiable: but the difficulty was that with only about forty minutes left, three divisions would occupy nearly all the time and then a fourth could not be finished by 11.00 pm

Three divisions would be required before the Bill could be reported to the House for its third and final reading, so the Bill's passage could be prevented merely by forcing some more divisions. Dennis decided to follow the Nelsonian principle of putting the telescope to his blind eye. When, at 10.45 pm, a member attempted to raise a point of order, Dennis said he could not hear him but gathered the member wanted to complain about something he had done, but he was not conscious of having done anything wrong. His narrative continues:

> At 6 minutes to 11, Clause I having been passed, I hurriedly called Clause II. Eyres-Monsell, in his excitement, attempted to move the Closure: if I had accepted such a motion and put it to the Committee another division was practically certain, and even without a division the clock would probably have beaten me if I had accepted a Closure motion. I ignored his attempt and "did not see" any member rise to speak, put the question that Clause II stand part of the Bill, declared it carried, then put the formal questions of the Title and of the Report to the Committee and left the Committee Chair at 3 minutes before

11.00 pm. The Bill being reported "without amendment", the third reading was at once put from the Chair of the House and carried without a division less than two minutes before the hour. So ended an exciting and, for me, anxious forty minutes.

The House of Lords had been kept in session and duly approved the Bill and the remaining technicalities went without a hitch, the Treasury rapidly making use of its newly-granted power to prohibit the export of gold. Thus, as Dennis wrote, the Bank's gold was saved for the nation. The incident, and the way he described it in his memoirs, typify Dennis's political career. He may have been, as one commentator put it, "a rather lifeless orator" but he had by general consent a cool head and a profound understanding of the rules of the House of Commons. He could be robust on the hustings, as we shall see, but he was certainly no sensationalist and he sometimes seemed to see life only through the prism of the House of Commons, which he so much loved. It was characteristic that he should head his account of saving the nation's gold, "Failure to suspend 11.00 pm Rule" and then, slightly more daringly: "A Race with the Clock". Yet paradoxically his political career was founded on a violent incident in the days before the General Election of 1910 when, as a new member of the Watford Conservative Club, he was physically assaulted by Liberal stewards at a rowdy political meeting. He and friends who came to his aid fought their way out of the hall intending to hold a protest meeting outside, but the police would not allow it. He stated, years later, that he had been asked by the Chairman of the meeting to go to the back of the hall and try to restore some semblance of order when he was set upon by the stewards, but the general interpretation was that he had been ejected. In any case the incident made him a local hero within the West Herts. Divisional Conservative Association and he soon became recognised as one of their leaders.

A couple of electoral victories for the County Council, two General Elections in which he worked hard for the Conservative cause, the suspension of political activity during the First World War, some good fortune and an increase in the number of parliamentary seats in Hertfordshire led to his adoption on February 16, 1918, as the prospective candidate for the Watford Division. At the General election of December, 1918, he supported the Coalition Government of Lloyd George and Bonar Law and won his seat by some 3,000 votes more than his Labour and Liberal opponents combined. This was an auspicious result, but his early days in the House of Commons were not. The air circulation system in the chamber gave him such bad headaches that he wondered if he would have to give up and retire, and he was so nervous when he made his maiden speech in April, 1919, that he twisted his notes into an unreadable mass, leaving most of what he had intended to say unspoken. His own verdict on the speech was "I was not pleased with it, and do not think I had any reason to be."

Dennis's interest in politics had been nurtured by listening to conversations between his father and his great-uncle, Dr. Richard Okes, who used to visit Hemingford Abbots from King's College, Cambridge, in his yellow coach. Both these pillars of the community were staunch Conservatives, but the Liberals were strong in Cromwell country and even one of the Okes uncles had shown Liberal tendencies, so Dennis, as he put it, recognised that Liberals could be "quite decent fellows". At King's School, Ely, where he went in 1883, and at Wadham College, Oxford, he at once joined the debating societies. He also joined the Oxford Union so had had plenty of practice in public speaking, but never overcame the shyness and nerves which made making a speech to any audience a hard task. At Oxford he had contemplated the Church, but in Eights Week at the end of May, 1890, he fell in love. The object of his passion was a Miss Adeline Jackson, the very pretty 24-year-old daughter of friends of his parents, but we know frustratingly little about the course of events because, though he kept a meticulous diary, Dennis subsequently filleted it, removing with scissors all the passages referring to A, as he called her. It appears, however, that he made some sort of declaration of love to her on May 29 and that her reply, though not completely dismissive, was less forthcoming than he would have wished. Nevertheless he was soon deciding that he must earn a living as soon as possible and consulting his tutor about trying to complete his studies in one year instead of two. (The tutor was properly dismissive and Dennis wrote resignedly "I expect I had better take the two years"). By the end of June, despite sending her John Ruskin's *Ethics in the Dust* as a birthday present, Dennis seems to have had a disappointing letter from his love. "Spent most of the day alone," he writes, "naturally feeling very down," and later "If only I could get at once into something where I might soon earn a living, I would give up Varsity at once." He went to Lords Cricket Ground in the hope of seeing A. and after much searching, caught a glimpse of her in the members' pavilion. At about this time he wrote in his diary: "I often feel inclined to be discontented with my lot and wonder why I have not the money that other people have, but we don't know what is good for us, and I have very, very much to be thankful for.

Courtship was no easy matter at the end of the nineteenth century and, though letters passed, Dennis was unable to see A. again for months. Then in the spring of 1891 his mother announced her intention of writing to invite the

Jacksons to stay. This threw Dennis into a fever of anticipation and he got up early every morning to check for an answering letter. He was at pains not to give too much away to his parents, but they must have known what was going on. When the Jacksons finally arrived Mary put him next to A. at dinner. Then began the difficult process of trying to get a few moments alone with A. They played tennis together and against each other at various parties, she rejected his offer of flowers for her corsage, he was prostrated by lack of sleep and nervous indigestion and fainted at the top of the stairs, then she kept to her bed with neuralgia and on a river trip his brother Teddie was boisterous and flirtatious with A. causing Dennis to complain to his father. Henry promised to do what he could and things did improve – but still Dennis had not managed a word with A. alone. On the third day he took a turn round the garden with his father:

> I talked to him about my plans after my degree: he quite fell in with my wish not to take orders, which I told him was largely because I did not feel I was prepared to live all my life alone and poor as might be required of me if I did: he found lots of difficulties and objections to my becoming a lawyer though not opposed to that as a profession at all, but we agreed that at present, whatever is to happen after, I cannot do better than give all my energies to doing well in the schools: as an alternative to the law, he could not suggest anything except tutorships etc. by which, he said, I might establish a connection and get a private secretaryship, but that would not do for me; it would be very uncertain and risky and there would be no scope for one much....We neither of us mentioned anything of marriage or anything of A; yet I cannot help thinking that M.H. and H.H. (certainly M.H.) must have some idea that there is something between us. They never put anything in my way at all, so I hope they would not object. I do not think they will at all interfere with anything I may wish to do as regards my profession. H.H. told me what I already knew, that he is spending capital on our education and that we must not expect anything to be left beyond his lifetime.

The bad news was that the Jacksons were intending to go to Cairo in the winter, then go round the Cape of Good Hope on the way home and then move to Switzerland. Already Dennis was wondering how he might get to Switzerland. He saw A. only once again as far as we know, paying a visit of a few hours later that month to the Jacksons' home in Surrey. As he had promised Henry, he returned to Oxford intent on getting a good degree. He was hoping for a First in history and was much devastated when he only obtained a Third. He found out afterwards that his written papers were on the borderline of a First, but for reasons which he did not explain, he made a mess of the *viva voce*. However, A., moving like some comet through his undergraduate years, had left him with a determination to follow a lucrative career and, with help from a Ruddock aunt, he was articled to a family solicitor in Gray's Inn. He implied in *Back-Bencher and Chairman*, that his ambition was sparked by a wish to make enough money by the time he was 40 to "retire into the House of Commons", but Miss Jackson had clearly turned his mind away from Holy Orders or private secretaryship and towards the the law. He made promising progress, being admitted a Solicitor in 1895, but he soon recognised that he was not going to fulfil his financial ambition and he was nearly 50 when he first entered the House of Commons. Moreover, by now he had a wife and three sons to support so he could not aspire to office. First love had faded in time and Dennis had married, on June 9, 1903, Mary Graeme Bell, the 20-year-old daughter of a Colonial civil servant, whose aunt Nora Lynch used to rent a house in Hemingford Abbots and invited the young lady to stay during the school holidays as her parents were in Jamaica. We cannot chart the course of his romance with May – no letters or records survive – but we know that Dennis proposed to her beneath the rose arbour in the back garden of The Rectory on July 22, 1902 and the match was welcomed on all sides. It was more than a decade since Adeline had broken his heart and the marriage came as no surprise in the village because May was a handsome, delightful and captivating girl. They set up home at No. 16, Scarsdale Villas, in Kensington, and Dennis George Ruddock was born on March 25, 1904, Valentine Henry Okes on June 4, 1905 and Robert John Grevile on January 6, 1909. During these years Dennis was making his way in the law firms Clarke, Rawlins & Co. and Beaumont & Sons. but living in London did not suit his health and in 1908 the family moved to Watford, then a small market town, where the air was clearer. Here, as we have seen, his political career began.

He made steady if unspectacular progress but it was during the election of 1923 that he hit the headlines. Once again it was because of the intervention of a woman – or rather a number of women linked together under the title The Six Point Group. As soon as the election was announced they published what one of them, Miss Vera Brittain, called an "inspired and disconcerting expedient" - a Black List of those who they felt had hampered the passage of legislation favourable to women and a White List of those who had been especially helpful in Parliament to the cause of women. Dennis's name figured prominently in the Black List and Miss Brittain and Lady Rhondda, descended on Watford in an attempt to damage his candidacy or even get him defeated. Their anger was chiefly aroused because of his attitude towards the

Matrimonial Causes Bill which was designed to remedy an inequity in the law on divorce and allow a wife to divorce her husband for a single act of adultery without having to prove cruelty and desertion as well. Dennis's view was that the Bill would make divorce (and particularly collusive divorce) much easier without in any way dealing with other serious defects in the laws on marriage. He knew that he would not get much support, but decided to oppose the Bill anyway.

On March 2, 1923, in a long speech in the Commons he described the present law as a fraud and a sham because if the parties to a marriage wanted to end it, they could do so by the wife writing to the husband asking him to come back, the husband refusing and sending her the address of some hotel where she could obtain evidence sufficient to obtain a divorce. If this fraud were to be ended it could only be done if a single act of adultery were not, by itself, grounds for divorce. It would be better to get equality between the sexes by saying that adultery could only be grounds for divorce if it were repeated or habitual. Then he went on to produce a more elaborate argument, saying:

> You may have identity of treatment between man and man, and you may have identity of treatment between woman and woman, but you can never make a man a woman, and you can never make a woman a man. You can never get over the actual physical difference which comes in in this question of divorce. [Interruption]. I am very sorry but if half a dozen hon. Members will make their remarks all at the same time, it is impossible for me to hear them. May I just put this question to Members of the House, who are themselves fathers of families? Is there any man in this House who is the father of a son and of a daughter who would regard the sin of adultery on the part of his son as being as serious as the sin of adultery on the part of his daughter?

There followed an exchange with a member who wanted to know whether that was what Dennis taught his children. He replied that it was unnecessary to discuss his particular teaching since he had only sons. Then Dennis returned to his main point again, saying that he would put it in a slightly different form:

> Is it not the case – regret it as much as you like – that throughout all ranks of society, from the highest to the lowest, the sin of adultery does not ruin the reputation of a man as it does that of a woman? (Hon. Members: "It should do!"). Will hon. Members be good enough to follow what I am saying and not what I am not saying? ....If the hon. Member who introduced this Bill and those who support him, would – I do not know whether it is possible –

amend or alter the Bill, or if they had introduced a Bill for the purpose which the hon. Member expressed to be his purpose, to bring about equality of the sexes, and if they would bring forward a proposal that adultery, apart from any other offence, should not be a ground for divorce except it be habitual or repeated, I would support them. I do suggest that, if you make divorce so easy, as you will do by this particular proposal, you will be putting obstacles in the way of other divorce reforms.

The House, of course, was overwhelmingly male – there were only two women members and neither took part in the debate – but Dennis's words brought him, as he put it, "a peck o' trouble". He claimed that this was as agreeable as it was unexpected, but should a politician as seasoned and experienced as Dennis have been surprised that his references to the consequences of adultery would be seized upon? Times were different then, but the word "serious" in his first passage was too ambiguous and enabled the Six Point Group to represent him as a misogynist. We have grown used to wilful oversimplification and the use of quotations out of context – and Dennis may well have had some cause for complaint on that score – but he was probably looking at it from a perspective too limited to the House of Commons when he argued that no one in the debate had attempted to deny the truth of what he said. It would have been unlike him deliberately to trail his coat with a provocative statement and we do not know whether the fatal sentence was pre-prepared or whether Dennis was ruffled by the interruptions he was getting from his opponents. At any rate the Six Point Group went to town, with the outspoken support of the magazine *Time and Tide*, accusing him of arguing that adultery by a man was of little or no moment.

The issue came to a head when the Six Point Group arranged a special meeting to denounce Dennis for professing a double standard of morality and hoping to get him defeated at the polls. Vera Brittain, in her book *Testament of Youth* claimed that she was extremely nervous about her speech, but the *West Herts Post* reporter was impressed:

> In appearance she looked incapable of the part of a militant agitator. Blessed with youth, evenly cut features, an abundance of black hair parted in the middle and trickily arranged over the ears, and neatly gowned in a black dress of simple design and soft material, she looked much too dainty for the hurly burly of acute controversy. But once she got down to her subject she proved she could hit and hit again, and keep on hitting without the least suggestion of nervous exhaustion, and never displayed the least tendency to be thrown off her line of attack by interjections, even from the "villain-in-chief" if

Mr. Herbert will permit that nomenclature to be used for the sake of convenience. Ruthlessly she set herself to examine from her point of view Mr Herbert's record as revealed by Hansard, the official report of Parliamentary proceedings.

Dennis, who had decided to come into the lioness's den, heckled Miss Brittain on several points of accuracy about his role in the passage of the Criminal Law Amendments Bill, which raised the age of consent from 13 to 16 and abolished in some cases the defence that a man had reasonable cause to believe that a girl was over 16. Several times he called on Miss Brittain to withdraw and apologise for saying that he had opposed the Bill, when he had expressly stated that he supported it, and when she refused there was what the reporter described as "a certain amount of commotion and howling at the back of the hall". Miss Brittain refused to withdraw, after which Dennis, at a follow-up meeting described her as sitting on the platform "like a sulky child". When he was told that he had been rude to his opponents, he replied: "I would sooner be rude than dishonest". He also told the meeting that Lady Astor, who was a supporter of the Six Point Group, had told him "that she would not be seen dead in a ditch with him if she could help it". For his part he was delighted not to be seen with her in the *Time and Tide* White List.

Dennis's objection to the Six Point Group had been as much due to their interference, as he saw it, between his constituents and himself and his efforts to correct what he saw as the misrepresentation of his views on women were directed at those Conservatives in Watford, of whom there were quite a few, who had joined in the protests against him. He issued a memorandum to them and addressed large meetings in several different towns in the constituency. He enjoyed the fact that many people took to referring to the Six Point Group as "Wild Women", amusing themselves by obliterating an "o" on their posters so that they became "The Six Pint Group". His tactics were largely successful, as exemplified by an adversary emerging from one of the stormy meetings, who remarked: "I don't like his opinions, because I don't like the Tory policy, but he's a jolly decent chap, and a thorough sportsman." The end result was that, in an election when results went heavily against the Conservatives, Dennis's poll was some 470 down and he was returned again with a substantial majority of 3,001. He was much gratified when the constituency party, recognising the financial strain on the Member of having to fight three elections in 18 months, collected and handed over to him, the £750 it had cost him.

In 1926 Dennis's strong belief in religious toleration and his anger at an inflammatory speech made by an extreme Glasgow Orangeman led to him taking on the task of piloting through the Commons a Roman Catholic Relief Bill, whose purpose was to sweep away a whole range of anti-Roman Catholic provisions. For example Roman Catholic priests were, in theory at least, prohibited from appearing in public in ecclesiastic garb or officiating in a building which had a steeple or a bell, and Roman Catholic charities were subject to income tax. His understanding of the arcana of parliamentary procedure allowed him to outwit the Government and get the Bill a second reading and then to outmanoeuvre a powerful group of extreme Protestants and anti-papists. In the process he was subjected to a death threat and much abuse, but he actually confounded the Clerk of the House, who was also Editor of *Erskine May,* the parliamentary bible of procedure. He claimed priority for an amendment of his which was designed to take the wind out of the opponents' sails. The Clerk said only the Government had that right, but Dennis proved him wrong and the Bill became law, to the delight of Roman Catholics all over the world. Dennis was understandably pleased with himself and was particularly delighted when Pope Pius XI honoured him, and two Roman Catholic associates who had worked with him, by presenting them with the Papal Gold Medal. So far as is known Dennis was only the second non-Roman Catholic to be so honoured, the first being Lloyd George, who had received the medal at the Peace Conference after World War I. The following spring, when the Pope heard that Dennis was in Rome with May on a business trip, he invited them to a private audience, at which Dennis spoke English and the Pontiff spoke French, each being able to understand the other with little need for an interpreter. Afterwards Dennis realised that the Pope had made them do all the talking by plying him with questions about unemployment in Britain and other current issues and May with enquiries about the family.

The kind of persistent use of parliamentary tactics and understanding of parliamentary procedures which had stood him in good stead on the Roman Catholic Bill, was also evident when Dennis succeeded, to local delight, in extracting Watford from the creation of a London and Home Counties Electricity Area, and in preventing the Church Assembly from overstepping the mark in the kind of legislation it brought forward for parliamentary approval. The details of how he did it are laid out in *Back-Bencher and Chairman,* and are too arcane to follow here but he was becoming a formidable parliamentarian and was a stickler for parliamentary rights. It can have been no surprise when in 1928 the Speaker retired, Dennis was elected as Deputy Chairman of Ways and Means or, in layman's language, deputy to the Deputy Speaker. For a few days he even thought that he might get the top job since the existing Deputy Speaker was known not to want it and his number two was not a lawyer and was not particularly well-known in the House, and it was thought, erroneously as it turned out, that the Labour Party, which had been disenchanted with the Chair, would not support either man. Dennis decided he should write to his eldest son, Dennis George Ruddock Herbert, who was a teacher at Achimota College in what was then the Gold Coast:

Very Private   Clarendon Lodge
                                                Clarendon Road
4th June 1928   Watford

My dear Dennis,
You are so far away & letters take so long, that I am going to write you a letter which quite possibly might well be torn up un-read by the time it reaches you: but if that be the case you will forgive me for having written what is to no purpose.

Today fortnight the Speaker retires, & on Wed. 20th a new Speaker will be elected: unlikely as it may be, there is at least a possibility that I may be elected in his place: whether that will be so or not, will probably be settled beyond much doubt by the end of next week, & somewhere about the time this reaches you, you should know certainly by cable (or from non-receipt of a cable!) whether I have been elected Speaker or not.

Now I have a special reason for writing this to you: because should I be elected, I shall probably want to submit a proposal to you, & I should like to give you a fair explanation of it.

Briefly & plainly, the question is whether if such a thing should happen, you would care to give up your present job & become Speaker's Secretary. Quite frankly, I believe you would say No, at once: and I shall not be the least troubled by your doing so. You are I believe well satisfied with the line you have taken in life – and so am I. But I should deeply regret it, if I assumed you would refuse & therefore did not give you the opportunity, & then found afterwards that you would have wished for it........

The letter is too long to quote in full because Dennis was so keen to emphasise that he was not pressing his son to abandon his career in Africa that he repeated himself several times, but he did reveal that the salary for the job would be £700, which was nearly double what "Young Dennis" (as he was known) was earning in the Gold Coast, and that it would involve living in Speaker's House, which would be inexpensive. A week later on June 10 his hopes were still alive, though fading and, writing to thank his son for his part in a silver-wedding present which the boys had jointly subscribed for, he wrote:

> Nothing is I believe definitely settled yet: but when the House adjourned on Friday evening I had come to the conclusion that probably it was practically a certainty for Fitzroy. I told your mother so: I know she had been naturally feeling very excited about it though I had tried to make her think that I had nothing but a very off chance: however she has taken it very well, & she had an enjoyable day yesterday to take her mind off it!

In the event Captain Fitzroy, despite his lack of legal background, was appointed Speaker and Dennis's dream faded. Moreover, James Hope continued as Deputy Speaker so Dennis had to be content with becoming Hope's deputy. This arrangement lasted for only about a year until a Labour Government came in and elected their own officers, who, however, insisted on resigning in 1931 and Dennis was then chosen as Deputy Speaker and Chairman of Ways and Means. He continued in this role for the next 12 years, being twice re-elected after General Elections, which meant that for the rest of his time in the House he remained in political purdah, unable to indulge in partisan party argument. In the first of these elections he even decided to adopt a self-imposed policy of not campaigning on controversial issues. Dennis never lost an election after he left Oxford and by now he had turned Watford into a safe seat.

He was still managing to combine his private legal work with his increasingly time-consuming duties in the House, but whereas he had managed in the early days to take May on a parliamentary visit to the United States and Canada in 1925 and a business trip to India at the end of 1928, he now had little time for travel. As he advanced up the Chairmanship ladder in parliament his constant presence was required when the House was in session and he had to hurry back from Calcutta, leaving May to spend a few weeks longer on her own. His travelling companions included the Aga Khan and the Maharaja Gaikwar of Baroda, whom he knew from a Watford connection. Dennis's father, that "dashing cricketer", would have been fascinated to know that he became friendly with two great Test players, Ranjitsinhji, the Jam Sahib of Nawanagar and F.S.Jackson, who was Governor of Bengal. Dennis had become a member of the Council of the Law Society in 1923, found time to publish a substantial work, *The Law as to Solicitors*, in 1932 and was also Chairman of Equity & Law Life Assurance Co. for several years. His speech at the latter's Annual General Meeting in 1936 was widely praised for both its delivery and its content. One commentator in the insurance journal *The Policy-Holder* wrote:

> It was sheer enjoyment, not alone for the thoughtful selectiveness in which the prosperity of the society was described but also for the clear diction and gently-persuasive elocution Sir Dennis habitually uses. Not a word was slurred, not a sentence hurried. I should guess that few men in the kingdom quite attain the Equity & Law chairman's pleasant mastery of the English tongue.

Such euphoria may have been inspired partly by a 34% increase in the company's gross business, but it showed that Dennis could at least captivate some kinds of audience. The *Guardian*, meanwhile praised as "able and interesting" his references to how assurance could be used to assist industry in extending credit. All this industry and service was recognised in June, 1933 when Dennis was sworn of the Privy Council of Great Britain - the prayer book on which he took the oath is among the family archives – and when, in 1943 a fund was set up to have his portrait painted, he chose to be shown wearing the Privy Councillor's uniform. The portrait, by George Harcourt, hangs in Watford Town Hall and is a very good likeness. A replica, also painted by Harcourt, hangs in The Old Rectory, where Dennis was born on February 25, 1869, and a copy was presented by the family to the Law Society, of which he was President in 1941-42.

At the end of December, 1938. Young Dennis received another "Very Secret" letter from his father. It was on the same topic as before because the possibility had arisen that Mr. Speaker Fitzroy was intending to retire. Dennis saw that this could put him in a difficult position. There were various possibilities – the House might think him too old to become Speaker or they might want him to do the job for one Parliament. If they did he thought he should accept as it would mean that he had to give up all outside duties and would therefore be less pressurised. However, if the Speaker did go and Dennis did not succeed him, it would be difficult for him to remain for long in the House of Commons; he would not much want to remain Chairman of Ways and Means under a new man and it would be difficult just to return to the back benches.

> They would, no doubt under such circumstances offer me a peerage, and if I were well off financially I should like to take it, as I would prefer being in the House of Lords to being out of Parliament entirely. It would be all right for me, but they will not adopt a system of life-peerages, and I feel that for you to be a penniless peer would be very burdensome.

> Of course it may be that none of these things will happen, but I should not like such a position to arise while you are abroad & without your ever having contemplated it.

This was a generous approach because Dennis had become so absolutely steeped in the traditions of the House that he was beginning to dread the thought of having to leave it. Events were, of course, to be overtaken by more fundamental problems. As late as April, 1939, Dennis was fairly sanguine about the possibility of war being averted, though he recognised the unpredictability of Hitler:

> One can never feel in the least certain what Germany will or will not do, & it all depends on whether Germany will start a war: we certainly shall not, nor can I conceive any other country in Europe doing so: therefore we can do nothing but await events & meanwhile press on with our preparations to meet any emergency.

He was in the House during the debates on Munich when Neville Chamberlain received support for his policy which critics described as sacrificing Czechoslovakia. At the end of the debate Chamberlain received a great ovation and many members went up to shake his hand. Dennis who was in his usual seat at the far end of the front bench near the Speaker's chair, turned to a colleague and said "Why can't they let the poor fellow alone, instead of putting him through all this handshaking." Then, to his surprise, Chamberlain, on his way out, stopped in front of him and shook his hand, saying "Well, that is a good finish." It was not, of course, and less than a year later Dennis was playing his part in the passage of no fewer than 41 Emergency Acts of Parliament in six sessions, which put the country on a war footing. He was in his place to hear that the country was at war and on that very first day he was among the many who crowded down into the room on the lower floors of the Palace of Westminster which had been prepared as air-raid shelters. It was a false alarm, but when the Blitz came May and Dennis took to sleeping under the dining room table at Clarendon Lodge and life became very difficult. May had turned the house at the start of the war into a headquarters for the Women's Voluntary Service and vast quantities of bandages, socks and other necessities passed through..

When the House of Commons was destroyed by a German bomb in 1941, Dennis was devastated and some said that he never quite got over it. He preserved a set of photographs showing the destruction wrought by the bomb and incendiaries and a much burnt and scarred inkstand, retrieved from the wreckage, with which he was later presented as a memento, now sits in the hall of his birthplace. It was, however, an even greater blow when, in October,

1942, he received the following letter:

> 10 Downing Street,
> Whitehall
> October 9th, 1942.

My Dear Dennis Herbert,

I have been wondering whether you would not be inclined to seek relief from your present duties as Chairman of Ways and Means when the new Session begins.

If this is agreeable to you, I should be very happy to submit your name to the King for a barony. This would enable you to carry on in an easier sphere the political mission which has occupied so much of your life. I shall be glad to hear from you.

Yours sincerely,

Winston Churchill

The letter reached him when he was ill at home and was accompanied by one from the Chief Whip, James Stuart, explaining that the move was in deference to Labour party pressure for representation in the Speaker's office now that they were part of the wartime coalition. He added: "You have been at this for some years and the P.M. felt that you might welcome a change which would enable you to retain your connection with Parliamentary affairs in the rarer atmosphere of 'another place'." It was not the kind of invitation to be resisted, however much Dennis might like to have done so. His answer to Mr. Churchill was delayed by his illness, but on November 11, 1942, he replied loyally that he would willingly comply with Churchill's suggestions and thanked him for the kind way in which he had made them. But the truth was he could hardly imagine what life would be like outside the House of Commons and he added: "While I should not have wished to retire from my post on my own initiative, my main desire, subject to my duty to the House, is to act in the interests of the country by helping you & your colleagues in the Cabinet in the best way I can."

He pleaded for a little time before an announcement was made and this was agreed with the Chief Whip, who replied that neither he nor the Prime Minister wanted to make the "unavoidably difficult negotiations arising from this contemplated change any more awkward than such affairs are, unfortunately, always bound to be." Dennis felt strongly that, as the Chairman of Ways and Means is elected by the House of Commons and not appointed by the Prime Minister or the Monarch, he should tell the House of his intention to resign <u>before</u> he accepted a peerage, which would then, of course, require his resignation. This meant that the change could not be made until the House met again in the New Year. There were also complications in the Watford constituency, where there was no obvious successor, and there were financial concerns. Dennis had resigned the chairmanship of Equity & Law in 1940 when the war had severely affected the company and new leadership was necessary. This had reduced his income, which was further depleted by the fall in the value of his shares. The loss of his parliamentary salary would make another dent in his finances. There was also the fact that Young Dennis was now in Uganda and, in wartime, even more inaccessible than he had been before, and Dennis wanted him to have a say on the choice of title. Should he become Lord Watford, Lord Hemingford, Lord Herbert of Watford, Lord Herbert of Hemingford or, his own initial favourite, Lord Dennis-Herbert? Letters sent by post, which were the only way of ensuring privacy, took about six weeks to reach Uganda, assuming that the ship in which they travelled was not sunk. Dennis took the precaution of taking carbon copies of his letters and sending the copies under separate cover a week or so later. Using this means of communication, though, meant that a full reply on confidential issues could not be expected within three months. Swifter communication was possible by Airgraph, which involved a miniaturised photograph being taken of a letter, but it was, of course, not secure. In one of his letters, dated November 1, 1942, Dennis summed up his mixed feelings:

> In the first place I should not have wished to retire on my own initiative just at present, because I have been glad to feel that I was pulling my weight in a post of national importance, & that in spite of my age & infirmities I was doing work of importance efficiently. Secondly I should have been glad to have continued to get my salary for at least another year or so, as I have very little other income to fall back upon. On the other hand I am bound to remember my age, & the possibility that at any time my health might so break down as to make my retirement necessary: it is better for an old man to retire while still capable, than to hang on till incapacity forces him to go.

> Had times been normal, & had I been better off than I now am as a result mainly of the war, I should have been only too glad to have been relieved of the rather exacting work of the Chair & of the Constituency, & to have been able to continue my interest in politics from the H of L. I must try still to look at the present position from that point of view, & possibly it may turn out in the end to be the best thing for me. As far as my purely selfish wishes are concerned the <u>only</u> objection on my part to going to the other House is that of Finance: but by moving into a small & cheaper house or flat & cutting down all unnecessary expense your Mother & I should be

132

able to scrape along, & there is the possibility of my being able to find some other way of earning something, though my age must make this rather difficult for me.

Even if communications had been faster, Young Dennis would have been badly-placed to play any helpful role for he was in the throes of the greatest crisis of his teaching career, as we shall see. Nevertheless, a series of short telegrams passed between them on the subject of what title Dennis Henry should adopt, the most memorable of which simply said "Considering Ousebank". To this Young Dennis replied instantly "Not Ousebank" But the idea of Hemingford seemed entirely appropriate. It was where he had been born, grown up and married and he retained a consequent affection for the village. And so it was decided; it certainly had a better ring than Ousebank.

It soon became obvious that the Prime Minister and the Chief Whip had been right. On December 19, 1942, Dennis was writing:

> Sorry as I am to have to confess it, I feel sure that it will be a good thing for me to be free from the work of the Chairmanship & of the House. I have got very much older in the three years since you left England: since my recent illness I still find that I easily get very tired: it is true (Dr.) Gough tells me I am now in really better health than I was before, but I shall have to be very careful during the winter: my chest & to some extent my heart are definitely weak spots: it therefore comes down to the only thing against my retirement being the question of money, and so (as we ought to be able to exist without my Parliamentary salary) there would seem to be a big balance of argument in favour of retirement from the personal point of view......So all things considered, I have become fairly reconciled to a course on which I <u>really</u> have little or no choice.

Watched by May and their daughter-in-law, Winifred, from the gallery Dennis announced his resignation to the House on Tuesday, January 19, 1943. It was, he later wrote, a sad and mournful occasion for him and he was in tears. He was at pains to dispel rumours that the resignation was on health grounds. On the contrary, his doctors had told him there was no reason why he could not continue. He went on to give as his reason that there were bound to be great changes in the years ahead and he believed someone younger should work his way into the job before the time for change came. He added that the Prime Minister permitted him to say that he agreed. Such are the glosses at which politicians are adept!

Churchill was in North Africa attending the Casablanca conference with

Roosevelt, so Mr. Clement Atlee, as Deputy Prime Minister, spoke of Dennis's long and devoted service as Chairman and Deputy Speaker and his other consequent responsibilities. He added:

> In all these activities his wise knowledge of procedure, his fair-mindedness and his accessibility have won him the esteem and, I think, the affection of this House. In this House the occupant of the Chair must have something more than knowledge of procedure. He must have a knowledge of human nature and human understanding, not only of formalities, but of the atmosphere of this House. Many members in the course of Debate have from time to time been pulled up, as I have, by our Chairman of Ways and Means, but despite his difficult duties the right hon. Gentleman has always managed to retain the friendship of Members in all parts of the House.

This was handsome but it was perhaps the words of the Liberal spokesman, Sir Percy Harris, - "a great House of Commons man" "a great master of procedure" and "a fine guardian of the best traditions of the House of Commons," which would have most pleased Dennis. A few days later he watched the election of his successor, Colonel Clifton-Brown, who within a short space of time found himself Speaker because of the death of Captain Fitzroy.

When he took his seat in the Lords soon afterwards it was as Lord Hemingford, of Watford, in the County of Hertfordshire, and some weeks later he was honoured with the Freedom of the Borough of Watford at a ceremony in the Town Hall, when May's contribution was also mentioned. The official Order of Proceedings noted that Dennis was a Justice of the Peace and a Deputy Lieutenant, that he had been instrumental in obtaining a Charter for Watford in 1920 and that he was A Governor of Watford Grammar School and Church Warden of St. John's Church. It added:

> Throughout the whole of the time they have lived in Watford Lord and Lady Hemingford have endeared themselves to the Townspeople and have interested themselves wholeheartedly in every movement appertaining to the welfare of the Borough.

He never really took to the Lords, but the great thing was that his peerage enabled him to continue monitoring his beloved Commons until the end of the war and to keep in touch with old contacts. Like others before and after, he seems to have found retirement busy, referring frequently to lack of time. There was time, though, to devote to his financial affairs and those of his two elder sons, for whom he held power of attorney, and, though finding a smaller house proved impossible, he gradually became optimistic that he could survive without so depleting his finances that he would be unable to leave them anything. His mind turned particularly to writing, perhaps a series of newspaper articles, as a way of earning some money and he came to the conclusion that the Abdication crisis would certainly figure in anything he might write. But he also thought that it would require much care and discretion and so he had better get it done carefully at once. Having written an account of it, he sent it privately to Stanley Baldwin, who had been the central figure in the drama, to ask if it contained anything better not published. Baldwin proposed the omission of one short passage and one other sentence, but described it otherwise as "a model of discretion & good taste". A newspaper friend put him in touch with a literary agent who read the piece, liked it and said he thought Dennis should write a book, but that it would not be published until after the war when perhaps paper restrictions might be less onerous. Dennis became quite enthusiastic, feeling that he had been given enough hope to put his heart into it and that he might be able to do it well. He was more or less confined to the house in the subsequent winter months and made good progress with the book. On Sunday, September 3, Dennis sat down to write the chapter which dealt with the outbreak of war exactly five years before. As he did so, there came the familiar roar of bombers bound for Europe. He counted 72 and more would follow – more aircraft, he calculated than the total number Britain possessed a year before the war began.

A series of periodical letters to his son Val, who was Officer Commanding the 23rd Parachute L.A.A., Anti-Tank Regiment in India and Ceylon, were designed to be read by the regiment and to give an idea of what people were thinking at home in the later stages of the war. The picture he painted was inevitably coloured by the need not to undermine military confidence, nor upset the censor, but it was interesting for the recurrent themes which he evidently thought important. Things were happier and more comfortable than in any other country in Europe, but there were many reasons to indulge in the traditional habit of grumbling. There was an acute shortage of people to do anything – he and May were having to shift for themselves with no domestic help - and cars could not be used except for essential journeys. Morale was good, but he was concerned about the number of unofficial strikes in the coal mines, ship yards, engineering works and other important industries. The Trades Unions seemed unable to prevent them and he returned to the subject several times, though stressing that the problem was relatively minor. Other recurrent themes were the great amount of work being done by the government on post-war reconstruction - education, pre-fabricated housing, plans for demobilisation - the wonderful successes of the Russians in the east, the importance of realising that it would take Britain a long time to recover after the cessation of hostilities and much suffering would be involved, and the likely need to provide troops for quite a long time to occupy the conquered countries to ensure that Nazism did not recur. All this was prescient, but Dennis was no great prophet. He had expected war to be averted almost until it broke out and now he thought Churchill would sail back into office in a post-war election.

With D-day approaching, people were bracing themselves for further privation. Dennis wrote "We at home are all just waiting, waiting, waiting. We are rather like a man about to undergo a painful and serious operation." At about this time the German flying-bombs, or "Doodle-Bugs", started coming over. Dennis was at first dismissive, but they gradually began to be a real nuisance, causing very frequent warnings, day and night. He clung to the thought that they must be expensive for the enemy because so many were brought down before they could do any damage, but "the machine is a beastly unpleasant and dangerous thing". One came down within two miles of Clarendon Lodge in July, 1944, destroying a dozen houses and killing a substantial number of people, mostly the elderly and young children. Dennis was on the spot a few hours later and was impressed by the speed and efficiency of the Civil Defence:

> What struck me was the cheerfulness of all the people who, while unharmed themselves, were left homeless, with their houses badly damaged and most of their household effects destroyed.

There were other diversions in 1944. In March Dennis was sued for libel, an unlikely fate for one so cautious, and had to appear in the King's Bench Division to defend himself. The case involved a letter he had written to a woman who was a friend of a Mrs. Taylor, one of his clients. Mrs. Taylor had become engaged and Dennis wrote that he was confident she would change her mind if he could talk to her about it, but he thought her fiancé might arrange a quick marriage before he could do so. The judge ruled in Dennis's favour on the basis that, though his words were defamatory, he was acting as a lawyer and the letter was therefore covered by qualified privilege. In September, following a successful testimonial fund, the Harcourt portrait was presented to Watford Corporation to mark Dennis's 25 years as M.P. The fund was oversubscribed and an extra £112 was presented to the local hospital.

In the last of his letters to India, dated May 28, 1945, Dennis described the twin emotions of relief (which he thought predominated) and rejoicing at the victory in Europe, but saw further hardships ahead. "It has become very clear to all of us that it is going to be a long time yet before life can be reasonably comfortable. We are not, so far, in danger of any serious food shortage, but rations are having to be reduced already." If this sounded rather doleful, it was nevertheless true, but things were a little easier to put up with in summer and it was good to be rid of the miserable and troublesome blackout.

For some time now Dennis had been hanging on, hoping to live through successive winters, so that he could see his sons again. As early as 1943 he had been speculating about this, but now with the war in the far east coming to an end, each winter he could survive brought the prospect nearer. Val returned in 1946 to his great delight and Young Dennis was back early in the same year. The winter of 1946-1947 was the severest for 150 years with heavy snow and freezing temperatures disrupting fuel supplies and transport and almost bringing the country to its knees. Despite a nasty and very painful attack, which his doctor called a spasm, Dennis managed to survive it by dint of staying in bed and relying on May to look after him, but he found it awfully boring. He finished *Back-Bencher & Chairman* and he wrote *What Parliament is and does*, a succinct distillation of all he knew about the British constitution, which he had been persuaded to do by the headmaster of Oundle School. He also paid his eldest grandson's prep school fees, looked forward to the boy going to Oundle himself and worried about how he would live up to the financial demands of the peerage, which he would eventually inherit. The strain of nursing Dennis day and night told on May and at the beginning of summer it was becoming too much for her. The invaluable Willie, with his wife Amy, came to help, despite a very gammy leg, and then arrangements were made for professional nursing. May was able to take a holiday with her sister, Lu, at Tenterden. They were buoyed up by the news that Young Dennis had got a new job back in the Gold Coast and would therefore soon be back in England again. Writing in July in his usual neat hand, Dennis was optimistic about his prospects of lasting out.

His next letter, written in September, must have been a shock to Young Dennis. The handwriting is that of a dying man. On November 19, 1947, came what was to be his last letter:

> My dear Dennis,
>
> I was just about to write to you you when I got got very very ill & have not been able to do so since then till now. I am however gradually by God's mercy getting better. I now hope that I may live to see you again when you return to England; I shall at least hope & try to do so & that will help me more than anything else. Then if I last just till the New Year, I may perhaps live another summer: but I

cannot expect to do more, nor indeed can I wish to unless I recover sufficiently to do some serious writing & be of some use which I am not not now.

Even writing such a note as this is not easy for me, so it will be only a brief one. I am immensely looking forward to your arrival here & devoutly hoping I may be still alive & no worse than I am now. I am too weak to do anything after months in bed, but now mentally quite fit & well but not strong enough to read the news intelligently as my sight prevents my doing so though I hope that may recover.

My very best love to you.

Your afffec.ate Father

Hemingford

P.S. Many thanks for kind parcel received today, which will be of great use to us, as we are hard up for food of that kind.   H.

Alas, the struggle was in vain. Dennis Henry died at 10.20 am on December 10, 1947, with Val, who had travelled all night, arriving just too late to see his father again and Young Dennis still awaiting a passage from Uganda. May wrote to the latter that same afternoon. "His mind was very peaceful, he had been very much worse this last week. It seems a dream to me to think he has gone and I have lost my best one in this world. I feel very sad to think you are not here, he had so hoped he would live to see you again."

The Speaker, Colonel Clifton-Brown, in a letter to *The Times*, paid tribute to his former chief, of whom he had been a little afraid when he was first appointed, but then found that serving him was a labour of love. "He was kindly, considerate, he helped me in all my difficulties, and I owe my present position entirely to his wise guidance and helpful advice," he wrote. The *Watford Observer* mourned "a man of infinite patience and courtesy and a dominant character in Watford affairs for the past 40 years." As the funeral cortège wound its way through the streets from St. John's Church, where the coffin had lain overnight, men stood to attention at the roadside and doffed their hats in respect.

Dennis Henry Herbert (1869-1947), Lord Hemingford, PC, KBE. Portrait by George Harcourt, RA. The uniform is that of the Privy Council.

Victorious!

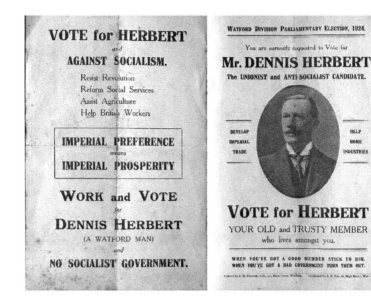

Dennis & Prince of Wales.

May Herbert (née Bell), Dennis Henry and L to R: Dennis, Oliver, Val.

Proposed Coat of Arms for the Lords Hemingford, rejected by Dennis Henry Herbert 1943-44.

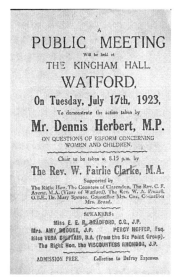

A

PUBLIC MEETING

Will be held at

THE KINGHAM HALL,

WATFORD,

On Tuesday, July 17th, 1923,

To demonstrate the action taken by

Mr. Dennis Herbert, M.P.

ON QUESTIONS OF REFORM CONCERNING
WOMEN AND CHILDREN.

Chair to be taken at 8.15 p.m. by

The Rev. W. Fairlie Clarke, M.A.

Supported by

The Right Hon. The Countess of Clarendon, The Rev. C. F.
Ayerst, M.A. (Vicar of Watford), The Rev. W. A. Powell,
O.B.E., Dr. Mary Spence, Councillor Mrs. Cox, Councillor
Mrs. Broad.

SPEAKERS:

Miss E. E. B. BRADFORD, C.C., J.P.
Mrs. AMY BROOKE, J.P.   PERCY HEFFER, Esq.
Miss VERA BRITTAIN, B.A. (from the Six Point Group),
The Right Hon. the VISCOUNTESS RHONDDA, J.P.

ADMISSION FREE.   Collection to Defray Expenses.

Poster for Group of Six Meeting

141

CALCUTTA, CEYLON & WALES

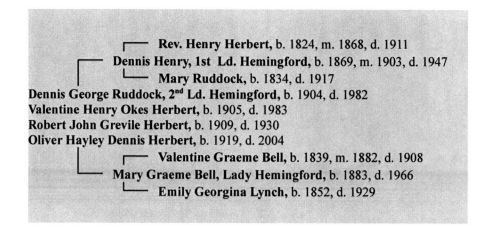

```
                  ┌──── Rev. Henry Herbert, b. 1824, m. 1868, d. 1911
          ┌──── Dennis Henry, 1st Ld. Hemingford, b. 1869, m. 1903, d. 1947
          │      └──── Mary Ruddock, b. 1834, d. 1917
Dennis George Ruddock, 2nd Ld. Hemingford, b. 1904, d. 1982
Valentine Henry Okes Herbert, b. 1905, d. 1983
Robert John Grevile Herbert, b. 1909, d. 1930
Oliver Hayley Dennis Herbert, b. 1919, d. 2004
          │      ┌──── Valentine Graeme Bell, b. 1839, m. 1882, d. 1908
          └──── Mary Graeme Bell, Lady Hemingford, b. 1883, d. 1966
                 └──── Emily Georgina Lynch, b. 1852, d. 1929
```

> Activity of youth,
> Activity of age,
> The like was never seen
> Upon a common stage. - Anon: *The Mummer's Play*

May felt "lost and vacant" for some weeks after Dennis Henry Herbert's death, but in truth it was a relief that the long months of intensive nursing and worry were over and her natural optimism soon reasserted itself. Life in Britain remained difficult. Rationing took an even tighter grip and it was difficult to keep warm, but the grinding pressure of the flying bombs was over and there was much to be grateful for. Another generation of Herbert men had survived a world war intact – Young Dennis, the new Lord Hemingford, was soon back on leave from Uganda, though it was sad that his father's long struggle to live to see him again had been in vain. Meanwhile her two other boys were back from India and likely to remain in Britain.

Valentine Henry Okes (1905-1983)

Val had spent the best part of 20 years in India, having initially failed to persuade his father that he should join the peacetime army when he left Oundle in 1923. He at once joined the Territorial Army, being gazetted as a Second Lieutenant in the 1st Hertfordshire Regiment on November 9, 1923, assisted no doubt by his four years of keen membership of the Officers Training Corps at school. He was also a keen rugby player, turning out regularly for West Herts as a half back. In October, 1925 he embarked for Calcutta, having got an appointment there as a General Assistant in the well-known firm of Balmer Lawrie & Co. Ltd. He signed a five-year contract which allowed him to leave the company's service only if two qualified medical men certified that he was unfit to carry out his duties and provided that this incapacity was not occasioned by "any impropriety of conduct on his part". The company had already been trading in India for over half a century and had a wide range of interests including tea, banking, coal, ice, shipping, flour, salt and engineering. It was in the last of these, in the metals department, where Val began to make his mark and determine the course of his future career. He of course enrolled at once as a Trooper in the Calcutta Light Horse and, over the next decade rose steadily to the rank of Acting Sergeant, at which point he inexplicably reverted to the ranks, presumably of his own volition as he was granted an efficiency medal in 1936.

An early love affair foundered when the girl turned him down – according to May she was not good enough for him – but it was in Calcutta that Val met his future wife, Winifred Mabel Pearson, whose father, Sir Herbert Pearson, was a judge in the Indian High Court. Winifred had, therefore, led one of those curious peripatetic British childhoods, apart from her parents, with she and her brother, Jack, spending school holidays with an aunt in Gerrards Cross. A talented pianist and singer, she was a Licentiate of the Royal College of Music (L.R.A.M.) having survived a training at the domestic science establishment in Atholl Crescent, Edinburgh, which she did not enjoy. They were married on October 3, 1931, in the Church of St. Margaret of Scotland, New Galloway, where the Pearsons used to spend their summer holidays. The bride's cream-coloured dress cut on close-fitted classical lines was enhanced with a train of old lace which her delighted mother-in-law had lent for the occasion. May travelled up the day before with Oliver, then aged 13, to be joined next day by Dennis, who despite an attack of neuritis, arrived in time by the overnight sleeper. The *Dumfries & Galloway Advertiser*, headlined its rather prosaic account "Interesting Stewartry Wedding". May describing the scene for Young Dennis, absent in the Gold Coast, was more enthusiastic:

> I wore my black satin beauté dress & coat & a hat which I got in Paris. Val looked very fine in his wedding clothes. We started for the Church, Dad and I, at about 10 mins. past 2 p.m.. Val gave me a nice bouquet of red carnations and asparagus fern. Lady P. had brown

carnations to tone with her beige lace dress.....Winifred looked very pretty but she was very white & nervous coming up the aisle. Val spoke up in a loud voice & held himself very straight.......I kept thinking of you and my darling Robert & wishing you were both with us. I felt very calm and cool – quite different to what I ever thought I could feel like at my son's wedding.

Sir George Rankin, Chief Justice of Calcutta, proposed the health of the bride and groom and Val acquitted himself well in reply. The only doubt concerned the bridesmaids' dresses of tulle net in shaded autumn colourings, for which she did not much care.

Val had signed up for another five years with Balmer Lawrie on the same draconian terms, but there was an extensive social life and holidays in Darjeeling or Kalimpong. It was not long before Win, as she came to be known, achieved the notable feat of giving birth to the first girl in the family since Caroline Herbert, Rev. Henry Herbert's sister, was born in 1822 – a span of 110 years. The new baby was Rosemary Anne to be followed two years later by another girl, Susan Jean. Susan, however, was a "blue baby" and her delicate condition seems to have played a part in the family's decision to return to England in 1936, four years before Val's latest contract was due to expire. Rosemary's earliest memories were of the long six-week sea journey home and particularly having to follow the tradition of throwing her topee into the sea and watching it float away.

Timothy William Okes was born in Beaconsfield in July 1936 and soon afterwards the family moved to The Tyddyn at Mold in North Wales when Val began a new career at John Summers & Sons, a large steel works on the north bank of the River Dee at Shotton, which was only just beginning to recover from the slump of the early 1930s and was installing a new hot and cold strip mill covering 27 acres. War broke out in September, 1939, and a few months later the family had to deal with the sadness of Susan's death in April, 1940, none the less distressing for the fact that it was not unexpected. Nevertheless, the Tyddyn, a handsome black and white house, standing above the River Alun in the valley outside Mold proved to be an ideal family house. It had nine bedrooms, which turned out to be a particular asset when Mr & Mrs Will from Birkenhead and their 11 children were billeted there. Win was by now heavily involved in W.V.S. work, organising the housing of evacuees from Liverpool and ferrying blood plasma around to various hospitals. She was thus allowed to run a car and, because she had always disliked cooking, she was pleased to pass the job on to Mrs. Will.

Val had, of course, joined the Royal Welch Fusiliers Territorial Association at Rhyl and was soon called up and on his way back to India as a gunner, the RWF having been turned into several battalions of which his was the 23rd L.A.A. Regiment, Royal Artillery. He remained in India and Ceylon throughout the war, his unit being eventually retrained as paratroops forming the 23rd Parachute Light A.A. and Anti-Tank Regiment of the Indian Airborne Division. They were destined for the war in Burma, but much to Val's disappointment the war ended before they saw active service. By this time he was an acting Brigadier and later became a substantive Lieutenant Colonel.

Back from the war Val returned to John Summers and began the difficult process of readjusting to family and civilian life after years away. It must have been hard to pick up where he had left off and difficult for Win and the children to get used to a new disciplinarian. As Rosemary wrote many years later, "No doubt we were a real pain and not how he thought his children ought to be." It was a problem being reproduced all over the country at the time. To a considerable extent the war had passed the children by, despite a drama when an incendiary bomb fell on Mold and the drone of German bombers heading south again after raids on Liverpool. A year or two after the war Celia and I were spending school holidays at the Tyddyn and I remember Val as a bit of a martinet, particularly in the matter of broken windows resulting from our passion for cricket. It must have been an added nuisance having to cope with a nephew and niece, but Val and particularly Win (who understood about spending school holidays with your uncles or aunts) were kindness itself. The absence of Dennis abroad also put an extra burden on Val.. Apart from being much more businesslike than his elder brother, he was also on the spot to deal with their mother's financial arrangements and with their young brother Oliver, who was already proving unsatisfactory. In 1948 Val and Dennis seem to have some kind of epic row, which they took pains to obliterate from the archives.

In a letter dated January 31, when Dennis was on the high seas on his way back to Accra, Val wrote saying:

> Thank you for your letter from the House of Lords, which I am about to tear up as I agree it should not be kept as an heirloom. There was no need for you to even refer to our argument at Clarendon Lodge. I had not considered it severe enough to warrant further mention – to be true to form we should all have fought like cats! But my apologies to you & I must say that I could never have considered that you lost your temper, a mere rise in temperature by both of us, & certainly no apology was due to me from you.

They were, of course, extremely different personalities - Val a man of the world, experienced in business, with a martial spirit and a view of the Empire directly opposite to that espoused by Dennis, whose military pretensions were extremely limited and whose grasp of business was rudimentary to say the least. Moreover, in the last 20 years they had seen very little of each other so some friction, in that difficult time after their father's death, was hardly to be wondered at. Nevertheless, if Dennis lost his temper it was an unusual event. But both men had a strong sense of family loyalty and once Dennis had settled back in England Val was a frequent visitor to Hemingford Abbots, visits which he much enjoyed though he refused to go on other family holidays. Any difficulties that arose between them were, in any case, obliterated by family events; in this case the birth in October of Sylvia Valentine aroused great delight.

The year 1951 heralded big changes. Val was promoted to be Managing Director of the Shelton Iron, Steel & Coal Co., a subsidiary of John Summers, which was located in the Potteries – too far from Mold for the family to remain at the Tyddyn. For reasons now obscure to do with their marriage settlement Win and Val's room for manoeuvre on house purchase was limited, but they bought a small house at Burland, near Nantwich, and set about enlarging it and converting the rather scruffy orchard into what became an attractive garden. The move was not a comfortable one. The children felt it was a "come down" from the spaciousness of the Tyddyn and it must have been difficult for the parents too. Much worse was to follow. In late 1953 or early 1954 Win felt a lump under her arm but did nothing about it until it began to hurt. Cancer was diagnosed and a mastectomy became necessary. After a period of remission the disease recurred, but in the manner of the times Win was not told, the fiction being maintained that it was arthritis. Val told Dennis, in confidence that, if a course of injections which Win was being given proved unsuccessful, the only hope was a ground-breaking operation for the removal of adrenal glands which was so new that it could be done only in London or Bristol. Eventually arrangements were made for Bristol and Val wrote:

> Win knows nothing of the Bristol plans & proposals & because news travels, all this that I've written you is confidential please – as we must try by every means to keep the truth from Win. This is important. ......Win understands that she is going to Royal Infirmary at Bristol because they have special experience with her type of arthritis & as yet has no idea of any operation.

He drove her down to Bristol on December 5, 1954. After some weeks she came home and was nursed there until she died on Sunday, March 20, 1955. She was 48, a person who radiated calm and competence even in the direst of circumstances.

In due course Janet Wigram, the daughter of Rev. Gerrard Wigram, arrived to keep house for Val, freeing Rosemary, who had given up her job in intelligence in Athens to come and run the household during Win's illness. In May, 1956, Val and Janet were married at St. Paul's, Quarndon, near Derby with Sylvia as the bridesmaid and Tim as best man. Val's career was also blossoming. He had become Director and General Manager of the Shelton company in 1950 and when, in 1964, he became Managing Director the appointment coincided with the construction of a radical new £19-million steel works next to the existing factory. Val told *The Times* that it should enable Shelton to live through future recessions "at the sort of prices which would cause conventional steel makers to wither away."

In 1970 when he had retired, he and Janet decided to go and live in South Africa. They sold the house in Burland and moved to Somerset West near Capetown, not far from Rev. Henry Herbert's old stamping ground more than a century earlier. Janet's brother lived there, and there were Ruddock and Okes relations in the vicinity and Janet enjoyed the warmth. They settled in well to a house with a swimming pool and made many friends. In September Val sent Dennis his first reactions:

> The Govt. here is just about as hopeless as Wilson & Co. in the UK, although in different ways. One day when I am better informed than at present, I will perhaps write you an essay on S.A. Politics, & you will probably agree with quite a lot of what I write???
>
> I shall soon have "blood pressure" if the exaggerations & untruths re S.A. continue. I wish you could come out here for a month or so, & I'm sure would at least modify your present opinions.........We are far more civlised than the U.K.... I can see you and Elizabeth snorting at these remarks?!!

As Val knew, a visit was indeed out of the question since Dennis had been sentenced *in absentia* to 40 lashes for his activities in opposing South Africa's apartheid policy. Nevertheless Val had always envisaged ending his days in Britain and he found it irksome that, as a foreigner, he could not take part in local affairs at the Cape and when, on a visit to England in 1973 they discovered how house price inflation was running, they decided that they should return. At short notice they managed to buy a house near Newbury, which was also where Rosemary and her husband, Brigadier Bill Turner, were based. In 1974 they sold up in South Africa and came back permanently.

Val began to get confused, irritable and difficult and Janet, who was a private and rather nervous person concealed from everyone the difficulty she was having with him. She herself suffered from insomnia and things evidently got on top of her until, in February, 1982, she took her own life at the age of 66. Val went into a nursing home nearby for some time, but had eventually to go into St Andrew's Hospital, Northampton, which was the only geriatric hospital in the country. There in January, 1983, he died.

Oliver Hayley Dennis (1919-2004)

The birth of Oliver in August, 1919, was much celebrated and his christening, in the House of Commons chapel, was pictured in the newspapers. As time went by he found himself, as the ewe lamb, tagging along at political meetings and being an object of some interest and attention outside the family. When his elder brother Robert died in 1930, Oliver was 11 and became even more cherished. The effect was not helpful. However, his career at Oundle was unexceptional and he went up to Wadham, where his progress was interrupted by the war. He was called up into the Queen's Regiment and went to France with the Expeditionary force. Here, he recalled years later, he was strafed by German fighters while travelling by train, but emerged unscathed, though someone in the same compartment was hit. In due course he was posted to India, where he was in the 1st Punjab Regiment, but fell victim to a virulent attack of dysentery, from which he took a very long time to recover. It was believed in the family that the Army decided to send him back to Britain, whether for reasons other than health is not known, but that his father exercised his influence to prevent this on the grounds that such a thing could not happen to a son of his. No record of any of this has come to light however. Oliver eventually served in Brigade headquarters of the 14th Indian Jungle Training Division.

His father, when he was putting his financial affairs in order in 1944, wrote to Young Dennis explaining a provision in his will which gave May the power to decide in what proportions the capital she would inherit should go to her three sons. He added:

> She knows that (unless some special and unexpected reason should happen) I do not want her to alter the equal division: but my reason for giving her this power is really the fact that Oliver's future is as yet so uncertain, and I do not want to overlook the possibility of his being (when the time comes) in difficulty with creditors which might make it right to "tie up" his money for his own protection: he has

148

> never shown any tendency to be extravagant or anything of the kind:
> but what sort of occupation or work he may go in for after the war I
> have at present no idea – nor as far as I know has he.

He went on to say that he strongly felt Oliver would not be likely to
succeed as a solicitor. The profession was now subject to so many complex
rules and regulations that the most honest and well-meaning person might
through carelessness easily find himself in trouble with the Discipline
Committee and, even if he avoided being struck off, could ruin his practice by
incurring fines.

> Oliver has of course had misfortunes in the matter of health & like
> every one else has his failings & weaknesses, but there is no vice in
> him, he has his very good points, & has shown signs of real ability in
> some directions, if only he would learn to cultivate it & apply it. At
> present, & I think for some years, he wants & will want guidance
> from his brothers: they may well be better able to help him than his
> very old father!

This estimation was to prove all too accurate and two years later Dennis
decided to relieve May of the responsibility of what could have been an
awkward decision. On December 31, 1946, less than a year before he died, he
constituted a trust fund, with Val as one of the trustees, which safeguarded
Oliver's inheritance. Oliver, who was back at Oxford, whence he emerged
without having taken his final examinations, was a signatory to this important
document. Very soon Oliver was living up to his father's fears and Val was
having to subsidise him from the D&V Fund, which had been set up for the
two older sons. A job as a political education officer in the Conservative
Political Centre seemed to augur well, but Oliver was soon in debt and by
1951 was living with his mother at her new home 15 Langley Way, Watford.
However, his lifestyle made life a misery for May and it was impossible to
keep any help in the house. He would stay up much of the night, demand
breakfast at 10.00 am and never do a hand's turn to help, and he ignored
May's pleas to keep his room tidy. Also, because he was not being successful
at selling encyclopaedias for Newnes, a job he had taken in the hope of
remedying his financial situation, he was not only making no contribution to
household expenses, but was getting into debt again and had actually
borrowed money from his mother and was using her car and petrol for his
own business. He was thus defaulting on promises made to Val in return for a
£100 bail-out of previous debts

On a visit to May in November Win found her in despair and at once
summoned Val. Prolonged negotiations followed over the next two weekends

in which Val's aim, with May's and Win's agreement, was to persuade Oliver to see a psychiatrist to help him with his mental difficulties, or to get a better job than selling encyclopaedias on commission or ask to be paid a salary, so that he could obtain a living wage. If he would not cooperate he could not remain at Langley Way. Oliver, who believed that his mother would never actually ask him to leave, relied on obfuscation and delay. By lunchtime on Sunday, however, he had agreed to see a psychiatrist and Val had given him £15 to pay off new debts. Then, just as the family were getting into the car for the long journey back home, Oliver ran out of the house recanting his agreement and saying that only the church could help him. More negotiations ensued and Oliver insisted that he would go on as he had done and would live his own life. May, in tears, told him that in that case he must leave her house at once. Relating all this to Dennis in the Gold Coast, Val wrote:

> Then I began to wonder if he was fit to be chucked out (even with the £15, which he still had) as I'm sure he is almost a mental case. So I weakened from my previous decision re his immediate departure & we told him he could stay at Langley Way till he had found out from Newnes if they would give him a salary.

Leaving Win and Sylvia to support May, he drove back north. Oliver had spoken much of a clergyman in London who he said mistrusted psychiatrists and could be helpful, so Win sought him out for advice. It turned out, however, that he could scarcely remember Oliver, but in conversation said he thought that Oliver must be made to support himself. Next Sunday negotiations resumed, Oliver having told May that he proposed to continue as he had been doing and she telling him that he must leave. Oliver greeted Val and Win affably as though nothing was wrong, but they told him he must go before they set off for home which would be at lunchtime.

> Oliver refused to go & stated that he would leave on Monday after he had time to sort out his belongings. We stated that we could not agree & mother insisted that he should go, as she said she could not manage him without Win & myself....He had made no arrangements to go anywhere else, & was obviously still trying to call what he thought was our bluff.

Finally, after much unpleasantness, he was got out of the house by lunchtime and told that he could come back in a day or two to sort out his belongings, that May would always be pleased to see him, but that he would not be provided for any longer. Val's final verdict was:

> There is still no evidence that he has been doing anything wrong in any way (i.e. no vices) but he has told untruths & we have learnt not

to believe what he says – he has been rude & unkind to mother. He will now have to sink or swim & I am fairly certain that we shall find he will go at last and take some job, as we now begin to think that he is not perhaps as mad as we thought, but just can't face the world & its troubles, which he will now be forced to do. I gave him another £5 so he has at least been chucked out with £15.

Part of the problem was that Oliver, perhaps because of his upbringing, was intent on solving the big problems which the nation and the Church of England were facing. He spent much time addressing the newspapers on the former subject and the Archbishop of Canterbury on the latter. (Years later when his great-niece became friendly with the daughter of an Archbishop, she found that the volume and persistence of Oliver's imprecations had left a lasting, but less than favourable, impression on the primate.). These issues loomed so large in his mind and he felt that his views on them were so important that he had no time to make up his mind on lesser issues like earning a living or deciding which job to take or where to live. At the end of a long life he left a large volume of half-finished and unsent articles and epistles on, for example, the dangers of the European Community or the importance of strict adherence to the principles of the Anglican Society. They mostly do not deserve quotation, but the following extract from a 1971 letter published in the *Spectator*, inveighing against the Treaty of Rome, gives a flavour of the self-importance and unreality which had begun to overtake him:

> Those of us who have given thought to this matter during the last two decades (and, indeed, since the war), have not in all cases been "politically active" in recent years – though not thereby politically unobservant: I am one such. Accordingly I would be grateful if I may state my viewpoint now in your columns for my many friends in politics and others here and in other Commonwealth countries among your readers, who may legitimately expect me to make known my views.

Val's optimism about Oliver's ability to support himself was, to a degree borne out, and he settled down seriously to living the life of a grey sheep. He had a number of (usually temporary) jobs, which allowed him time in between to set the world and the church to rights. There were reports from time to time, which caused consternation at Hemingford Abbots, where both May and Young Dennis were now living, that for example he was living in the waiting rooms of railways stations, but for a longish period in the 1960s and 1970s he had a flat in King Henry's Road, off Regents Park.

Then, on December 4, 1975, his brother Dennis received a sensational letter. It began, typically enough, with apologies for not having been in touch, with a passing reference to "items of concern in Church & Politics", with the thought that he might have been missing his vocation all these years and with an account of his elderly neighbour's bowel trouble. Then, half-way down the second page came this:

> However, the end of the year finds me contemplating rather a revolution in my life, which will more than intrigue you – Marriage! All rather unexpected, it began to loom in the autumn but only came to a head on Sunday and is as yet unannounced to the world.

> Rosemary Bate, aged 46, is the lass in question. She is the daughter of Canon Roland Bate, who was Vicar of Welwyn for 30 years till his retirement 10 years ago. She first came into my purview this August at Hoddesdon, where I was attending the annual conference of the Fellowship of St Alban and St. Sergius.

Reflecting universal relief at this turn of events, the wedding, at the Church of St Mary, the Virgin, Primrose Hill on April 19, 1976, was a great event, attended by an impressive array of relations covering three generations. The ceremony however, turned out to be a full nuptial mass, which was too much for some of the younger ones, who had to be removed before the end. The couple settled in to Rosemary's house in Tewin, Herts. If the more seasoned members of the family felt it was all too good to be true, their scepticism was sadly justified because seven years later in July, 1983, at Luton County Court, on Rosemary's petition, the marriage was annulled on the grounds of non-consummation. Oliver, who claimed that he had not been given notice of what was happening and that anyway Christian marriage was indissoluble, refused to accept the verdict and barricaded himself in at No 36, Lower Tewin, refusing to answer the telephone or the doorbell. Eventually he was evicted by the bailiffs but, despite his niece Cass Moggridge's best efforts, refused to accept accommodation from the council because it would have involved signing a document which recorded the end of his marriage. The true story, as related by Oliver to me later, was indeed extraordinary. He said he had written two letters, one proposing marriage and the other not; he had then posted the wrong one, by mistake. Rosemary, he claimed, having recently been rejected by another person named Herbert, had decided to accept him instead.

After the eviction he decamped to the Victory Services Club near Marble Arch, a place designed for ex-service people to spend an occasional night or two, and there he took root, moving out every 10 days for one night in an attempt to abide by the rules. At about the time of his marriage Oliver had been told that the ligaments in his hips were contracting, and now, unbeknown to the family, he began to be seriously disabled by this condition. His right foot became locked behind his left foot so that he could only shuffle forward by moving one foot at a time. The Club, with admirable patience, put up with all this for almost a decade, at which point they declared that he could no longer reside there because, in the event of fire he could not get out of the building quickly enough and his room was such a mess that it could not be let to other people. Alerted to this his nephews and nieces combined to hi-jack Oliver into a taxi, resisting his protests that he needed to go and retrieve some papers from the Club, took him to a doctor, by prior arrangement, made sure he kept a hospital appointment and forced him to decide between three or four nursing homes in the northern home counties, which because of his father's prudence in 1946, he could still afford. As a result he ended up living at St. Audrey's in Hatfield, having both hips replaced so that within a few weeks he could walk up and down stairs and finding that he could, after all, live a rather more straightforward life. He continued to bombard the Archbishop with his views on the indissolubility of marriage and the public prints with his political opinions and he complained about the mealtimes at St. Audrey's, but his financial affairs were regularised. He had been declared bankrupt in 1998, when he owed the Inland Revenue almost £25,000. Now he was discharged. He lived to a greater age than any of his brothers - his 80th birthday being marked by a lunch with some of his relations – and he died in January, 2004. His ashes were interred across the road from St. Audrey's in Hatfield. Rosemary Bate, despite having sent his letters back unanswered for the past several years, attended his funeral. She died four years later in May, 2008.

*Valentine Henry Okes Herbert
(1905-1983).*

*Valentine married Winifred Pearson,
New Galloway, Oct. 3, 1931*

*Nineteen descendants of Dennis Henry Herbert among others, at Oliver's wedding,
1976.*

Part II

-------------Chapter 15 -------------

A DAWN RAID

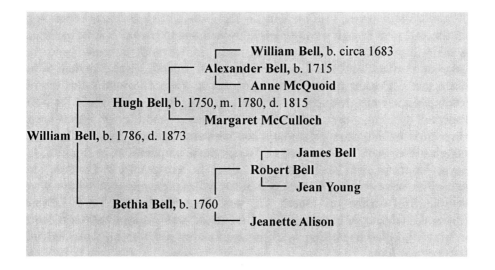

Our ancestors are very good kind of folks; but they are the last people I should choose to have a visiting relationship with.- *Sheridan*

Hugh Bell was, in the language of 1798, a Radical Reformer. Born in Dublin of Scots-Irish descent, he was a prosperous merchant in the City of London, provisioning the Royal Navy and running a Wine and Spirits business. But he was perhaps not wholly surprised when, at 8.00 am on the morning of March 7, while he was still in bed at his London house in Charterhouse Square, a King's Messenger, supported by a posse of Bow Street Runners came to arrest him on suspicion of high treason or what would now be called terrorism. The proceedings of a dawn raid were more gentlemanly than they would be nowadays. The King's Messenger, a Mr. Cox, allowed him to dress and take a little breakfast, using the time to search the bureau and desk for papers, intercept the prisoner's letters and survey Mr Bell's bookcase where he found a suspiciously revolutionary volume, Tom Paine's *The Age of*

Reason. "I must by your leave, Sir, take this book with me," said Mr. Cox. "Certainly", replied the prisoner, "if you will also take the volume next to it." It was Bishop Watson's *Apology for the Bible*.

It was not until 11.00 am that the prisoner was conveyed to the office of the Home Secretary, the Duke of Portland, who had signed the warrant for Mr. Bell's arrest. After appearing before the Privy Council, the prisoner was - at half past one o'clock - discharged on the orders of the Under Secretary of State, one George Canning, with whom he was acquainted. The problem was that Mr. Bell had been playing host for several days to an Irish friend, Arthur O'Connor, who was a leading light in the United Irish Society, which was plotting to invite French intervention in Ireland and to rise up in revolt as soon as their forces landed. The movement was riddled with informers and the Duke of Portland and the Lord Lieutenant of Ireland, Earl Camden, were aware that O'Connor himself had been over to Paris 18 months earlier and concluded a secret agreement for a French landing. In the event the ships were dispersed by a big storm and the invasion came to nothing. O'Connor spent some time behind bars in solitary confinement, but was now in London, though still on bail. Fresh reports of French naval preparations in Dunkirk, Le Havre, Honfleur and Calais had again raised the temperature in London. The authorities were moving in on O'Connor's colleagues, many of whom were arrested in Leinster on March 12, and in particular on Lord Edward Fitzgerald, who, after escaping the initial arrest, was surprised at his hideout on May 19, killed one of his would-be captors but was himself wounded and died early in June.

Hugh Bell's own origins were in Ireland, whither his forebears had migrated in the 16th Century from the Scottish Border country; his father, Alexander (1715-), son of William (1683-) and Anne, née McQuoid, was a distiller from Greyabbey on the shores of Strangford Lough. His uncle Samuel, was the father of General Robert Bell, of the Honourable East India Company, of whom we shall hear more later. In London Hugh Bell belonged to the group of Whigs who had some sympathy for the French Revolution and with whom the United Irishmen were on familiar terms. Whiggish sympathy for the United Irishmen was all very well when the movement was a political one, aiming to secure emancipation for Roman Catholics in Ireland so as to unite the populace and separate from England, but once George III's obduracy had killed their hopes of a political solution and they turned to military means, it became more dangerous. The Government had the problem that its informers declined absolutely to identify themselves publicly or give evidence in court so that the chances were slight of being able to prove what the

Ministers knew to be true.

O'Connor had been introduced to Hugh Bell some years previously by a mutual friend, General John Knox, who lived in the Isle of Wight, but was now in command of a district in Northern Ireland. The Duke of Portland was alarmed, therefore, to find among Hugh Bell's papers a letter from Knox expressing views about Ireland which His Grace did not find attractive. The Duke wrote at once to Camden:

> I cannot let the extract of Brig. General Knox's correspondence with Mr. Bell be sent to yr excellency without acquainting you that had it been known or suspected that Gen. Knox entertained the political sentiments he has there expressed, or had been capable of imparting to a person of Mr. Bell's way of thinking, (to which it is evident that the General was not a stranger), or indeed to anyone but his superior officer, the opinion which he has given to Mr. Bell upon the plan of defence which he had been directed to execute in the north of Ireland, His Majesty's Confidential Servants would have considered it to have been their duty to represent against his being employed at least in Ireland..."

Camden mounted a strong defence of the General, whom he described as a man of honour who would never act in a cause which he intended to betray. He had to concede, though, that for the General to communicate his sentiments "to a person of Mr. Bell's opinions" was, to say the least extremely indiscreet. It emerged that Knox and O'Connor knew each other well, which surprised their Lordships not a little and the Duke was outraged by Mr. Bell's testimony that even now (he underlined the words) if Knox's house had been fit for O'Connor's reception, O'Connor would have had the use of it. Finally Camden persuaded the Duke that more harm than good would result from General Knox being relieved of his command and the Duke agreed that their concern about Knox should be kept secret, especially from the General himself, but he assumed that it need never become public. If it did, though, it would "entirely disqualify him from serving His Majesty in any public capacity."

How much O'Connor told Hugh Bell, we can only guess, but Bell did know that O'Connor was travelling under a false name and that he was without a passport because he was still on bail. He helped O'Connor to try and get passage to the Continent and he ordered for him some Louis d'Or, the foreign currency of choice. He also allowed O'Connor - who was usually more cautious - to bring to dinner an associate known variously as James O'Coigly or Quigley, about whom neither of them knew much. George Bell, writing almost a century later, assumed that his grandfather had been, in effect betrayed by some of his servants who had elaborated imaginatively upon what they had heard of the dinner-table conversation between the their master and the two Irish conspirators, but another century later that looks less likely. The authorities had a good deal of more tangible evidence.

A week before the arresting officer's arrival at Charterhouse Square, Arthur O'Connor, James O'Coigly and three associates had been arrested in a pub in Margate and charged with three species of High Treason - compassing the King's death, aiding and abetting the King's enemies and inciting the French to invade - and seven other so-called "Overt Acts" of treachery. In fact the Government threw the book at them. Their papers were seized and O'Connor's doubtless included some references to Hugh Bell. O'Coigly's coat pocket turned out to contain a much more explosive document, nothing less than an address from "the Secret Committee" to the French Executive, urging an invasion of England. No wonder O'Coigly told his companions that he hoped the arresting officers would lose the papers on the way back to London because there was one among his which could hang them all.

In the event, when the trial began in May before a court of *Oyer and Terminer* in Maidstone, the names "Hugh Bell, Charterhouse Square, Merchant; J. Wallis and J. Morris, Servants to the said Hugh Bell" were high on the list of witnesses. Nor were they likely to default. Among the records of the trial in the National Archives is a recognizance accepted by Hugh Bell in the enormous sum for those days of £500, which he would forfeit to the King if he failed to turn up to give evidence at Maidstone, and other witnesses had to make the same commitment. At the trial in May Hugh Bell did his best for his friend. His memory was a little rusty on how he had come to address a letter to O'Connor, using his assumed name, or precisely when O'Coigly had dined at Charterhouse Square, but he did not allow himself to be intimidated in cross-examination by the Attorney-General, Lord Eldon. He testified that he had bought Louis d'Or for O'Connor, had tried but failed to get him a cross channel passage and that he did not believe O'Connor was a member of any English society or club. This was an important point because England and Ireland were separate kingdoms and the prisoners were accused, in this instance, of treachery towards England only. Bell also said O'Coigly had visited O'Connor several times at his house but their only connection was that they planned to leave the country together. The prisoners had agreed to be tried together, but there was not much solidarity between them. When O'Connor himself intervened to ask Hugh Bell whether he had appeared to know O'Coigly, Bell replied that he had not. O'Connor, he said, received visits from many Irishmen but was careful to avoid making acquaintances and behaved in a guarded way in England. When Bell added that O'Connor had not wanted to travel with O'Coigly because he was indiscreet, the judge intervened to stop O'Connor's questioning. "Mr. O'Connor, do you not see how much this is to the detriment of the other prisoner?, " he said.

The specific points made by Hugh Bell in his evidence were of considerable technical importance, and he was followed into the witness-box later by a bevy of like-minded Whig notables offering evidence about O'Connor's character and aims. Charles James Fox himself paid O'Connor a generous compliment, Richard Brinsley Sheridan said he had been particularly keen to meet him because of the good recommendations he had received from Ireland and other encomiums came from the Duke of Norfolk, Lord John Russell and several Earls. O'Connor's biographer says "These were gentlemen whose word was a matter of honour. The court did not consider them capable of perjury. They were professional orators and chose their words with great care when questioned both by the defence and by the prosecution. There is no reason to believe they lied.". Nevertheless they must have been embarrassed some years later when O'Connor admitted his offence.

O'Coigly lacked such luminous support and he was found guilty of High Treason and ordered to be hanged, drawn and quartered - a sentence which the King munificently commuted to mere hanging. The other defendants, including O'Connor, were acquitted. The Government were furious that their main quarry had escaped punishment in England, but they were determined to get him in Ireland. The atmosphere was so highly charged that a near-riot ensued. Two Bow Street runners tried to seize him while he was still at the bar, but the courts prevented this abuse. So great was the crush that O'Connor could not escape, swords were drawn and two of the ex-prisoner's friends who stood in the way of the bailiffs ended up being prosecuted and imprisoned for a year for attempting to rescue him. Whether Hugh Bell was embroiled in this unprecedented rumpus we do not know, but he kept faith with his friend and when, four years later, O'Connor was released from prison and sent into exile, it was Hugh Bell who took on the job of getting to him in Paris the income from his Irish land; he seems to have gone on fulfilling this function until his death in 1815 - a few weeks before the Battle of Waterloo.

Before that, though, the story was to take one more twist. In 1810 some letters written by Arthur O'Connor to his brother were published and in the process of commenting on these the *Morning Post* picked up verbatim an allegation in a Dublin journal that Hugh Bell had been confined in London on

159

a charge of high treason. The arrest 12 years before had, however, been on *suspicion* of high treason and Bell felt sufficiently strongly to mount a libel action against the Editor of the *Morning Post*, Nicholas Byrne, as a result of which he enjoyed a moment of fame or notoriety and was held out as a champion of those who had been falsely labelled as traitors. Byrne was defended by no less a person than the Attorney General, who tried to argue that it had all happened so long ago that no injury had resulted, but, since Bell had never been charged, it was an open-and-shut case. Bell was victorious and was awarded damages of £500, though these were apparently never paid because of a technicality. A grovelling apology was, however, published, to the effect that the paper never intended to wound the feelings or injure the character of Mr. Bell and had never inserted the paragraph concerned from any knowledge or belief that Mr. Bell had been confined on a charge of high treason. The case enjoyed some high-profile notoriety, arousing comment on the law of libel. In particular the conduct of the Attorney General in defending the *Morning Post* aroused the ire of that fiery journalist William Cobbett, who had himself recently been fined £1,000 and sentenced to two years' imprisonment for upsetting the government with his views on military flogging. In the Bell case the Attorney had argued that as he himself was well known from boyhood, the case he was putting should be credited. Cobbett's comment on this was: "There may, perhaps, be, and I dare say, there are, some people who have known him all that while. Most of us have been known all our lives by somebody or other; so that there was nothing very rare in his case. Like the rest of us his beginning is known, but there is nothing to boast of in it being known. If he could have foretold his *end*, indeed, there might have been something worth hearing."

Cobbett, who was also an old enemy of the *Morning Post*, added:

> I cannot help writing a word or two here upon the manner of Mr. Bell's proceeding against this calumniator. He did not pursue him by way of information or indictment; he did not prosecute him for publishing falsehoods, and at the same time leave him no chance of proving his innocence; he took no unfair advantage of any sort of the foul and malignant asperser of his character; he appealed to the old common law of the land; he brought his action against him, for damages; he left him at full liberty to justify his conduct, by praying that what he had done was no *wrong* to Mr. Bell; in short, Mr. Bell put it upon this issue; if what you have said be *true* you are innocent; if what you have said be *false* you are guilty. Mr Bell did not shut up the lips of the accused, at the moment that he preferred an accusation against him. He did not tie his hands, while he set others on to beat

him. He acknowledged in his mode of prosecution, that *truth* is not a libel. The Morning Post of the 20th has the impudence to insinuate, that the Jury acted contrary to their consciences, in giving a verdict of £500 damages. Have the men who write in this paper, or who publish their lucubrations through it, forgotten that they thought, or at least took occasion to say, that the sentence on me was too light The public are obliged to Mr. Bell for pulling out this Byrne by the ears, and holding him up like a pole-cat dragged from his hole.

Hugh Bell had married in 1780 another Bell, "a distant Scotch cousin". She was Bethia, daughter of Robert Bell of Dundee and his wife Janet (née Allison) and she was to bear him eight daughters and four sons. They seem to have been a close-knit family. Not all of them, inevitably, lived to adulthood. Of those who did, Hugh noted in his Will the two sons William and Robert, who had followed him into the family firm of Bell & Higginson. He left them a sum of £6,000 provided that they continued to work together in the company "in the like manner as now used by my said partner, Joseph Higginson, myself and my said sons". This act of kindness, he added, arose from the confidence he had in their integrity, their industry, their rare attention and caution in business and, still more, from the love and affection for their mother "towards whom I trust with the greatest confidence, they will always act a part truly kind and liberal as well as towards their sisters and brother". Until the sons married, he wanted them, their mother and their unmarried sisters to continue to live together. He also made provision, of course, for Bethia with a legacy which was to be kept out of the control of any future husband of hers and he included special provision for his daughter, Anna Maria, of whom he wrote charmingly that it had pleased God to send her into the world to lead a careless and inoffensive life, though not exempt from pain and troubles.

The eldest surviving girl, Margaret (1784-1851) married, as his third wife, General Robert Bell, of the Honourable East India Company, her father's first cousin, by whom she had one son. The General, who began his military career as a private, rose to be the senior General in Her Majesty's Service, which was no mean achievement, even if, as was alleged, a five-month voyage out to India with Sir Eyre Coote, the Commander-in-Chief, gave him a good start . He served for over 40 years in India and fought most notably in the second siege of Seringapatam in 1799, which established British supremacy in southern India. He appeared as Lieutenant Bell, of the Madras Artillery, in Robert Ker Porter's enormous 2,550-sq. ft panorama of the storming of the fortress, which toured the nation to great acclaim before being accidentally burnt. By his first wife, Sarah (née Sydenham) he had four children, one of whom, William, married Henrietta Bell (1793-1844), who was Hugh Bell's daughter and therefore his second cousin . The General's second wife, Jemima (née Scott), bore him two sons and five daughters, one of whom, Louisa married as her second husband, Ambrose Poynter, father of the renowned painter, Sir Edward Poynter, thus establishing a rather tenuous connection between the Bells and Rudyard Kipling and Edward Burne-Jones, who were both married to sisters of Sir Edward's wife.

When Hugh Bell died at Merton a few weeks before the Battle of Waterloo, on March 10th, 1815, the fact was briefly noted in *The Times*.

Hugh Bell's eldest son, William, was 29 when his father died and he did, in accordance with his father's wishes, continue to run the family business with his brother Robert. When the senior partner, Joseph Higginson died, the firm became Bell Brothers & Co. Doubtless Robert also helped William to care for their mother and unmarried sisters, and it was not until 1820, on July 5th, that William married. The bride was Elizabeth Fearne Kinnear, the daughter of George Kinnear, a wealthy Edinburgh banker.

William does not seem to have been as political as his father, though he did evidently keep in touch with Arthur O'Connor because his son, George William, describes in *Recollections* seeing O'Connor at dinner at the house in Aldersgate Street in about 1842, though this will have been a purely social visit. Another account describes O'Connor as having become so Frenchified that he told his hostess: "I'm sorry I am late, Elizabeth, but my cheval has lost its clou". George William described his father as "an excellent man of business, a singularly upright, honourable man". His main other interest was music and, as he was said to possess the best tenor voice in the country bar one, he was much in demand. To the relief of several professional singers, one of whom said he would be nowhere if Mr. Bell sang opera, William declined to go on the stage, resisting all blandishments, including a large salary, but he sang at the coronations of George IV, William IV and Queen Victoria and, as a member of the Harmonists' Glee Club, moved in musical circles. He took George William, for example, to meet Attwood, the organist at St Paul's, who had been a pupil of Mozart, and the conductor at Queen Victoria's wedding, Sir George Smart, was a family friend. But it was Elizabeth who was the primary influence in the family. She was a loving mother and a woman of great ability, with a belief in parental discipline derived from her Scottish background. She had a particular love of literature, which she imparted to her children by reading aloud to them while they got on with their needlework, knitting or drawing. She began with fairy tales and nursery rhymes, Maria

Edgeworth's *Early Lessons* and other stories. *Robinson Crusoe* and *Pilgrim's Progress* were favourites, but it was at reading Walter Scott's *Waverley Novels* with her native Scottish accent that she particularly excelled. She also took the children to evensong at the nearby St Paul's Cathedral and it was she who held the family together when, on November 21, 1842, as reported in *The Times*, "The failure of Messrs Bell Brothers & Co, a firm of old and respectable standing in the Irish trade, was announced on the 'Change today. Beyond the mere fact of their stoppage, no well authenticated particulars have transpired."

A week later *The Times* returned to the subject, indicating how serious an event it was. The Dublin correspondent reported that the news had inflicted a severe shock to the mercantile community both in Dublin and Cork, where the Bells had many agencies, and local firms were expected to suffer. Although the names of the Messrs. Bell did not appear in the list of persons who contracted for the last Government supply of beef and pork, the firm had an interest through its Irish contacts. The consequences of this distressing failure first manifested themselves at the Smithfield cattle-market, where prices had to be cut in order to promote sales.

> The house in question had correspondents in almost all the large towns in Ireland, and, as the firm was connected with the execution of the navy contract for beef and pork, their stoppage of course took several buyers out of the market yesterday. Hence the extreme difficulty of effecting sales.....The next advices from Cork, Limerick, and Waterford, are looked for with great anxiety. The fact of the failure of Bell Brothers is announced in the *Cork Reporter* of yesterday evening on the authority of private letters to parties having extensive commercial connexions. It has excited great surprise in that city.

According to George William Bell, the Company had "found it imperative to place their books in the hands of their creditors"; however, William Bell does not seem to have been bankrupted and both he and Robert soon obtained their discharge from the creditors upon honourable terms, but it was nevertheless a disaster for the family. Elizabeth's reaction to it was typically robust, despite the fact that she had given birth to her 13th child, Grace, only nine weeks before. Her fortitude was described by her eldest son:

> I desire to record the gallant struggle of my dear mother to keep the house and its inmates bright and hopeful. She sustained my father in his trouble, and made her arrangements for retrenchment of all household expenses without troubling him about them. My sisters at once determined to earn their livelihoods, and soon bravely obtained

situations as governess. For myself, a commercial clerkship seemed the easiest and speediest source of an income, and, in a very short time, a post was found for me in the Atlas Fire Insurance Office, carrying on its business in Cheapside."

For George William, as the eldest son, his father's bankruptcy was a particularly bitter blow as he was just qualifying as a barrister. It must have been Elizabeth Fearne (1821-1896), Anna Louisa (1824-1900) and possibly Leonora Georgiana (1827-1914) who became governesses, for the others were too young. Thomas Evans (1825-1887) had already embarked on what was to be a controversial career in India; Hugh Reid (1828-1858) was 14, Isabella Bethia (1829-1835) had died at the age of six, Octavius Plunket (1830-1845) was 12, Frederick Hayley (1832-1895) was 10, Archibald Hamilton (1834-1864) was eight, Mary Caroline (1837-1844) was five and Valentine Graeme (1839-1908) was three. Grace Henrietta Hamilton was born on September 12th, 1842 and Louise (1845) was yet unborn.

Hugh Bell(1750-1815). Portrait by Thomas Hickey.

Bethia Bell(1760-1834). Portrait by Thomas Hickey.

Chapter 16

FROM LONDON TO NAGPORE & SHANGHAI

┌─── **William Bell,** b. 1786, m. 1820, d. 1873
1.Elizabeth Fearne,   **8.Octavius Plunket Bell,** b. 1832
2.George William Bell, b. 1822   **9.Frederick Hayley Bell,** b. 1833
3.Anna Louisa Bell, b.1824   **10.Archibald Hamilton Bell,** b. 1834
4.Thomas Evans Bell, b. 1825   **11. Mary Caroline Bell,** b. 1836
5.Leonora Georgina Bell, b. 1827 **12. Valentine Graeme Bell,** b. 1839
6.Hugh Reid Bell, b. 1829   **13.Grace Hamilton Bell,** b. 1842
7.Isabella Bethia Bell, b. 1830 **14.Louisa Bell,** b. 1834
└─── **Elizabeth Kinnear,** b. 1799, d. 1888

The dead are still able to influence and guide us even more than when they were alive. - *F. W.Sanderson*

William Bell had good connections and it was not long after the financial disaster that he was appointed to the lucrative post of Official Assignee in the Court of Bankruptcy and in 1845 the family moved to 36, Woburn Place, where they lived among the good and the great for many years.

George William (1822-1910)

George William records meetings with Alfred Lord Tennyson, Benjamin Disraeli and Thomas Carlyle, among others, but these were sufficiently rare occasions to require a mention and, unfortunately for him, the family of his intended, Jessie Hawes, who also lived nearby in Montague Place, did not consider him a suitable match for her. Their courtship was long, partly because George William was not well off and partly because of what he described as "the shadow of an unreasonable opposition on the part of my future wife's parents". Jessie had to show considerable fortitude in the face of the family's hostility and even had to face down her brother-in-law when he pointedly preached a sermon on the Fourth Commandment with special reference to the wickedness of daughters who married against their parents' wishes. She refused to invite this censorious cleric to conduct the wedding ceremony and was delighted when George upstaged her parents by inviting the well-known and fashionable F.D. Maurice to do so instead.

When he finally tied the knot for them in 1860, Jessie's mother, by way of revenge, gave her a poor trousseau and a going-away dress that had been rejected by her elder sister. William Bell, however, as her new father-in-law, settled £100 a year on Jessie, which gave them a disposable income of £335, not counting George's £100-worth of Life policies, without which, as he said, "marriage would have been wicked". They lived frugally, refusing invitations which would require them to take a carriage or a cab, holidaying at William's country quarters at Colwyn Bay, or Tinwell near Stamford or Torquay, and raising a family of four children. This may have been no particular hardship to Jessie, whose upbringing had been so sheltered that, when she was married at 28, she had never been to a dinner party or read a book not approved by her parents.

Known as "Gaffie" by his grandchildren, but addressed as "Sir" to his face, George would regale them in later life with tales of how he had seen two pirates hanging in chains near his boarding school in Wandsworth and, while studying in Germany, had been taken by a fellow student to see a woman beheaded. He was evidently supposed to enjoy the spectacle but when the executioner, dressed in red, struck the victim's head off with a sword, he was sick. No wonder, perhaps, that he sought to satisfy his love of music by taking up an introduction to a musical family in the Jewish ghetto in Frankfurt. After a month of these visits, however, the Professor with whom he was staying told him to stop going to a Jewish house or to leave the country.

In 1845 George had been appointed Chief Clerk and later, in 1868, Secretary, of the newly-formed Law Fire Insurance Office which turned out to be his life's work. He never quite got over the loss of a legal career, but he was a very worthy character, whose good works included starting (in 1858) and running a Boys Home as "a nursery of young Christian workmen" which was the first of its kind and eventually grew to accommodate 150 boys. He assisted various of his younger brothers in their tussles with authority, helped to organise relief for the families of soldiers fighting in the Crimea, fundraised for the building of a church in St. Pancras, joined the Committee of King's College Hospital and supported a Nursing Sisterhood – St. John's, Norfolk Street, just off the Strand. Normally an uncontroversial figure, he became involved in a spectacular row when the entire nursing staff resigned rather than submit to the medical staff of the hospitals they served. A ferocious correspondence ensued in the columns of *The Times* and one of the founders of the sisterhood, taking the part of the Charing Cross Hospital, alleged that King's College Hospital had secured too strong a position on the committee, and denounced George William for betraying the nurses.

George William dabbled in journalism and he turned down the opportunity of becoming Secretary of the company which later became the Canadian Pacific Railway because they would not confirm the conditions of his appointment in writing until he reached Canada. He became a Fellow of King's College, London, a member of the Garrick Club and a diligent attender of meetings of the Councils of the Royal Botanic and Humane Societies. Despite their indigence he and Jessie managed a trip to Rome in the year of their Silver Wedding anniversary, a "vast and momentous undertaking" which he described in detail in published letters, and thereafter they became inveterate travellers to places as far away as Scandinavia, Prague, Naples and Biarritz. The family were poleaxed in July 1891 by the death of the eldest boy, William -"one of those sudden and utterly mysterious deaths which call for a deep faith in the Almighty and Merciful Ruler of all earthly events", but eventually the pain eased and, when he died he did so feeling that he had given his remaining son and two daughters a good education, literary and artistic, foreign tours and allowances which, though small, had been willingly granted.

His obituary in The Times said:

> His kindly judgement and sound experience in matters of industrial training and practical Christian education earned him the respect and affection of all with whom he came in contact. In his business career and in his private life he was no less esteemed. He had a large fund of reminiscences of a busy London life, and some years ago printed his Recollections for private circulation (reprinted 1906).

Anna Louisa ((1824-1900)

Anna Louisa married Henry Chisholm, a civil servant who became in charge of weights and measures. Their son, Hugh, was an eminent journalist, City Editor of *The Times*, and achieved fame as Editor of the renowned 11th Edition of the *Encyclopaedia Britannica*. Their daughter, Grace, became the first woman in any subject to be awarded a doctorate at a German university, her thesis being on T*he algebraic groups of spherical trigonometry*. Anna

Louisa had been firmly against Grace studying medicine, her first choice, so she opted instead for mathematics, in which she obtained a First Class degree while at Girton College, Cambridge. and later cooperated with her husband and former tutor, William Young, in producing a large number of mathematical works. For most these she was given no credit on the basis that William was the breadwinner and she had the children to look after, but *A First Book of Geometry*, which used paper-folding to introduce the subject to children, bore her name too. Their eldest son, Frank, was killed in action in the Royal Flying Corps in the first world war. In later life the Youngs lived in Switzerland but when World War II loomed, Grace brought two of her grandchildren to England early in 1940. She had intended to return, but was unable to do so and William could not get to England. They never met again as he died in 1942.

Thomas Evans (1825-1887)

Thomas Evans Bell, William's second son was a bookworm; his every waking hour was devoted to reading and he cared little for sports or exercise. A cadetship in the army of the East India Company was, therefore, a rather improbable choice for him, but on being told by his father that this was his destiny, he very characteristically at once began learning Hindustani. Towards the end of 1841 he embarked on the *City of Poonah* for the three-month passage, via St. Helena and the Cape, to Madras where, arriving in 1842 he was posted to the 2nd Madras Europeans. His military career was unremarkable, but in 1854 he was plucked from his regiment as a Lieutenant to become one of the Civil Staff employed to administer the newly-annexed province of Nagpore, where his literary abilities apparently earned him quick preferment to Assistant Commissioner and Assistant Agent to the Governor-General. The occasion of British annexation had been the death of the Rajah, Raghuji III, without an heir and one of Evans Bell's jobs was to liaise with the Rajah's widows, the Ranees, and some of the principal ladies of the harem, who had been allotted pensions by the British, which they considered inadequate. The feeling was understandably heightened by the decision of Lord Dalhousie that the personal property of the ruling Bhonslah family and their private treasure was now the property of the state of Nagpore. Since, he argued, the state had ceased to exist, he "conveyed" these riches to the British exchequer in Calcutta. Much heat was also generated by the fact that no provision had been made for the late Rajah's adopted son, Janojeeh - a youth who needed to marry and required some substance in order to be able to do so.

Evans was persuaded that the Ranees had a legitimate complaint and got his Commissioner, George Plowden, to visit the palace and formally promise the Ranees that he would apply to the Government for the grant of a title and stipend for Janojeeh. Plowden, however, though not particularly ill-intentioned was a slave to procrastination and did nothing to redeem his promise. Even when the Ranees, against popular opinion in Nagpore, came to the aid of the British at the time of the Indian Mutiny, (thus in the opinion of many preventing the spread of the insurrection to Southern India), Plowden could not stir himself to action. The Ranees naturally grew peeved and Evans, as the go-between, was the object of their annoyance. He had been pestering Plowden for some time to take action and he roped in his brother, George in London to print every detail of the case and lobby the Minister for India, Lord Derby. Now he took the extreme step of writing himself directly to the Government in Calcutta and letting Plowden see copies of his letters. Plowden still failed to react; he neither explained himself to the Government, nor forbade Evans to write to Calcutta. Evans, having got the bit between his teeth, poured in a stream of increasingly outspoken letters until, eventually, on July 27th, 1860, both Plowden and Evans Bell were dismissed, Plowden for manifest neglect of duty and Evans for "insubordination". An official told Evans that the volume of his correspondence had delayed action for at least a year, to which his response was "This is correct enough. I was doubtless very irritable and impatient."

Summoned to Calcutta, Evans was told in no uncertain terms by the Governor-General, Lord Canning, that his insubordination was intolerable, that he could not necessarily expect another appointment and that he had been treated very leniently. Canning was, piquantly, the son of the man who had helped Evans's grandfather when he was arrested on suspicion of treason, and he now softened the reprimand by adding that he understood Evans's frustration and by shaking hands with him when he took leave. Canning had decided to re-appoint Evans to a job in India and he soon took up a position as Deputy Commissioner of Police in Madras on January 3, 1861. He had the satisfaction of knowing that the authorities had officially described his conduct not only as insubordinate but also as "honest, fearless and unselfish", and that the Ranees and their followers had received all the benefits for which he had argued. His taking leave of them was accompanied by tears and prostrations and offers to load him with gold and jewels, which he doubtless refused. A dinner was given him at the palace and Janojee's father put on a lavish entertainment in his honour.

Evans had now got himself a cause and, after two years' police work, he retired from the Indian service on a small pension, and became a professional critic of British conduct in India. For this role he was perfectly qualified. As his obituarist in *The Statesman* explained:

> Stoicism was, we take it, the prevailing moral element in Major Bell's character, all through his life. He gave one the impression of a man who tolerated life rather than enjoyed it. A favourite saying of his, indicative of this habit of mind, and taken from the Persian poet Saadi, was - 'This too will pass'; and on one occasion when he was asked by some friends to give them a motto, he said, 'Never advise, never explain; never give your reasons, never complain'. Quite in accord with this stoicism of mind was his indifference to the things which the majority of men delight in. In his personal habits he was frugal even to asceticism. Seldom taking either meat or wine, weak milk and water was his chief beverage. He cared neither for sport nor games of any kind. His pleasures were exclusively intellectual - either reading or writing, and therefore it was that he acquired so complete and accurate a mastery over the complicated Indian subjects he took up. The distasteful labour, as it would have been to most men, to find their way through the colourless intricacies of blue-books and official reports was a positive pleasure to him."

Here was a man who, once he had got his teeth into you, was not going to let go. *The Statesman's* description may have been rather too bleak, however, because, although it is clear that Evans Bell had very little small talk, he was evidently quite "clubbable", being a frequent visitor to the National Liberal Club, and immensely courteous and unsnobbish. At any rate he became a pain in the neck to the authorities, inveighing against the policies of the former Governor-General, Lord Dalhousie, who took the view - and acted upon it - that annexation was usually of great benefit to the people annexed and always good for the annexer. Evans also championed the cause of individuals like the Maharajah of Holkar, who he believed had been traduced in connection with the Indian Mutiny and Duleep Singh, who had been detained in Britain. Duleep sent one of Evans's books, *The Annexation of the Punjab and the Maharajah Duleep Singh*, to Queen Victoria, whose private secretary, Lord Ponsonby, quoting another official, said: "Major Evans Bell is a professional agitator. He is a clever but entirely unscrupulous writer, & he has used his pen against us as a paid agent in every single annexation or settlement we have ever made." The Queen was rather partial to Duleep, but she certainly agreed with Dalhousie about annexation so Evans Bell's trenchant views will not have gone down well with her. Here is a sample of his style:

> Lord Dalhousie might have gained the hearts of the Princes and

people by a plain statement of what had been done, and what was intended to do in the Punjab. Instead of doing so, he violated treaties, abused a sacred trust, threw away the grandest opportunity ever offered to the British Government of planting solid and vital reform up to the Northern limits of India, and by an acquisition as unjust as it was imprudent, weakened our frontier, scattered our military strength, and entailed a heavy financial burden upon the Empire. That, I believe, will be the verdict of posterity and history."

Even the great Liberal statesman, John Bright, seems to have been a little nervous of Evans Bell's views. Writing to him when he was due to leave for an American tour in 1883, Bright said: "You are supposed to judge somewhat harshly of our Indian Government. In describing its course I do not doubt that you will give it credit where credit is due, and that you will point out how much the people of England are disposed, so far as they are concerned, to govern wisely the vast population conquered by their fathers." Evans would certainly have tried to do so. Whatever else he was, he was not unscrupulous. All the evidence is that he was particularly careful to stick to verifiable facts upon which to base his arguments. As to his being a paid agent, he accepted that not all his work had been unpaid, but he rejected the suggestion that an advocate being paid was enough to destroy the effect of his advocacy. He was an officer on half-pay with negligible private means, his work had been conscientiously done and he had never advocated a cause which he believed to be unjust, incapable of resolution or injurious to the Empire. As *The Statesman* put it, "Major Bell has made himself poor that he might make others rich."

For a wife he had chosen someone with absolutely complementary attributes to his own. Emily Ernst Magnus was the daughter of George Eugene Magnus, the Jewish proprietor of the Pimlico Enamelled Slate Works, who made billiard tables for, among others, the Prince Consort. She was an elocutionist, dramatic reciter and actress best known under her professional name of Mrs. Fairfax. They were married in 1865 and had two daughters. Of her a friend wrote: "She had all the brightness, ambition, and invincibility of her race. From her childhood she had a passion for the stage, where, with the great personal advantages of beauty and enthusiasm she possessed, had continuous opportunity befallen her, she would have excelled. As a teacher of elocution she more than excelled - she had inspiration." She seems to have shared Evans's love of liberty and sense of duty and their marriage was happy, though blighted by the death, of typhoid at the age of nine, of their elder daughter, Mynie. Emily was so devastated that it was said she never smiled again and she gave up all ambition to succeed on the stage. This further depleted the Bells' meagre income, but they remained generous in support of those still less fortunate. For example, when others shunned the Pre-Raphaelite painter, Simeon Solomon, who had been convicted of a homosexual offence in a public lavatory and was reduced to begging, the Bells continued to offer him safe haven. After Evans had died Emily recalled: "A tramp we had much befriended and visited in the work-house, one day being denied admittance, screamed out a volley of abuse. I said I should never have anything more to do with him, but Evans only said 'He is still more pitiable now, give him a shilling'."

That they inspired the love, admiration and affection of many Indians, was evidenced by the voluminous coverage in the Indian press when Evans died. *The Statesman* of Calcutta, for whom he had been a correspondent for many years, described him as India's greatest benefactor and ran an extensive three-part Memoir, the *Tribune* described his death as a national calamity and the *Indian Spectator* said he possessed a noble soul rising above the ordinary temptations. Hearing that, as a widow, Emily was in straitened circumstances, the Maharajah of Mysore, to general acclaim, granted her and the family an annuity of £180.

Shortly before his death a public meeting at the Westminster Palace Hotel adopted an address of thanks to Evans Bell for his eminent services to the princes and people of India. He was too ill to attend, but his brother George William, replying to the motion, told of an encounter he had with an official to whom he complained that his brother had been treated with obloquy. The reply was: "Well, you know, but he is so indiscreet. (Laughter) He attacks the Government and Government bodies, and you cannot expect any good to come out of that." George added: "But I will tell you something more. He is loyal to Britain. (Cheers). If you consider India is of value and should be kept, it will only be kept by carrying out his reforms. (Cheers). To a deputation which called upon him at home to present the address, Evans said: "I accept it gratefully as having a greater value in my eyes than any mark of official approval - as an expression of your appreciation of the objects to which I have devoted my life, as well as of the motives by which I have been actuated."

As Freethinkers, who did not believe in a church hierarchy, the Bells could nevertheless be buried with Mynie at Brompton - Evans on September 12th, 1887 and Emily on July 12th, 1893. At both ceremonies an address was given by George Jacob Holyoake, founder of the Secularist movement, who had once been imprisoned for denying the existence of God. He abjured any such controversy at the graveside, saying of Evans that he was true to his colleagues, true to his principles, true to the authority he served, true to the princes of India whom he defended and true to the people of India whose civil rights he advocated. Of Emily he declared that she was a worshipper of liberty, a friend of all who were wronged. "She believed that duty was the only good, reason the only torch, and love the only priest. She added to the sum of human welfare."

No wonder that their daughter, Ernestine, who married Dr. Herbert Mills, turned out to be a "New Dawn Woman," as described by her great niece, Irene Cockroft in her book of that title. Tina, as she was known, was a suffragette - her mother, after all, had signed the 1866 Suffrage petition to parliament - and a talented enamellist in the Arts & Craft movement. Her first teacher was Frederic Shields, whose Life she wrote and who was a friend of the Pre-Raphaelite poet and artist, Dante Gabriel Rossetti. Her daughter, Hermia Mills, became a Doctor in Kensington, where three generations of her family had lived.

Leonora Georgiana (1827-1914)

Leonora Georgiana, William and Elizabeth's fifth child, is reputed to have gone to the Crimea with Florence Nightingale. I have not been able to substantiate that, and Leonora is recorded as running, during the war, a home and school for the children of soldiers who were fighting in Russia, but the conflict lasted over two years, so she might have been able to do both things. The story must be given some credit as it was recorded by my father, who knew Leonora and her husband, William James Gillum (1827-1910). As a junior officer in The Royals, he lost a leg at Sebastopol in 1854-55 and the theory is that he was nursed by Leonora, with whom he fell in love. What is certain is that they were married in St Pancras in 1860. Gillum was a man of means and an amateur painter. Two years earlier he had become a founder member of the Hogarth Club, a short-lived organisation set up by the Pre-Raphaelites in opposition to the arts establishment. Here he got to know Dante Gabriel Rossetti, whom he commissioned to produce a series of watercolours, Ford Madox Brown, from whom he took lessons, and the architect and furniture-designer, Philip Webb, a friend of William Morris.

According to one authority, soon after his wedding William Gillum was walking past No 44 Euston Road which he noticed was an "Industrial Home for Destitute Boys". He went straight in, was shown round, joined the management committee and was so inspired that he went off and founded a supplementary institution. This makes his involvement seem much more accidental than it surely was and takes some liberties with the timing of events. After all, Gillum had just married the sister of the founder and presiding genius of the Boys' Home, George William Bell. Leonora must have had a hand in introducing him to the concept, but she must have done so long before the wedding because two years earlier, at about the time that the Euston Road Home was opened, William Gillum and some friends had bought a 48-acre section of the Trevor Park estate in East Barnet, which they converted into a farm for the training of destitute boys who had not been involved in crime. The Boys' Farm Home, or Church Farm Home, opened in 1862 with four boys and suffered many difficulties in the early years but by 1889 the complement was 88 boys between the ages of 10 and 16. The farm was no more financially successful than other farms (the same agricultural depression that hurt Rev. Henry Herbert at Hemingford Abbots took its toll), but a school-house was added in 1868, a new school-room in 1876 and a play-room in 1881. The initial outlay seems to have been down to William Gillum himself, but later a committee headed by the Bishop of St. Albans became the governing body. "The Colonel", as he was known, was appointed superintendent and treasurer, both posts honorary. The latter particularly was no sinecure as it cost £1,400 a year to run the farm. Leonora was heavily involved too. An admiring visitor paid tribute to her contribution:

> The influence of Mrs. Gillum is apparent in the manners the boys exhibit at all times; in their devotion to their teachers and masters, their affection for each other, their ministrations to those more destitute than themselves, and in the deep love expressed in letters from all parts of the world. In one respect this Farm Home is remarkable beyond all other Homes, and that is in the connection maintained with the lads after they go away. This part of the work is wholly the creation of Mrs. Gillum, and in order to foster it a printed sheet called 'A Flying Leaf from Church Farm,' is forwarded to every old boy once a year. This contains the names and addresses of every boy who has written, together with extracts from their letters, and short addresses from Colonel, or Mrs Gillum, Mr. Bowden, the master, and other officers. The 'Leaf' for December, 1886, contained the names and addresses of a hundred and twenty eight 'old boys' some in New Zealand, others in Australia, Queensland, Ontario, Quebec, River Darling, New South Wales, Egypt, Cyprus and Italy; while others were serving on board H.M. ships in various quarters of the world.

The regime was heavily practical. Boys were taught to darn, sew and make their own shirts, going on later to the tailor's bench or shoemaking (repairs for local people produced some useful income). Under the direction of a farm bailiff and two labourers, they worked hard at looking after the animals - cows, pigs and horses - gardening, labouring in the fields and dairy work, They were also taught cooking, sold their produce and kept the accounts. The day began at 5.30am with classes until breakfast at 7.45 am, followed by play until 9.00, then farm and school work until 1.00 pm lunch, more work from 2.00 pm to 5.00 pm. An hour of gymnastics, drill or band was followed by supper at 6.00 pm, more play, prayers at 8.00 pm and bed shortly before 9.00 pm. One of Her Majesty's Inspectors of Schools reported: "I seldom see so many intelligent boys in one school at any one time."

Amidst all this activity "the Colonel" stumped vigorously about on his wooden leg, inspiring everyone. Tall and soldierly, with white hair and long white beard, he was possessed of grey eyes which seemed able not only to take in everything going on, but also to read the characters of those with whom he conversed. He played chess with the boys and supervised cricket, football and the fife-and-drum band, welcomed returning pupils with their wives and children and was hero-worshipped by everyone. In true Victorian style, our visitor concluded that Colonel and Mrs Gillum's self-denial and Christian labours had been the means of improvement to almost all the boys that came under their care and established in East Barnet's pleasant hills one of the most successful training homes in the country.

Personally they were waited upon by the Colonel's batman, Mr. Richer, and his wife, Mrs.Richer, who was a great comfort to nephews and nieces when they came to stay. One of them, Maud Bell, recalled:

> Aunt Leonora firmly believed that they had very small appetites, which dear Mrs. Richer supplemented by secret suppers in bedrooms.....Aunt Leonora was small with a head of naturally frizzy hair smoothed to flatness in front with the aid of a horrible grease called Bandoline, and worn in a mass of tight curls at the back, done up, we all believed, with safety pins. Very interesting people stayed at East Barnet, but Aunt Leonora believed that children should be seen and not heard and we considered all the lions and lionesses most boring.

Though devoted to each other, the Gillums disagreed about many things, and the more they squabbled, the more affectionate their language became. Leonora would begin with "But my dear William," and progress to "dearest", "my dear heart" and "my dearest dear". When at family prayers Leonora prayed that they might be "amiable in every temper of their lives", one bright spark of a nephew said it meant getting more and more affectionate the more you squabbled.

The Gillums retained their contacts with the Pre-Raphaelities, some of whom took an interest in the farm, a poster for which appears in one of Ford Madox Brown's paintings, and a circular table, now at William Morris's house, Kelmscott Manor, is said to have been made by the boys at the Euston Road Home. Philip Webb designed a terrace of shops and workshops in Shoreditch for William Gillum and the house to which the Gillums moved to be near the farm in Barnet, the original drawings for which are preserved in the Victoria and Albert Museum. In their old age the Gillums moved to No 1 Pembridge Place, Kensington, and Philip Webb designed some interior alterations for them. The Colonel died in 1910 aged 83 and Leonora in 1914 aged 87.

Frederick Hayley(1832-1895)

When Leonora was running the home for soldiers' children in Hounslow, her younger brother Frederick Hayley Bell, was paid secretary of the Association for the relief of Soldiers' Wives and Children with their eldest brother, George William, fulfilling another of his numerous honorary tasks, as treasurer. Their father, though, seems to have felt that the East offered much and soon after the war, Frederick found himself despatched to Shanghai to work for a firm run by Jo Mackrill Smith, whose daughter he married, but he had no interest in money and went bankrupt in 1893. They had six children, one of whom, Francis Hayley Bell, was a romantic character. He explored Madagascar, Egypt, Ethiopia, Russia, was mauled by a tiger in Pakhoi, befriended the Dalai Lama and spoke seven different dialects of Chinese as well as Mandarin, Russian and other languages. He fought in the Boer War as a trooper in the Natal Carbineers and was eventually sent to the Formosan island of Amoy to "settle down". There he married the strikingly beautiful Agnes MacGowan and became the father of Mary Hayley Bell, the playwright and wife of the noted actor, Sir John Mills.

Her word portrait of her father, who called her "Muggins", is vivid:

> He was tall, thin as a Ghurka blade, with piercing dark blue eyes and a nose like Wellington's - which unfortunately he has handed down to all of us. A strong, complex man, spiritually proud, with the heart of a lion; sometimes *too* strong, and in his early years viewed with benevolent intolerance or amusement by many; though the friends he

had he kept always. Only my mother knew his private heart. To Francis Hayley Bell, love was the mainspring of his life; susceptible, he was ever in search of the ideal, and demanded and was dependent upon unstinting affection. He idealized those in whom he placed his affections, clothing them with the reflection of himself, often suffering the searing pains of disillusionment. Yet he never looked at himself for the cause of any failure, but blamed it elsewhere!........

My father's gay, towering personality reacted on all who came into contact with him. Passionate; emotional with a thundering temper; sometimes arrogant and self-indulgent; selfish on his own admittance; never amenable to censure from others; slightly ostentatious and grandiloquent at times, with a splendid rhetoric: 'I must know everything of something, Muggins, and something of everything.' His vitality was unbounded. His laughter filled the house, for he could and did laugh at himself continuously. Yet I have looked up into his face in church when he was singing, seen his lips trembling and the tears splashing down his cheeks, but if I dared to slip my hand into his, he would draw sharply away.

He made headlines in 1926 when, as Commissioner of Customs at Canton, he closed the port in order to safeguard the revenue. Armed pickets had removed a large consignment of goods and were refusing to return them for examination by customs. Francis discovered where they were holding the goods, went there and demanded their return. The pickets refused. Francis declared that he would remain until they complied. At noon the Commissioner's servant arrived to serve him lunch, he then settled down for the afternoon, but when the servant reappeared with dinner, the pickets told him he could remove the goods. His reply was that, as they had removed them, they must return them, which they eventually did.

Six years later, by now retired, he and Mary were involved in a harrowing bit of derring-do during the Sino-Japanese War. This is how *Time* magazine described it:

Lieut.-Colonel Francis Hayley Bell, retired, is British, indomitable. With his daughter, Lieut-Colonel Bell rushed into the smoking, crumbling ruins of 'No Man's Land' (the Chinese Chapei District) and in rushed Father Jacquinot with 13 nuns. Other good people offered their help. By heroic efforts, working against time (four hours) they evacuated scores of wounded men and women, piling them hastily into six motor ambulances.

Archibald Hamilton (1834-1864)

Archibald Hamilton Bell was also a military type, a Lieutenant in the Royal Artillery. He died at the young age of 30 but not before contributing to the family story by marrying Augusta Ramsbottom, who was descended from William IV and Mrs Jordan. She long outlived her husband, dying in 1919 at St. Ives, Huntingdonshire, where her son-in-law, Rev. Oscar Wade Wilde, husband of her daughter, Cecilia, was the Vicar. Archibald's son, Kenneth Frederick Hamilton Bell, a private in the 1st (City of London) Battalion, The London Regiment (Royal Fusiliers) from the Inns of Court Officers Training Company, was gazetted second lieutenant on April 9, 1915, rose to become a Lieutenant-Colonel and was awarded the D.S.O.

Archibald shared an interest in scientific subjects with his younger brother, Valentine Graeme Bell, who is dealt with separately.(See Chapter 18)

William Bell (1786-1873)

Elizabeth Bell (née Kinnear)
1799-1888

George W. Bell (1822-1910)

Col. William Gillum (1827-1910)

Major Evans Bell

Emily Ernst Bell with her two children, Mynie & Ernestine

Ernestine Mills (nee Bell) as a suffragette. Her husband, Dr. Herbert Mills in a top hat.

Mary Hayley Bell, Sir John Mills & family.

181

FROM EDINBURGH TO BLOOMSBURY

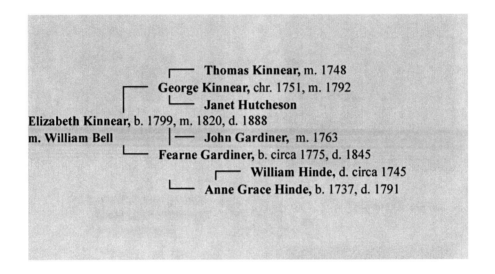

> For beautiful manners and courtesy and hospitality, as well as for real culture, give me those old Scots families – *Maud Anna Bell*.

Old Mrs Kinnear, née Fearne Gardiner, believed even after death that her family could not do without her. After she died in 1846 her ghost, clad in lavender silk with a lace shawl, was seen by many people at Cargilfield, the big house at Trinity, outside Edinburgh, where she lived in the early-19th century. So legendary was she that her great granddaughter, Maud Anna Bell, recording these sightings a century later, described her as an alarming person. Yet the attractive portrait of her by Henry Raeburn, which hangs in the Scottish National Gallery, shows a rather soncy lass with a beautiful complexion and a wistful look in her eye. You could take her for a milkmaid, were it not for the elegant, black lace shawl draped over her white gown that befitted the wife of a wealthy banker. The contrast is evident and is perhaps due to nothing more than the fact that the elderly can be terrifying to the eye of the young. The testimony of Fearne's grandson, George William Bell, is less grim. He used to go from London on visits to Cargilfield, taking a 36-hour boat trip rather than suffer the discomforts of the coach and he describes her as an exceedingly shrewd clever lady and a very kind one.

There is no doubt that she was grand. Her husband, George Kinnear was one of a numerous family of well-established bankers and her father, Dr. John Gardiner was President of the Royal College of Physicians in Edinburgh. He was therefore an eminent scientist, but he was better remembered in the family for taking a spoonful of crushed oyster shell daily for the sake of his digestion. Otherwise little is known of him, except that in old age he was blind.

Fearne had strong views. She married her daughters off young because she said Kinnears only loved once and she did not intend to have a lot of spinsters at home. In the 20 years between 1794 and 1814 she had 13 children herself, of whom five were daughters. There was, therefore, an enormous cousinhood, whose various doings became enshrined in the family history, recalled a century later by Maud in a letter to a newborn Bell baby. Marion Kinnear, the daughter of Fearne's son, John Gardiner Kinnear, married into the family of Sir Walter Scott – her husband was Robert Lockhart and when he died Marion moved to keep house for her brother, Alexander Smith Kinnear, who became Lord Kinnear as a result of a distinguished career in the law. As a Scots Lord of Appeal he preferred the commercial cases with which he had grown up and, if required to deal with a case of murder would be much put out. His butler at Fingask Castle would inform the family "His Lordship is a bit distressed" and they would all behave with the utmost decorum.

Another Fearne Kinnear, daughter of Fearne's son, James, belied the dictum that Kinnears only loved once. She fell for a young, impecunious naval officer, James Forbes, who returned her affection but, with nothing but his pay to look forward to, disappeared to the Far East, leaving her broken hearted. Some time later she went to stay with two elderly sisters, whose brother, a well-known poet and historian, Professor William Aytoun, had fairly recently become a widower. He took a fancy to Fearne and proposed to her after breakfast every day for a month. Eventually she succumbed and they were married, but Aytoun's health was failing and he died after about 18 months of a reportedly happy union. In the best traditions of romance Captain Forbes, meanwhile had been promoted and come into a fortune. He hurried home to propose to his one and only love and must have been put out to find her at Waverley Station clad in the blackest of black widow's weeds. All was well, however. They married and had seven children, and everyone was delighted except the sisters, who never forgave Fearne.

It was Elizabeth, the third of George and Fearne Kinnear's daughters, who, when she was not quite 21, married William Bell in front of her father's sideboard at Cargilfield. On the eve of the wedding William and Elizabeth signed a marriage contract which reflects the canny approach that had made George Kinnear a wealthy banker. He contributed £4,000 and William undertook to arrange for his wife to receive an annuity of £400 per annum payable in two tranches, at Whitsun and Martinmas, if he should pre-decease her. A sum of £6,000 would go to a single child of the marriage, but if there were more than one child £8,000 would be divided among them. Elizabeth would have the right to leave £2,000 to be paid by William to whoever she chose if she died first. Implementation of this pre-nuptial agreement, to which the bride's mother, Fearne, was also a party, would rest in the hands of any of a bevy of Kinnear relations, who might be alive at the time - David the bride's brother, who was also a banker, Isaac Nicholson, George's son-in-law, and the bride's four oldest brothers, Thomas, John Gardiner, George and David. Provision was also made for there being no children but in the event Elizabeth went one better than her mother and the marriage was blessed, as we have seen, with seven daughters and seven sons – a family of remarkable talent.

Raeburn's Portraits of Fearne Kinnear (c.1775-1845) and her father,
Dr. John Gardiner (Courtesy Scottish National Gallery)

Chapter 18

FROM THE ALPS TO CADIZ & SPANISH TOWN

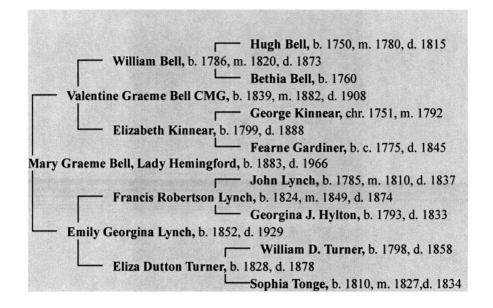

We have crossed, we have crossed, o'er the great Mont Cenis. - *Capt Tyler.*

William and Elizabeth's youngest son, Valentine Graeme Bell, was arguably the most successful of them, but his career was marked by severe ups and downs. He served an engineering apprenticeship with Messrs. Wren and Hopkinson, of Manchester, and later trained under the well-known entrepreneur, James (later Sir James) Brunlees. After a brief spell in 1861 on the Pembroke & Tenby Railway in South Wales, he became Brunlees's chief Assistant and from 1863 to 1865 was resident engineer on the Cleveland Railway in North Yorkshire. In June 1864 he married his cousin, Rebecca Dalzell Filson, daughter of Dr Alexander Bell Filson of Portaferry, Co. Down and of Jane Dalzell. Rebecca's grandmother Mary Filson (née Bell) was a sister of Valentine's grandfather, Hugh Bell.

The steep inclines Valentine encountered on the line between Stokesley and Battersby fitted him well for his next, and notable, job – resident engineer in charge of building the Mt. Cenis Railway which ran over the Alps between

France and Italy more or less due east of Grenoble. He and Rebecca were admirers of Garibaldi and named their daughter Anita, born in 1866, after Garibaldi's wife, so they must have been delighted to be going to Italy. The route of the railway, from St. Michel in Savoy to Susa in Piedmont, was challenging, following the path of an existing road, rising to a height of 6,828 feet at the frontier on the col of Mont Cenis and being subject for much of the way to avalanches and landslides, from the which the line had to be protected by covered ways built of timber and corrugated iron. Tunnels, embankments, and viaducts had also to be constructed to accommodate the more gradual curves of a railway. The locomotives used were of a revolutionary design by J. B. Fell, who used a centre rail gripped by two horizontal wheels to assist in braking. The technique was effective but was complicated when it came to the many level-crossings, which required a special means of raising and lowering the centre rail. The whole project, under the Chairmanship of the Duke of Sutherland, was also fraught with financial difficulties, having been launched in the midst of the 1866 economic slump. The shareholders, or at least those of them who were well-informed, were also aware that a tunnel was being drilled through the mountain which would, in time, render their railway redundant, but they hoped (in vain as it turned out) to have seven years of profitable operation before the tunnel came into use.

Valentine had assisted Brunlees in laying out the line and he was appointed resident engineer in 1866 when work began. There were inevitable dramas and setbacks. Unseasonably warm rain melted deeper than usual snow, causing flooding which, in the words of the surveyor sent to report on the damage, "rolled down the valley and carried all before it". A young Italian employed on the French side slipped into a crevasse in a glacier where his companions left him for dead, but a week later his father climbed down and found the young man still alive. There was a shortage of horses and fencing off the road from the railway was complicated by the need to blast holes in the solid rock for posts. The construction of the locomotives was required by French law to be done by French manufacturers and they fell behind. In the midst of all this Valentine undertook the construction of a temporary, and eventually a permanent, road between St. Jean de Maurienne and Lanslebourg, which had also been washed away in the flood. To cap it all Valentine suffered a personal tragedy in 1868 when Rebecca contracted scarlet fever and died, leaving him with two small children, Archibald Graeme, an infant, and Edith Jane Anita aged 2.

Despite all this, everything was more or less ready for the official opening though the train carrying about 50 people on the inaugural passage had to proceed slowly over the first few miles, where the track was unfinished. Brunlees himself was driving and Valentine was almost certainly among the passengers. His contribution to the spontaneous cheers when they reached the top were probably particularly heartfelt. *Dejeuner* was served at the summit and the train rattled at good speed into Susa in time for the consumption of "sundry bumpers in loyal and characteristic toasts". It was the first time a train had ever travelled from France to Italy. Captain Tyler, the surveyor, composed a song, which acknowledged Valentine's part in the great enterprise:

> The Alps have succumbed to the skill of Brunlees
> Six Thousand seven hundred feet mounted with ease.
> The engine of Fell in Italia you see
> We have crossed, we have crossed, o'er the great Mont Cenis....
>
> Sharp curves and steep gradients may add to the load,
> The snow and the ice may encumber the road,
> The precipice yawns, and mists hinder the sight,
> But with wheels on the central wheel safely we bite.
>
> The Alps have succumbed to the skill of Brunlees.
> Bell, Blake, Derbyshire, Baylis are now at their ease......

In truth the project, though doomed to a very short life by unexpectedly rapid progress on the tunnel, had made Valentine a considerable reputation. He was elected in 1869 a member of the Institute of Civil Engineers, was sent to Paris to design and supervise the construction of further locomotives, but escaped the siege of Paris in 1870, being despatched to examine and report on a projected new railway at Marseilles. This work, which was put on hold during the Franco-Prussian war, was interrupted for Valentine by a commission to go to the United States to visit and report on the East Eureka Mining Company's mine at Grass Valley, California, and other mines in Nevada and Utah – a pioneering journey in the 1860s.

Emboldened, he decided to go into practice in London as a civil engineer on his own. In 1872 he became joint consulting engineer to the Railway Company of the Old Port of Marseilles and chief engineer to the Cadiz Waterworks Company, an English venture to bring clean water to the Spanish port. He designed and supervised works for both of these, shuttling to and fro between the south of France and the Atlantic coast for the next three years. Cadiz had a high death rate because both the drainage and the water-supply were inadequate but, although there seems to have been nothing wrong with

Valentine's designs, the populace did not appreciate the benefits of clean water and the Company foundered. Unfortunately, whereas on Mt. Cenis Valentine was a mere employee and thus escaped any financial damage, in Cadiz he had been induced by the promoters to invest in the company and, when it failed with much consequent litigation, he lost a great deal of money. Nowadays you have to pay 70 euros to buy a £100 bond certificate for the Cadiz Waterworks on the internet, but in 1875 they were virtually worthless. In the words of his obituarist, "Although he had established his reputation in London as one of the ablest engineers of his day, these circumstances had their effect in reconciling him to give up his prospects at home and take up a career in Jamaica."

He was sent initially to Jamaica by the Colonial Office in 1880 to investigate the condition of the miserable 12-mile stretch of railway which had been built 35 years earlier between Kingston and Spanish Town. Confronted by a line in utter disrepair which was hardly safe to travel on, Valentine refurbished the track, extended it north to Ewarton and west to Porus and in three years had converted it into a railway that was regarded as a credit to the island. He very quickly fell for Emilie Georgina, the daughter of the Clerk to the Legislative Council, Francis Robertson Lynch, and on February 21,1882, they were married at St. Andrew's Church, Half Way Tree. He was 43 and she was rising 30, a large, talkative lady well-connected in Jamaican society, whose family, as we shall see in a later chapter, were worthy of note. Emilie's relationship with her husband was graphically described as follows:

> Very vivacious, very talkative, whereas he hardly ever opened his mouth, when somebody had slandered Bell for some quite unjustifiable reason, she went about entreating everybody to "raise the Negroes" against that person. She was a very lovable person, but also inclined to take "possession".

She and Valentine had three children. Mary Graeme, known as May, was born in 1883, Valentine Hylton in 1886 and Ethel Louisa ("Lu") in 1890. In later life Emilie was fondly remembered by her grandson for her appetite. He used to say that it was from her that the family inherited a hamster-like need to be fed every 20 minutes. She herself, to guard against any sudden pang of hunger, travelled invariably with two hard-boiled eggs and a pot of cream in her handbag, snacks of which modern dieticians would surely disapprove. In Kingston her fierce defence of her husband was soon to be required. Valentine's administrative record as Chief Engineer had so impressed the Governor, Sir Henry Norman, that he appointed him in 1886 to the Legislative

Council, which governed the island. But change was not long in coming. Writing to his brother George in January 1889 about money matters and expenses for his older children, Edith and Archie, who were then in England, Valentine added by way of postscript that a new Governor, Sir Henry Blake, was due shortly, adding: "The reports here have been that he and Lady Blake are very grand & stuck up & try to do things in viceregal style. We are not accustomed to that here: the Normans were very unpretentious & hated all pomp & ceremony."

However, Sir Henry Blake proved popular in the colony and had his term of office twice extended by popular demand. To begin with the Blakes and the Bells got on well, but, after Valentine, as a favour to the Governor, had taken on the duties of Inspector of Railways in addition to those of Director of Public Works, the two men got into a wrangle over the detailed arrangements. Valentine maintained that he ought to be paid for doing two jobs at once and that a deputy inspector of railways should be appointed. Sir Henry disagreed. Valentine then said he thought he should resign as Inspector of Railways. Sir Henry claimed that he could not do that without surrendering both jobs; he agreed, however, to refer the matter to London. Nine months later Valentine discovered that the matter had not been referred and was told that the Attorney General in Jamaica had confirmed that he could indeed resign one job without the other. This victory turned out to be pyrrhic because Sir Henry then appointed a friend, P.A. Fraser to be Inspector of Railways and Fraser found fault with Valentine's work. Describing what had happened, Valentine wrote to his brother George asking him to intervene with Lord Ripon, the Colonial Secretary, with whom George had been acquainted in the past:

> From the end of July until December Mr. Fraser was sending in reports to the Governor finding fault with the two sections of the Railway which had been taken over by me, & in fact charging me with having acted wrongfully. The Governor accepted all he said as Gospel, never consulted me on the various points, & although we lived for six months in the hills within a mile of each other on terms of intimacy, constant communications taking place between the two houses, he never spoke to me on the subject.

> Finally, he wrote me a private letter saying he felt it his painful duty to have an enquiry into my conduct. I replied saying he was acting on very insufficient grounds & that a little delay & further enquiry would satisfy him that there were no grounds for the enquiry. Thereupon he summoned a Privy Council, without summoning me, either as a member or as the person implicated, & next day appoints this Commission to make an enquiry in public.

190

Valentine was sure that the Commission would exculpate him, but he was nervous that it would try to gloss things over to ease the Governor's feelings and let Fraser off as lightly as possible. He wanted to be sure that Lord Ripon understood the background. His expectation was proved more or less correct, the verdict being in favour of Valentine, except that it criticised him for not communicating more fully with the Governor. As a result, perhaps, the report was not made public, though the island's leading newspaper, *The Gleaner*, reported in January, 1894, "it is generally known that Mr. Bell was completely exonerated from the charges brought against him." Fraser, it added, had not returned from England where he went on leave of absence.

Blake's handling of the case was, indeed, odd. Once the Commission had reported, he wrote, in February, 1893, to the Colonial Office saying he no longer had confidence in Valentine and asking for Lord Ripon's support in asking him to resign and, if Valentine declined, to bring him before the Privy Council with a view to his suspension. He added: "It is my duty to tell your Lordship that the course that I propose will be followed by considerable ill feeling, as Mr Bell has married a Jamaican lady who is widely connected." Ripon's advisers took a gloomy view of the Governor's approach. One wrote in the margin:

> It is quite clear that Mr Bell has failed to protect the Government as he might have done. But the report of the Commission seems to me to have a great tendency towards whitewashing Mr Bell and it implies that he has, in departing from his legal obligations, procured the Government a better line than was expected. This is awkward. Further it is indubitable that proceedings against Mr. Bell will be most unpopular.

The view in London was that it would be much better if the Governor were to take responsibility and then ask for support. Ripon told Blake, by telegram: "I approve of proceeding as proposed; but in the event of the council suspending Mr. Bell I must reserve to myself full power to decide whether I will confirm." The words "Mr. Bell" were sent in cypher.

The issue was ludicrously arcane. It turned on whether Valentine had passed as satisfactory 14-foot railway embankments when the specification given the American construction company had been for 16-foot embankments. Valentine claimed that, if the measurements taken from the middle of the rail were seven feet on one side, he had insisted on 9 feet the other side, making 16 in all. The only concession he was prepared to make was to accept that some engineers might require 8 feet on both sides and that there may have been some misunderstanding. Inconveniently for the

Governor and Mr. Fraser, most of the experts brought in to adjudicate seemed to agree with Valentine. Pages and pages of reports with Valentine's comments and Fraser's comments on Valentine's comments and Valentine's comments on Fraser's comments are to be found in the public records at Kew. Although Valentine was not named, the issue was raised in the House of Commons when the Under-Secretary of State for the Colonies, answering a question, stated "The officer who has been impugned has appealed to the Secretary of State; but no action will be taken on his appeal pending a further inquiry by an expert whom the Secretary of State is sending out from England." Valentine addressed a lengthy memorial to Ripon complaining that although the Commission's report relieved him of all moral blame, it did so in such grudging terms that he must ask the Secretary of State to review all the evidence and to express his disapproval of the Report. In the end the long-suffering Lord Ripon wrote a minute: "I am prepared to accept Sir George Berkeley's opinion and to relieve Mr. Bell from all censure except that involved in the passage in the report which I have marked. That amount of censure is, I think, deserved." The passage marked said that though Mr. Bell had taken at least the usual amount of care, "nevertheless in my opinion it would have been more judicious....... if he had reported difficulties to the Governor or other proper authority."

Valentine had told George that so long as Blake remained Governor, life would be awkward, but he continued in post for the remaining four years of Blake's tenure and beyond. Relations seem to have been at least proper and when Valentine died years later and reference was made to friction with Blake, the former Governor wrote to *The Times* from his home in Ireland:

> May I say that there was no personal friction; simply a difference of opinion as to the discretion allowed to the Director of Public Works under the terms of the agreement made with the American syndicate which had undertaken the railway construction to Montego Bay? As Governor I interpreted the agreement very strictly and literally, and intimated my disapproval of a departure from its terms without previous approval of the Legislature, by consent of the Director of Public Works who, as a railway engineer of great experience, was satisfied that his consent to the divergence from the letter of the contract was justifiable and expedient. But at no time did I regard Mr. Bell as other than a perfectly upright and honourable gentleman, nor did the episode affect a personal friendship that was, I believe, as sincere on his part as on mine. From no official in the colony did I receive more constant and valuable support in the legislative and other work of the island, and I have never varied in my high estimate

of his character and ability.

There is no evidence that Valentine saw it like that. At any rate his reputation survived and in 27 years he left a very tangible mark in Jamaica, having by the time of his retirement, built 110 bridges and added 1,166 miles of road to the 801 which existed when he arrived. In 1903 he was decorated with the order of Commander of the Order of St. Michael & St. George (C.M.G.). But fate had one more blow to deal him.

On the morning of January 14, 1907 Jamaica was struck by a fearful earthquake. Within half a minute Kingston, a town of 46,000, was wrecked and hundreds of people lay dead. Brick walls bulged and collapsed, carriages were flung through the air, telegraph poles swayed like leaves in the wind and huge structures, whether of iron, wood or stone, crumbled into rubble. People were tossed about like puppets and those who managed to get out onto the streets were enveloped in a thick yellow fog of dust. Then fire broke out and burnt for four days, completing the devastation. The damage was assessed at over £2m and over 800 people died. The insanitary conditions gave cause for huge concern, but it was considered a mercy that little rain fell in the next few months on the many who were living in the open air. However, it was an opportunity to build a new, better-designed capital, and once the immediate clearing up was done, Valentine began the job, but the stress and the insanitary conditions had taken their toll and, though advised by his doctors that he ought to rest, he insisted on going to work. Then things got better and the doctors thought they may have been mistaken and, when in April, 1908, he retired there was universal pleasure at the prospect of his enjoying a long retirement. The Legislative Council passed a resolution, whose proposer said that, after a great many fights, always for what he considered right, Mr Bell was going from among them, and they were now about to bid goodbye to a comrade who had fought against them and with them: and therefore it became them to give him a valedictory address. Many members joined in the eulogy, Valentine gave a modest reply and the *Daily Gleaner* devoted almost a column to its own praise:

> Railway and buildings, tracks, tunnels, great highways and splendid bridges – all stand as a memorial to his energy and skill and he will be remembered by them. He has made mistakes – no one need be afraid to say that....but what other British tropical colony has a finer systems of roads and bridges than we have today, the difference in financial conditions being allowed for?

Two days later his own departmental colleagues presented him with a purse and a lengthy address, singling out his ground-breaking use of arched concrete in the construction of bridges, which had been recognised far beyond the shores of Jamaica. So, after 22 years at the head of his department Valentine sailed off into the sunset feeling, as he said in reply, that his life in Jamaica had been on the whole a useful one – and promising to come back to show them what he had bought with their kind gift.

He never managed it. Within two months he was dead – of a bowel complaint said to have been brought on by the atrocious aftermath of the earthquake. He had the satisfaction of knowing that his son, Archie, had been appointed Director of Public Works in another West Indian Island – Trinidad, in which job he was also in due course to be honoured with the C.M.G.

Before he died Valentine knew three of his eventual five grandchildren – Archie's daughter Margaret and May's two oldest sons, Dennis George Ruddock and Valentine Henry Okes – and he was spared the knowledge that his other son, Valentine Hylton Graeme Bell, suffered a severe attack of sunstroke in Los Angeles, which sent him out of his mind so that he spent the rest of his life in an asylum. He too had been an engineer - in Los Angeles. He eventually died in 1962, by which time his wife, Beatrice, had divorced him and married Robert M. Shipley, though she kept in touch with her first husband's family. Valentine's two other daughters remained unmarried. Edith Jane Anita had intellectual interests and what were known as "advanced views", which presumably unfitted her for matrimony. She was friendly with Ramsey Macdonald's family. The youngest girl, Ethel, known as Lu, lost her fiancé in the First War. She inherited the beautiful golden red hair and porcelain complexion, which had come into the family via her grandmother, Eliza Turner. For many years, after her mother died, she made her home in Sèvres, in France, and later at Tenterden, Kent, with her cousins Muriel and Gladys Hylton-Hylton.

Valentine Graeme Bell (1839-1908)

Emilie Bell (née Lynch) 1852-1929

Left: The Bells at a Fancy Dress Party, Jamaica, January, 1891.

Emilie, Countess of Argyle;

Valentine, Civil Service;

Valentine Jr. Little Jack Horner;

May, Titania.

Chapter 19

FROM GALWAY TO THE RIO COBRE, HAMBURG TO HAITI & BOMBAY TO THE SEYCHELLES

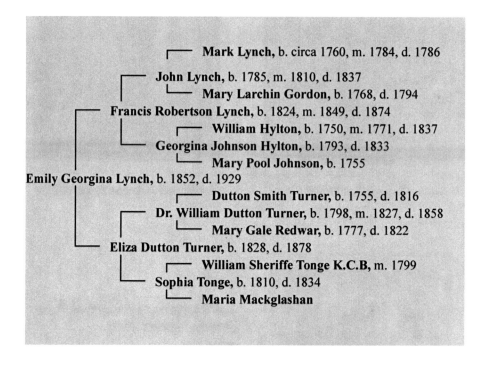

Mark Lynch, b. circa 1760, m. 1784, d. 1786
John Lynch, b. 1785, m. 1810, d. 1837
Mary Larchin Gordon, b. 1768, d. 1794
Francis Robertson Lynch, b. 1824, m. 1849, d. 1874
William Hylton, b. 1750, m. 1771, d. 1837
Georgina Johnson Hylton, b. 1793, d. 1833
Mary Pool Johnson, b. 1755
Emily Georgina Lynch, b. 1852, d. 1929
Dutton Smith Turner, b. 1755, d. 1816
Dr. William Dutton Turner, b. 1798, m. 1827, d. 1858
Mary Gale Redwar, b. 1777, d. 1822
Eliza Dutton Turner, b. 1828, d. 1878
William Sheriffe Tonge K.C.B, m. 1799
Sophia Tonge, b. 1810, d. 1834
Maria Mackglashan

It seems as if the Lynches liked to live in faraway exotic places.
They all seem to have a quixotic streak - *Renée Hays*

Mark Lynch was, in October, 1786, a bright young Irish lawyer, a Master in Chancery, on the staff of Governor Campbell in Spanish Town. He had made a good marriage two years earlier to Mary Larchin Gordon, whose Scottish parents were cousins belonging to prominent landowning families in Clarendon Parish; he had a young son of one and Mary was expecting another child in four months' time. The future must have looked bright, but Mark did not always keep wise company among the hard-drinking, hard-gambling community on the island and was inclined to be a bit wild. At dinner one evening he made a foolish bet that he could ride his horse at full gallop across a rocky and precipitous stretch of the Rio Cobre, which flows down from the central massif of the island into the Caribbean at Kingston Bay. He stood to win £100, which was a substantial sum in those days, if he could do it, but the odds were ridiculously against him. Whether he told Mary about it when he got home we do not know, but sure enough, the next day he fell from his horse, broke his neck and was killed.

The young widow, who was only 18, once she had given birth to her son, Larchin, in the following February, decided to make her home in England with the two boys. She settled in Wimpole St. in London and in January 1794 she married again at St. George's Hanover Square. Her husband was Colonel Henry William Brooke, an official at the War Office with a house on the Isle of Thanet in Kent. It was a happy occasion after seven years of widowhood, but the marriage was tragically short and before the year was out, on December 30, 1794, she died at the birth of another son. She lies buried at St. Mary's Church, Swansea, but why she should have been there at the time is unknown. Her sons by Mark Lynch, John and Larchin, were nine and seven respectively and were brought up by their step-father with his own baby son, Gordon, who however also died when he was only nine. The young Lynches grew up to inherit land in Jamaica and, after a legal training, went back to the island, where John became a partner in the firm of Munro, Bullock & Lynch of Kingston and Spanish Town. He married Georgina Johnson Hylton, the daughter of a much-respected sugar planter, William Hylton and his wife Mary (née Johnson) and they raised a large family of nine sons and four daughters.

Of these Francis Robertson Lynch, who was born in London in 1824, was the ninth child in the family and became, like his father, a lawyer. As a young man he fell in love with his cousin, Charlotte Frances Hylton, the daughter of his mother's younger brother, Samuel Barrett Hylton, but the family would not sanction such a relationship and Francis had, after much distress, to give her up. Later, when he was 25, he married Eliza Turner, a beautiful red-headed Scottish girl, and they had seven children, but the story had a sad ending. Soon after the wedding in 1849, it is said that a "friend" told Eliza that Francis had married her not for love but on the rebound. Eliza was shocked to the core, did not talk to Francis about it, but became withdrawn and morose, with the result that the marriage was unhappy and Eliza spent long periods in Europe, leaving the hard-working Francis to earn enough money to finance her shopping and school fees for the children. The strength of this story is difficult to assess. Eliza was undoubtedly rather eccentric and left most of what would come to be regarded as essential motherly duties to her nannies, while she carried on with her singing and studying - activities which were probably regarded as a bit odd in mid-nineteenth century Spanish Town. By contrast Francis was warm-hearted and much-liked. However, the picture is filtered mainly through the daughters of the family, who saw rather little of their father and thus were inclined to idolise him and regard him as hard done by, whereas dealing with their mother was a day-to-day matter.

The eldest girl, Sophia Caroline Lucille (b. 1849) made a big social splash in Jamaica when she married Edward Henry Howard, the Captain of *H.M.S. Raccoon*, whose aristocratic connections made it the wedding of the season. It should have been a fair wind all the way, but the marriage was tinged with tragedy. One of twin sons died in infancy and the son and heir, Midshipman Edward John Howard, was killed at the age of 22 in an accident at Vadsö in Norway when he fell from the futtock rigging of his vessel. Poor Sophia, for all her grace and beauty, never recovered from that disaster and became overprotective of her remaining children, who never married and lived genteelly together in Bexhill in an old rambling house, where they nursed stroke victims. Sophia, whose nickname was Totie, was, however, a keen family historian and was responsible for much of the detail in the notebooks kept by her great-niece, May Graeme Bell.

The next daughter, Nora, was unlucky in love. She rejected her first fiancé and her second died just before the wedding. She mismanaged her money, travelled a great deal and had a chip on her shoulder, but she was responsible for her niece, May, meeting Dennis Henry Herbert, because she used to rent a house in Hemingford Abbots to which she invited May in the school holidays.

Louisa Marianne Steventon married into the Bravos, a prosperous family of Spanish Jews, who had achieved prominence in Jamaica through Alexandre (1797-1868), a successful politician. Though he owned about 1,000 slaves, he was the leading advocate of emancipation in the island and held a number of important posts, culminating in Receiver General in 1867, a year before he died. With her husband, Stephen John Bravo, Louisa went to Australia, where they lost a lot of money, and later to Paris, where their two daughters, Muriel and Gladys, ran continental tours for Americans and Australians. In the face of Nazism, the girls adopted their grandmother's surname of Hylton , but had to flee Paris before World War II, moving to a house in Tenterden, Kent, which they shared in respectable indigence with their cousin, Ethel Graeme Bell.

There were two sons William, who became an American citizen with a rich but expensive wife, and Francis George Mackinnon, an engaging character who played one first-class cricket match as a wicketkeeper (two stumpings and innings of 0 and 6) for the Born in Jamaica XI in 1895. In 1902, when he was a Clerk in the Postal Service, a warrant was issued for his arrest on a charge of embezzlement, but before it could be served he had decamped on a ship bound for Port Lemon, Costa Rica. His fate is one of those loose ends of which family historians always have a few. Before his marriage to Maud Isaacs in 1885 his sister, Emilie Georgina looked after him in the family home. The father of this diverse brood, Francis Robertson Lynch, had a legal training and was a successful civil servant and politician, whose career covered that turbulent period of Jamaican history when, after the abolition of slavery, the island experienced hard times, revolution and political and constitutional uncertainty. Matters were complicated by the fact that an insurance company, into which he had put a lot of money in life assurance premiums, collapsed leaving the family impoverished and leading to his early death on December 9, 1874 from renal failure brought on by overwork.

Two extraordinary developments occurred as a result. First Eliza became almost completely reclusive. She took to spending all day in a kind of bath, hewn from the enormous trunk of a cedar tree, where she sat, writing and complaining of her fate. Secondly, an extraordinary deal regarding the future of the Lynch's youngest daughter, Ella, was carried into effect. Realising that they were short of money, a German family friend, Ernst Carl Corty, offered to be responsible for the cost of bringing up Ella on the understanding that, when she was 17 she would become his wife. Precisely when this remarkable arrangement was agreed, and therefore whether Francis was a party to it before his death, is not clear, but the impression left is that it was Eliza who agreed it. Ella grew up believing, rightly or wrongly but understandably, that her mother disliked her. She was certainly not fond of Eliza, but as one of the main witnesses on the subject of her parents' marriage got her information from Ella, it is necessary to exercise a little scepticism. At any rate, two years after Francis died, when Ella was 16, she was sent over to Hamburg to stay with her prospective mother-in-law and a year later the marriage took place in Lewisham. It was conducted by Robert B. Lynch, Francis's younger brother, who was Vicar of Lilbourne, Northants, and among the witnesses were several other members of the wider family.

Ernst Corty was a difficult man. He fell out with his two British business partners, who defrauded him of a large sum of money and then set up separately without him, and he was not an easy husband. He made excessive demands on his young bride who was a sexual innocent, and after she had borne him 11 children, several of them stillborn, she finally jibbed when he proposed a round dozen. Only four grew to adulthood and three of them were said to have given her nothing but trouble. Embittered by his business failure, Ernst decamped with Ella to the backwoods of Haiti, where they had steel shutters on the windows to deflect the gunfire produced by successive revolutions. They re-emerged eventually in New York, where Ernst abandoned her to hunt butterflies and beetles in South America. When eventually he sent her a telegram instructing her to purchase a menagerie of animals and go off to Colombia, where he planned to start a farm on the Alto Piano, she replied "Definitely not". This offended Ernst, who stayed away for five years and, on his return, finding that Ella had made ends meet by taking a job with a firm of tailors, flew into a rage. Apparently he would have preferred her to borrow money rather than sully her hands with work. In the home, however, he expected her to do everything. When she bought a Christmas pudding and he found that she had not made it herself, he shouted "Take it away, take it away!" and he gave away a dining room suite which Ella had bought with her own hard-earned money. On arrival home in the evening, he would clap his hands and require all members of the household, from his wife to the youngest servant, to line up before him in the entrance hall. He did once send Ella a present from Colombia. It consisted of a box of ostrich feathers which were just then in high fashion for ladies hats, but Queen Victoria knocked the bottom out of the market by declaring that she was against the killing of the lovely birds. His end was just as bizarre. Back in Jamaica in 1900, he went to the window to observe a thunderstorm. Suddenly he clutched his heart, said "God have mercy on me", and fell down dead.

These exotic details come mostly from a series of letters written much later by Ella's daughter-in-law, Aline Johanna Hofer (1892-1975), the German-born wife of Ella's second surviving son, Luis, whose own life was nearly as remarkable as those of his father and of his siblings. Ella took the family to Germany when Ernst died and set up house in Darmstadt, but the elder boy, Basil Francis (c.1894-1932) never settled there and, as soon as he could, sailed for Mexico and later Honduras, where he became a bank manager in the capital, Tegucicalpa. One day a customer he did not know applied for a loan, which Basil refused him. In the resulting argument Basil took offence and challenged his opponent to a duel. As his daughter described it later:

> The duel (the only one known to have taken place since colonial days) took place on a small island in the middle of the big river that crossed the town. It was all done properly, with pistols & witnesses – the only problem was that the opponent was a military man, a pistol

expert, while my father was a poor shot. He was shot in the abdomen
& had his right hand badly hurt.

The sequel was happier. A kindly lady, whose German husband Herr
Hartling, was a music teacher and author of Honduras's national anthem, took
pity on the young Englishman dying of peritonitis in the hospital where she
did charitable work, and helped nurse him back to health. The consequent
friendship resulted in the marriage of Basil to Enriquetta, his rescuer's
daughter. His relations were astonished that someone who affected to dislike
Germans as much as Basil, had ended up marrying a German girl and the
marriage did end in divorce, though whether the bride's nationality had
anything to do with it is not known. However, Basil and his assailant were
eventually reconciled and the island where they had fought came to be known
as "Corty's Island". Basil went to New Orleans in 1923 and eventually to
Chicago, where in 1932 he shot himself, leaving a sufficient sum to pay for
the education of his daughter. According to Aline, he had told his mother
years before that he would end his life once he had accumulated the necessary
fees. She had made him promise never to fight against Germany, which she
much regretted later, fearing that it may have somehow influenced his suicide.
Aline was told that, though she was mercifully unaware of it, he hated his
mother and even indulged in far-fetched speculation that he may have been
trying to hurt her as she had become a Roman Catholic in youth and would
therefore see suicide as meriting "eternal damnation". There were two Corty
daughters, Freda (b.1877) and Maria, of whom little is recorded, in one case,
at least, because even Aline, with her zest for scandal, could not bring herself
to write about it. This was because Freda, who had become a nun, much
against her mother's advice, then ran away and married a coloured man. She
was thereupon written out of the family's history and nothing more is known
of her. Maria married a man called Jansen and had two children.

Luis, Ella's younger boy, was too young to escape Germany before the
First World War and was conscripted into the German army when he was just
17. He declined to try for a commission and became a corporal in a heavy
machine gun unit on the Eastern front, where he was slightly wounded but
more seriously caught a heavy attack of dysentery in Rumania, where the
troops were living mainly on plums. Miraculously he recovered sufficiently to
be transferred to the Western front, but at the end of the war was again in
hospital. For some years he drifted until, in 1925, with the benefit of his
knowledge of English, he got a clerkship at the Behring-Werke, a Serum
Institute at Marburg-an-der-Lahn. There he met Aline who, having been head
nurse at a Red Cross hospital in charge of 120 seriously wounded patients

during the war, was now librarian. Though she was seven years older than he, they married in 1927. A year later Luis was sent to India, but it was another year before Aline could join him. The marriage was happy, though the presence of Ella living with them from the start made it difficult, especially as she conceived an intense dislike of Aline. As an Englishwoman, Ella had suffered in Germany in the war, though she was allowed to have paying guests, and both she and Luis lost all their money in the galloping inflation afterwards. As she looked back over her long life before she died at the age of 89, she must have wondered why fate had dealt her such a difficult hand. For fortitude and resilience she would be hard to beat.

Luis himself fell ill and suffered much, but the Swiss pharmaceutical firm, Gebrüder Volkart, which he had joined in India, were generous to him and to Aline, to whom they sent 5,000 Swiss francs when they heard that she was seriously ill. By then she was living in the Seychelles, where they had gone when Luis retired and it was there, soon after writing my father a long letter about the history of the family, she died on February 18th, 1975, and was buried at sea. We owe her much for recording an extraordinary story in such vivid detail.

John Lynch (1785-1837)

Georgina Johnson Lynch (née Hylton)
(1793-1833)

Francis Robertson Lynch (1824-1874)

Chapter 20

FROM INVERNESS TO DARIEN AND FARENOUGH

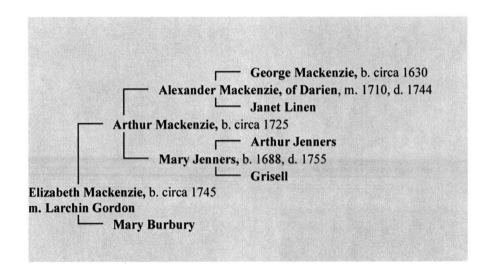

George Mackenzie, b. circa 1630
Alexander Mackenzie, of Darien, m. 1710, d. 1744
Janet Linen
Arthur Mackenzie, b. circa 1725
Arthur Jenners
Mary Jenners, b. 1688, d. 1755
Grisell
Elizabeth Mackenzie, b. circa 1745
m. Larchin Gordon
Mary Burbury

I struck the board, and cried,"No more;
I will abroad." - *George Herbert*

Among the great disasters of Scottish history, the attempt in 1698 to found a colony at Darien ranks high. Twelve hundred men set out in five ships, established themselves at what is now Panama, were ravaged by disease, blockaded by the Spanish with the connivance of the English, who did nothing to encourage this exercise in Scottish colonialism, and finally, after desperate privation, disease, extreme incompetence and internal disputes, dispersed, leaving nothing but a few temporary buildings behind them. Only 36 eventually returned to Scotland and among them were Alexander Mackenzie and a kinsman from the Gordon clan.

Two hundred years later, on May 4, 1898, their fifteen-year-old descendant, Mary Graeme Bell, sat down to record in a thin notebook the details of her family.

> The Gordons & Mackenzies were cousins. Gordon of Auchendolly and Mackenzie of Ord, Inverness. These families were staunch

adherents of the Stuarts and in the rebellion of 1740 joined with other Jacobite gentlemen, for which they would have lost their heads as well as their possessions had they not been lucky enough to have younger brothers who were in the Duke of Cumberland's Hanoverian Regiment, and who took over the estates of their elder brothers. Consequently the younger branch of the family are now in possession of the old family properties in Scotland with a large sum of money. They were abroad with their families and bought land in the Isthmus of Darien. Not finding the land prosper there they sold it and went to Jamaica, W.I. where they bought a great part of Clarendon and settled. These cousins seem to have intermarried a great deal and the Mackenzies in Jamaica have quite died; the Gordons also in the legitimate white male line though there are several through the female white legitimate descendants like ourselves.

May was working on information supplied by her Lynch aunts, primarily Aunt Totie Howard, whose capacity for euphemism crops up from time to time in the notes but nowhere more egregiously than in this description of the Darien venture. The date 1740 is presumably a mishearing of 1714, and there is confusion about which Jacobite rebellion was involved, but the essential facts are there, as confirmed by subsequent research, although Aunt Totie, like many others was clearly defeated by the intermarriages of the clans. What she was quite clear about was the racial purity of her Gordon ancestors – a point which she must have felt it was particularly necessary to make because she and May were writing only a generation after the great Jamaican rebellion, led by the mixed-race George W. Gordon, had been brutally suppressed by Governor Eyre.

The descent of the Mackenzies of Ord is well-documented and need not be elaborated here except to say that it is from the Lords of Kintail and Earls of Seaforth. The Gordons of Auchendolly, at least in so far as our family is concerned are less easy to track down. What we know about the Mackenzies is that John Mackenzie, of Ord, co. Ross, was the father of George Mackenzie, who married Janet Linen. Their son Alexander, born in Scotland in 1663, took an active part in the Darien expedition, survived to return to Scotland and subsequently settled in Jamaica. In 1703 he was, somewhat mysteriously made a Baronet on the same day as two other Mackenzies – Mackenzie of Scatwell and Mackenzie of Gairloch. No patent exists for Alexander's baronetcy and it is not registered in either the *Great Seal Register* or the *Registrum Preceptorum cartarum pro Baronettis Novae Scotiae*. The remainder was said to be "haeredibus quibuscumque", meaning that it could be inherited other than through the direct male line. Alexander's descendants do not seem to have been particularly keen on the title, but it was successfully assumed between 1900 and 1904 by Sir James Dixon Mackenzie, of Findon, co Ross, who was an acute genealogist and made a particular study of the Mackenzies.

Anyway Alexander, having got back to Scotland from Darien and having avoided being ruined by his Jacobite tendencies thanks to the precaution of installing some of his siblings in the anti-Jacobite army of "the Damnable Duke of Cumberland", decided to cross the Atlantic yet again. In Jamaica he finally settled down for good in Clarendon parish, where, perhaps unsurprisingly, he called his estate Farenough. There he married Mary Jenners and *pace* the record books which record one son and heir only, they produced two sons, George, the next Baronet, and Arthur. It was the eldest of Arthur's three daughters, Elizabeth, who on April 15, 1762, married her cousin Larchin Gordon, and became the mother of the unfortunate Mary Larchin Lynch, who was widowed by her husband's rash bet.

Chapter 21

FROM SOUTH SHIELDS TO NEW YORK & CHATEAU PEN, JAMAICA

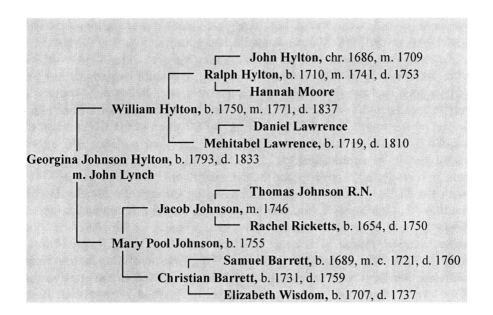

Hilton's line dishonoured falls;
Your course of crime the soul appals;
Your strong walls shall broken lie;
From their deep holes the owlet cry;
Ghosts and harpies walk your grounds,
Making dismal cries and sounds.
- The Cauld Lad of Hilton

In 1788 William Hylton, while on a trip to England from America, decided to pay a visit to Hylton Castle in County Durham to see, out of curiosity, the home of his ancestors. During the visit he and a lawyer friend from Newcastle came upon the 1640 will of Henry Hilton, which convinced him that he and his father had been done out of their inheritance and were the rightful heirs to the castle and to the so-called Barony of Hylton. This soon became an obsession and William spent the next 59 years trying to establish the claim. We have much to thank him for – it must be his genes which led to a strong interest in genealogy in May Graeme Bell's family – but he exemplified the danger that family historians, like golfers, can overdo it; he became a crashing bore on the subject and expected everyone else to be as interested in his claim as he was. When he was 83, for example, he wrote his grandson a long letter upbraiding him for being indifferent and silent on the subject.

The Hyltons were a rum lot, exceptionally martial, inclined to be short-tempered, gloomy and violent, but Henry, who was known variously as The Mad Baron or the Pious Baron, depending on your outlook, was the rummest of them all. He had been married off at a young age, but did not live with his wife, preferring to double up with his cousin, Nathaniel, who was Vicar of Billingshurst in Sussex, and later moved in with Lady Shelley at Michelgrove near Petworth. In his will he was insistent that he had no heirs of his body and he tied up his wealth by leaving it in trust for 99 years to the Corporation of London so that they could make gifts to 38 specified parishes and install young people in apprenticeships. The effectively ruined the family, which sank into respectable poverty and in the senior male line died out in 1746, when the castle and the Barony were passed on through the female line on condition that the name Hylton was adopted. But the Mad Baron had an uncle, Henry Hylton, of South Shields, who was a Captain in the States Service under Maurice, Prince of Orange, and our William's father, Ralph Hylton, born in 1710 was descended from him. This branch of the family were seafarers, but they were impecunious and Ralph decided to emigrate to the New World where, however, he was allegedly ignorant of what had been going on in the family at home. His marriage to Mehitabel Lawrence on Long Island, New York on December 27, 1741, produced five children, of whom William was the youngest. Mehitabel, as we shall see, brought another colourful collection of ancestors to the family history. With his dying breath, according to William, Ralph had expressed his confidence that one of his children would live "to possess those rights which their fathers fought, bled & prayed piously for from the reign of King Ethelread who they descended from by marriage with Elgiva, his daughter." The Hylton's had certainly done plenty of fighting and bleeding - the death toll at the following battles was : Faversham (1), Normandy (1), Metz (1), Crusades (4), Bordeaux (3), Agincourt (1), Berwick (2), St. Albany (2), Market Bosworth (5) and Flodden (4). Records of their piety are fewer.

Poor William had done his best during his long life (he was 88 on the day before he died at his estate in Jamaica) to bring about his father's wish. As he wrote to his grandson:

> Cherishing almost from infancy every legend of their history, I treasured up every information which tended to strengthen a belief that some part of my good father's prophecy would be fulfilled. I surely have raked, as it were from the ashes of the dead, a knowledge of the dignities & wealth which have been withheld from the lawful heirs of Hylton Castle since the death of Henry the Pious or as others called him the Madman.

On his own death-bed William's last words were that he had been cut off by God before he had obtained the great object of his life, but how gratified he would have been by the verdict of T. Arthur, chronicler of the Hiltons, that he was right and that he and his descendants were the legitimate male representatives of the blood and honours of the Hiltons of Hylton Castle. The Castle is now in the hands of English Heritage and has an energetic friends organisation, which is seeking to refurbish its empty shell. The Cauld Lad, a kind of benevolent poltergeist who took delight in rearranging the kitchen utensils, tidying them when they were untidy and vice versa, is now underemployed, but is supposed to be still present.

William was born in New York. He went to Jamaica from Virginia in about 1770, bought a sugar plantation and married Mary Pool, 4th daughter of Jacob and Christian Johnson of the nearby Springfield estate. They returned to the U.S. in 1792 intending to settle there, but because of what he called mismanagement of his affairs, he had to return to Jamaica in 1801, settling on the Delve Estate in the Parish of Westmoreland in the extreme western part of the island. He was a slave owner (in 1816, for example, on his estate at Porus in Clarendon Parish he and his son had 70 slaves) but his views on the subject of abolition were relatively liberal. He was personally acquainted with the Bishop of London, and in a letter to him dated June 25, 1808, he commented on the destructive effects of hard manual work on slaves when beasts with ploughs could better do the work. He was an advocate of estate schools jointly financed by owners offering moral, religious and vocational training, but he opposed a scheme for allowing slaves to work their own land at weekends as a violation of the Sabbath and a temptation to excess. His obituary in the *St. Jago Gazette* said he took a prominent part in all measures designed to benefit his adopted country particularly "those relating to the abolition of the slave trade and slavery".

He and Mary had fourteen children – nine sons and five daughters – in the space of 28 years. It was their youngest son, Samuel Barrett, who married

Margaret Campbell, whose daughter Charlotte Frances was the cousin with whom Francis Robertson Lynch fell in love but was not allowed to marry. She eventually married another member of the Bravo family.

Mary Johnson's mother, Christian, was a member of the extensive Barrett family who had been on the island since it was captured at Oliver Cromwell's instigation by Admiral Penn and General Venables in 1655. Among their force, which was far less well trained and equipped than the one in which Captain Andrew Ruddock had figured in Ireland a few years before, was one Lieutenant Hearcey Barrett. He came from Cornwall, where his family were known to be staunch Royalists so Hearcey's presence may have betokened a family rift. Penn and Venables met with several setbacks in their attempt to replace the Roman Catholic Spanish in the West Indies with good British Protestants, but at Jamaica they met little resistance since there was not much wealth there to defend. Within a week the Spanish governor had surrendered to a force which was described as consisting of "common cheats, thieves, cutpurses and such like persons". No wonder it took them another three years to clear the last of the Spanish soldiers from Jamaica. Hearcey, however, soon began to accumulate property and build up what became a rich inheritance for his descendants. His first wife, who had come with him from England, died and he married again Eleanor Miten in the Parish of St. Catherine. Their son, Samuel, born in 1662, married Margery Green and had two sons, but was killed in 1694 when resisting a French invasion of the island which had been weakened by the Great Earthquake of 1692. By this time his estate at Withywood on Carlisle Bay was the richest settlement in the island bar St Jago de le Vega (now renamed Spanish Town) itself. He and Margery had two sons, but the older one, Richard, was shot by a neighbour's boy, Cudjoe, while at dinner in 1718. The younger son, Samuel (1689-1760) the sole male heir, established himself at Cinnamon Hill, now the site of a lush golf course, and had eight children by his wife, Elizabeth, daughter of Henry Wisdom. One of these was Christian (1731-1759), who became the mother of William Hylton's wife, Mary Johnson. Another was Edward, whose grandson was Edward Barrett of Wimpole Street, father of the poet, Elizabeth Barrett Browning. In later years, the Lynches were proud of being acknowledged as kin by the Barretts, though this probably had more to do with their wealth than with their literary descendant.

Hylton Castle in 1726

Chapter 22

FROM WEXFORD TO NOVA SCOTIA & JAMAICA

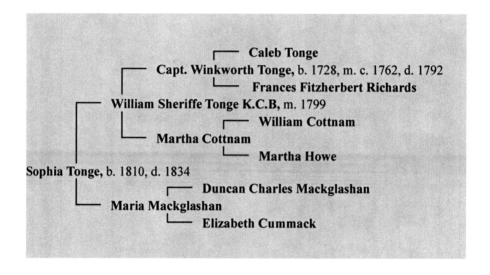

A live trout swims against the stream.- *Canon Churton.*

Captain Winckworth Tonge acquired his unusual first name from his grandmother, a Miss Winckworth, who marrried Rev. Caleb Tonge, the Rector of Ross in County Wexford. She had inherited an estate in County Limerick because all her three brothers died without children so she was a good catch for the young clergyman, whose own roots lay in South Yorkshire. They had three children – William, who died without issue, Rebecca who, while at school was kidnapped "after which nothing more could be discovered about her", and Caleb, who was Winckworth's father. Winckworth's mother, Frances Fitzherbert-Richards, as later generations were fond of pointing out, had aristocratic connections, being somewhat remotely descended through the Fitzherberts from the 3rd Lord Swinnerton.

Winckworth Tonge was born on February 4, 1727, in Wexford and when he was 16 took part as a volunteer in an expedition against the Spanish American settlements. This launched him on what was to be a distinguished military career beginning in the 45th Foot stationed on Cape Breton island from 1746 to 1749 and subsequently at Halifax, Nova Scotia. He took part successively in the capture of Fort Beausejour (1755) the capture of Louisbourg (1758), and Wolfe's campaign at Quebec (1759) – the main North American battles of the Seven Years War which dislodged the French from that part of the world. Winckworth then acquired some land north of Halifax and settled down to civilian life on what became an impressive estate which he called with becoming modesty, Winckworth. He was a Justice of the Peace, and represented three different Counties in the House of Assembly from 1759 until his death in 1792, but his most significant job was that of naval officer for the colony. His duties included the regulation of shipping between Nova Scotia and Europe, Asia, Africa and America, but the job also amounted to being chief tax-collector, never the most popular of activities. Winckworth, however, lost no time in making himself some powerful enemies. Within months of his appointment in 1773 he had alienated the governor, Lord William Campbell, who had been used to appointing the deputy naval officers throughout the land. Winckworth declared that *he* was going to do that from now on and furthermore was going to claim half of their fees for himself. He then put the fees up and sat back waiting to see what would happen. The worlds of business and politics were outraged and sent off urgent appeals for help to the Board of Trade in London, only to be told by Lord Dartmouth, the secretary of state for the American Colonies that Mr. Tonge was technically correct. He did, however, add that if Winckworth insisted on claiming the fees for himself, he would have to forfeit his salary, which he could not afford to do. The next governor, Francis Legge, tried a different tack and actually recommended Mr. Tonge, as a "Gentleman of Good Character & Reputation", for a seat on the Council, noting also that he had spent over £3,000 on agricultural improvements on his estate. But Winckworth was not going to be suborned so easily and rejected the Governor's overtures, which were then withdrawn. When the American War of Independence broke out Winckworth decided to tackle the widespread smuggling by a strict enforcement of the navigation laws, but vitiated this act of rectitude by again starting to collect fees for himself. The Attorney General protested and the assembly even debated whether to abolish the post of naval officer, but Winckworth was unabashed:

> I do declare & can prove, I have not in any instance demanded anything but what is fully authorised by Acts of Parliament....and that, so far from being exorbitant in my demand of fees, they are by no means adequate to the trouble and expense of keeping offices open.

The dispute between him and the assembly and the maritime community continued for another four years until, in 1790, the issue was settled with the establishment of a table of fees. This represented something of a restriction on the naval office, but it was still intact when Wickworth died on February 2, 1792, two days before his 65th birthday.

In about 1762 Winckworth had married Martha Cottnam, daughter of William Cottnam and Martha (neé Howe) and as soon as he was of age their firstborn son, William Cottnam Tonge, was appointed by his father to one of the controversial deputy naval officer posts. What would now be regarded as an outrageous provocation seems to have got lost in the general argument and William served for many years. Moreover, when his father died, the temporary governor appointed him to the main job. Within months William was at loggerheads with the new Governor, Sir John Wentworth, who was soon describing him as a subversive. William became the focus of a new populist movement in Nova Scotia but in the end Wentworth summarily suspended him a few months before he was himself removed from the Governorship.

We are more concerned, however, with a younger son of Winckworth and Martha. He was William Sheriffe Tonge, who trained as a lawyer and moved to Jamaica, where he was licensed to plead before the High Court. He married Maria Mackglashan, the daughter of another prominent civil servant and among their children was Sophia, who became the mother of the eccentric Eliza Turner and was, therefore, Emilie Georgina Lynch's grandmother. William Tonge died two days before the news arrived from England that he had been appointed Attorney-General of Jamaica and was to become a Knight of the Bath.

Chapter 23

FROM BRISTOL TO ANTIGUA & RHODE ISLAND

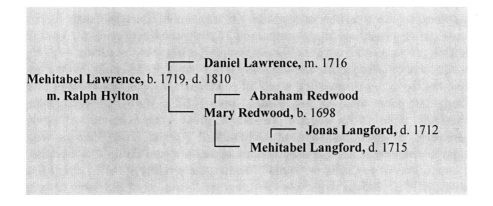

> Take heed you fall not into wantonness as all the disobedient do, whose end will be woe and misery for all, except they repent. - *Jonas Langford's last Will & Testament.*

When Jonas Langford went to Antigua in 1660 the British authorities were encouraging settlers, and a reduction had been made in the size of land grants to accommodate as many as possible. But Jonas was not quite the type they had in mind. The main need was for more men to bolster the armed forces to defend the island from attacks by the Kalinaja indians from Dominica and St. Vincent, but Jonas was a Quaker and steadfastly refused to compromise his religious and pacifist beliefs. Nevertheless when he got there and called on the Governor, Christopher Kayneth, he was given a kindly reception and told he could settle wherever he liked. So he bought a piece of land on the north coast and sent for his family in Bristol to come and join him; it was the start of a roller-coaster career, which brought considerable tribulation but eventually considerable wealth.

In September Mrs. Langford arrived and two months later Justinian Hollyman, who had been banished from Nevis for being a Quaker, also turned up. This was enough for a Meeting so the three duly got together "to wait upon God and worship him". The Governor, alerted no doubt by gossips, sent for the two men and interrogated them, with no more than an admonition that they should report back when called upon to do so. Colonel John Bunkly, however, when he became Governor, took a harder line and clapped the two men into prison for holding a meeting with another newly-arrived Quaker, who was also gaoled and, not being an inhabitant, deported. This began a long battle of wits between the gradually-increasing number of Quakers and the authorities which was to last for years and was meticulously chronicled in Joseph Besse's famous *Collection of the Sufferings of the people called Quakers*. In this Jonas bore his share of tribulation. He was fined, or had horses or hogsheads of sugar confiscated, for not providing arms for himself and his servants and frequently for not paying his share of the parson's upkeep and he was imprisoned for allowing his staff to work on a fast-day. In the last case the Governor responsible was Philip Warner and by a nice twist of fate, about 330 years after he imprisoned Jonas, Philip Warner's eighth great-grandson, John Witt, married the ninth great grand-daughter of Jonas Langford, Elizabeth Herbert, at Hemingford Abbots. The Warners were important people in the Leeward Islands at the time and Philip's half-brother, Thomas, known as Carib, or "India", Warner, the product of their father's first marriage to an Indian wife, was Governor of Dominica at the same time as Philip was running Antigua. At a "peace conference" arranged between them a quarrel arose as a result of which Philip was accused of murdering his half-brother and sparking a massacre of the Dominican delegation. Though he was unsurprisingly acquitted by a jury of planters in Barbados, he did not get back his job in Antigua and some time later, as the Quakers duly recorded:

> The above-mentioned Col. Warner, as he was riding, his horse stumbled and fell upon him, so that he died a few days after of the hurt he received.

This fate seems to have been more or less what Jonas and his Quaker friends would have expected. They noted other examples of divine retribution. Thus Major Mallet, of the Militia, who had been a particular scourge, harassing, fining, beating and torturing Quakers, was suddenly surprised by a deadly fit, fell from his horse, remained speechless for 10 days and then died.

> Some who made their observations on the manner of his exit, were of opinion, that it was a token of the divine vengeance upon him, who had been a busy persecutor, and seemed to delight in oppressing his innocent neighbours.

No doubt the Quakers were difficult to deal with. One of Jonas's letters of complaint to Governor Lea, who was one of the more sympathetic officials, ran to over 1,500 words and warned him not to abuse his power by using the sword against those who had put the sword in his hand lest he be judged as

216

not fit for the service of God. Some of the Governor's henchmen had interrupted a Quaker Meeting and ordered them at the point of the sword to disperse. Jonas was eloquent in complaint:

> Friend, I cannot but in God's fear warn thee to take heed what thou dost in this matter for it's safer for thee to take the counsel of wise Gamaliel to the persecuting Jews, than to be forward and hasty in a matter of so great a moment as this. Now consider seriously, whether the carriage of these men towards us were not rather heathenish than become true Christians, for men to lie in the woods with guns and swords, and then being called, to come rushing in upon us, more like beast of prey than mere mortal men.

Small wonder, perhaps, that one official report in 1676 said that the "singularity and obstinacy" of the Quakers had given the Governor more trouble than anything and complained that, while they were happy to enjoy their peaceable existence, they would neither watch over nor ward against the Indians, "whose treacherous and barbarous murders, rapes and enormities" discouraged the planters more than anything else. Jonas, however, was certainly numbered among the latter. He had already been in Antigua for 24 years, and built up a sizeable holding of land, when in 1684 Sir Christopher Codrington arrived from Barbados to see if the island was suitable for growing sugar. Up to then Jonas had been growing mainly tobacco, but he cashed in on the resulting boom in sugar with substantial estates called Popeshead, Soldiers Gut and, particularly Cassava (or Cassada) Gardens and a good deal of property in the blossoming capital, St. John. Jonas's first wife died after bearing him three (or possibly four) sons, all of whom also predeceased their father, and a daughter, Mehitabel. He then married a second wife, Anne, the widow of his kinsman, Harry Langford. Sometime in about 1667 he was joined in a partnership with a sea captain, Abraham Redwood, whose roots were also in Bristol. Abraham gave up the sea, married Mehitabel, and eventually inherited Cassada Gardens, which was a very prosperous estate and is now on the very edge of Vernon Bird International Airport. When eventually Jonas died at a great age in 1712 his will was found to have attached to it lists of the names of all his slaves. There were 158 slaves on the Popeshead and Soldiers Gut plantation with 44 cattle, 18 horses, 74 sheep and 13 goats and 79 on Cassada Gardens with 8 horses, 65 cattle, 56 sheep and 12 hogs. Even in death Jonas could not resist a homily:

> And now, my dear wife & children, having distributed my outward estate among you as I have thought most proper according to the best of my understanding, the last and best legacy I can give or

217

recommend to you is to commit you to the grace of God which bringeth salvation to all those that receive it and this grace will teach you to deny ungodliness and to live goodly and soberly in the present wicked world as I have found by long and good experience, and therefore I do charge you to take heed to it and live that holy pure life it calls for and take heed you fall not from it into wantonness as all the disobedient do, whose end will be woe and misery for all except they repent. For assuredly, except you be obedient to this grace and be taught by it, you cannot be true Christians. Therefore fear and obey the living God and beware of all the vain fashions, customs and pleasures of this world which grieve the spirit of the Lord and keep the soul in bondage to sin and Satan...........

and so on (brevity was not Jonas's strong point). It would be another two generations, in 1770, before the Society of Friends adopted its anti-slavery policy and by then Jonas's grandson and heir could not be prevailed upon to set his slaves free.

For some years before Jonas died Abraham and Mehitabel had acquired interests in Rhode Island. Now they settled in Newport, where Mehitabel died in 1715 leaving a young family. The eldest surviving son, Jonas Langford Redwood, was killed in a fall from his horse at Newport in 1724, but the next son, Abraham, made the most of his inheritance and established the first public-lending library in what became the United States, the Redwood Library in Newport. He seems also to have adopted a lifestyle, which would have incurred his grandfather's severe displeasure and, when he married it was out of the order of Friends. Abraham and Mehitabel's daughter, Mary, however, was married within the Quaker fold. She had been born in Newport in 1698 and her marriage to Daniel Lawrence took place in Newport a year after her mother's death and in the same year that her father remarried. Daniel was a prominent merchant and landowner who lived at Tew's Neck, Flushing on Long Island, New York, and was descended from one of the original settlers. It was their daughter, Mehitabel, who married Ralph Hylton and became the mother of William, who spent so much time pursuing the barony of Hylton.

Chapter 24

FROM KINGSTON TO WATFORD & HEMINGFORD

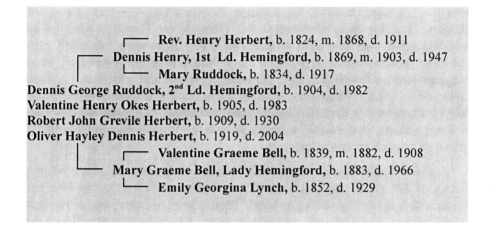

Rev. Henry Herbert, b. 1824, m. 1868, d. 1911
Dennis Henry, 1st Ld. Hemingford, b. 1869, m. 1903, d. 1947
Mary Ruddock, b. 1834, d. 1917
Dennis George Ruddock, 2nd Ld. Hemingford, b. 1904, d. 1982
Valentine Henry Okes Herbert, b. 1905, d. 1983
Robert John Grevile Herbert, b. 1909, d. 1930
Oliver Hayley Dennis Herbert, b. 1919, d. 2004
Valentine Graeme Bell, b. 1839, m. 1882, d. 1908
Mary Graeme Bell, Lady Hemingford, b. 1883, d. 1966
Emily Georgina Lynch, b. 1852, d. 1929

*Better be than seem. Better do than dream – Motto of The Beehive
School, Windsor*

When May Graeme Bell, Valentine and Emilie's elder daughter, was 15 she
sat down with a thin marbled exercise book and began to record details of her
family. "My great great grandfather, Mark Lynch," she wrote, "went out to
Jamaica on the staff of Governor Campbell." There followed many pages of
information gleaned in the main from her Aunt "Totie" Howard, who, having,
as we have seen, married into the aristocracy, was keen on tracing
relationships with important people. Being a Lynch, though, she was also
interested in the eccentricities of her relatives and she had an encyclopaedic
memory for the ins and outs of of the large families in Jamaica into which
they had married.

May herself was born in Jamaica – on February 4, 1883 – but she was by
1898 in England, where she had been sent to board at The Beehive School in
Windsor. The school opened in 1876 with a prospectus which began: "Miss
Browning, living with her mother, receives into her home a limited number of
pupils," and, although by the time May arrived in the 1890s, a slightly less

informal atmosphere had developed, there was, in the words of one of her contemporaries a warm welcome, a well-appointed house, a liberal table and ungrudging and attentive service. In its earliest days it had been little concerned with academic success and was designed chiefly to fit the sisters of Etonians for lives in society, but Miss Browning was a stickler for thoroughness and from 1881 had arranged examinations by Cambridge University, though the thought of girls actually entering that university was still regarded as eccentric or worse. From the time they got up in the morning until they finished work in the evening the girls had to speak French on Monday, Tuesday and Wednesday and German on Thursday and Friday, though English was permitted at tea time. Their baths were frequently cold and they incurred penalty points if they indulged in slang or used loose language such as "awfully jolly". They played tennis and cricket and hockey, curtseyed to Queen Victoria in Windsor Great Park and were given P.T. and drill by a sergeant in the Life Guards. And, of course, they spent a lot of time reciting collects, psalms and gospels. They wore boaters decorated with the school colours of black and yellow.

May was happy there, was a keen Old Bee (she was delighted when a history of the school was produced the year before she died) and in later life would often quote the school motto: "Better be than seem; better do than dream", to her grandchildren. As we have seen, during the school holidays she used, from time to time, to go and stay with her Aunt Nora in Hemingford Abbots. So it was that May met Dennis Henry Herbert, the son of the Rector, who was an aspiring young lawyer in London. Their romance was sealed when she accepted his proposal under a rose arbour in the garden of the Rectory and they were married at St. Mary Abbots Church in Kensington on June 9, 1903.

The service was conducted by Rev. N.H.C.Ruddock, a cousin of Dennis's, assisted by Rev. R.B. Dickson, who had married Henry and Mary Herbert 35 years before. May was given away by her father. She wore a dress of white crêpe-de-chine embroidered in silver with a long train of duchesse satin, carried by two smartly dressed pages in white sailor suits. Her five bridesmaids' soft white silk dresses were complemented by long mousseline-de-soie fichus and pale blue belts. They carried bouquets of pink carnations and wore écru-coloured straw hats trimmed with forget-me-nots.

After honeymooning in Warwickshire, May and Dennis settled down at 16 Scarsdale Villas, Kensington, where their first two sons, Dennis George Ruddock and Valentine Henry Okes, were born. In 1908, for the sake of her husband's health, the family moved to Watford, and the following year Robert John Grevile was born, to be followed a full ten years later by Oliver Hayley Dennis. Meanwhile May watched her husband embarking on a political career in tandem with his legal work and, when eventually he was adopted as the Conservative candidate, she turned out to be a formidable campaigner both at his side and on her own when his duties as Deputy Speaker kept him in Westminster. At the announcement of the Poll after the 1923 election, for example, when Dennis had been under attack by feminists who objected to his views on divorce and adultery, she stole the show. Mr R.A.Bateman, the Liberal candidate, began the process by saying that though he gave Mr. Herbert no bouquets, he would like in the spirit of chivalry to offer one to Mrs. Herbert. He then stepped forward and presented her with a large bunch of yellow chrysanthemums – yellow being the Liberal colours. May received them gracefully, but made sure that they did not obscure the enormous blue rosette which she had sported throughout. When there were calls later for her to speak, she stepped forward and let Dennis's feminine opponents have it:

> Thank you very much indeed for your kind words and cheers. I have been working very hard and all the ladies have been working even harder (Hear, hear). I feel perfectly certain we should not have won but for the women. We have had women up against us, and my delight is that right has conquered wrong. (Loud applause) They have said terrible and untrue things about my husband. I have lived nearly twenty years with him, and I do know him (Loud applause and laughter). Thank you all very much; we cannot thank you enough. If we have to fight another election in three months, we will win again (Loud applause and renewed cheers).

She was equally unabashed when actually confronted by his political opponents. One of these in 1923 was Lady Astor, who said she would not be seen dead in his company. In his 1944 memoirs Dennis said that Lady Astor must have forgiven him because she now regarded him as a friend, though previously they had quite often disagreed and he had perhaps succumbed to the temptation of "ragging" her. He then told the story of a memorable exchange which took place at a party given by the Speaker not long after the 1923 General Election:

> Another M.P., who was a great friend of mine, and who also knew Lady Astor well and often quarrelled with her on political questions, thought it would be fun to introduce my wife to her and did so, explaining to her that she was my wife. Lady Astor exclaimed: "What are you the wife of that awful man? How long have you been married?" - "About twenty years," said my wife. "And you've put up

221

with him all that time! But there ------"(mentioning a lady friend of hers who had known me for a long time)"tells me he really is quite a good fellow in private life." Perhaps therefore among the many good services my wife has rendered to me, may be the starting of friendly relations between Lady Astor and myself.

The family legend that something like this exchange took place when Dennis was filibustering against some piece of legislation of which he disapproved and the two women met by chance in the gallery of the House of Commons, though attractive, must yield to Dennis's version.

Their Silver Wedding day in 1928 coincided with the first, though outside, chance that Dennis might succeed to the Speakership and was spent quietly because Dennis was "too busy to do anything dashing". What exactly they did we do not know since May was the one who was to describe it and her letter does not survive. However, musing on the past 25 years Dennis wrote to their son in the Gold Coast:

> We have much to be thankful for, & indeed our troubles have been trifling to what they might well have been, & our successes more than we had any right to expect. But the one thing which far above all else makes us happy is that we have been so fortunate & happy in our good sons. Good luck to you & God bless you all!

Alas! The family was soon to be struck with a disaster. The third son, Robert John Grevile, a tall, handsome, much-beloved lad of 20, was diagnosed with an incurable brain tumour in 1929, believed at the time to have been caused by a blow from a cricket ball. His sight was affected and he soon became gravely ill. With both their elder sons abroad, "Young Dennis" in the Gold Coast and Val in India, other friends and relations rallied round. Dennis's brother, Willie, and a nurse, Nurse King, came to help. On January 23, 1930 it was obvious that Robert was dying. The Vicar came in twice daily to say prayers, Robert rallied briefly and May and Dennis stayed up with him all night on the Friday and Saturday but at 5.30 am on Sunday, January 26 the end came. It was less than three weeks after his 21st birthday. Next day May, in her grief, wrote to her son, Dennis:

> Our darling is at rest and he looks so beautiful. He had a very peaceful passing over and Dad and I and Nurse King were with him to the last. He just slept away & never had any pain.....We will have a lot to learn from Robert, his unselfishness & patient endurance was wonderful and I feel he has gone to higher work.

May's old friend, Ellen Kinder, had come to stay and was a tower of strength, helping to take the parents' minds off their loss. She also wrote to Dennis in the Gold Coast a reassuring letter about the state of affairs at Clarendon Lodge:

> They are so wonderful – your mother in the midst of trouble able to be bright, and your father never for one moment thinking of himself. Dear Willie is wonderful. He looks after us all and what they would have done without him I dare not think.......Robert breathed his last at 5.30. Your mother then seemed better – she knew her darling was quite safe and could see her more plainly than he had done for weeks. Your father, as usual just thinking of her and us all, made Bovril. I did not offer to help for I thought better for him to be busy.

May had accompanied Dennis on trips to the United States in 1925 and India in 1928, but his opportunity for travel was limited by his duties in the House. He had to hurry back from Calcutta, for example, but May was able to spend longer there with Val and Winifred. In 1937 they managed a brief trip to Copenhagen in connection with a small company which Dennis had helped, in his legal capacity, to form. Thirty years later one of the directors remembered:

> Your mother then seemed gay and surprisingly young and one evening after your father had retired to their hotel, even took part in tours on the switchback of the famous Tivoli Gardens, together, I believe, with the much younger Peter Heering of Heering Cherry Brandy fame.

Back in London May continued her support, dividing her time between Clarendon Lodge, in Watford, and a flat in Dolphin Square, which was conveniently placed for the Commons. She frequently filled in for Dennis in the constituency when he was unavoidably detained in Westminster. She opened fêtes and bazaars, she chaired meetings, she sang in the Watford Conservative Mixed Choir, she distributed prizes and often managed to captivate her audience with some homespun wisdom. In the space of a few weeks in 1931, for example, she gave away prizes at Gartlet School Speech Day, opened a bazaar in support of the Church Missionary Society, stood in for Dennis at a political meeting and divulged to a meeting of the Primrose League that she had become a Girl Guide. She advised the Gartlet girls to be punctual ("unpunctuality is selfishness"), courteous towards parents, teachers and schoolfellows and loyal to God, to King and Country. There was more to life than kicking up your heels. The churchgoers she told: "Do not think you are doing the church a kindness by helping to finance the missions overseas. It is your duty.", and to the politicians she explained Dennis's absence by saying that he was opposing the Finance Act: "He is quite good at obstructive work and the party were rather anxious that he be there."

When the war came in 1939 with its blackouts, bombing raids and rationing, May gamely moved their bed under the dining room table for air raid protection and turned the house into a depot for W.V.S. Hospital supplies, serving the 30 work parties in the district. At the time of Dunkirk, when convoys of wounded poured into Leavesden hospital, the depot supplied thousands of surgical dressings and later equipped 70 first-aid posts for the Invasion Committees and Housewives' Services. Thousands of woollen garments were made and sent to the Forces, the Red Cross and to the Russian allies. As Chairman of the W.V.S. Hospital Supplies for Watford and District, she was a very hands-on worker, but she had also served on the General Association for the W.V.S., organised working parties to help the Red Cross and been active in War Savings campaigns. She was a national vice-president of the Y.W.C.A. At Christmas-time in 1943 a colleague of young Dennis's at Budo, Margaret Hamand, came to call and described the dominance of Blackie, the cat who had enslaved May and Dennis, to the point where the latter would miss a train rather than deny Blackie a scratch. She was enchanted with May:

> She did, of course, have me well under her thumb with her charm
> from the start and I did like her awfully because it is not an outside
> charm, but an inside charm, which does seem such a rare thing in
> people.

Dennis's retirement from the house and elevation to the peerage prompted another sea change for May, but she took it with typical resilience. She had continued to patronise the theatre during the war, when she and Dennis were at their Dolphin Square flat and would seize the chance of a day out with passing relatives. On the day after Dennis resigned she took Val's wife, Winifred, in hand:

> On Friday I met her in town & we went to W.V.S. Headquarters to
> see Mrs. Holmes, the wife of Val's late Colonel who Val liked so
> much. Then we had some lunch at a Fuller's tea shop & then went to
> the Vaudeville Theatre to see 'Men in Shadow' by Mary Hayley Bell.
> It is a very thrilling & amusing piece. John Mills takes the leading
> part in the play & is excellent. I took Lu & Pamela as well as
> Winifred. We had very good seats in the stalls

This was an archetypical May occasion, involving a lunch, a theatre, a sister, Lu, a daughter-in-law, Win, a cousin, Mary Hayley Bell, and her husband, John Mills, and Pamela Maddison, a young friend of the Clark family from Haltwhistle, who had stayed at Clarendon Lodge while working in London. Aunt Totie would have understood.

Now May and Dennis were looking for a smaller house. The W.V.S. moved out, though she continued her work for the service, but in he event their own move became impracticable and they had to do the best they could. Gradually May found herself devoting more and more time to nursing. Domestic help was impossible to obtain and not until the final days of Dennis's life was she able to arrange satisfactory nursing assistance. When the end came she was exhausted, but at peace, happy that Dennis's struggle was over, though sad that he had not achieved his ambition of living to see his eldest son again.

It would be a wrench to leave Clarendon Lodge after 25 years, but she was able, at last, to find a smaller house and moved into 15, Langley Way, Watford, with Blackie the cat. This animal she outrageously spoilt, feeding him, even in the midst of rationing, on the most expensive diet – May complained once of his having declined sirloin of beef with fish sauce, which some of her grandchildren might well have lapped up, though the combination was not perhaps ideal either for cats or children. The recipe she had contributed towards the end of the war to a publication called *Fare-Ye-Well with Ladies of the Realm* was much more modest. Hemingford Toast consisted of melted cheese, chutney and cayenne pepper spread on thick slices of toast and served very hot – a dish, as she said, that was simple and quick to make, tasty and satisfying. The book was a compilation of recipes donated by prominent women in aid of a fund for Russian children and May's inclusion among the 42 said something about her war work, particularly for the W.V.S., of which she had been one of the earliest members.

But all this, and the years of loyal political service to the Conservative party in Watford, was now, largely behind her and she could devote more time to her first love – her family and friends. She was, *par excellence,* what would come in later years to be known as a "networker", keeping in touch, by letter or at least Christmas card, with an astonishing number of people, the ins and outs of whose lives she could instantly call to mind, though she sometimes employed a baffling shorthand. For example, when asked once about a distant relation, she replied "Well, he died and she married again." Now the prospect of seeing more of her grandchildren was particularly welcome to one so family-oriented, and she embarked on a programme of taking them out individually for a day in London, usually incorporating a matinee at the theatre and lunch at the Trocadero. Though she was now The Dowager Lady

Hemingford, she retained her skittishness and sense of humour and took very much to the new genre of American musicals like *Oklahoma* and *Annie Get Your Gun* which were taking London by storm.

In 1952 May bought Littlecote, an attractive thatched cottage in Hemingford Abbots, a long stone's throw from the rose arbour where she had become engaged, and the Old Rectory, where her eldest son and the family were now ensconced. She at once began a new life of busily getting to know everyone in the village. She was soon a parish councillor, president of the Village Hall management committee, a regular worshipper at St. Margaret's Church, a member of the Mothers' Union and Women's Institute and an unofficial counsellor for anyone who wanted to get a problem off his or her chest. Though crippled with arthritis – she could scarcely bend her legs at all – she drove her little Morris GGK 101 with careful élan, though reversing was a particular problem. Her companion, Mona Roberts, who had come to May via her daughter-in-law Winifred in Wales, was a tower of strength and became a village character in her own right.

These were happy years in the bosom of the family she had done so much to strengthen and chronicle. At the wedding of her granddaughter Celia in May, 1966, she appeared happy but frail and two months later she died. The volume of mail which her son Dennis received, contained many heartfelt tributes from all sorts of people. Two were typical. One, from Nancy Lennox, of Epping in Essex, read in part:

> It is 61 years ago last April since I came to live with your mother and I was with her for nearly six years. She has corresponded with me and taken a great interest in my family. She was such a dear friend and gracious lady and I was very fond of her.....The one great comfort is that she did not suffer a long illness at the last and she is now at rest from all the pain and suffering that she has endured for many years.

The second came from Lucy Boston, the children's author who lived at The Manor House, Hemingford Grey:

> I am very sorry to hear of your mother's death. It does not alter the long beauty of her life, but the interruption of so much love, given and received, is startlingly painful.

Mary Graeme Herbert (née Bell), later Lady Hemingford, 1883-1966

May with her Jamaican Nannie

May aged 18

May as a girl

May with a "tushie" hat

Part III

--------------Chapter 25------------

FROM THE MERSE TO FEATHERSTONE

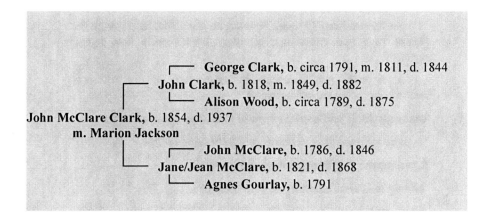

George Clark, b. circa 1791, m. 1811, d. 1844
John Clark, b. 1818, m. 1849, d. 1882
Alison Wood, b. circa 1789, d. 1875
John McClare Clark, b. 1854, d. 1937
m. Marion Jackson
John McClare, b. 1786, d. 1846
Jane/Jean McClare, b. 1821, d. 1868
Agnes Gourlay, b. 1791

I fear the English have a tendency towards softness and I welcome a leavening of the more rugged character of the Scottish race. - *Dennis Henry Herbert, Royal Caledonian Society Dinner, 1934*

In January, 1867, the same year that Rev. Henry Herbert finally achieved a stipend upon which he could marry, John Clark, away in Northumberland, was making a career move. For the last 19 years he had been employed as land agent at Featherstone Castle, near Haltwhistle, which belonged to the Hope-Wallace family, scions of the Earl of Hopetoun. There he had met and in December, 1849, married, Jane McClare, from Musselburgh, east of Edinburgh, who, with her mother Agnes (nee Gourlay) was in service at the castle. Now, 18 years later, John and Jane had produced three children who survived infancy and, according to family legend, a string of 13 stillborn babies, because Jane's blood group was rhesus negative. To add to their distress their daughter, Agnes, had died at the age of six in 1862 as a result of diphtheria, another condition then imperfectly understood and frequently fatal.

At Hallbankhead, the long, low stone cottage, which had been built for him and his bride-to-be at the top of the hill above the castle, he sat down and wrote out, in his bold handwriting, a circular letter advertising his services to one and all:

> I beg to intimate that the Drainage, Repairs and Improvements on the Featherstone Castle Estate are now so complete than Mr. Hope Wallace has permitted me to undertake other Agencies and kindly permits me to refer gentlemen to him as to my qualifications.

> I have been 19 years Steward on this Estate and during that period have had experience in every branch of a land agent's business.

> I have had considerable experience in the following departments of estate management

Drainage works and improvement of land connected therewith

Negotiating loans for Designing and Improving estates

Rearrangement of farms & mapping designs

Valuing land and Reporting on Improvements

Repair and Improvement of Farm House and Out Buildings

Constructing and Repairing Roads

Inclosing and Draining Hill Pasture

Planting Plantations and Ornamental grounds

Transplanting large trees for Improving Park scenery

Management of woods and Plantations and Reporting on improvements

Thinning Pruning and Management of neglected Plantations

Sales of Timber and Timber Valuations

Management of Sawmills for Estate Purposes

Improving Water Courses

Overlooking Collieries

Estimates of Improvements

Overlooking Tile works

Manorial Rights & Collection of Land Rents

Conducting Arbitration cases

Valuation for purchase or sale of land

Receiving Rents of Royalties and Estates

Interests intrusted to me will be appreciated and the duties discharged with prompt attention and solicitous care.

I am Sir

Your obedient Servant

John Clark

When he sat down to list this impressive portfolio John probably had no inkling that his wife had only 12 months to live, though it is possible that her fatal breast cancer was already manifesting itself. However, on January 9, 1868, Jane died at Hallbankhead and was buried in the churchyard of the little church at Knaresdale, a few miles up the valley towards Alston. John's two sons, George and John McClare, were 16 and 14 respectively and it may well have been at this juncture that John decided to send them away to school. They were enrolled at Montrose Academy, a long-established institution with a history going back to the 14th Century – the 1871 Census shows John McClare boarding with a Mary Galant in Montrose.

John's own education had been hard-earned; he is reputed to have paid for it himself by breaking stones in the evenings for the road-building programme. But, as indicated by his manifesto, he enjoyed the full confidence of his employer, who used him as a political confidant and seems to have reposed complete trust in him. Now he was, by any standards, a well-educated man - no mean achievement for the son of an agricultural worker from the borders of England and Scotland, where schooling was rudimentary for boys of his station. John was born on August 21, 1818 at Blackhouse near the delightfully-named village of Bunkle, or Bonkyl, in the low-lying, slightly marshy area known as The Merse, at the foot of the Lammermuir Hills west of Berwick-upon-Tweed. Watered by the Blackadder and Whiteadder rivers, its drainage in the late eighteenth century made it prime agricultural territory.

There is not much hard evidence about his father, George, but we know that he was at various times described as a labourer, a shepherd and a ploughman, or hind. Hinds were responsible for a pair of horses and were usually expected to supply a second member of the team, usually a woman, and perhaps a boy as well. They would present themselves at the beginning of March at the hiring fair in the larger towns like Duns or Lauder, wearing a sprig of hawthorn in their hats to distinguish them from the carters, who wore a piece of whipcord and shepherds, a tuft of wool. Sometimes there might be no work and a hind might wait all day without an offer of employment. If a deal was done with a hind, he would be offered accommodation – in the farmhouse if he was single, or in a cottage if married. In the rich agricultural fields of the Merse at the turn of the century when George was making his living, ploughmen were in greater demand than in the uplands to the north and west and the total value of a hind's wage might amount to £13 or £15 or, exceptionally, up to £20 a year, which was regarded by many others with envy.

At what stage George graduated to this relative prosperity is not known, but there is a persistent – and as yet unverified - family story that he "carried a pike at Waterloo" in 1815. It does seem improbable, but the timings do not rule it out and four George Clarks are listed among the participants in the battle. George was born in 1786, the second son of George Clark and Sarah Hogg, and would, therefore, have been 29 at the time- a good military age. His first marriage – to Isabella Cockburn – took place at Duns on August 27, 1807 and they had two daughters, Margaret and Agnes. Mysteriously their dates of birth, given as February 22, 1812 and November 25, 1813 respectively, were not entered in the parish register until 1821.

On April 21, 1811, however, George and Alison Wood, the daughter of a shepherd, John Wood, and his wife, Mary Lidgate, appeared before a session of the Associate Burgher Congregation at Lauder and "acknowledging themselves before the session to be husband & wife tho' irregularly married, were rebuked accordingly for their irregular conduct". This may not have been quite as bad as it sounds because the Burghers took a highly-coloured view of sex and marriage. Their registers are full of blood-curdling denunciations of couples who had indulged in "ante-nuptial fornication" and other forms of immorality, which seem in their eyes to have included being married in any other church. George and Alison's reprimand was very much on the low end of the scale. The Burghers had a turbulent history of opposition to patronage and to allegiance to earthly monarchs who might, after all, be Roman Catholics. Much later, in 1847, they became a constituent part of the United Presbyterian Church. Presumably the Woods were dissenters and Alison must have retained some links with the Burghers because, when George's eldest daughter, Margaret, was married in 1832 to Walter Fairbairn, the ceremony was conducted by the Minister of the Burgher Congregation from Duns. However, her son, John's baptism, on September 20, 1818, was recorded in the parish church at Bonkyl, and John later became a pillar of the Church of England.

John's early years will have been spent in fairly primitive conditions. The housing with which hinds were provided was anything but lavish. Cottages were typically built of rough stone with clay or dung plaster, a thatched roof and a clay floor and usually consisted of one room, very likely without a chimney so that a pall of smoke hung about most of the time. Box beds divided up the living accommodation. However, in his essay *The Border Farm Worker*, Michael Robson concludes that, with a good manager for a wife, a worker could save a little and even prosper.

> It was possible to live 'decently', although close to the edge of poverty, save a little, spend a little on education, Sunday clothes, fair day entertainments, and occasionally on books and foodstuffs. There were also times when the hardship of work was relieved by cheerfulness if not quite by a real holiday....It is certainly not possible to accept that the life of a Border farm worker prior to, say, 1850, was one of downtrodden misery, drudgery and squalor.

Alison's managerial skills seem to have been up to the mark because it is obvious that young John received a good education, and when he reached working age, he was sent to work for the Duke of Norfolk's agent in the Sheffield area. Here, in his spare time, he became a prolific contributor to the *Sheffield Iris,* a paper whose editor, the evangelical hymn-writer, James Montgomery, had toned down his politics after spending two terms in gaol for libel, but remained fervent for the abolition of slavery, reform of the poor laws and revolution in Scottish court procedure.

How exactly John Clark's move to Yorkshire came about we do not know, but a bright young lad would be likely to attract the attention of the local landowners. Significantly, although the Home family were pre-eminent round Duns, the 4th Earl of Hopetoun lived about 30 miles away at Luffness, near Haddington across the Lammermuir Hills and it was to his relative at Featherstone Castle that John eventually went in 1848 when he was 30. As we have seen he flourished there. A year after his arrival he married Jane McClare and settled into Hallbankhead, which had been speedily prepared for them. Jane was a native of Musselburgh, a fishing community east of Edinburgh, where her forebears were in the weaving trade. They lived in a small community called Newbigging which adjoined another property belonging to the Hope family, who were no doubt responsible for giving Jane her job at Featherstone. Jane McClare's mother was Agnes Gourlay from whom the connection with Mrs Dows derived (she was Coz Jane's great-aunt).

Some major work done to the castle was already complete when John arrived, but much of the experience he listed in 1867 was gained there. One of his early preoccupations must have been with the railway company which obtained authority in 1846 for the branch line from Haltwhistle to Alston. The line, it is believed, would originally have passed close to the castle, but in 1851 when the first trains ran, they were comfortably over the brow of the hill. The "Alston Puffer", as it was affectionately known, became a notable addition to the valley and managed to survive until 1976. James Hope-Wallace died in 1854 and for the next six years John was responsible to his executors as John George Frederick Hope-Wallace, the heir, was still a minor. That this period was a success is evident because at the end of it the tenants all clubbed together and presented John with a black marble clock with a plaque paying tribute to his "zeal, tact and energy", a phrase which has echoed down the generations.

His relationship with John George Frederick was particularly close. The young man consulted him about his plans for entering politics as well as more germane issues such as the letting of shooting rights or the installation of a new school teacher. They remained close even after John spread his wings beyond Featherstone and moved from Hallbankhead to Haltwhistle as Manager of the newly-opened branch of the Cumberland Union Bank, into whose "handsome building" he moved his living quarters. This was in November, 1875, only days after the death, at Manderston, Duns, of his mother, Alison Clark, who must have been immensely proud of how far her son had gone up in the world. Alison was buried, with her husband George, in the little village of Fogo, but whether John was able to be there we do not know.

At Haltwhistle he was turning out to be something of a polymath – banker, land agent, arbitrator, geologist, journalist, antiquarian, public speaker and pillar of the community, serving two terms on the Board of Guardians and doing spells on the Parochial Committee and the Highway Board. His major work was to survey 20 potential sources of water for the municipal water-supply and to take part in the establishment of a sewerage system for the town. His report on water resources was recalled in the *Hexham Herald* in these terms:

> We know that he must have trodden many a sinuous mile over hill and dale, by babbling streams and along the tortuous winding of mountain brooks, over rolling expanses of green meadow, and across dark stretches of lonely fell, measuring the flow and testing the quality of every possible source of water supply for the elaborate

report, which, written in his own characteristic calligraphy, was presented to the Sanitary Authority as the result of those pleasant wanderings, and which formed the primary basis on which they proceeded to determine the selection of the source of supply. He knew every inch of the district, and even its wild flowers were familiar to his observant eye.

The *Herald* may have been pulling out all the stops on behalf of one of its own because John was a contributor to their columns as well as to those of the *Carlisle Patriot*, but he does seem to have been a keen and knowledgeable naturalist and an agreeable character. The town's other paper, the *Hexham Courant*, said that in all his transactions, "he evinced an amount of sagacity, forethought, and sound common sense that entitled him to the confidence which he ungrudgingly received from those whom he so conscientiously served. His varied knowledge of practical and scientific subjects, added to his genial temperament and broad sense of humour, rendered him an agreeable companion, and lent a charm to his conversation."

He had come a long way from The Merse, but he remained devoted to the area of his birth and used regularly to entertain audiences at the Haltwhistle Mechanics' Institute with readings about it and his reading of these favourite selections was inimitable, according to the *Courant*. His favourite book was *Tales of the Borders,* a miscellany of stories about the myths, murders, castle-rustling and raiding in which the borders delighted and which would have given John free reign to indulge his Scottish accent. He was in demand as a speaker, the paper said, because his demeanour was genial and his language forcible, a quaint illustration, thrown in as it were at random, or on the spur of the moment, giving pith and point to his argument and plausibility to his advice. The paper even forgave him for being a Scotchman, observing that "although he was not a native of the town, he had in the course of a long series of years identified himself so closely with its public interests and social welfare as to be looked upon by the inhabitants as being in all essential respects as one of themselves." In Haltwhistle, you could get no higher praise than that!

John's death had come suddenly. He had suffered for some years from a weak chest, one of the more dramatic remedies for which was an enormous beard stretching almost to his waist, which was supposed to add protection, but fundamentally he was healthy. In August he was well, but soon began to go down hill. A spell away from home was tried, but only made him worse and on October 19, 1882, he died at his home in Edens Lawn, Haltwhistle, the cause of death being given as "Embolism, Softening of the brain." He had been a widower for 14 years, but now he was buried at Knaresdale with Jane and Agnes and, as the *Courant* put it, "some children who died in infancy,"- the only known reference to all those poor little stillborn siblings.

The tombstone reads:

Faithful unto Death.

In loving memory of John Clark, 34 years steward at Featherstone Castle, born August 16, 1818, died October 19, 1882. This stone was set up by his sincere friends John and Mary Hope-Wallace.

Also his wife, Jane Clark, born 11 March, 1821, died 9 January, 1868, and their daughter, Agnes Janet, born 16 January, 1856, died 10 June, 1862.

The link with the Hope-Wallaces remained strong after John's death because, not only did John McClare Clark take on responsibility for the Featherstone estate, but his elder brother, George, was agent for Admiral Charles Bethune, of Balfour, Fife, who was Mrs. Hope-Wallace's father. John McClare had been preferred as partner in Haltwhistle as being more reliable than George. Perhaps the Admiral was felt to be a sufficient disciplinarian to cope with the wayward George, who was at this stage in his early 30s. In his youth George was reputed to be so fast on his feet that he could catch a hare without the aid of a greyhound and for a time made a living by touring the agricultural shows and taking bets against his being able to jump over a five-bar gate, which he was well able to do. The family must have felt that the Bethune treatment had worked when George became engaged to a local merchant's daughter, Euphemia Tosh, and his younger brother hastened north to witness their marriage on June 17, 1884, at Anstruther Wester, on the Fife coast. Euphemia, who preferred to be known as Phame, was 22, ten years younger than her husband, who was living at Kilrenny Mains and managing a 500-acre farm employing 24 men and women and a lad.

By the time of the 1891 Census they were back in Haltwhistle, where George's skills as a draughtsman were useful, and in 1901 they had migrated to Cumberland, where George was agent to the widowed owner of the Dovenby estate near Cockermouth, and her 19-year-old undergraduate son. Alas a discrepancy occurred in the books and, as one of his nephews put it, George went off to build railways in South America. Phame may have had her doubts about the venture because whereas a G. Clark is recorded as applying for a passport on November 27, 1902, it was not until December 24 that Mrs. E. Clark's application was noted. It is not certain that these entries refer to our couple, but instinct suggests the probability. Nor do we know for sure whether

Phame actually went to Argentina, where it is believed George worked on the building of the Trans-Andean Railway and crossed the mountain-range into Chile himself.

Little else is known. I have reluctantly discarded for lack of evidence, a family legend that he became *Victor Ludorum* at the National Athletics Championships of Peru. Unless he made an unrecorded trip to South America after 1871 when he was in England, returning again to appear in the 1881 Scottish census, he would surely have been too old – by 1902 he was 50. Eventually he reappeared in Haltwhistle, bearing a large glass case containing a selection of stuffed South American birds and little else. Phame had left him and he took up residence in the offices of J.M.Clark & Sons, bedding down on a mattress supported on piled-up bound copies of the *Estates Gazette*. As this publication did not come in regular deliveries of four at a time, his bed was on an awkward slope for about three years out of four. By now he was Uncle Geordie to his brother's six children and he is remembered chiefly for looking like Edward VII and for infuriating everyone by running down the accumulator of the radio. When he died in 1927, at the age of 76, the *Haltwhistle Echo* recorded euphemistically that "he was well-known in the district".

It was his younger brother, John McClare Clark, however, who really made an impact.

John Clark (1818-1882)

The Bothy (much altered) where John Clark was born

Hallbankhead, where John and Jane (née McClare) lived.

Featherstone Castle, Haltwhistle

John Clark's "manifesto"

239

FROM BELLISTER TO ASHCROFT

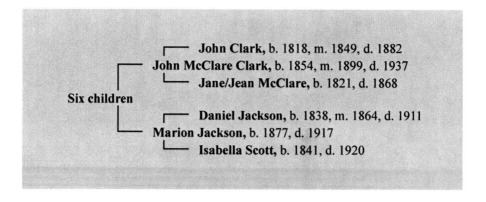

```
                          ┌── John Clark, b. 1818, m. 1849, d. 1882
                   ┌── John McClare Clark, b. 1854, m. 1899, d. 1937
              ┌    └── Jane/Jean McClare, b. 1821, d. 1868
Six children  
              │    ┌── Daniel Jackson, b. 1838, m. 1864, d. 1911
              └── Marion Jackson, b. 1877, d. 1917
                   └── Isabella Scott, b. 1841, d. 1920
```

Toiling – Rejoicing – Sorrowing,
Onward though life he goes,
Each morning sees some task begin,
Each evening sees it close;
Something attempted, something done,
Has earned a night's repose. - *Longfellow.*

The week beginning February 26, 1917, was a momentous one in world history. The Russian revolution came to a head and the Tsar resigned, the Germans concentrated their forces on the Hindenburg Line preparatory to the great battles to come and there was a crisis in relations between the French and British generals. All this paled into insignificance for John McClare Clark however. He had got back to Bellister Castle on the Monday from a business trip to London to find his young wife, Marion, suffering from a sore throat. Then suddenly, unexpectedly and disastrously, she died on Tuesday morning. She was only 39 and had given birth a mere seven months earlier to their fifth son and sixth child, William Donaldson. John himself was rising 63 and had never expected to be a widower. He was crushed by the tragedy and was not the same again for the remaining 20 years of his life. He took to walking every morning from Bellister to the cemetery in Haltwhistle to visit her grave – a round trip of about two miles, which involved fording the fast-running South Tyne. On the day of Marion's death John came, in tears, into the nursery and told his children they would have to be good in future, but the younger ones understood very little of what had happened and a well-intentioned maid told Betty that God had taken away her mother, thus damaging her faith for ever. The children remembered in later years, the caparisoned horses with their black ostrich feathers pulling the hearse, but they were considered too young to attend the funeral at Haltwhistle Parish Church on the Friday, March 2. Only John, aged 13, and David, just 10, were among the mourners.

Their father contemplated farming the young Clarks out among various Jackson relations, of whom there were many because Marion was one of 16, but this plan was, mercifully abandoned; it would surely have only increased the children's sense of loss. Instead Jane Jackson, or Auntie Jenny, Marion's eldest sister took a special place in the household, though it was not so permanent as to forge particularly close personal relationships with the family. This may have been because John Clark was inclined to bully members of the household, not excluding Auntie Jenny, treating them as "silly women". A high-spirited Jackson would not put up with much of that and Auntie Jenny was soon succeeded by a governess, Miss Pooler, of whom more anon.

John McClare Clark was a man typical of an age, in which people were defined by their standing in the social scale and he was rising up the ranks of the middle class. As we have seen, his grandfather had been a hind; John McClare was now a respected Land Agent, a national authority on valuation, a retired Colonel in the Territorial Army and a magistrate. His eldest son had recently started at a public school, he ran a chauffeur-driven car and was head of the family firm of Land Agents. The family were now living in the comparative grandeur of Bellister, which was let to John by his father-in-law, Dr Daniel Jackson. He was proud of this progress but was not at all vainglorious about it and was not personally pushy. As a young man John rode enthusiastically to hounds and was celebrated for his ability to cope with awkward mounts; he would make the horse face into a corner of the stable block and then, according to legend, vault into the saddle from behind. This was said, improbably, to work well. He suffered from periods of acute depression, akin one supposes to those which Winston Churchill called his "Black Dog", and at times his friends used to keep a close eye on him for fear that he might harm himself. Perhaps because of this he affected a kind of bluff heartiness which showed itself in a love of puns and party games. Marion's death must have tested his resolve to the utmost, but, though he was devastated, he did not allow the tragedy to ruin his life. Though keen on country pursuits, he disliked "smart" shooting parties and shunned grand social events. His one-time pupil, Willie Vane (later Lord Inglewood), recalling these characteristics years later, added that he was not at all snobbish and much disliked inverted snobbery among the working class. Some even said that he was unduly humble and was held back by his strong disapproval of the trades unionists' feeling that Jack was as good as his master. His dislike of this egalitarianism was so great that he refused to set foot in a Co-op store and would not allow his family to shop there.

However, though he believed that people should know their place, and therefore regarded his clients as his superiors in the social hierarchy, he was not sycophantic and was quite ready to give them blunt advice even if he knew it would be unpopular. When he took over another land agency business in Hexham in the late 1890's, he took on his first pupil, T.J.Young, who left this description of his boss:

> His tremendous energy at the time, when nearly all the office correspondence was written by his own hand, continued with very little diminution right up to the last few years....With all his great devotion to the large business which he so strenuously built up, he loved a day's hunting with the Haydon Foxhounds, and knew a lot about this branch of sport. He had a warm heart, never forgot a friend, and was always ready with kind advice and help to others – especially the younger members of the profession.

Because of his age he had had to retire from the colonelcy of the 4th Battalion of the Northumberland Fusiliers in 1912 and, in his valedictory address he noted that recruitment was not up to strength. He had no doubt that young men would flock to arms if war came – and he prayed that it would not – but the time to join up was before an emergency arose. It was fortunate for the firm that John was ineligible for service in the war because it depended wholly on him, and at the time of Marion's death he was much in demand as an arbitrator, particularly in cases involving moorland and sporting rights, all over the country. He was one of the original referees under the Finance Act, 1910, the Acquisition of Land Act, 1919 and the Agriculture Act, 1920. Election to the Institution of Chartered Surveyors came in 1892, ten years after he took over the banking and land agency work on the death of his father. He became a member of the Council in 1912 and he was President in 1922-23, the first man from the north to be so honoured. In a lengthy inaugural address he sketched the similarities between agricultural conditions after the Napoleonic War with those faced by farmers after World War I, and issued a call to government to follow a policy of "Speed the plough". He was involved in acquiring land for water supplies and for the War Office at Catterick Camp. He was a director of the Newcastle and Gateshead Water Company, Chairman of Border Counties Wood Sales, Ltd. and local director of the British Law Insurance Company. He was also – and this proved to be his Achilles Heel – Chairman of the Naworth Coal Company, an unlimited company which owned a number of mines between Haltwhistle and Brampton.

On June 11, 1924, his eldest son's 21st birthday, the disastrous news came that the Naworth Company had collapsed. It is not clear exactly what had happened, but the records show that between 1923 and 1925 there was a sharp drop in the number of miners employed at all four of the Company's mines, two of which were abandoned in 1925. John had guaranteed the Company and his liability was about £6,000 or three times what his firm was earning annually from land agency. Moreover he lost an income of some £4,000 a year from the colliery. No wonder he said, as recalled by one of his sons, "Mr. Scott (the bank manager) will be balancing me up the wrong side soon." The disaster certainly put a serious crimp in the family finances and it spurred John into further ventures. One of the most successful of these was his appointment as a valuer for the Agricultural Mortgage Corporation, in the counties of Northumberland, Westmorland, Cumberland and Durham. This he achieved, to the fury of his competitors, by offering to do it at two-thirds of the standard fee. He was also involved in the production of a seminal work called *Parry's Valuation Tables,* which remains the bible in the field of valuation of, for example, leasehold property. He was sent a copy of this tome with an inscription thanking him for his assistance. At some stage in his career he is believed to have been offered a partnership in Smiths Gore, who wanted him to do valuation work for them, but he turned it down because he could not countenance living within 25 miles of London.

About five years after Marion died, John began to think that he was going to do so too and decided that he should have a home of his own to leave to the family so he acquired Ashcroft, a large house near the Parish church in Haltwhistle and the big move from Bellister took place. At Ashcroft John began the process of never throwing anything away, which gave his children such trouble, and was inherited by at least one of his grandsons. As something of a connoisseur of port (he could identify a vintage with a sip), he generated a good many empty bottles, but even these were preserved. A telephone was installed, though he never quite came to terms with it, seeming to believe that one had to shout sufficiently loudly for the voice to be heard at the other end without benefit of wires. One of his most important decisions was to install, as governess to the younger children, Miss Louie Pooler, who had previously looked after the children of the Viceroy of India. The children were quite a wild lot and spent much of their time tormenting Miss Pooler, whose red hair and florid complexion inspired the name of the Anti-Magenta-Nose Club, which they formed for the purpose. Reacting to the new circumstances by uniting against the rest of the world, they developed a vocabulary and a set of sayings of their own, based on shared experiences, anecdotes and puns of their father's and quotations from books like *Eric, or Little by Little*, which must have been baffling to those not in the know. Years later I composed a "dictionary" of this language, which I gave to David's second wife. It ran to many pages and contained about 200 entries.

Thus, at moments of crisis, they would declaim: "The cook's put her foot in the pudd'n and the blank mange has slippered awa' doon the back stair." When calling for help, especially at railway stations, the cry was "Porter, porter, I've a tin chest." 'I dinna care if you've a wooden leg, it's up the stair and ower the brig for Aberdeen'." The Scottish origins of these cries is obvious but there were several sayings which purported to be French, and were attributed to their father, who is reputed once to have crossed the English Channel. Toast, for example, was invariably referred to as 'Dew pang o rotey" and "Passer m' lore the buttery vous," is self-explanatory. In church when others sang the *Magnificat*, the Clarks sang "Manny coos are hard to keep" and when play acting, they would chant, with one voice, "A druiy stoo' in a dar' ol'woo'," or "Madam, I cannot control the dog." The former was supposed to be an accurate rendering of a recitation given at the Haltwhistle Mechanics' Institute (but history does not relate what the druid did next) and the second was the only line which Betty was given to say in her first play. If the temperature rose to anywhere near most people's comfort zone, they would mop their brows and exclaim: "It's het as Hawick - but gimme Peebles for pleesure," or "I can scarce thole me breeks". When out motoring they greeted every steep slope with "Hills? Down 'em in a jiffy", and all solicitors, medical partnerships or estate agents were known as "Ivans, Kellets and Childs". Cries of "Fah, Lah, Pannicker tanta see" or "Kommarashantu" were harder to pin down, but a favoured "Old English Joke" was "Carry your bag, sir?" "No, let her walk."

Poor Miss Pooler, who had to put up with all this, seems to have been a kind woman, but she was the victim of what was perhaps a natural resentment among the older children for having "replaced" their mother and they gave her a hard time. However, in William, the youngest, for whom she became a genuine mother-substitute, she kindled a lasting affection and he kept in touch with her. He described her in later life as "a sentimental old pussy". There must have been times when she wished she was back with the Viceroy; perhaps that is why she talked of India so much - in Rudyard Kipling idiom.

Although she and Betty were the only females in a very masculine household, there did not develop between them any particular bond and Betty teamed up with the boys. John went off to school at Oundle in the autumn after his mother's death and it was David who masterminded the A.M.N.C.

In 1923 much effort was put into the composition of some execrable verses on the Clark family. These were lovingly typed up and have survived:

> There is a familee called Clark
> Some are fair and some are dark
> There never was such a familee
> From old Paw down to wee Billee
>
> They lived in a hoose twas called Ashcroft
> With a garden and flowers and an apple loft
> They had a farm with sheep and cows
> And an Amurrican cousin called Mrs Dows

Some supplementary verses were evidently considered so scurrilous that they were declared secret. They dealt with the wretched governess:

> Miss Pooler was a sicht to see
> She always adored miseree
> She felt an earth tremor in the night
> Which gave her an unholy fright
> Her nose was a magenta hue
> Her cheeks they were magenta tu
> She did exercises every day
> In training for our Jenny's fray
> One day she said "Upon my soul
> "The whole of Japan in my camisole".

Dennis Herbert, whose introduction to all this we shall come to, preserved the document formally making him an honorary member of "The Ashcroft Military and Naval Club, otherwise called The Anti-Magenta-Nose Club". It was dated 1926 by the President, David, who was by then cruising in *H.M.S. Vampire* in the Adriatic. Under the heading:

Oyez! Oyez! Oyez!

To all whom it may concern

it granted Dennis permission "to sing the club song and attend all meetings, dinners, suppers, breakfasts, teas, luncheons, beanfeasts, thé dansants, café chantants, cocoa drinkants, or any other function of eating given by the club. Also to take part in any outing, games, jousts, tournaments, matches, picnics, or other sports connected with, or organized by, the club" and to see all documents and other writings of the club and wear any apparel or regalia which may from time to time be approved as uniform.

The "Amurrican cousin", another of the children's enemies, was Coz Jane, otherwise Mrs. Dows, a rich Scottish relation of their father's, whose American husband had memorably been the Sheriff of Oyster Bay. He had left her a fortune (allegedly garnered from the sale to churches of Dows Port) - and an American accent. She owned a Rolls Royce and a substantial pile called Rock House at Washington in Sussex, to which the family were frequently bidden and which acquired a legendary quality in their folk lore. Though they were only second cousins (they shared a great grandfather, James Gourlay) Coz Jane and John Clark were quite close and he naturally relied on a female relative after Marion died. She admired the way John had coped with the death of Marion, stepping in, as she described it, to the place of mother as well as father. Coz Jane was, therefore, a frequent visitor, but her visits were regarded with dread by the children because she was very demanding. Betty told Dennis she wished she liked her godmother better, but the Dows habit of laying down the law and always being right was too much to take and the Rolls Royce made her car sick. At brother John's wedding to Audrey Irwin in 1928 she insisted that Betty, who was a bridesmaid, should powder her nose. Betty did not agree! Part of the problem may have been that the Clarks always thought *they* were right, but it must have been trying to have all their activities run down in broad American tones. Coz Jane complained that the pictures were hung too high, that the children had too many shoes, that the churchyard was untidy and the weather too bleak. Nor was she always rational. Convinced, for example, that the gas lighting gave her sunstroke, she wore a hat at table and insisted on one of the two lights being turned out. Because their father tended to support her, she had enough authority to require the children to toe the line. How Miss Pooler must have envied her that.

John McClare himself survived for the most part by busying himself with his enormous workload, but he wrote regularly to his children when they were away and kept a lively interest in their doings. A complete set of his letters to the youngest boy, William, survives and consists of short, but encouraging notes, sent every week. In one, responding to William's "decision" at the age of 16 to take Holy Orders, he summed up his view of family relationships:

> I am quite glad to know you think of taking Orders but you are still

246

very young to decide and we will see what you think in a year or two. You must not think you annoy me in any way. When people love each other there are always times they vex each other but it is soon over & forgotten. Don't think about that sort of thing at all. I want you to be your own natural self and quite open & free with me. None of us is perfect & never will be. So long as we strive to do what is right & love each other all is well.

William, as we shall see, was never able to achieve this ideal and, as John grew older, his children did find him increasingly difficult. They dreaded the sessions of cribbage which they were required to play with him and, at the very end, they grew impatient with their father's inclination to hypochondria. But the warning signs manifested themselves. In early 1937 Ken took his father to the dentist in Carlisle because he was complaining that his teeth felt sharp. After examining the patient, the dentist took Ken aside and said: "I think I ought to warn you that your father has only about six months to live." When Ken asked him how he knew, he replied: "His teeth are like dust. It is always a sure sign." Ken then summoned his uncle, Noel Jackson, who though not John's doctor was on close terms with him. His verdict was that when the autumn leaves began to fall, John would die. One morning in September Ken noticed at the family prayers which were always said at Ashcroft, that John was rambling and repeating himself; he had quickly to usher the staff out of the room. John was still *compos mentis* enough to assert, against all prevailing opinion, that war with Germany was going to come, but the final illness was uncomfortable with the old man wanting to get up and go to a big meeting he believed was taking place. On October 17 he died at the age of 83 and was buried with Marion in the churchyard at Haltwhistle. The *Haltwhistle Echo* reported:

> The church of the Holy Cross, Haltwhistle,was unable to accommodate all who gathered to pay their last respects to Colonel John McClare Clark on Tuesday.

John McClare Clark (1854-1937)

Colonel John McClare Clark on a docile horse.

Ashcroft, Haltwhistle

Miss Pooler, Betty & Billy

FROM HALTWHISTLE TO ALL FOUR CONTINENTS

```
                    ┌── John Clark, b. 1818, m. 1849, d. 1882
            ┌── John McClare Clark, b. 1854, m. 1899, d. 1937
            │     └── Jane/Jean McClare, b. 1821, d. 1868
John Clark, b. 1903, d. 1977
David George Clark,  b. 1907, d. 1960
Elizabeth McClare Clark, b. 1910, d. 1979
Daniel Nicholas Clark, b. 1911, d. 2000
Kenneth Allan Clark, b. 1911, d. 1986
William Donaldson Clark, b. 1916, d. 1985
            │     ┌── Daniel Jackson, b. 1838, m. 1864, d. 1911
            └── Marion Jackson, b. 1877, d. 1917
                  └── Isabella Scott, b. 1841, d. 1920
```

There is a familee called Clark
Some are fair and some are dark
There never was such a familee
From old Paw down to wee Billee – *Family song.*

John (1903-1977)

John McClare and Marion's eldest son, John, was destined for Eton but sometime in the early years of the war, probably through the agency of Coz Jane, the parents became aware of Frederick Sanderson and the great work he was doing at Oundle in the teaching of science and practical subjects. So, in September, 1917, still grieving over his mother's premature death, young John arrived at Bramston House, Oundle to find that he was one of 29 boys new to the school and, therefore, all about the same age, a circumstance which had arisen because the government had raised the age at which boys entered the army. Fewer boys than expected, therefore, left at the end of the preceding summer term and emergency arrangements had to be made for the new intake.

A London lawyer, Dennis Henry Herbert, had been involved in the sale of Laundimer House to the school's governing body, the Grocers' Company, and Bramston House was also purchased during the summer.

Clark, J. soon struck up a particular friendship with Herbert, D.G.R., the lawyer's son, with important consequences which will emerge later. He flourished as a runner and a prefect and achieved those academic goals, which allowed him to go on to take a diploma in agriculture at Armstrong College, later part of Newcastle University. He joined his father in 1924 when the firm of J.M.Clark & Sons was formed, anticipating correctly that one more son, at least, would take to land agency. In 1928 John married Audrey Dorothy Irwin after a courtship that was fraught with difficulty. Breaking into the tightly-knit Clark family was no picnic. John's first love, Joan Cobb, whom he had met while training in Kent, took fright, ostensibly at the prospect of a life in Northumberland, and now Audrey was subjected to much ridicule and some cruelty and she and John had to conduct their romance at the Irwin's weekend retreat in Alston. She would go there to prepare things for a family visit and John would ride up to Alston so that they could have a bit of peace together. The fact was she was rather fussy, a bit sentimental and inclined to be demonstratively affectionate to her fiancé, qualities which the young Clarks especially affected to despise. David particularly disliked her, referring to her as "a fat bitch" and Betty was inclined to think her rather dim, though in later life she became more appreciative. Nick, in adulthood actually wrote to her apologising for the way she was treated by him and his siblings. At any rate she made John happy and presided over a friendly, well-run household. In 1929 their daughter, Maud Marion, was born, to be followed in 1931 by Ruth Irwin, in 1933 by Susan Elizabeth and in 1937 by John Malcolm.

A keen territorial soldier, John went to France with the B.E.F. in 1939, as Lieutenant Colonel, second in command of the 4th Battalion of the Royal Northumberland Fusiliers. He was lightly armed - with a tennis racket and a cricket bat - as he was on the train south after leave when the phoney war, which he had expected to continue, turned nasty. Evacuated from Dunkirk with his diminutive batman, Morris, he liked to tell how, as they were wading out to the rescuing boat, the water began to rise up to Morris's face. An encouraging seaman shouted to him: "Come on, another foot and you'll be there," to which Morris replied, "Yes, and another foot and I'll be oonder!" They both made it home and John was assigned to the War Agriculture Department. He used to go back to Haltwhistle once a month to keep an eye on the firm, which was being run, as a favour and without pay, by a retired land agent. In 1942, as a Lieutenant Colonel in the Directorate of Quartering,

John earned the Territorial Decoration and was awarded an O.B.E.

The authorities commandeered Bellister Castle, to house members of the Halbert family who had come to start the Kilfrost factory. To Audrey and the children this must have seemed rather unfair, but they had to move out to Hallbankhead, the house at Featherstone which had been built for John's grandfather when he first came to Northumberland in the mid 19ᵗʰ Century. It was was cramped and there was no bathroom so they all trooped out once a week for a bath at the nearby Wallace Arms.

John had early become involved in the professional organisations, the Royal Institution of Chartered Surveyors and the Land Agents' Society. After the war he became Chairman of the Northumberland and Durham branch of the former and rose to become the national president in 1969, having already been President of the Chartered Land Agents Society in 1956. By this time the firm had expanded with offices at Hexham, Newcastle and Carlisle and was managing some 120,000 acres of agricultural land. John and Audrey were living in the castle at Featherstone and John, following family tradition, was Chairman of the Haltwhistle Rural District Council, the Hexham and District Employment Committee and the Newcastle and Gateshead Water Company, a Justice of the Peace and Chairman of the Northumberland Juvenile Court. He died in December 1977 at the age of 74.

David George (1905-1960)

If John demonstrated some of the qualities of stolidity and orthodoxy of his paternal forebears, the next son, David George, was a much wilder and more tempestuous character. When he had finished tormenting poor Miss Pooler, he passed out of Dartmouth in March 1924, and continued to run the Anti-Magenta-Nose Club from various of H.M.Ships. The Royal Navy spent a lot of time showing the flag, which involved balls, dances, dinners and other social events interspersed with sporting activities. David relished these and recorded them (though not of course any compromising details) in the official logbook which he kept from 1924, when he joined his first ship, *H.M.S. Royal Oak*, as a Midshipman. He became a specialist in torpedoes, commanding the 2nd Flotilla Motor Torpedo Boats on the China Station, and he had an exciting World War II, being sunk three times and suffering a period of internment after *H.M.S. Edinburgh* went down off the north Russian coast. His favourite story of this period was that the Russian sailors were all fans of Hollywood films but when asked which was their favourite, replied "Twenty thousand foxes"- their version of Twentieth Century Fox. At least one of his torpedoes was reputed to have sunk the German battleship *Scharnhorst* in the Battle of the North Cape in December, 1943 and he was promoted to Commander later that month.

David had red hair, of which more anon, great charm, the social graces learnt on the Royal Naval circuit and a warm heart. Inevitably he was a bit of a *bon viveur* with a liking for fast cars, wine and song, but a broken heart made him, for a while, wary of too close an association with women and he was, with one final exception, unlucky in love. In 1938, while serving on *H.M.S. Royal Sovereign*, at Sheerness, he fell madly in love with a girl who did not reciprocate. As he told his brother William:

> It is all over now, and I have sworn not to see her again, but it was all very disturbing and depressing, and has left me rather bewildered. Take a tip from me, William, and don't fall in love too deeply, because it hurts like hell, during and after. Find a thoroughly reliable girl and get her to love you, not the other way round!!

Unfortunately he did not take his own advice and, when after the war while stationed in India, he met and married Patricia Hazeldine, it was a disaster and ended in divorce. David was so upset that he attempted suicide with the inevitable result that his Naval career was blighted. He was in charge of the battleship *King George V* when she was in dry dock in 1949 and much impressed the author, then aged 15, by inviting him to stay and putting him up in the Vice Admiral's quarters. A day out shooting with David was both extremely energetic and a master-class in naval invective since he frequently missed, but he was also a master of such important works as *1066 and All That* and the *Hunting of the Snark*, an enthusiasm which he passed on to at least one of his nephews. Under the aegis of Mrs. Dows at Rock he got to know Handasyde (Handy) Buchanan, a humorous bookseller with an owl-like demeanour, with whom he shared a liking for gin, a boyish sense of humour and an addiction to croquet fed by an appalling book called *Galore Park*, of which Handy was supposed to have the only surviving copy. David had lost most of the teeth in his upper jaw and wore a rather uncomfortable plate; he therefore used to keep it in his right-hand jacket pocket and, when he was suddenly introduced to someone, developed a complicated scooping gesture which installed the teeth preliminary to a handshake. Weekends when they came to stay were always unusual and occasionally riotous. Handy's wife, Molly, who kept the bookshop accounts, thought David was a bad influence. By now, though, David had married Violet Grant. As a former Wren officer and the daughter of an admiral, with an independent career as a journalist on the books page of the *Daily Telegraph,* she knew how to handle any bumptiousness and was an admirable foil for him. David became Librarian of the Royal Naval College at Greenwich and they set up house in The Paragon, an elegant eighteenth century crescent. When David retired in January, 1957, they moved to Mayfield in Sussex. He died of a heart attack in 1960.

Daniel Nicholas (1911-2000)

Daniel Nicholas, the next brother, the elder of the twins, who was known as Nick, could hardly have been more different – intellectual, religious and a little squeamish about blood sports, preferring to walk over the fells unarmed – but he was a good rugby player and runner, a ready participant in the family high jinks and a courageous soldier. Head of the School at Oundle and a another product of Bramston House, he had a struggle to persuade his father that he should be the first of the family to go to university. He was helped in this by his first choice of career – the church, for which, of course, a degree was necessary. He went up to Balliol to read chemistry and emerged three years later with an upper second class degree. He then embarked on a course at Wycliffe College, but he found he could not entirely accept the 39 articles. This turned out to be typical of Nick's spiritual journey through life; he never quite found an established creed which entirely fitted his own carefully thought-out beliefs, to which he adhered with single-minded honesty. He had already, after a brief flirtation, rejected Frank Buchman's Oxford Group because he could not accept that absolute honesty must be practised even if it inflicted unnecessary hurt on others. Now, with a diploma in theology, he abandoned the idea of ordination and embarked on a career as a schoolmaster. By this time he was known as Nick Clark-Lowes, having added the surname of his godfather who had left him a farm, Allens Green near Hexham, on condition that he do so.

He flirted with pacifism, but decided once the war had begun that it must be carried through and so, in the Royal Northumberland Fusiliers, he was involved in the retreat from Dunkirk and was mentioned in despatches for his role in the rearguard. Characteristically he recalled the moral dilemma of keeping the roads clear of fleeing refugees in order to speed the retreat of the British forces. Later, commanding an Eighth Army anti-tank gun company in a mortar battalion, he was overrun by Rommel's tanks in the Battle of the Cauldron outside Tobruk. The unit ceased to exist as a fighting force with only three officers and two platoons surviving, but Nick re-formed these into an independent anti-tank brigade and went on fighting for another two months. He had various narrow escapes; including one while he was standing on top of a tank as communications had failed, and a tank shell passed through his legs. His siblings used to say it was a good job he had "bow-and-arrow legs," the result of knee trouble, which became a family failing. Repatriated in order to form a new battalion, he made the long journey back via the Cape and New York.

In 1941 he had married Audrey Dixon, daughter of the headmaster of Hillbrow, and their early married life was peripatetic until Nick embarked for the Middle East. Audrey was an artist of some talent, slightly fey and unworldly, for whom housekeeping was of no interest. After the war Nick became Chemistry master at Shrewsbury, but his next career move was a disaster. His father-in-law, W.S.Dixon, had stayed on as headmaster of Hillbrow for too long, causing uncertainty as to the school's future and a consequent fall in numbers. A successor was finally appointed, but fell foul of some of the existing staff and eventually of the Dixons too. Nick was persuaded to take over, which he did in 1954, but things had gone too far, the numbers could not be got up to the required 50 and amalgamation with another establishment seemed the only option. A bad choice was made and relations with the other party went from bad to worse. His son, Francis, wrote of this period:

> This was the nadir of Nick's career. Everything he had worked for had collapsed. In retrospect it seemed clear that he should have heeded the strongly-stated advice of several good friends not to involve himself in this particular amalgamation. He often asked himself later whether he should not have stayed and fought a legal battle with the ex-headmaster. Others would have done so, and might have won. It was, however, very much a part of Nick's character to avoid bruising confrontations; better to wipe the dust from off his feet and move on. The agreement effecting his separation resulted in him taking the debts of Hillbrow with him. There must be a question about the justice of this arrangement, but he accepted it without great protest. The alternative, he said, would have been to go bankrupt, and this would have left the local traders in the lurch.

He got a job as assistant master at Haberdasher's Aske's, a direct grant school near Watford. Here, though he found the adjustment to day-school life and the less-committed attitude of staff difficult to come to terms with, he was successful, but had to supplement his income by selling petrol in two different garages for many years. Another stage in Nick's spiritual journey began when he became Librarian of the Psychical Research Society, which was concerned with the study of ghosts, poltergeists, telepathy and clairvoyance. As he explained in a newspaper interview:

> I was born and brought up in Bellister Castle in Northumberland. It
> was supposed to be haunted by the ghost of a minstrel murdered in
> the 13th century. The owner of the castle was constantly warring with
> other local lords along the Border region. He suspected the minstrel
> was a spy. He set his bloodhounds on the poor man and they tore him
> to pieces.
>
> I come from a religious family and I've taught chemistry most of my
> life. Combine the two and you can see why I'm interested in the
> paranormal!

He was, as ever, strictly practical in his assessment of the reports which the
Society received. Out of an average of 20 received every week a fair
proportion were "plainly crackers" but others were more considerable and
about six a year merited a full investigation. He believed that the right
approach was neither to try to fit evidence into the accepted scientific view of
the universe nor into the accepted religious view, but to start with knowledge
and then add faith. He had an abundance of both knowledge and faith, but
when he died in July, 2000, I suspect that he had not resolved the issue to his
own satisfaction.

Kenneth Allan (1911-1986)

May 10, 1940 was the day Winston Churchill became Prime Minister and
the phoney war came to an end with the German invasion of Belgium and
Holland. On that day Kenneth Allan Clark, the younger twin, found himself at
the age of 28, in command of the 4th Battalion of the Royal Northumberland
Fusiliers because his brother John, who was second in command, had gone on
leave the previous day and Colonel Wood was cut off by the suspension of
sailings from England. He thus led the British Expeditionary Force into
Belgium. Forty-five years later Ken told me how it happened.

He was woken at 6.0am by Morris, John's batman, who said in his chirpy
Northumbrian accent:"Meestor Ken, you are wanted immediately at
heedquarters." He was taken by surprise that neither of his superiors were
there, but he went off to H.Q. which turned out to be General Montgomery's.
There were a lot of top brass there and Ken concealed himself behind the
piano, but Monty said the person he really wanted to see quickly was the C.O.
of the 4th Battalion, Northumberland Fusiliers. So he stepped forward and
saluted. Monty said "You are very young," and Ken began to explain, but
Monty interrupted, saying "I don't mind. I am sorry to tell you that the
Germans are advancing very fast. I want you to go now and capture the bridge

on the River Dyle. You had better go at once." Ken saluted and turned to leave. Monty said " You are a territorial aren't you?" Ken said he was. "Well", said Monty, "I have a great respect for territorials but you can tell your chaps that this time there is no need to wait to close the gate." He added, "I will be over to see you this evening."

Ken rushed back and set off for the bridge. On the way they came to a level crossing with a train shunting to and fro across the road. Ken realised that it was a tactic to delay them. He took his pistol, which he had never fired before, went to the driver of the train and indicated to him that if he didn't get out of the way he would shoot him. That solved the problem. They got to the bridge just before the Germans, but they were very short of weapons and ammunition. They had three-inch mortars and Ken ordered them to be used, but all the ammunition turned out to be smoke (for practice) and there was no high explosive. He ordered his men to let off everything they could, including the smoke, which persuaded the Germans that they had a formidable force ahead of them and they held back. When Monty came round that evening, he congratulated Ken and said he was recommending him for a medal, but nothing ever transpired. Monty asked whether Ken needed anything and Ken told him that they had nothing to fight with. Monty said he would sort it out and he did. John Clark returned from leave on the next day and took over command.

A few days later, the Germans counter-attacked with tanks, continuing to fight after dark, which Ken said he thought at the time " a bit much". The French gave way on the right and the Northumberland Fusiliers were surrounded. Ken remembered sheltering behind a bank opposite a field, green with waving corn. Then the Stuka bombers attacked. When the raid was over the field was completely ploughed up. Yet only two or three of his men had been hit. Later, when he was leading his men from the middle ("You weren't supposed to lead from the front") on the line of march, they were bombed again by Stukas. They had been trained to dive into the ditch. Ken noticed, though, that the bombs came out sideways from the bombers and invariably fell in the ditch. If you walked down the middle of the road, you were all right. After that he had to lead from the front. Eventually Ken was hit on the head by a piece of shrapnel and was knocked out. He had recovered consciousness by the time, hopelessly surrounded, they were captured on Sunday, May 26th, 1940 – the day the evacuation from Dunkirk began.. He thought it might be a good idea to try to escape "But that was when the Germans were really rather brutal." They knocked him about with rifle butts, breaking off all his front teeth.

257

It took a month for the news to reach Haltwhistle, where on successive days Audrey, at Bellister, received a telegram from the War Office saying that he was missing and a card from him saying that he had been captured but was "quite all right". If this was something of an exaggeration in view of the lost teeth, it was nevertheless very welcome news and was prominently reported in the *Haltwhistle Echo*. It is said that an obituary of him was printed at this time and that, when he returned five years later, he was one of the few people to read his own death notice.

Ken said he was one of the very first British prisoners captured by the Germans. They numbered them from 200 and Ken was number 209. At one time he was in Colditz, where he kept in touch with the progress of the war by listening to the nightly nine o'clock news on the camp's illicit radio, put together from bits and pieces of stolen material. When they moved from camp to camp, the bits of radio would be concealed in the medicine balls used for exercise. One day General Alfred Jodl, Chief of the Operations Staff of the German High Command, came to the camp. He told the prisoners they would soon be home because Germany would have won the war. Jodl arrived in a superb Mercedes, which was at once surrounded by admiring prisoners, who flattered the driver, saying "No wonder you are winning the war if you can build cars like this." Meanwhile they stole all the light bulbs (to make radio valves) and numerous other bits and pieces. When Jodl came to leave, the car had to be pushed out of the camp.

At Laufen camp, about midway through the war, Ken helped to dig an escape tunnel. In order to get below the constant probes of the guards, the tunnel had to be deep and the entrance trap door had to be well covered by sand. This meant that it took about 20 minutes to get in and out which increased the claustrophobia from which Ken had always suffered. One day when he was down the tunnel, filling sacks with the earth dug back by the front people, one of the diggers cut through the taut electric cable they had rigged up for light and fan ventilators. The wire snaked back and the live end hit Ken on the forehead, imparting a considerable electric shock. "The trouble was that, as I was sitting in a pool of water, every time I moved I got another one." The fan stopped working and air became short; he pulled the alarm bell, but he knew that it would take at least 20 minutes to get him out. Over forty years later when he had a heart attack and was similarly breathless every detail of the incident would flash through his head night after night and he could not get it out of his mind.

In all Ken made three escapes, after one of which he had his toenails pulled out, but on another occasion when plans were made for an escape over the wire, using scaling ladders, he drew an administrative job in the ballot, which meant that he had to stay behind. However, it also involved "the worst job I ever had in my life" - scraping the insulation off the main electric cable into the camp so that the lights would fail. If he didn't go far enough, the escape would fail; if he went too far the lights would go up with a bang and so would he. But he managed it, the lights went out and 150 men escaped over the wire, three of whom eventually made it back to Britain.

When the end of the war came, Ken was at Regensburg, where he was liberated by General George Patton with his pearl-handled revolvers. He met Patton because he had been put in charge of a lot of very bolshie white South African prisoners and he had to make representations on their behalf. Patton told him "Stay put and don't try to get away. You will be taken care of.." The Americans had said repatriation would be strictly block by block with no favouritism, but all the Americans went first. He and his South Africans were eventually flown out in Dakotas to Rheims, where they arrived on VE Day. They were supposed to be flown to Britain the next day, but the aircraft never turned up - not unnaturally the R.A.F. had been celebrating. The South Africans were getting restive; Ken saw a group of high-ranking officers talking on the airfield. He went up to one who had a lot of rings on his arm and told him what he thought. He said if something didn't happen soon he could not be responsible for controlling the South Africans any more. "I used plenty of unparliamentary language." The officer said he was equally unhappy about the non-appearance of the aircraft, but Ken had his assurance that they would come the following morning. Afterwards one of the lower-ranking officers said to Ken, "Who the hell do you think you are? Do you know who you were talking to?" Ken replied that he neither knew nor cared. "Well it was Air Chief Marshal Tedder!" The aircraft were there in the morning.

They were bombers and Ken remembered sitting on the floor looking out through the bomb doors at the sea below. It was only his second flight. They arrived at Brize Norton, where many of the service people were WAAFS. Ken was astonished because he had never before seen a woman in trousers. It soon became apparent that more prisoners were arriving than the authorities were expecting, and anyone who had accommodation to which he could go was allowed to leave. A friend of Ken's knew that his father had a flat in London so together they went there. Champagne flowed and eventually he was shown up to a very comfortable bedroom, but he could not sleep in a soft bed and had to move onto the floor. It took him a long time to get used to a bed again.

Next day he took the *Flying Scotsman* to Newcastle, where he was met by John, who, however, did not recognise him (before the war Ken had weighed 11 stone, but he now weighed eight). When they met they said "Hello" and shook hands. As Ken remarked: "We're not like the French who kiss each other on both cheeks and we couldn't think what to say. But it seemed somehow inadequate." Next day Ken went into the office and resumed work, but some weeks later he was summoned to a hotel and told that he still had two months to serve in the Army. "What would you like to do?" the officer asked. "I told him that, quite frankly, whatever he said, I was not going back. I had started work again and was going to carry on." And that was what happened.

A few days after he got back he went down to London and had a celebration with his brothers David and Nick and Handy Buchanan. It was a considerable pub crawl. He remembered getting back to the place in Shepherd's Market from which they had started out and the restaurateur meeting them at the door, holding up his hands and saying "Gentlemen, I beseech you, not again!"

As a prisoner of war Ken had run a correspondence training course for land agents, by which means he trained over a dozen new recruits. He also made contacts which enabled him to bring new business to J.M.Clark & Sons. He was resident agent for one of these, Lord Barnard's Raby estate, while John looked after the old clients. Ken settled into a house in Staindrop, where he had a long, low MG sports car which he drove extremely fast. In March, 1949 he announced his engagement to Joan Aileen Noblett, who came from Chard in Somerset, but she was diagnosed with a serious malady and very sadly fell from a train and was killed. Ken's sister, Elizabeth, who was on leave from Africa, hastened to Staindrop to console him, but it was a difficult period. Two years later, however, he became engaged to Patricia Ann Trotter of Staindrop and they were married in November, 1951. They moved to Loughbrow House in Hexham where twin daughters, Vanessa Jane and Ursula Sarah, and a son, Kenneth Nicholas, were born to them.

In youth Ken had followed his Jackson uncles to Durham School, where he emulated their athletic prowess and went on to become an extraordinarily versatile sportsman. He played fly half for Blackheath and was on the verge of the England Rugby XV, but broke his collarbone in the trial match, he set a new Army record for the mile, which lasted 20 years, he played cricket for Durham County and he was an accomplished horseman - a successful point-to-point rider and a member of the England show-jumping team. He gave me

260

much kudos, deputising for my father in the Father's Match at Hillbrow, when he hit our best fast bowler for several lofty sixes over the castle perimeter wall before getting himself out. But his top-class sporting days were over and he began to concentrate on other matters. He and John did not always see eye to eye, but the division of labour within the firm enabled them to rub along and business flourished. One particularly proud boast was that he succeeded, on behalf of a client, in investing £1m in property between Christmas Eve and New Year, not the most promising time of year for such a task. He was Chairman of Norwich Union and of the appeal which raised £100,000 in 18 months for the CARE village at Ponteland. He joined the board of the Northern Rock Building Society and, after a five-year spell as Deputy Chairman, became Chairman in 1977. He was also High Sheriff of the county. Though, in general, he shared King George V's view that "abroad is hell", he was even persuaded in retirement to make the occasional foreign trip. At the end of his life Ken suffered from heart trouble. After an attack in 1984 he wrote to me:

> I did have a very frightening few days but thankfully that is all over and I am now on the mend, but it is going to be a long haul and I will have to do what I am told and be patient; neither of which figure largely in my characteristics; but I got a big enough fright to make me think twice before I try to do too much.

He began to work on a book about three generations of Clarks, but the work was cut short and he died on March 29, 1986.

William Donaldson (1916-1985)

Billy, as he was known in youth, though he grew up to become William, was the brightest of all the children and had considerable athletic ability too. He was head of the school at Oundle (Bramston House, of course), and gained a scholarship to read history at Oriel College, Oxford emerging with a First class degree, and a clutch of honours, including a prestigious Gibbs prize. He was captain of gymnastics at school and won a half-blue as a hurdler. These achievements owed much to strong sibling rivalry and a lack of parental empathy. As William himself put it: "I looked to my father as the source of all personal promotion, and only by pleasing him could I hope to advance to a position where I might rival or even excel my elder brothers."

This may seem unfair to John McClare Clark, who was a conscientious and caring father, but the fact was that, with a gap of 62 years between them, William saw the relationship as distant and cool – effectively non-existent.

261

Paradoxically this seems to have been a greater difficulty even than the loss of his mother when he was still a baby. It was said of Boswell that he was an eternal disciple, in constant search of a prophet whose mantle should cover him – of guides, philosophers and friends – in short of father substitutes. The author, F.L.Lucas, called it a Telemachus-complex, after the son of Odysseus who found fame seeking his lost father, and one can see William's life as the search for a succession of Dr. Johnsons. He himself recognised it. He was going to call a personal autobiography *Four Fathers*, to tell of the dominating influences of his life, but in the event what he wrote was a more political book *From Three Worlds* so he did not develop the theme. Looking at his career through the prism of these recurrent father figures, one can see that the first was John McClare himself, whom William only knew after he was of retirement age, lonely and inclined to be depressive. It is sad that their relationship was not better, but at least in its effect on William, we have to accept that it was galvanising but unhappy.

He departed for Oundle with the benefit of a talk from William Dixon on the technicalities of sex, which astonished him, and an injunction from his father, who said: "If a boy wants to do something with you, tell Matron, but I don't think they will because you are not good looking."At school he tried God as a father figure and shortly before his 17th birthday announced that he had decided to take Holy Orders. With his brother Nick he became involved in running Christian conferences, but God failed to fill the bill and William pronounced himself agnostic. He is revealed by a diary he kept at Oundle for a few months in 1934 as suffering typical teenage problems::

> Depression came on very badly at night. I do so terribly badly want someone to talk to, someone to halve the weight of the burden by sharing it. I know if I could find him or could laugh at many of the things that now seem so disheartening. My prayers have lately descended to saying "Oh God" with varying degrees of bitterness, perhaps I will now try saying "Oh God be a friend or find me one."

However, it was more complicated than that; he did have friends and indeed was much preoccupied by what he called a series of "amicitates"- friendships with other boys which would appear to have been platonic, but were intense and represented that longing for approbation. Obliquely he discussed this with Dudley Heesom, his history teacher, who was a real friend and was to remain so for life:

> We also discussed shortly the knotty problem of friendships between boys of very different ages. It is a problem that I am very little fitted to speak on because it has never occurred to me. The dangers seem

to be the danger of immorality, which is a danger that some people would never dream of letting enter their heads. There is also the effect it has on the younger boy when his Maecenas has been inevitably withdrawn. On the elder boy it has the bad effect of withdrawing him from his own proper set so that it is improbable he will make any of those valuable casual friendships that are born and die at school, but which do give colour to life at school. He will in fact be driven in on himself in those long periods when he is parted from his friend. Yet really Pat, Mills, Gregg all seem to have made casual acquaintances – in the two first cases with me – which have blossomed into quite good friendship.

The diary ends abruptly in March and, though there is evidence of an active social life at Oxford, he does not seem there to have found a father figure. When he departed for the United States in 1938, with a Commonwealth scholarship to the University of Chicago, it was different. It was typical of William, who collected the friendships of the famous, that Bertrand Russell should arrive in Chicago as a visiting fellow on the same day. He taught William to question received wisdom, but he was not authoritarian enough to fulfil William's other needs. He was followed by the historian, R.H.Tawney, whose vision of a Europe without nation states was inspirational, and Lord Halifax, who as Ambassador in Washington, was concerned to counter American isolationism but foresaw the need for the "Big Three" to take notice post-war of other important nations like India. Finally Maynard Keynes, who arrived in 1944 to begin constructing the post-war economic world, inspired William with "a dizzying vision" of a brave new world without beggars.

William's version of the family knee problem had ruled him out of military service and added to his many complexes another one – a feeling that he was not doing his bit as his brothers had in the war. In 1941 he began three years with the British Information Services in Chicago and a spell as Press Attaché at the Embassy in Washington., doing his best to counter isolationist opinion in the Middle West which was determined to keep America out of the war. This was valuable work, but William could never quite equate it with putting one's life on the line and when, years later he fell mortally ill, he took comfort from the thought that it enabled him to look death bravely in the eye, which he duly did.

After the war William went to London to edit the *Encyclopaedia Britannica,* but he found the job offered less scope than he had expected and soon migrated to the *Observer* where as Diplomatic Correspondent he could

263

deal in some of the big ideas which his former father figures had inspired in him. Here he also came under the spell of perhaps his greatest father figure, the Editor, David Astor. Astor had an extraordinary ability to get the best out of a motley collection of wayward geniuses, whom he collected around him and who, for a couple of decades produced some of the best journalism of the century. Softly spoken, unflappable and courageous, he had the quality of calm authority which William needed. He was also dedicated to ameliorating the problems of Africa and the Third World, which fitted in neatly with Keynes's "dizzying vision". William gave something in return. According to Astor's biographer, he became the Editor's closest personal confidant, was ostentatiously brilliant and contributed much by becoming the court jester on the staff. When, at an editorial conference, staff were discussing who had proposed T.S.Eliot for the Order of Merit, William's contribution was: "I have heard it was the Ministry of Agriculture because he had written a poem called 'The Waste Land' and that it was the Archbishop of Canterbury, who's hoping for another murder in the cathedral."

When William wrote to Astor, expressing frustration at not doing more hard work, and asking for help in stretching his intellectual abilities further, Astor replied, in longhand, advising him to calm down and allow the psychoanalysis which he had encouraged William to undergo to take effect. It would, he said, reduce inner tensions and enable more sensible decisions to be made. He added:

> Now, TAKE HEART. All is not lost. There's a good time coming.
> You're in amongst friends. You're doing fine. *Continuer mon brave.*
> I'm on your side. We're all on your side.

This, of course, was just the kind of language which William needed to hear and his admiration for David Astor became even greater when the inadequacies of his next chosen father-figure became apparent. Early in 1955 William had been approached about the possibility of becoming Press Secretary to Anthony Eden. It was not an opportunity that he had it in him to refuse. He was flattered to be asked, he was attracted about the prospect of power and he felt that he could work with Eden, whom in many respects he admired. So he moved into No. 10 Downing Street. At first things went well. William found the Prime Minister far stronger, far tougher, far more decisive and even more fundamentally decent than he had supposed. He told his analyst he was enjoying it, despite the frustrations and the fact that the novelty was wearing off. But it soon became apparent that Eden was not going to be Doctor Johnson to William's Boswell. The problem was that he too craved adulation. When William suggested that he would be judged on the success of his team, Eden's reply was: "But what if the captain never scores any runs?" And true to form William himself began to be jealous of the other civil servants who surrounded the P.M. and to feel that Eden did not love him because he associated him with "the beastly Press". By May, 1956, after the Soviet leaders, Bulganin and Khruschev had been on a visit to London, William's verdict was much more severe:

> Eden is a fascinating character to watch, especially to an ex-analysee. He is very nearly mad, & has a great deal of genius. During the Russian visit I saw him at his public best (the world owes him a great debt) & at his private worst.....He bullied us, swore at us, was silly, absurd, vain, cruel – all the things he was <u>not</u> to the Russians, to Parliament & to the public.

> Personally I am having to learn (& you'll see how hard it is for me) to get all the blame, & give <u>all</u> of the credit back. People say the P.M. is vain; it is true to say he is pathologically in need of all possible praise. He sucks it up, inverts it if necessary, passes on none of it. Very different from David Astor, whom I admire more in retrospect than I could as a colleague. I see that in a curious way David was a great character: Eden is a mean, cruel, silly character; yet – yet he is very good at the game of international politics. No sense of humour at all, no breadth of vision, little wisdom, really very little learning – yet, again, with good instincts; to prevent class war, international rivalry, American hegemony, even German revival to too great an extent.

Worse was to come with the invasion of Egypt in November, 1956, a venture with which William was completely out of sympathy. Once this was evident he was frozen out of the information loop and was acutely unhappy. He knew that he must resign. On November 4, the eve of the Anglo-French landings in Egypt, he went down to his country cottage, Sheepbrook, near Watlington, to clear his mind and next day told the Cabinet Secretary, Sir Norman Brook, in a letter which he personally typed so that the contents should not leak, that he was going. He asked for advice on how it should be done so as to do the minimum damage to "the Master I have served to the best of my ability faithfully". He added:

> Let me make one thing clear at once. I have held a very privileged position as a Civil Servant. I will make no demonstration on leaving, nor when I have regained freedom will I use past privilege in any immediate way. (I mean this far beyond the bounds of the Official Secrets Act.) Indeed I intend if I can to go abroad for a year.

The following evening he wrote to Eden:

> When you asked me to come here a year ago I agreed to try my hand
> at the job for a year. When that year was up you were in the midst of
> the Suez crisis.
>
> Tonight's good news of a cessation of hostilities provides an
> opportunity for me to say that in present circumstances I feel you
> should have the services of a stronger advocate than I can be.

He went off to minister to Hungarian refugees in Austria and then, reverting to type, to become the *Observer* correspondent in India. It had been a bruising experience, especially for one with William's susceptibilities, but he was buoyed up by the many expressions of admiration and support which he received – and cast down by some of the others which included criticism from some of his siblings. After a year in India and two years back in London under David Astor's wing editing a digest of the week's news which the *Observer* was pioneering, the pull of the North-South divide became too strong to resist and he left to run, as its Director, the Overseas Development Institute, whose benevolent realism was a rarity in the field. He flourished during this period but had little hesitation in taking up the next offer he received – a return to Washington to be Director of Information for the World Bank. Arriving on the same day as the Bank's new President, Robert S. McNamara, William very quickly elevated him to father figure status, the last in a line of distinguished paters. They were to spend 12 years working closely together and both said they found it extremely rewarding. McNamara had the kind of determined strength of character that William expected in his father figures. McNamara found William a valued friend and colleague:

> To be a desk-bound bureaucrat was his idea of purgatory; he needed
> to see at first-hand the progress made and the problems remaining.
> Upon them he brought to bear a lively perspective, often seeing or
> sensing what others, including me, would miss. And how we enjoyed
> the name-filled anecdotes told by this man who could so happily
> laugh at himself. A man of boundless energy too, who could remind
> us of the athletic triumphs of his youth and then delight in claiming
> that he now had the fastest limp in the free world!

When he left the World Bank, as a Vice-President in 1980 it was only because another authoritarian figure was demanding his presence. Though she could hardly be categorised as a father figure, Dame Barbara Ward, Lady Jackson, had for long been an inspiration to William and now, in her last days, she appealed to him to succeed her as President of the International Institute for Environment and Development, a body designed to focus attention on

266

economic development, the environment and human needs. He could not resist and it proved a rewarding final move.

William's search for the ultimate Dr. Johnson was, inevitably, never to be realised and it was mirrored in the history of his personal relationships. Unable to commit himself completely for fear of being smothered, he gave women with whom he had affairs (including Lord Russell's third wife) the impression that he was using them, and his competitiveness sometimes got in the way of his friendships with men. Although he never completed his course of psychoanalysis, he did get some relief from it. Writing to his analyst, Mrs Hoffer, in 1956, he said:

> I tend now to feel that I am stuck in the way of life I have got, whereas I used to feel that analysis (=Mrs Hoffer=father=God) would pull me out of my bog & without effort by me make me great, famous, rich & successful. Specifically I feel that I shall not now grow out of being a 'homosexual', at least that I shall not marry. I feel that I shall not grow into being a famous writer etc. Partly this is being 39¾ years old! partly guilt, partly fact. Perhaps too it is the process of reconciling myself to being me, and to not being a Walter Mitty capable of everything – or capable in whimsy of being anything.

William learned that he had incurable liver cancer on All Hallows Eve in 1984, not long after the publication of *Cataclysm*, his prediction of the world economy collapsing because the Third World refused to pay its debts – a prediction much bolder then than now, 20 years later. He faced death bravely, sustained by the award of an Honorary Fellowship at Oriel, a wish to complete his memoirs and design his own tombstone, by his many friends and particularly by his niece Celia Goodhart and his friend and associate of 25 years, David Harvey. Not long before he died in 1985 William wrote:

> Poverty can be as devastating as plutonium; the South presents as great a challenge as the East, and at least as urgent.

Famous almost-last words.

John Clark (1903-1977)

Midshipman D. Clark (1907-1960)

Elizabeth Clark (1910-1979)

Nicholas Clark (1911-2000)

Kenneth Clark (1911-1986)

William Clark (1916-1985)

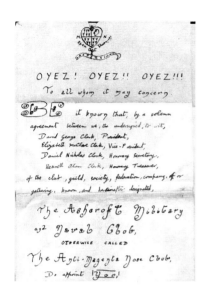

Shooting Party. L to R:Nick, John,David & Ken.

Anti-Magenta-Nose Club certificate

The last time all were together - the author's wedding, Harrogate, November, 1958.

269

Part IV

-------------Chapter 28 ------------

FROM CARMUNNOCK TO HEXHAM

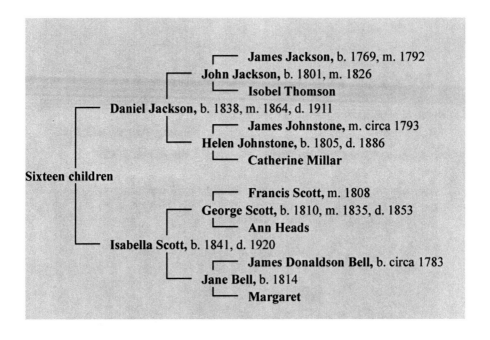

James Jackson, b. 1769, m. 1792
John Jackson, b. 1801, m. 1826
Isobel Thomson
Daniel Jackson, b. 1838, m. 1864, d. 1911
James Johnstone, m. circa 1793
Helen Johnstone, b. 1805, d. 1886
Catherine Millar
Sixteen children
Francis Scott, m. 1808
George Scott, b. 1810, m. 1835, d. 1853
Ann Heads
Isabella Scott, b. 1841, d. 1920
James Donaldson Bell, b. circa 1783
Jane Bell, b. 1814
Margaret

Who shall find a valiant woman;
Her children rose up and called her blessed. - *Proverbs, 32*

When Daniel Jackson first came to Hexham in 1861 it was a very noxious town. A few years earlier a sanitary inspector had pronounced it filthier, more overcrowded and neglected than any town of comparable size in the country. The stench of dead horses being rendered down for fertiliser hung in the air, and human and animal excrement mingled in the water supply with the output of several slaughter houses. There was virtually no sewerage system and piles of ordure had to be removed from time to time by men with carts. This awful situation had been allowed to persist because there were in power on what was laughingly called the Hexham Board of Health, a group of men who came to be known as "the dirty party" and whose guiding principle was that the rates should not be increased.

A couple of years after Daniel took a room in Orchard House on one of Hexham's main streets, and was recorded there in the 1861 census as a surgeon of Glasgow University, things began to improve. Three men with some reforming zeal were elected and slowly began to make progress. Amazingly some of their main opponents were medical men, which must have seemed extraordinary to a young man who in Glasgow had sat at the feet of the great Joseph Lister, promoter of antisepsis in surgery.

Why Daniel should have come to Hexham is not certain but it is believed that friendship with a young Glasgow contemporary, Francis Scott, was responsible. At any rate the move was to have a fundamental effect on Daniel's personal and professional life. The Scott family lived just round the corner from Orchard House, in Fore Street, where Jane Scott continued to run the tobacconist and grocer's shop that she had shared with her late husband, George. Their 19-year-old daughter, Isabella, was away staying with an aunt in London when the census was taken, but on June 9, 1864, Daniel Jackson and Isabella Scott were married in the parish church – and a very extraordinary union it turned out to be.

Daniel's origins were comparatively mundane. He came from farming stock in a rural area of Lanarkshire which was soon to be submerged by the exponential growth of Glasgow. Carmunnock, which had a population of about 700 when Daniel's father John and grandfather James were born there in 1801 and 1769 respectively, is still a conservation village, but the Jackson farms, Netherton and Carntyne, are long gone. Cambuslang, where Daniel's grandmother and he were both born, is now indistinguishable and is known as the largest village in Scotland.

At first sight Isabella's forebears were no more remarkable than her new husband's, but a persistent legend suggests that she may have been descended from the Dukes of Buccleugh and therefore from Charles II via his beautiful but insipid mistress Lucy Walters. The story is that the Duke of Buccleugh fell in love with his gardener's daughter and fathered a son by her. The boy was given the most mundane of the Buccleughs' many surnames, Scott, was

271

named George, was "looked after" at a safe distance from the Ducal estates in the borders and became the father of Isabella. Though one is duty-bound to be sceptical of such stories, there are a number of circumstances which can be adduced in its favour:

1. Henry, the third Duke of Buccleugh (1746-1812) was known to fraternise with "the lower orders", visiting their cottages in disguise, ostensibly to learn about their way of life.

2. George Scott's baptism is registered at Hexham on October 30, 1810 and he is shown as the twin of Margaret Scott, both being born on October 24, children of Francis and Ann Scott, tobacconist. The entry is in handwriting quite different to those of all the other entries on the page and they are the only children whose dates of birth are given. An explanation for this could be that George had been "added" to another family and the entry in the register arranged accordingly. Within reason the children would not have to have been exactly the same age; otherwise the coincidence of the surname might have stretched credulity.

3. An entry for the marriage of Francis Scott (Tobacconist) and Ann Heads, by licence on July 30, 1808 in Hexham gives the bride's name and other details in pencil while the bridegroom's name is in ink. Could Ann have been the gardener's daughter?

4. The story was subscribed to by several of Isabella's grandchildren, including one who was actually mistaken for Alice, Duchess of Gloucester, who was a Buccleugh. The occasion was in 1941 when she went shopping at Liberty in London and found that the larger-than-usual crowd of shoppers parted respectfully when she arrived, thinking that she was the Duchess, who was expected shortly. In 1960 William Clark was touring the Hermitage Museum in Leningrad and saw a family portrait of the Buccleughs in which the Duchess bore a striking resemblance to his mother Marion and his sister, Elizabeth. Apparently the Intourist guide noticed that William Clark himself bore a resemblance to the Duchess in the portrait. My wife and I once saw a Buccleugh portrait of a red-haired man who looked very like David Clark, R.N., but we have not been able to locate the picture again.

Readers will bring their own degrees of scepticism to bear on this tale; many may agree with Francis Clark-Lowes, who postulates that George was indeed illegitimate but that the story was got up simply to make the best of a bad job. Alternatively, noting that the Duke concerned died only two years after George was born, he wondered if it might have been George's father,

Francis (incidentally, a Buccleugh name) who was of royal descent.

Whatever her origins Isabella turned out to be a remarkable mother. She gave Daniel 16 children in 23 years. The complete roll is as follows:

Jane Jackson, b. 1865, d. 1946
John Archibald Jackson, b. 1866, d. 1951
Helen Jackson, b. 1867, d. 1940
George Scott Jackson, b. 1869, d. 1946
Isabella Jackson, b. 1870, d. 1955
Daniel Noel Jackson, b. 1871, d. 1945
Katherine Jackson, b. 1873, d. before 1961
Donaldson Bell Jackson, b.1875, d. 1958
Marion Jackson, b. 1877, d. 1917
Frances Jackson, b. 1879, d. 1961
Robert Jackson, b. 1881, d. 1888
Letitia Mary Jackson, b. 1881, d. 1962
Gertrude Octavia Jackson, b. 1883, d. after 1963
Charles Strathnairn Jackson, b. 1884, d. 1955
Agnes Nona Jackson, b. 1886, d. 1948
Edythe Jackson, b. 13 Nov 1888, d. 1960

Of these only one, Robert who died of Scarlet fever aged 7, failed to reach adulthood. Indeed only three of them failed to reach 70 and a healthy seven lived to be 80 or over. All bar three - Jane, Charles and Edythe – were married. Their descendants, at the end of 2002 were approaching 500 in number, scattered over four continents.

In his early years in Hexham Daniel, who had gone into practice with a Dr. John Nicholson, concentrated on his medical career, but in 1876, alarmed perhaps at the high death-rate in the town, he was appointed Medical Officer of Health and began a battle to clean up Hexham which was to last for many years. He may also have been motivated by the work of Robert Koch, whose work on anthrax demonstrated in that same year for the first time that disease was not, as hitherto assumed, caused by miasms or polluted air, but by microbes. In his first quarterly report he set out the principal causes of the high death rate, suggested remedies and urged speedy action. Nothing happened and three years later he offered this stern comment:

> I regret that my suggestions have not been carried out, and in
> consequence of this neglect the death-rate of the district, of which
> the sanitary condition has been to your care, instead of decreasing

has been steadily increasing until it has become higher than that of
any other place similarly situated in Great Britain.

What he wanted dealt with were the badly-built and badly-sited
slaughterhouses, the inefficient system of refuse collection, the huge
uncovered middens, the pools of stagnant water which made the streets almost
impassable, houses without gutters, the failure to flush and ventilate the
sewers and the absence of an isolation hospital. However, the opposition were
determined and when Daniel urged the Board to increase the water supply,
they claimed that the town was groaning under the weight of taxation and
there was no need for further supply; they proposed to use water which had
been previously rejected because it was believed to be polluted by farm waste.
Daniel went into battle. He pointed out that the water was coming between a
pigsty and a farmyard midden and a few feet away was a cesspool gathering
liquid manure. He wrote to the Board accusing them of not showing proper
consideration for the health of the inhabitants and he sent a copy of his letter
to the Local Government Board in London. The chairman in Hexham
responded by charging Daniel with "unparalleled impertinence" and a year-
long campaign of denigration was mounted against him. Daniel's next report
was described as "most unmitigated lies," one-sided and false, but he stuck to
his guns and in 1881 had to fight a contested election for the job of Medical
Officer of Health. His opponent, who had no experience of public health,
nevertheless came within a single vote of defeating him. The *Hexham
Courant*, expressing surprise that in view of the hard things said about him,
Daniel had even allowed his name to go forward, reported , however, that he
had received the votes of people who had previously criticised him. After this
things did begin gradually to improve and the Local Government Board
proved obdurate allies. When he finally retired in 1910 a new drainage system
was in place and an improved water system had been secured. The death rate
had dropped from 34 to 16 per thousand and an isolation hospital had been set
up.

These public-spirited battles did not, however, take up all of Daniel's time.
Beside his medical practice, and service on the bench as a Justice of the
Peace, he was certifying surgeon under the Factory Acts and medical officer
to several societies including the Free Gardeners, the Oddfellows and the
Forester Friendly Societies. He joined the Hexham company of the Volunteers
as a private, becoming eventually its surgeon and he won several shooting
trophies. He also subscribed to the construction of a tennis club and was a
keen farmer. His first farm was Highford, south-west of the town, but in 1882
a grateful patient left him Bellister Castle, Haltwhistle, a 13th Century pele

tower with a castellated farmhouse and associated land, which he later increased by purchase. He and his burgeoning family moved in to the castle, which he restored, and he became known locally for his excellent shorthorn cattle and Leicester sheep, which he successfully exhibited at agricultural shows.

Then, on Tuesday, February 6, 1900, disaster struck, as reported in *The Times*:

> Bellister Castle, residence of Dr. Jackson, was destroyed by fire yesterday morning. The outbreak which is supposed to have been caused by mice eating matches, was discovered between 6 & 7 o'clock & before help could be obtained from Haltwhistle, a mile distant, the flames had obtained such a strong hold that all the firemen could do was to remove part of the furniture on the ground floor. The building itself and the most valuable part of its contents were destroyed. The water taps near the house were frozen and the water supply, as a consequence, was inadequate for extinguishing fire. The family and the servants were, with difficulty, rescued, many of them in their sleeping attire. The manor of Bellister dates back to the 12th Century, and the castle had in recent years been restored by Dr. Jackson. The castle was insured.

It is reassuring to find that the cause of the fire, which was always attributed in the family legend to mice eating matches, has obtained the imprimatur of *The Times*, and if the story seems a little odd to a modern reader, it is necessary to remember that in 1900 the safety match had not been invented and friction on the head of the match could ignite it.

After the fire the family moved temporarily into a house at Bridge End, but they soon settled in to Netherton in Hexham, while the surgery and other offices were at Carntyne, both houses named after his ancestral farms in Scotland. It was typical of Daniel Jackson that he had Bellister well insured – he was a highly competent businessman and he built up a substantial portfolio of property during his years in Hexham. When he died in August, 1911, his will, drawn up in 1905, listed, besides Bellister, three dwelling houses – Carntyne, Netherton and Abbey View – several cottages in Hexham and Park Village, near Haltwhistle, and farms at Bellister, Wydon, Broomhouses and Linnshields in Northumberland and Low Row in Cumberland. All these he left, in a complex web of arrangements, for the benefit of most, but significantly not all, his many children. In the original will, dated 1905, he had left Carntyne to his eldest son, John Archibald, who succeeded him as Medical Officer of Health at Hexham, but in a codicil made five years later only a year before he died, he revoked this legacy without making any other provision for John Archibald. What the reason for this was I have not discovered, but there is evidence that it led to a fierce feud in the family. Donaldson Bell Jackson, the fourth son who was a solicitor, was an executor of the will and to him and his heirs was left Bellister, the jewel in the crown. This alienated him from his eldest brother and other siblings took sides. It is said that when, after years of non-communication, two brothers found themselves on the same bus, they exchanged a perfunctory "Hello" and went their separate ways.

Whatever divided them, Daniel and Isabella's sons were mostly athletic and were all eclipsed in athletic achievement by their sister Helen (1867-1940), whose glittering career as a tennis player culminated in her appearing in the Wimbledon Singles Final in 1895. That she lost 5-7, 6-8 to Miss C.R.Cooper was always attributed by the family to their having plied Helen with too much gin before the match because of the need to calm her nerves even though she was a seasoned campaigner. It was her only Wimbledon singles final, but she held the All-England Doubles Championship and was a frequent winner of the Scottish championships. She and Miss Cooper were old adversaries and there was not much between them. In the same year the magazine, *Pastime*, featured Helen on its front page and summed up her career:

> As one of the best of lady players as well as one of the most enthusiastic, Miss Jackson is a welcome competitor at such of the leading tournaments as she honours and adorns with her presence; and, fortunately for lawn tennis, whose votaries owe her a debt of gratitude for the share she has taken in its promotion among her sex, these are many in number.

> Her style is a model of activity, and it may be doubted whether any of her rivals can vie with her in the speed with which she runs about the court, or the pluck and perseverance which she shows in reaching an opponent's best-placed returns. Her persistent adherence to ground play – for she is seldom or never known to attempt the volley – gives her frequent occasion to exhibit these qualities in rallies of long duration. In attack, her principal strategy consists of remarkably well-placed drives of good length, while in defence her admirable steadiness is conspicuous.

She married George Murray Atkins in 1902 and had a daughter in the following year. Her brothers may not have managed quite such eminence, but their sporting achievements were still notable.

John Archibald (1866-1951) the eldest boy was an exception, his distinction being in medicine with a medal in anatomy to his name at Glasgow University. He later succeeded his father as Medical Officer of Health in Hexham. His descendants live in the United States.

George Scott (1869-1946), another doctor, played cricket and rugby for Glasgow University, was West of Scotland tennis champion for three successive years and also commanded the 7th Battalion, Northumberland Fusiliers, in France from 1915 to 1918. He was mentioned in despatches six times, was awarded a military C.B.E. and, "for gallantry and distinguished service in the field" in 1918 won a bar to the D.S.O. he had been awarded two years earlier. The citation read:

> He successfully assembled his battalion under very heavy fire. At a
> critical stage he made a personal reconnaissance under heavy fire,
> and by judicious use of his reserves gained the battalion's objective.

After the war Scott, as he was known, became a Deputy Lieutenant of Northumberland, an office which he resigned after 15 years when his first wife died and he moved from Alnwick to London. His descendants are still mostly in the north of England.

Daniel Noel (1871-1945), also a medical doctor, played rugby in 1888 and 1889 and lawn tennis for six years from 1888 for Durham University and represented Northumberland at lawn tennis, football and hockey. His sisters Isabella and Marion at various times assisted him in his practice in Corbridge. His daughter, Kathleen, endured a three-month trek out of Siam via the Shan states to Calcutta in World War II; her husband Evelyn van Millingen, was captured but escaped. Kathleen's son-in-law, Charles Backhouse, compiled in 2002 a comprehensive record of the descendants of Daniel and Isabella Jackson.

Donaldson Bell (1875-1958), inheritor of Bellister, played rugby for two years in the Durham School XV. He was a Solicitor in Newcastle. His son Edward gave Bellister to the National Trust in 1976.

Charles Strathnairn (1884-1955) captained Durham School at cricket in his fourth year in the XI and played for three years in the rugby XV. At Christchurch, Oxford, he was also captain of rugby. He was ordained, was a convinced Socialist and was described as "a popular, if eccentric, priest". He was unmarried.

Daniel Jackson (1838-1911)

Isabella Jackson (née Scott) (1841-1920

Edythe Jackson's 21ˢᵗ birthday party. L to R. Back:Edythe, Charles, Gertrude, Scott, Nona, Noel, Isabella, Donald, Fannie. Front: Kitty, Marion, Helen, Isabella (mother), Daniel (father), Jenny, Leta, Archie.

October

7#. Thomas s. of Thomas and Eleanor Leek
7. John s. of Francis and Barbara Campbell, Painter
10. Robert s. of Francis and Elizabeth Scott
10. Ann D. of Jasper and Mary Lowes, Taylor
14. Henry s. of John Dodd Taylor
14. John s. of Robert Lowes, Beacon, Husbandman
22. James s. of William and Hannah Hall, Labourer
31st Isaac s. of Isaac and Martha Watts Gardener
30— Margaret D. } of Francis and Ann Scott Tobacconist (Twins)
30. George s. } born 24th Instant—

November

4# James s. of Prudhoe and Isabella Svison, Hatter

Record of George Scott's baptism in the Hexham Parish Register, October 30, 1810. Note the handwriting differs from other entries. (Courtesy of Hexham Abbey)

Bellister Castle. Home to Jacksons and Clarks for three generations.

Helen Jackson on court.

Chapter 29

FROM HEXHAM TO HALTWHISTLE

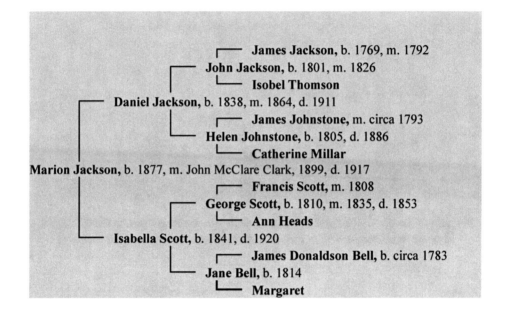

```
                              ┌─── James Jackson, b. 1769, m. 1792
                   ┌─── John Jackson, b. 1801, m. 1826
                   │       └─── Isobel Thomson
        ┌─── Daniel Jackson, b. 1838, m. 1864, d. 1911
        │          │       ┌─── James Johnstone, m. circa 1793
        │          └─── Helen Johnstone, b. 1805, d. 1886
        │                  └─── Catherine Millar
Marion Jackson, b. 1877, m. John McClare Clark, 1899, d. 1917
        │                  ┌─── Francis Scott, m. 1808
        │          ┌─── George Scott, b. 1810, m. 1835, d. 1853
        │          │       └─── Ann Heads
        └─── Isabella Scott, b. 1841, d. 1920
                   │       ┌─── James Donaldson Bell, b. circa 1783
                   └─── Jane Bell, b. 1814
                           └─── Margaret
```

So, when a child on some far morn astir
With April promises, runs in, and spills
Beneath the portrait of his ancestor
A tumbled heap of meadow daffodils;
He will not know his eyes are bright because
A child of long ago loved flowers too,
And that strange lady in the picture was
As pleased as he when April skies were blue. - *Carla
Lanyon Lanyon.*

In 1873 Marion Jackson went to stay with a German family in Goslar in
the Harz mountains. It must have been an unusual and exciting adventure for
a 16-year-old girl from Haltwhistle, Northumberland, but the Jacksons were
an enterprising family and took such things in their stride. Indeed, but for an
extraordinary sequel three-quarters of a century and two world wars later, no

record of her visit would have survived. In 1947 a Frau Lattman, by now an elderly widow, wrote a letter addressed to Daniel Jackson at Bellister Castle, in which she recalled Marion's visit with pleasure. The Lattmans were in some distress after the war – nothing had been heard of two sons who had been at Stalingrad and three other sons were all unemployed and living on their mother's small pension. With happy symmetry, two of Marion's sons, John who was now living at Bellister and William, who had connections in the United States, managed to send them some food parcels from Chicago.

Though we know no details of Marion's visit, we know that she continued with her German lessons because two diaries she kept between 1896 and 1900 make frequent references to them in the early years; in 1896 there was even a resident Fraulein to supervise the process as well as other lessons. The diaries catalogue an active life - much walking, golfing, cycling, sewing, darning, mending, letter-writing, a medley of visitors, frequent train journeys, dances at Christmas and New Year, siblings' birthdays, occasional bouts of "feeling very seedy" - but one is left with the impression that Marion was not being extended. One entry, for January 15, 1896, gives the flavour:

> Bellister. Wet. Walked into Haltwhistle about 11. Shopped. Saw no one nice. Walked in again in afternoon, very windy. Fannie & I were dying to speak to someone, as we were so tired of each other's society. Only saw Dr. Rose. Bought sweets. Read & worked till bed.

But the tone is generally upbeat and one can sense that romance was in the air as early as 1896. Whenever she saw Mr. Clark, or J.M.C. as she soon called him, even for a few minutes and without speaking, she logged it faithfully. Often he was "in very good form", sometimes she teased him, he came to tea and supper, he brought flowers at New Year for Marion's mother, Isabella, he discussed horses with Daniel while Marion sat quietly in the house. After a while the entries reveal a growing relationship "Mr. Clark came home with us for supper. Talked etc.", then greater intimacy. On Good Friday, 1898, for example:

> Bellister. Glorious day. Church morning, Leta & I went up to Gemini, others all biking. J.M.C. came along about 2.30, came to Gemini & was <u>awfully nice</u>. Noel & Ravenstone party biked up about 4.30. Tea. J.M.C. went away about 6. to church.

On Easter Sunday and Monday he walked home with her after evening events, on Tuesday she "saw J.M.C. to bow to", on Wednesday he accompanied her to the station, on Thursday she saw him to wave to and on Friday he came to the station to see her and her sister Fannie off to Dovenby, near Cockermouth, where they were to stay with his elder brother George and his wife, Euphemia for four nights. Marion and Euphemia were friendly; they exchanged letters and presents and seem to have met whenever they could, but Marion always referred to her formally as Mrs. Clark. In later family mythology both George, who was regarded as unreliable, and Euphemia, or Aunt Phame, as they called her, had a rather bad press, but at this stage they appear to have been well-integrated and popular, though in Marion's case it is possible that it was a matter of reflected glory.

Family holidays cannot be comprehensive when you number 18 as the Jacksons did, but a goodly gathering was present at The Imperial Hydropathic Hotel, Blackpool in May 1896 for Marion's 19th birthday when they went for a sail in very rough conditions - "awfully jolly" - and later watched the comedians on the pier. J.M.C. was not there but he weighed in with a "lovely umbrella" as a present. For the month of August that year a large contingent went to Rothesay, from where they toured the western isles, admired the beauty of the scenery and, being Jacksons, took plenty of vigorous exercise. By now Marion had moved in with her brother Noel along the South Tyne at Corbridge, where he had set up his surgery and was in partnership with the eldest brother, Archie. She evidently had some receptionist duties and also devoted a lot of time to dispensing, but still had an active social life with golf, tennis parties and tournaments, the occasional play in Newcastle, dancing and visiting. She covered miles on foot – 10 miles a day was not unusual - and bicycle - on one trip from Alnwick she suffered seven punctures. Back for a stay at Bellister she walked with J.M.C. after supper and (enigmatically) "pitched into him", but he was soon "very nice" again and a few months later was "just too awfully nice", an entry which merited sidelining in the diary and ended "<u>very</u> happy". This day, February 7, was probably when the die was cast and a few weeks later came the following entry:

> Sunday May 14th Bellister. Few showers morning, lovely afternoon & evening. My 22nd birthday. Church morning. J.M.C. walked along with me & gave me lovely gold chain with pearls. After dinner sat in Dining Room with Fanny & Edith. J.M.C. came 2.30 ------------- After tea told Mother of my engagement to Mr. Clark. Everyone very excited. J.M.C, and I went walk up Brae. Very very happy.

And so it was settled, J.M.C. at once became John or J., preparations were put in hand, the happy couple went to stay with his brother George at Dovenby, Marion decamped from Corbridge to Bellister, and:

> Wednesday, Sept: 20. Bellister. My Wedding Day. Fine, very windy. Wrote letters thanking people for presents all morning. Church 2.30:

> Fannie, Leta & Beryl my bridesmaids, Reception at Bellister
> afterwards. John and I left at 4.12 for Preston. Arrived there 8.30.
> Dinner.

In the next two days, in London, they went to see "H.M.S.Pinafore" at the Savoy, and "Gay Lord Times" at the Globe, visited the London Zoo and Earl's Court and then set off for the Isle of Wight. At the Royal Pine Hotel at Ryde, however, first John and then Marion was "very seedy". In her case she felt very ill with a bad throat and a doctor was summoned, but she recovered after a couple of days. By now it was time to go home where Marion was again stricken, and was confined to the house for a week, the doctor prescribing poultices and steam. Settling in to married life in the Bank building in Haltwhistle seems to have been a seamless process. There was no more surgery work or dispensing, but otherwise the diary reflects continuity - frequent visits from her numerous siblings and short trips away, for example to Cumberland and to North Berwick. After one such trip in the New Year – to Glasgow for her brother Noel's wedding – she began to feel unwell. There was 'flu in the air, but her indisposition was longer-lasting and she reported regular bouts of nausea until, after a month, she recorded:

> On Feb. 24 was at Hexham for play "My Friend, the Prince". Had
> felt very seedy for some weeks, felt very ill all the Sat. & on Sunday
> 25 was very <u>bad</u> & was in bed for three weeks.

This was a retrospective entry because she stopped writing the diary for seven months and it looks as though this was the time when she suffered a miscarriage, but the immediate cause of the break in entries was the Bellister fire, after which she had to put up various members of the now homeless Jackson family. The weather was Arctic. It was a depressing time. By August, however, things were back to normal and two years later she was pregnant again. This time all went well and her son, John, was born on June 11, 1903, to be followed by David George (1907), Elizabeth McClare (1910), the twins Daniel Nicholas and Kenneth Allan (1911) and William Donaldson (1916).

Then, as we have seen, when the baby was only seven months old, disaster struck. The old malady – sore throat – was the start of it, but she saw no need to tell John about it while he was on a business trip to London. She was able to get about over the weekend, but then things took a rapid turn for the worse and, only hours after John's return, she died in the early hours of Tuesday, February 27. Because Marion was young and healthy and had not seemed to be seriously ill, dark stories began to circulate that her condition, described as a quinsy, or abscess between the tonsils and the wall of the throat, had been misdiagnosed and the doctor had given her the wrong treatment or an overdose of morphia. These gained some credence within the family, but there is no hard evidence that it was so and the Clarks continued to use the services of the same doctor, which suggests that any doubts they may have had were later banished. The death certificate listed as the causes of death 1. septic tonsillitis and 2. endocarditis, a rare condition which causes inflammation of the lining, muscles and valves of the heart and can arise, in acute form, from a streptococcal infection. The *Echo's* obituary said:

> The deceased lady, who was the daughter of the late Dr. & Mrs. Jackson, of Netherton, Hexham, was held in high esteem by all classes at Haltwhistle, where she had made her home for many years. She took an active interest in the different organisations connected with the Haltwhistle Parish Church, the Girls' Friendly Society, and the local Nursing Association and had been an untiring worker in the various benevolent agencies connected with the war. Indeed, there were few institutions of a philanthropic character but found her a whole-hearted and generous supporter, and her loss will be keenly felt throughout the district. Deep sympathy is felt for Col. Clark and family of 6 young children in their great bereavement.

For them life had to go on, of course, but it was not easy. Marion was hardly ever mentioned after her death - it was simply too painful a subject - and so her memory faded and the children remembered very little about her. Most recorded comments about her are complimentary but largely platitudinous - she remains a difficult person to capture, though her diaries show her to have been lively, energetic, sociable and devoted. Twenty-one years before she died, when she was eighteen, Marion had written in the back of her diary some lines from Longfellow:

> Enjoy the Spring of Love & Youth,
> To some good angel leave the rest,
> For time will teach thee soon the truth,
> There are no birds in last year's nest.
>
> Maiden that reads't this simple rhyme
> Enjoy thy youth, it will not stay
> Enjoy the fragrance of thy prime,
> For, Oh! It is not always May!

Below this she had written: "Into each life some rain must fall. Some days must be dark & dreary."

Marion Clark (née Jackson) 1877-1917.

Fannie &Marion, 1897

Marion's mother, Isabella, as a girl.

Ten Sisters, 1897. L to R: Back: Fannie, Jenny, Marion. Middle: Bella, Kitty, Edythe, Isabella (mother), Leta. Front: Gertrude, Helen, Nona.

Part V

-------------Chapter 30 -------------

FROM ARDMORE TO BRAMSTON

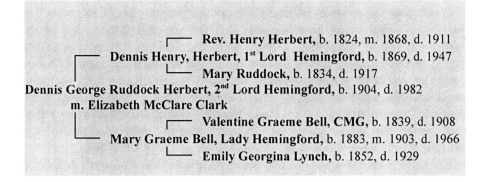

Rev. Henry Herbert, b. 1824, m. 1868, d. 1911
Dennis Henry, Herbert, 1st Lord Hemingford, b. 1869, d. 1947
Mary Ruddock, b. 1834, d. 1917
Dennis George Ruddock Herbert, 2nd Lord Hemingford, b. 1904, d. 1982
m. Elizabeth McClare Clark
Valentine Graeme Bell, CMG, b. 1839, d. 1908
Mary Graeme Bell, Lady Hemingford, b. 1883, m. 1903, d. 1966
Emily Georgina Lynch, b. 1852, d. 1929

Some fellows would cheerfully go in for any amount of exams. -
D.H.Herbert

When Dennis George Ruddock Herbert could not make a modern gadget work he would say, "The trouble is that we didn't have it at Ardmore," recognising that people learn most of what they know in their early years. In fact Ardmore, a rather solid house in Cassio Road, Watford, remained his parents' home until he was at University so he was giving himself plenty of latitude.

Though he was actually born in Scarsdale Villas, Kensington, on March 25, 1904, the family soon moved to Watford so that his father could embark on his political career there, and it is fair to say that Dennis's formative years were indeed spent at Ardmore. It was, therefore, the venue for some of the episodes of his youth with which he used to entrance his children and grandchildren when he was in story-telling mood and, as a teacher and a practised mimic, he told stories very memorably. The best-loved was probably "The Lake". Two small boys, Dennis and Val, had been sent up to rest in their bedroom while their mother, May, entertained friends in the dining room below. Suddenly in the middle of the meal she detected the sound of dripping water – Plop! Plop! Plop! in the corner of the room. "Oh, I say, what are those boys doing," she said, hurrying upstairs. There she found Dennis, in a bed, and Val, in a cot, jumping up and down excitedly chanting "Gading-aling-aling, we've got a lake on the floor." When she told them sternly what naughty boys they were, Dennis at once began to blame Val for emptying the contents of the brass ewer from the washstand onto the linoleum floor. Val at once said "Oh Mummy Dennis told me to, Dennis told me to."

The mopping up process began. "Well, you are very naughty boys," said their mother, "but Val is too young to have thought of such a thing. Dennis, I shall tell your father when he comes home how naughty you have been." In due course, after much apprehension, father returned and was very cross. Then, indignity of indignities, he put Dennis into Val's cot. Dennis protested shrilly, "Daddy, daddy, this is Val's cot. I'm too big to be in a cot." "Never you mind, my boy," said his father in his best legal tones, and left him there. Sometimes the story would merge with another about a family picnic in the nearby village of Sarratt. In this case, Dennis's punishment was to be left at home when the picnic party set off and dramatic representations of his protests would have the listening children in ecstasies of sympathy mixed with delight. The familiarity of the stories only added to children's delight in them, a fact which Dennis well understood and would, from time to time, make deliberate mistakes in the re-telling that would bring down upon him fervent protests from his audience.

It seems unlikely now that his earliest but undated letter was from a relatively rural Ardmore, but in the early years of the century it could well have been. "My dear Daddy," it said, "A nice old horse came to the window yesterday and we gave him sugar. Lots of love from Dennis." Anyway it was from Ardmore that he went to Shirley House School in Watford, reporting on September, 1911, to his father, who was holidaying in Scotland: "I like school very much. There are seven boys in my class. I am not the youngest. Val and I go to drilling tomorrow." The Ardmore writing paper was edged in black as the family were mourning the death in July of Dennis's grandfather, Rev. Henry Herbert, at Hemingford Abbots. Dennis's next school was Seafield School in Bexhill-on-Sea, where, the Headmaster, Mr. Coghlan, had Dennis marked down as a future judge and, under parental urging from Ardmore, coached him into winning a scholarship to Oundle. His father had been unable to conceal from Dennis how keen he was for him to get a scholarship and had been writing to Dennis regularly on the subject – on the basis of those letters which survive, indeed, he rarely wrote to him about anything else. In his delighted letter of congratulation, his father wrote:

> Of course your Mother and I are both very pleased & she is quite

excited! I am not very surprised at your success as I quite thought you had a chance as I told you: but I did not want to say too much about your chances because I did not want you to be disappointed if you did not succeed. Well, I am very glad about it: it is your first big achievement in your life & I hope it will only be the first of a lot of successes. It will give you a little confidence in what you can do if you try!

Once again the letter was edged in black. Dennis's grandmother, Mary Herbert, had died five months earlier in February, 1917.

His mother wrote too expressing pride and delight, quoting Sanderson's telegram from Oundle: "Your boy been elected to a £30 scholarship" and promising to buy him his reward – a new bicycle. Less than a year later, the question of scholarships was again an issue. Dennis must have written to his mother expressing some anxiety on the subject, so his father tried to put the matter in perspective:

Now I don't want you to be worried about this scholarship business; but I will try & explain to you exactly what my idea was about it & then you must settle what to do, & I shall not be annoyed if you still settle not to go in. First of all, I do not want you to do extra work for it, or to let it interfere with your other exams: my idea was that without extra work you should just do the papers as well as you can & see the result.

Last year you got one of the lower (house) scholarships & I think that if you had done the maths papers you might have got a higher one - & that at any rate you would very likely do so this year as you have probably made more than a normal year's progress since then, & if you are good enough for one of the higher schools, I don't see why you should have only a lower one!

As to the money I am not thinking about that at all, because I care much more about your general success in work & in health than about money – though incidentally the money is perhaps more useful than you think & I am not rich enough to feel I've no right to take advantage of what you can get: but don't let the money question affect your decision: I only mention this because I don't want you to get any idea that I have got plenty of money! It may perhaps be that it is not considered the right thing when you have got one scholarship to try & get a better one? If that is so, tell me so, & don't do it.

Some fellows would cheerfully go in for any amount of exams (as long as it did not mean doing extra work for it) & just try their luck:

> that I know is not your way, as you always take it very seriously &
> are inclined to worry about it - & that is one of the things you must
> try to get over! But, again don't go in for it if you really feel it is too
> much for you, or will spoil your chances in the other exams. If you
> can go in for it without extra work or worry (& if there is no other
> reason against it) then go in & try your best without worry. But
> otherwise <u>don't</u> go in for it, & I shall quite understand & not mind.

For a boy known to be inclined to worry and overwork, this well-meaning attempt to cover all angles, was surely ill-advised Anyway, it was the beginning of a process which inculcated in young Dennis an aversion to scholarships, or at least to any parental pressure about winning them. But it did not stop him striving for academic success, and it was prolonged bending over his books later in his career that was to be the cause of the curvature of the spine which prevented him from playing games in his later time at Oundle and left him with a permanently hunched back.

History does not relate what it was that led John and Marion Clark to send their eldest son to Oundle. We do know, however, why Dennis Herbert was sent to Oundle. His father was instructed as a London solicitor to sell Laundimer House to the school. In the course of doing so he met the headmaster and was so impressed with him that he abandoned the plan to send Dennis to Rugby and decided on Oundle instead. Although John Clark was 10 months older than Dennis Herbert both boys started in September, 1917, and both were put into a new house, Bramston, in the Market Square. A handsome 18th century building, it was destined to play a very important part in the family's history. Initially Dennis Sr. was not best pleased when told that there was no room for Dennis in School House. Young Dennis described the scene:

> On the first day of the September term he himself took me to
> Oundle, presented me to the rubicund but awe-inspiring Headmaster,
> whom we met on the steps of School House, and told him that he felt
> sure I should wish to transfer to School House as soon as possible.
> Sanderson, his heavy hand resting on my shrinking head, said he did
> not feel sure about that, for I should be very happy with Mr. Jones -
> the most experienced housemaster he knew - who, wanting to do his
> bit in the War, had come out of retirement to start the new house.

Jones soon fulfilled Sanderson's expectations. His address on why the boys should be proud to be "the fathers of Bramston House" prompted urgent messages home urging abandonment of any thought of School House. Here is part of Dennis's description of how the house was organised:

> If, in 1981, a new house were to be founded with 29 boys of

approximately the same age, great care would be taken to prevent any of them from thinking that he was accounted less worthy than the others. The House would probably be formed into a council to decide how its life should be organised, and different members would be detailed to discharge various responsibilities in rotation. When all had had opportunities of showing their capabilities, some might perhaps be selected, or at least nominated, by their fellows for permanent appointments. No such egalitarian ideas were in vogue in 1917. What was considered necessary as soon as possible was to set up a hierarchy, and this would naturally be done by the Housemaster. "Juggy" Jones therefore considered that one of his most urgent responsibilities was to establish what he called a "House order". This would not be based on exact age, intellectual ability or athletic promise, though it might take all these into account: the theory was that it would reflect the general character and potential value to the community of each of the 29 individuals, which would soon be evident to a schoolmaster of Mr. Jones's experience and wisdom.

Though he was the second youngest of the 29, Dennis found that, when the House Order was published, he was ranked 10th and he wrote proudly to tell his parents. By return his mother wrote to ask "Who are the other nine?" Sixty four years later Dennis wondered what Mrs. Morris or Mrs. Brown thought about their sons being ranked 28th and 29th and what the effect was on the boys. "Fortunately," he wrote, "they will often have heard Sanderson declare that every member was of value to his community. Fortunately, too, there was no bullying in the early Bramston." So Dennis remained in Bramston and he prospered. Egged on by his father, against the advice of Sanderson who wanted him subjected to less strain, he was entered for a history scholarship at New College, Oxford, when he was 17 but he failed to obtain an award and seems to have been discouraged. At the foot of his report that term, Sanderson wrote: "I doubt whether the experience of taking the scholarship exam has been a good one – but I have no doubts at all that he will do well in the university & afterwards. He must have a good rest & we are arranging his work a little differently next term." The result was success and Dennis obtained an open history scholarship at Brasenose the following year.

Dennis's reflections on Bramston were prompted by another of the 29 writing his memoirs and inviting Dennis to comment It took him months to do it because the subject was of such moment. "The reasons for Oundle meaning so much to me are that through Sanderson I found my main work in life, which was teaching in Africa for 26 years, and through John Clark, of Bramston, whose sister I married in 1932, my life-partner."

Dennis, Robert & Val

Dennis & Val

Ardmore, Cassio Road, Watford

Dennis as a page at friend's wedding.

Bramston House, Oundle, where three generations of Herberts and two of Clarks were at school.

L to R: Dennis, Oliver, Robert

Dennis at Oxford

FROM THE NURSERY TO THE ALTAR

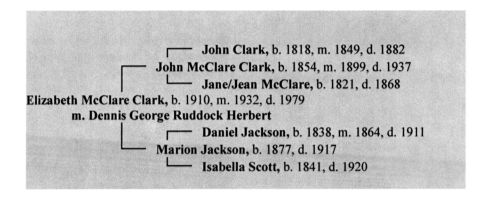

John Clark, b. 1818, m. 1849, d. 1882
John McClare Clark, b. 1854, m. 1899, d. 1937
Jane/Jean McClare, b. 1821, d. 1868
Elizabeth McClare Clark, b. 1910, m. 1932, d. 1979
m. Dennis George Ruddock Herbert
Daniel Jackson, b. 1838, m. 1864, d. 1911
Marion Jackson, b. 1877, d. 1917
Isabella Scott, b. 1841, d. 1920

Aren't the cobbles cobbly? - *Elizabeth Clark.*

"Boys will be boys! Dennis has got two cuts and a black eye." With this typically exuberant telegram John McClare Clark announced to the boy's parents that 17-year-old Dennis George Ruddock Herbert had suffered a rather nasty bicycle crash. Freewheeling down a steep bank near Haltwhistle in Northumberland, he had failed to make the back-pedalling brake work properly, run out of control, caught his front wheel in the ruts made by carts turning into the nearby sawmill and gone over the handlebars. His injuries were a little more serious than the telegram suggested - among other things he had severed the tear duct under his eye which meant that, to the delight of his young friends, he cried for a week.

Swathed in bandages and mopping at his involuntary tears, he was confined to the company of the younger siblings of his school friend, John Clark. They were Betty (11), the twins Nick and Ken (10) and Billy (6). They took him to their hearts and he took them to his. The following Christmas they sent him some cider and he gave Betty a box of chocolates. He kept her note of thanks for over 60 years until he died in 1982. It read:

Jan 10, 1922

Dear Bird,

Thank you very much indeed for the topping boxs of chocalates you sent me. I am glad you like the cider and I hope you won't be too boozed. I told John all you asked me to tell him. I had a lot of Xmas presents and I hope you did too. I am very sorry I have not written to thank you before but I have not had time. I go back to school on the 18th, Wednesday.

I have no more news.

Yours   Betty

Hereafter his visits to Haltwhistle became a regular entry in the calendar. Young Billy recalled in a memorial address sixty years later that Dennis had turned up just before his sixth birthday in July, 1922. He was much flattered until he realised that, since Betty's birthday was the day after his, his own anniversary may not have been the primary reason for the visit. This story clearly owed something to hindsight, but nevertheless there does seem to have been some special quality to the relationship between Dennis and Betty from a very early stage. Not only did Dennis keep the first letter, but he kept the next one a year later - this time thanking him for toffee and commenting "You must look awfully posh now you have left Oundle. You were bad enough before." - and all the subsequent ones, however trivial, including several ostensibly written on behalf of the Anti-Magenta-Nose Club. To begin with these letters were couched in the jocular language of teenage, sometimes interlarded with references to the mannerisms of John and Dennis's housemaster at Oundle, "Yes!, No! (Sniff!). One written from Coz Jane's country house in Sussex in 1926 began:

> In order to prevent another moustache I hasten with all speed to send your razor strop which you left hanging on the end of your bed. I was amazed, staggered and devastated to see that you, in spite of the excellent memory, had forgotten it!

Gradually, however, the letters took on a more personal note and the pretence that she was writing as Secretary of the AMNC was dropped.

Coz Jane's relationship with Betty was, as we have seen, not particularly easy and unfortunately her Rolls Royce made Betty car sick, but she did get credit for the important decision that her god-daughter should go to a good girls' school - Hayes Court at Bromley, which was run by a remarkable headmistress, Katherine A. Cox. This is how Betty remembered her:

An M.A. of Radcliffe, Miss Cox introduced into her own school many of the philosophical and psychological ideas she learnt from William James. Many of her old pupils will remember with gratitude what was a very remarkable school for its day. Forty years ago it was unusual for young ladies to be allowed out for walks in twos and threes, for about 70 girls to sleep on the lawns on summer nights and for staff and pupils to meet regularly together to discuss the administration of the school. This "court" was run by the girls and the memory of its strict democratic procedure has served many of us well when faced by public committees later.

Miss Cox believed passionately that only the best was good enough for the young and that their spirits should be stimulated by contact with the best adult minds. I remember particularly visits from Solomon, Wanda Landowska, Segovia, Jelly d'Aranyi, Roger Fry, Walter de la Mare and Virginia Woolf whose advice was "never read a book because you think you ought to, but because you think that you will enjoy it." Sometimes we were not so highbrow: a Red Indian Chief, Oskenonton, was even allowed to make a fire on the drawing room floor. Here we used to sit listening to Miss Cox reading Henry James and Joseph Conrad, her two most admired novelists, Aldous Huxley, Yeats, Swinburne and Frances Cornford. A love of literature was perhaps her most enduring legacy.

An acknowledged agnostic, she did not force girls to go to church, but she did insist on girls thinking things out for themselves. Clichés were anathema and we were never allowed to accept conventions at their face value. Perhaps this over-stimulated our critical faculty, but it has certainly helped us to understand a new generation's uncertainties.

Miss Cox had a natural style and elegance but she could be alarming though her love and care for each individual made her approachable. She always said goodnight to each girl individually and, though we might be too alarmed to tell her she was sitting on our feet, we were not afraid to discuss our problems with her.

Many of these ideas, original in their day, have become commonplaces of education, but her small school produced contemporaries who ultimately became Head of a Cambridge College and the Governor of Holloway Prison - a sign that her influence was catholic enough.

The school magazine, *The Hayeseed*, of which she was Editor in 1927, records that Betty was awarded colours for tennis and lacrosse - she had the alarming job of keeping goal – was a member of the Dramatic Committee,

President of the Classical Society, Treasurer of the Library Committee and, in the Summer term of 1927, was elected President of the Court. Miss Cox remained a friend and Miss Parsons, who taught English, was a genuine soulmate and remained on intimate terms with Betty for the rest of her life. Some of Betty's letters to her are among the most vivid she ever wrote.

It is difficult to tell exactly when romance first blossomed between Dennis and Betty. The surviving letters are intermittent and, of course, do not cover periods when they were together, but a close analysis suggests that they reached "an understanding" during 1928, when Dennis was on leave from the Gold Coast and that they became engaged on the 9.5 train from Euston to Watford in the summer of the following year. A fragment in Dennis's handwriting, headed Review of 1928, speaks of the joy of seeing Betty again in January that year and introducing her to the family. "We took her & John & David to *The Desert Song* and to the dance at Oxhey, and to Oxford. We had a wonderful time, all due to the thoughtfulness of Mother." In September, addressing him as "Bert my darling," she was already looking forward to his next leave; such were the difficulties of conducting a romance across two continents in the days when the boat trip to Accra took 14 days and letters were intermittent. Dennis was again on leave for three months in August, September and October, 1929. Here is Betty's letter written the day after they had said goodbye for another nine months:

>   Ashcroft
>   Haltwhistle
>   Northumberland
>
> 8-10-29
>
> My darling - (I've now got to the stage when I don't know whether to call you Bert or Dennis so I put neither! I rather incline to the latter it is such a pleasant name!) I have nothing to say (nothing fresh at least, after last week nothing in the way of "I love you" is left to say) but I'll say it again just for the pleasure of seeing it written.
>
> My dear, I love you now as I loved you yesterday and the day before and the day before and so on ad infinitum! I wish I could see you; all I can remember at present of what you look like is those very sparrow-like photomatons which is not flattering but perhaps better than a vague sort of Heath Robinsonish blur which is generally all I can focus of you when you are not there for me to see! Did the prolonged scrutiny you took of me help you at all; can you remember in the least what I look like? I almost trust not.............

Today I have been quite successful in bottling you up into your little compartment in the back of the brain and only producing you at given moments but yesterday was grim and the journey the longest ever and it was only by reading "Olivia" very violently and crunching grapes with some vigour that I prevented myself from leaping out at Rugby and taking a slow train via Bletchley back to Watford! What would you have said if I had? I shudder to think.

I suppose nine months is quite a short time - it doesn't seem so after one day. However, your letter will come tomorrow. I hope it's nicer than this -- oh! I forgot no apologies.

What a marvellous fortnight we have just had; evenings from 10.30 till 11.30 were the nicest parts generally, though the day you were in bed was very pleasant - but so were all the days and nights and evenings and mornings and every minute. It is lovely to have all that "canoodling" stored up behind us, like water for a camel to cross the desert on. What an excellently apt simile, dear, don't you think so? Very clever indeed. Katherine A. would approve strongly.

Luckily everybody here has decided it is very informal and unofficial and so I have not been congratulated unexpectedly any more, in fact no one has spoken to me about "the affair" at all as yet, the only reference to it being Audrey's cry "Ah! Betty, little do you know the trials and tribulations of married life." Not encouraging! But it won't deter me; nothing ever will - except you could, I suppose! But I don't think you will somehow!

This letter, significantly, was signed "All my love your Betty or Elizabeth, which?" They were beginning to be Dennis and Elizabeth rather than Bert and Betty though it would take some years before the change took absolute effect. It is clear that at this stage she was expecting this to be their last separation.

Meanwhile, there was a cloud on the horizon. Dennis's younger brother, Robert, now 21 had been diagnosed with a brain tumour and was dying. Dennis had to say goodbye to him in the knowledge that they would not meet again. Sure enough, only a few weeks later came the sad news, in a telegram followed by a letter from his mother, that Robert had gone very peacefully:

He left us at 5.30am on Sunday morning 26th. I know he is at peace and I know he will always be very near us to help us in our difficult times. His unselfishness and patient endurance was wonderful and I feel he has gone to higher work. He certainly had done his bit here. We have a lot to be proud of having had such a wonderful child. I had such a nice letter this morning from Elizabeth, she is a dear.

Consent was given for Dennis and Elizabeth to announce their engagement the following summer when Dennis was on leave and John Clark wrote to give his blessing too. "As you know," he wrote "I am very pleased to have you as a son-in-law & I am sure that you will make Betty happy." But it would have been very difficult to arrange a wedding before Dennis's leave was over. So Elizabeth had to wait again - and this time there did appear some of the doubts and uncertainties which in 1929 had seemed impossible. An ominous gap in the preserved correspondence masks the details, but in May, 1931, on his way back to England again, Dennis had a letter from his father which indicates that all was not well.

> You may rely upon it we shall all do our best in every way to make you happy during your leave; you may have a difficult task before you I know; but I feel confident God's guidance and your own good sense will enable you to get through difficulties or doubts satisfactorily. Of course, we have not seen - nor indeed heard anything from - Betty lately & have no idea what her real feelings or ideas are. But you are older & have much more experience than she has, so that what ultimately happens may rest more upon you than upon her. I am very sorry for her because I expect she is rather 'lonely' in her thoughts & probably finding great difficulty in seeing her way. I am sure you will not only make allowances for her doubts & difficulties but also, in your own & her interests, try & consider her point of view & what she is really fitted for. If you and she do decide to marry one another you will have my love & best wishes, & if you decide otherwise I will do my best to sympathise with you & cheer you up. As you know, I do not think I ought - & do not want - to influence any decision on your part; whatever you decide I shall do all I can to help you, & the more you like to confide in me or talk to me about things the more I will try & help you to find out & know your own mind.
>
> Ever your affec.ate Father,
>
> Dennis Herbert

This excellent letter throws a light on the relationship between father and son which does not emerge from most of the rest of the correspondence between them. Sir Dennis, for all his formality and preoccupation with worldly success, was able to come up with genuine and heartfelt support when it was most needed. And it was probably all the more heartfelt because the previous morning the parents had received a letter from Dennis about a bathing accident in which a child had been drowned and Dennis himself had narrowly escaped with his life.

299

The passage of the letter well illustrates the problems of communication which were then in force. Sir Dennis had first thought it too late to write, but then had elicited from Elder Dempster's office in London that a letter posted that evening could be delivered. Written on the business writing paper of Beaumont & Son, the solicitors of which he was a partner, on May 12th, 1931, sealed with red sealing wax and the "Herbert" crest of seven arrows, it was addressed to Dennis c/o Messrs Elder Dempster & Co., Sierra Leone. It duly arrived in Freetown on May 23rd in time to be delivered to Dennis on board the S.S.Accra - good value for a penny halfpenny.

Just what the difficulty was which Dennis was confronting is known in outline. It would be hardly surprising if, after all this time, Elizabeth experienced doubts, but the truth was that a rival for her affections had appeared on the scene. This was Willie Vane, a scion of an aristocratic Durham family, who had become a student Land Agent in J.M..Clark & Sons, and was destined, in later life to become Lord Inglewood. He was young – a year older than Elizabeth – attractive, recently down from Oxford and, what was particularly relevant, he was present. He was clearly attracted by Elizabeth, who by now had been grappling with the difficulty of relating to Dennis's circumstances in a completely unknown and different environment for three tours. She and Dennis had been unofficially engaged for over two years but had probably spent less than two months in each other's company. Dennis had many like-minded colleagues, several of them young women, and Betty was bound to wonder whether he might not fall for one of them. Indeed a year or two before, when Dennis had suffered a heart flutter after cross country running, she had commented "for heavens sake take care and don't run any more fearful cross country races! I suppose that was because there was no Miss Witten present to look after you! I thought Andrew Fraser was a woman-hater and now you announce his engagement. Truly Achimota is a dangerous place!" On another occasion she admitted "Till this time I always feared rather that someone 'perfectly amazing' would turn up for you". She did add "But now I feel sure they won't! How NICE!" Nevertheless it was natural that such thoughts would occur to a 20-year-old woman stuck with the uncongenial task of running her elderly father's household in remote Northumberland while her unofficially-betrothed 26-year-old fiancé was thousands of miles away in the company of like-minded women colleagues.

She had reason to be worried. Mary Witten was headmistress of the girls and young children at Achimota, had a strong personality and a great gift of inspiring friendship and loyalty. Moreover she was in love with Dennis, although she had not declared herself. Mary knew about Dennis's relationship with Betty. As early as 1928 she wrote "I'll be patient about Betty, but it will be a great day when you let me meet her." Two years later she resigned and returned to the Far East, where she had previously worked. This time it was Burma, where her health, always suspect, deteriorated seriously. Just after she had agreed to become my godmother in 1934, she asked her doctor to write to Dennis telling him that she was dying and a week later she herself wrote from the Ellen Mitchell Memorial Hospital in Moulmein, Burma:

> Dennis, I've been – am – so terribly proud to be your friend & never can I tell you how much you've inspired & helped me. I like to think that, even if the old pump does give out, I'll go on loving you for ever. Not many people in the world have had so great a friend as you – bless you!
>
> I am doing my best to be a miracle of the first water and get better. And if I do, I'll be a wee bit shy of having said in so many words how dearly & how deeply I love you. It is a luxury to have told you & probably unnecessary for I have an idea that you knew all the time! God be with you. Yours always, Mary.

Miraculously she recovered enough to go on leave to the United States in 1936, but by 1940 she had suffered another stroke and was all alone, being nursed by two Burmese nurses 67 miles from the nearest doctor. Finally in June, 1941, a few days after getting a letter from Dennis with news of her godson, she died weighing just over eight stone and with a temperature of 109.6 degrees. She left some books and a box labelled "Pictures of God Children".

There is no evidence, or suggestion, that Dennis's attitude towards her was ever anything but platonic. She was some years older than he and he would hardly have confided in her about Betty if he harboured romantic feelings about her. But he clearly shared other people's admiration for her and it would have been easy for Betty to build her up as a rival. Meanwhile back in Haltwhistle Betty had little to stimulate her mind. She hated housekeeping and German lessons with an uncongenial colleague do not seem to have lasted long. At one point she was teaching a young girl privately - she mentions in one letter doing "Simple Interest" with her. But, after the stimulating atmosphere of Hayes Court and with at least one of her close friends, Lucy Bosanquet, coming up for a degree at Oxford, it must have been a very difficult period for her. Besides, her confidence had been dented by a surprising failure to pass her Higher Certificate exam in her final term at Hayes Court. She claimed not to be surprised herself because she did not do any extra work "for which reason (perhaps!) I have failed which is a rotten show". She wrote apologetic letters to Miss Cox and her other teachers, who urged her to re-take the exam in the autumn. To Dennis she wrote: "I think I shall tackle it again at Christmas as I rather hate being beaten by a mere exam (I can hear you snort with horror at that remark!) as it's still the same syllabus and if I fail again I'll give myself up as a bad job! And as I'm sure to, it's rather a pity." Given his views on education for women, it is difficult to believe that Dennis would not have supported her in this - surely he would not have snorted with horror at her reluctance to be beaten, but we do not know his reaction, or how he replied when, just after she left school, she voiced the following doubts about the propriety of carrying on with academic work:

> I went down to Hayes on my way home from Paris and Katherine A and everyone there is very anxious that I should go on working a bit up here alone, with perhaps a lesson once a week from someone in Newcastle. They all think, of course, that there is still hope of my going to college, but I know that I shan't for more reasons than one, only they can't all be explained there. Of course I should like to keep up Classics for a bit as they interest me more than anything. I do simply love them, but the point is do you (knowing, I think, more of the points in the case than anyone else!) think it would be a waste of my time and Dad's money if I go on. Of course it is very dull here in a way and there is nothing much to do and I would like to go on working, but equally, of course, it's to no immediate end and might be considered a waste.

In her later life it was always regarded as a shame that she did not go to university and I think it is clear that she would have liked to do so, but the contrary pressures were strong. Her father in 1928 was approaching 75 and needed looking after. Besides, he was unconvinced of the merits of university even for men - until Betty's younger brother Nick went up to Balliol in 1930 no member of the family had ever done so and he was given permission only because he was contemplating taking Holy Orders, for which a degree was required. Betty was unofficially engaged to Dennis and was expecting to decamp with him to the Gold Coast and a married life in Africa. Tuition in Newcastle and retaking the exam would not have been either popular or particularly simple to arrange. So the opportunity was let slip. In the summer of 1931, however, they did not let their relationship slip. Again we know no details but, when letter-writing resumed in September Betty wrote :"I feel just calm and happy and sure now and it is very nice. All my love."

Weddings were now feasible and when Sir Dennis and Lady Herbert's second son, Valentine Henry Okes, married Winifred Pearson in October, 1931, Betty and her brother John were the only non-Herberts on the bridegroom's side of the church and May and the youngest boy, Oliver, went to stay at Ashcroft afterwards. Dennis's tour ended on May 28 in 1932, by which time arrangements for his wedding in Haltwhistle Parish Church, were far advanced. The great day was fixed for June 25. Here is a newspaper account:

> Crowds gathered around the church to catch a glimpse of the happy bride. The sun was shining brilliantly as she entered the church to the singing of the hymn "Praise my soul the King of Heaven."
>
> The bride's lovely dress of silk marocain was cut with a cowl front, the skirt forming a small train behind. A train of old Limerick lace, lined with silver tissue, fell from her shoulders. Her tulle veil was over a Juliet cap of pearls and orange blossom, and she carried a sheaf bouquet of yellow roses.
>
> Her retinue consisted of three bridesmaids and a train-bearer, Miss Pamela Maddison. The bridesmaids were Miss Lucy Bosanquet, Miss Celia Richardson and Miss Kitty Armstrong (cousin of the bride). They looked charming in 'Jane Austen' dresses of yellow organdie over deeper yellow crepe-de-chine, with yellow velvet sashes and elbow capes. They wore wreaths of real buttercups and carried Victorian posies, and were wearing amber necklaces presented by the bridegroom. The train-bearer was prettily attired in a yellow organdie dress, with yellow velvet sash. She wore a wreath of buttercups and carried a small posy. The best man was Mr. Charles Woodhouse, Achimota College.
>
> At a reception held at Ashcroft about 200 guests were present.
>
> The bridal couple left later for their honeymoon, which is to be spent motoring in Scotland. For travelling the bride wore a blue silk dress and coat, with stitched hat to match.
>
> Lady Herbert, mother of the bridegroom, was attractively attired in a dress of black lace, with a hat of Batu straw.

The bride was given away by her father and all her five brothers were present. So was Coz Jane, who seems to have approved of the match – at any rate she paid for Betty's wedding dress. Symbolically the plants and flowers decorating the church came from nearby Featherstone Castle, where the bride's grandparents, John Clark and Jane McClare, had met and married in the same church 82 years earlier. Typically the bride and groom's main recorded memory of the occasion was Elizabeth's remark on the way from the church "Aren't the cobbles cobbly?"

BOY AND GIRL ROMANCE OF M.P.'s SON

MR. D. G. R. HERBERT COMES BACK HOME FROM GOLD COAST FOR HIS BRIDE.

The West Herts Post's headline, June 30, 1931

First picture of Elizabeth (left) & Dennis (top right) together?

Elizabeth behind Miss Cox, Head of Hayes Court School.

Elizabeth & Dennis's Wedding. L to R: Kitty Armstrong, Celia Richardson, Charles Woodhouse, E.M.H, D.G.R.H., Pamela Maddison, Lucy Bosanquet.

Elizabeth with the bridegroom's parents and her brothers.

FROM WATFORD TO THE GOLD COAST

To make the most of ourselves for the welfare of others; to make ourselves more efficient, more capable of adding to the well-being of the world – this is life.

To advance the knowledge of things; to add to the safety, resourcefulness, and well-being of the world; to relieve the hardships and distress in the world, by sacrifice, by labour, by attitude of mind; to join with those who love the pure and beautiful – this is life. – *F. W. Sanderson*

When the newly-weds left for the Gold Coast, Dennis for a sixth tour and Elizabeth on her first visit to Africa, Achimota School - or to give it its formal name, the Prince of Wales School, Achimota - was just seven years old. Already it was in financial straits because its grant from the British Government had been reduced from £60,000 to £48,000 as a result of the economic crisis of 1931. It was operating at well below its capacity of 700 pupils because few African families could afford the relatively high fees, but its indomitable founder and inspiration, Rev. A.G. Fraser, had three more years of his headmastership to run and Dr. Aggrey, the famous African scholar, who had spent much of his life in the United States, was on the staff.

Alec Fraser's brand of muscular Christianity particularly appealed to Dennis and it was a letter of his, describing his plans for Achimota which, in 1925, had made Dennis decide that his future lay in Africa and in education rather than in Holy Orders. In his first year at Oxford he had drafted a letter to his father saying that it was the Church rather than the Law to which he felt called. His father accepted this, with perhaps a tinge of regret but without surprise, and revealed that he himself had gone up to Oxford expecting to take Holy Orders. Dennis took an enthusiastic part in Christian activities, including the Student Christian Movement and the work of the Oxford University Missionary Campaign, of which he was in 1925 the Secretary. Its particular aim was the creation and increase of interest in foreign missions and it was led by Christopher Chavasse, Rector of St. Aldate's, Oxford, who was an important influence on Dennis (he later became Bishop of Rochester). In

1923, after a Campaign in Carlisle, he wrote to Dennis expressing pleasure that he had determined to take Holy Orders. However, it was at a conference at Swanwick, near Derby, in 1925, at which both Fraser and Dr. Aggrey were present, that the die was probably cast in favour of teaching. With Chavasse's blessing, Dennis summoned up all the testimonials he could muster from both Oundle and Oxford and applied to Fraser for a job. In a long letter dated February 12, 1926, he wrote

> I am still very keen to join the Achimota staff, if possible next autumn. So this letter is to ask you to accept this as my formal application, and, if you are still ready to have me, to take the necessary steps. I shall be more than grateful if you will.

To the surprise of at least one of his tutors, Dennis was not awarded a first class degree, but the great career decision having been made, it did not seem to matter very much. Useful testimonials for Fraser were forthcoming. From Oundle, the new Headmaster, Kenneth Fisher, said that when he succeeded Sanderson after the latter's sudden death, he had appointed Dennis head of the school on the recommendation of the masters who knew him. "He shewed himself to be a boy of most remarkable character, discretion and common-sense, and he discharged his duties at a most difficult time in such a way that I shall always be grateful to him." He added that he had discussed Achimota twice with Fraser during the past year and "Herbert has just those gifts of mind and character which should make him an invaluable and loyal helper in the important work there." An even more thorough recommendation came from J.A. Higgs-Walker, who had taught Dennis history at Oundle before going on to be headmaster of Sevenoaks.

> Mr. Herbert was closely associated with me in the foundation of what is now a flourishing History Sixth Form at Oundle School - he was, in fact, the winner of the first History Scholarship gained from that Form. He also rendered great service to the school by the energy and ability with which he supported me in the foundation of the School Classical Society, and in the revival of the School Debating Society.

> Mr. Herbert joined energetically in all School games and sports and was a particularly fine runner. As Head of his house, his good influence was quite clear even to those who, like myself, were associated with other houses.

The Principal of Brasenose, C.H.Sampson, was equally enthusiastic.

> He is a man of high ability as a student of history, trained in the best

307

traditions of Oundle School under its great Headmaster, Mr. Sanderson. In college he has been a leader in all matters connected with the Student Christian Movement more particularly in regard to missionary work. He has powers of organization and soundness of judgement. He will be most valuable on the staff of Achimota College both for his own special gift as a student of history and for his general outlook on all social & educational questions.

Even allowing for the hyperbole frequently employed in testimonials of this kind - and Higgs-Walker's praise of Dennis's athleticism failed to mention the restriction which his damaged back had caused - these were nevertheless gratifying accounts of Dennis's career to date. Higgs-Walker lent weight to his encomium by adding that he wished Dennis were applying to work for him at Sevenoaks. His letter expressing this wish survives, but Dennis was already under Fraser's spell and there was never any chance that he would settle for Kent instead of the Gold Coast. Years later Dennis said the following passage from Fraser was decisive in his choice of career:

> Most of us need not be so vague as we are about the character to be reached, for we call Jesus Lord and Master. His ideal character is summed up as one who shall love the Lord his God with all his heart, with all his soul and with all his might, and his neighbour as himself.
>
> Of course, it is a desperately high standard, and the nearer a man gets to it the more he sees the amount of ground to be covered between him and his goal. But that is no reason why we should not hit out for it. We start science or art, knowing that no one yet has been the complete scientist or artist; and always we will have to reach beyond our grasp. Why in character should we aim at mediocre or attainable standard?
>
> Our Lord tried to train men to the character He desired, and He did this first by living His life in closer communion with God and, second, by living His own life in closest communion with His students. Each had the chance of seeing how He lived, and each in his own way was able to live his own life after His pattern. The result was that His students caught fire from Him. His point of view became theirs, and they went out aflame. Like those who saw the King invisible, they never wavered or flinched. None became as their Teacher, but they got a long way towards it, and His pupils could be recognised afterwards.

This was the vision to which Dennis aspired and to which Elizabeth was going to have to adjust. It would not be easy. After being told that God had taken her mother away, she could never unreservedly accept the benevolence of the Almighty and she was, in general, of a much more sceptical cast of mind than her new husband. In later years this scepticism led her, for example, to disbelieve in life after death, but at this stage there is evidence that she was a believer. For example, sending her condolences to Dennis when his brother, Robert, died she wrote:

> He is happier, far happier, than we can conceive, happier than he could have been ever on earth........This morning in church when I tried to pray to God to help you all to bear it and to give you His comfort, it all seemed so remote and impossible; his death so senseless and cruel. But thinking of it tonight it all seems smooth and calm again. God will send you His comfort, such a comfort as we can't conceive who have never known it, and the joy of knowing that Robert is in the best place of all and in the presence of Christ, will come to you.

Many of the major decisions Dennis was to take about his life and career were rooted in an absolute certainty that he was doing God's wish. Elizabeth found this frustrating at times, being unpersuaded of the certainty that God would provide, but she understood and rather admired Dennis's conviction even as she found his neglect of the affairs of Mammon infuriating. Much of this, though, was still in the future. Meanwhile the task would be to remain healthy in a place designated as "the white man's grave" because of the prevalence of malaria, yellow fever and dysentery, and to cope with the mosquitoes and the termites and the fearsome heat and the baneful effect of the Harmattan, the drying wind off the Sahara which caused the furniture to shrink and crack. The immediate challenge on arrival off Accra, however, was to get across the surf. Here is Dennis's description of how his landing was accomplished.

> Passengers were slung over the side in a device called a 'mammy chair' and were lowered into a canoe bobbing about on the surf. After 20 minutes' exciting ride through the surf, I was lifted up by one of the canoe-men and carried pick-a-back onto the shore.

One of Dennis's favourite stories about Alec Fraser was of his arrival off Accra, as headmaster-designate of Achimota. When the Governor's Aide-de-Camp came on board with messages of welcome, he told Fraser that a house had been set aside in the so-called European Reservation for him and his European colleagues and that Dr. Aggrey would be accommodated elsewhere in town. Fraser told the A.D.C. to inform the Governor that, unless he could have all the members of his staff under one roof, he and his party would not disembark but would return to England. The Governor gave in and Dr. Aggrey lived with his colleagues. It was not long before Aggrey proved his worth. He had coined the philosophy that black and white must work together like the keys on a piano because you had to use both to produce fine music. This had been depicted in the school's badge but now Aggrey was required to counter a view among some Africans that Achimota had been invented by the Governor in order to condemn them to second-rate education, since first-class schools could exist only in Europe. Fraser was well able to disarm those Europeans who objected to the idea of trying to teach Africans more than very basic skills. In this he was helped by many of his designated staff, Dennis among them, who were brought out before the school was opened so as to acclimatise themselves and act as ambassadors for Achimota.

Fraser's vision was of a school that was to be "as living water for a thirsty land," and in that crusade Dennis was in his element. His admiration for "the Chief "- he called him "that most practical of mystics" - was immense, and the admiration was mutual. Fraser was soon writing to Fisher at Oundle:

> Herbert, your representative here, is first-rate, and I am looking forward to a very useful service from him in years to come. He is quite one of the very best. He has taken to the place like a duck to water and he is always serving somebody & growing in the power to do it as he practises. He really is one of the very best.

However, all was not perpetual sweetness and light because Fraser's temper was legendary. W.E.F. Ward described it in *Fraser of Trinity & Achimota* as "a tempest of blind fury like that of his Highland ancestors whose charge overwhelmed the redcoats at Killiecrankie and Prestonpans." Dennis told Ward what happened when he and some colleagues played a joke on another member of staff, the joke miscarried and the Chief decided that his son, Sandy Fraser, must have been responsible. Dennis happened to overhear Sandy being given the full force of his father's rage. Knowing that Sandy was not involved, Dennis took apprehensive counsel with his collaborators. They agreed that they must confess. Fraser summoned them one by one, Dennis among the last. He entered the dread presence. 'Did you take part in this affair?' 'Yes, sir; I'm very sorry.' 'You're a damned fool. Get out!' And that was all. For the time being the Chief's anger was exhausted.

By the time he brought his new bride to Achimota, Dennis had moved from the primary school, where among the usual subjects – reading, writing, mathematics – he was required to instruct the young boys and girls in clay-modelling and knitting. None of his previous seats of learning had equipped him for these latter tasks, but the headmistress taught him the patter to

310

accompany the actions of knitting: "Kofi goes into his house; he puts on his scarf; he goes out and his father goes after him." This he found successful but trouble came when learners got their knitting in a tangle. Fortunately a girl in the class called Emily already knew something of knitting and Dennis referred the tangles to her.

After three happy years teaching these young pupils in their native Twi language, which he had spent six months learning before the school opened, Dennis was transferred to teacher-training and became Housemaster of Livingstone House in the secondary school, where (probably to his relief) English was used in class. He therefore had a couple of years under his belt in this new job when Elizabeth came to Achimota and he was loving it. The school was run on the familiar lines of an English public school, but not all the activities were drawn from English traditions. As Dennis wrote:

> There were debates, plays, concerts and an orchestra. There were also moonlight performances of tribal drumming and dancing, deliberately encouraged by the Principal despite criticism from the local churches. On these, and on other, great occasions, the pupils wore gaily-coloured African cloths, which at that time were despised by many of their educated elders. There was a social service society, which sent staff and senior students out into the neighbourhood to clear swamps, dress sores and do anything else that they could to help the villagers. Each student had a course on the school farm, where there were both crops and livestock. Everyone had to cooperate in doing domestic chores; and, because the Europeans took part in manual labour, the prevalent notion that a "scholar" should not soil his hands soon died. Mr. Fraser was determined that Achimota should not divorce boys or girls from the life of their people.

This became an article of faith for Dennis too and it was probably from Fraser that he learned the doctrine that, as he put it to Achimotans in 1951, "The true man or woman is content to be, if necessary, in a minority of one." Fraser seems at times almost to have sought such isolation. He was irascible, impatient, outspoken and he loved a fight. Those who knew him best, Dennis among them, almost worshipped him, and a congregation of distinguished English public-school heads agreed that he was the best headmaster they knew, but there were many who could not abide him. His own views on missionaries perhaps explain why:

> Ninety per cent of our missionaries have no gospel except pharisaism and negatives. It is true! Of course they talk of the Love of God – but they don't know what it means. It is nothing radiant and full of life.

311

> It is full of death, and has more commandments than the Law. It is
> ghastly.

Dennis would never have expressed himself so undiplomatically, though he could be just as obdurate. You might even say that, whereas Fraser's bark was worse than his bite, with Dennis the bite was sometimes preceded by too little bark. Nevertheless, when in 1929 the staff at Achimota were looking for a spokesman to undertake the delicate job of putting to the Chief some concerns about the way the school was going, it was to Dennis that they turned. As Ward put it: "Someone was needed who was a tactful and polished speaker, and whose devotion to Achimota and affection for the Chief were beyond question. Dennis Herbert was invited to present the case, and did so to the admiration of all." What they wanted was a greater involvement by the head with the pupils, more leisurely staff meetings, greater responsibility for monitors and prefects and some other relatively reasonable measures. The Chief reacted badly at first, but later mellowed, and agreed to see what could be done.

Dennis described a number of interesting students training to be teachers:

> One, named Seth, was so clever that he was given a scholarship to enable him to transfer from the Teacher-Training Department to the Secondary School. Another, named Francis was difficult to train as a teacher because he talked so much. He was angry when, after giving a lesson on teaching practice, he found that I had written in his notebook, "You are being trained as a teacher, not a preacher."
>
> "Sir," he said, "have you not told us that what matters is interest?!"
>
> "Yes, I have."
>
> "And weren't my children interested?"
>
> "Yes, they certainly were."
>
> "Very well, then, Sir…"
>
> "Ah, but what they were interested in was a sermon not a lesson."
>
> Being an intelligent lad, he saw the point: and he finished his course well.

There was another teacher-student, whose name was Robert Baden-Powell Botsio. The name was typical of that time, when everything English was admired and everything African was considered inferior. We shall meet these characters again later in the story.

Elizabeth settled in to the life of Achimota and to married life

312

simultaneously. The contrast with her former existence was extreme and there must have been times when she yearned for a Scotch mist on the fells of Northumberland, but she liked the Achimotans, particularly those with a literary bent. They liked her too - their nickname for her was "Soldier Woman", which reflected, perhaps, her rather formidable mein and long-striding gait. Livingstone House had already developed a strong team spirit – many of the letters sent to Dennis by his pupils and former pupils testify to that – and must have been a stimulating community. Besides, she had Dennis as a companion and, busy as he was, he was on the spot now. By November, 1932, Sir Dennis was writing from Clarendon Lodge, the senior Herberts' new house in Watford, "I am very glad Betty seems to have taken so kindly to Achimota, & that apparently you & she are both settling down comfortably." Her first tour was of nine months so they were back in England for three months from May to August, 1933. Later that year there was significant news. On Christmas Eve, May wrote thanking them for their letters and a pretty cloth which they had sent. She went on:

> I was simply delighted and thrilled to hear about "the descendant". I trust all is going on well and that Betty you may soon pass over the stage of being sick. I had my fortune told at the Y.W.C.A. Bazaar in a teacup from the tea leaves & the girl said "you will hear some news that will simply thrill you & you may cry tears of joy before the 1st Jan." I never however thought of "the descendant", but evidently that was the news. I think a child makes a home and I am sure "the descendant" will bring you joy and although he may cause you work it will be worth it. I do sincerely hope & pray he may be a boy and I like Nicholas & Dennis for names. But I think it ought to be "Dennis Nicholas" & you can call him Nicholas all the same. For Dennis is always the eldest of the Herbert family. For a girl I like Diana & Alison. I don't like Jane much. I like Elizabeth, Bethia, Rowena. Oliver likes Elizabeth, Mary, Myrtle, Dorothy, Eleanor, Vivien, Sheila, Margaret, Helen.

> I hope you both like the large choice of names we have given you.

Betty had apparently suggested that she might go to a nursing home at Corbridge in Northumberland for the birth, but the grandmother-to-be could scarcely conceal her wish that she might choose Watford instead, while scrupulously deferring to Betty's possible preference for the north. Then, more planning:

> I can let you have a cot and I will have it all recovered for you – a collapsible white one that Dennis was put into & all the others of this family when they were born and I will cover the Herbert family

> basket for you if you like. I also have 6 quite good nightgowns I
> think, I will look over the things I have put away. I will start
> collecting for "the descendant". He or she will be a sweet little thing
> I know & will take after its Grannie Herbert!! I have just had a line
> from Mr. Clark who seems very pleased at the news & says "No
> marriage is a success without a child." He looked ever so well last
> Tues. when I saw him at the House of Commons. I must try and
> think of all the news since I last wrote to you. Oh! I will be delighted
> to see you here Betty about 14th April and hope you will keep well
> till then.

This kindly enthusiasm, so typical of Dennis's mother, proved
irresistible and in February she was in further transports of delight at the
decision to make Watford the place.

> I never ever thought Betty would choose Watford, but I am very
> complimented and honoured. I will do all I can for you & "the
> descendant," I promise you. Last night we saw Dr. Gough and he
> will take the case on & directly you arrive here in April he would
> like to examine you. He is putting his holiday off to attend you and I
> believe he is quite good at the job. He is considered the cleverest
> doctor in Watford. Dr. Gough advises that you should go to Mardale
> Nursing Home. They have a very good maternity block there. The
> charge would be 8 guineas a week but you would be comfortable.
> Sister Williamson & Sister Player are the very nice nurses. I could
> soon get you to Mardale when the event starts and you could return
> here as soon as you could travel & I could look after "the
> descendant" for you & give you a real rest. None of my sons married
> near Watford but my grandson will be born here. I was so thrilled I
> shed a few tears. I hope all goes well and the young man or lady is
> starting to move about. Dad is very pleased at all this & I can see we
> shall have a happy summer.

There followed a catalogue of detailed preparations already accomplished
and many still to come. Evidently she had become reconciled to Jane as she
approved either Dennis Nicholas or Alison Jane as names – no mention here
of Lavinia which according to legend she vetoed on the grounds that the girl
would be called "Little Lavvy" at school. In the event all these preparations
were well made and Dr. Gough's expertise was to be stretched to the full.
Four days before Elizabeth's 24th birthday, Dennis Nicholas put in his
appearance at the Mardale Nursing Home, weighing a whopping nine pounds
and six ounces. Complications ensued. Elizabeth's kidneys began to fail and
for three weeks there were fears for her life. Then she began to improve and,
though told that she should never have any more children, she made a good,

but inevitably slow, recovery. Mary Ruddock's christening robe came into its own on September 16th and soon thereafter Dennis, who had been in England since July, had to go back alone to Achimota for a longer-than-usual tour.

Alec Fraser retired from Achimota early in 1935, his health, if not wrecked by long years in the tropics, severely damaged. His successor was Canon Myers Grace, headmaster of King's College, Budo, in Uganda. This turned out to be significant for Dennis for reasons which we shall discover later. Meanwhile Dennis did not get back to England in 1935 and so missed the Jubilee celebrations in London in May. He got a typically colourful description of this from Betty (she was still signing herself thus). Sir Dennis had pushed the boat out for the occasion, inviting Betty to stay in town at the Hotel Metropole. He also impressed her by buying tickets for all the Clarendon Lodge staff to watch the King's Procession and giving each of them 10 shillings to defray expenses. Here are her observations:

> You would love to be here, and I do wish you were. By nature I think you were just built for a jubilee, perfervid loyalist coupled with amused commentator on human nature!!.........
>
> We rose at dawn and breakfasted in splendour at 8.00. Sir D. encrusted in gold lace and swearing a lot at the tightness of his collar and boots – he has, I know, an outsize in necks, but I did not know in feet too! The Lady was very chic in her Marina frock and a new coat, smart but unbecoming (I thought but didn't say) in the new sac style! She wore, however, a hat that even you would approve, bought at Clements and trimmed with pink. With it was worn two pink carnations to tone! (at my instance, the Lady wishing to wear some old mauve ones that she had "put by"!!).
>
> We then stept into a lordly Daimler, driven by a friend of Gilpins, with footman complete, and swept through cheering crowds to the Mall where our seats were.

There they found Sir Herbert and Lady Pearson, and their daughter, Val's wife, Winifred. Lady Pearson was described as wearing a toilette that was meant to be red, white and blue but burst out in unlikely places into yellows and browns, while Sir Herbert wore a bowler when everyone felt that he should have had a topper. During the morning they were diverted by the Speaker's Coach "which creaked by with unbroken dignity except for the trainbearer who had to sit on the floor with his chin just level with the window and facing it so that he looked out at us all like a monkey in a cage", the Lord Chancellor's procession and various taxis containing well-known personages, whom they were hard pressed to recognise.

The Prince of Wales's bearskin kept falling over his nose and he had to jerk it back with his head, it not being *de riguer*, I suppose, in the army to do anything so sensible as touch it with the hand! He was pleasant and smiling, the Queen of Norway had apparently dyed her hair red for the occasion. I never knew it wasn't always red but everyone else seemed to know. The third and last carriage contained the Duke and Duchess of York and the children, the Duchess obviously on two cushions to make her taller, Princess Mary, Harewood and the two children, dressed in kilts but looking very German all the same, and the Duke and Duchess of Kent, very handsome both, she lovely in an enormous hat that would have delighted your heart.

This epic letter ran to 10 pages, double-sided and must have made Dennis ache to be going home instead of taking a laborious trip to the Volta river, which he did in June. Not to be outdone he plied Betty with two very long descriptive letters, just as acutely observed as hers. Amused commentary on human nature was one of the things they had in common. Here is Dennis on travel in the Gold Coast:

What a journey we had here on Thursday! I had a breakfast of bananas and Bourbon biscuits at 5.30, and we left Larteh at 6.00 in a lorry chartered from an Achimotan parent. I hope Achimota makes the son more honest than the parent, who (I found out) had instructed his representative to try to get £3 out of me. I beat the man down to £1 and agreed to pay that much, only to discover afterwards that £1 was twice what should have been charged. The lorry did perhaps have a pound's worth of shaking, for we went over the worst roads I have ever struck. At 7.15 we reached the Volta and at about 9.00 we set sail in a small and noisy launch. For an hour or so I sat in some discomfort in a crowded closed-in deck, conversing with Mr. G, the father of Violet and one of the most plausible rascals in the Colony. I then retired into a cabin, where I could stretch my legs out on a couch, and read *Moor Fires* by E.H. Young, which I greatly enjoyed. There were portholes on both sides of the cabin and in front of it, and the view of the Volta was magnificent. It was really refreshing to be on a great wide river, with beautifully green banks, but as the view was almost exactly the same throughout the nine hours of the voyage, it grew monotonous....When we reached Alitete, our destination, I was startled to see a crowd of young women greeting me vociferously and even running into the river. I gave them a somewhat half-hearted wave, which doubled their frenzy. They turned out to be the local porters and were soon marching off with baggage on their heads........

> We walked a few hundred yards to a lorry bearing the appropriate text over the windscreen, "Life is not a victory but a struggle". Then began a long struggle to pack far too much luggage into the trailer, and far too many passengers into the lorry. These two feats having been accomplished, the driver had a long wrangle with the lady porters, no doubt about "dashes". As the launch had been over an hour late, this was annoying; however I sat calmly in the front seat and comforted myself with *Moor Fires*, and exchanged an occasional word with Mr Kpeglo, another Achimota parent, who giggled at my every remark. At last we started, the enraged lady-porters giving us a terrific send-off as though they were wedding guests speeding the bride and bridegroom on their honeymoon; they had thoroughly enjoyed the riot.

The journey continued through scenery that made Dennis feel he had at last come to the Africa of magazine-covers and cinema with palm trees strangely contorted by the wind. They stopped for the Kpeglo family to alight. Naturally the Kpeglo luggage was at the bottom of the pile. Unpacking it by the light of one hurricane lamp and a candle was difficult.

> Then came the shattering discovery that Mr Kpeglo's "rubber-bag", containing his suits and shoes and four mosquito nets – his most valuable possessions – was missing. Mr. Kpeglo, who had seemed the mousiest creature I could imagine, became a demon of excited abuse, and everybody, except myself, joined in a deafening altercation between him and the driver. They just managed not to come to blows, and it was at last concluded that the "rubber-bag" had been given by Mr. Kpeglo to a girl attached to another lorry, and that it would come on later. Therefore everyone surged round Mr. Kpeglo exclaiming, "It can never lost", and we then left him standing disconsolate by the roadside with his ninety and nine packages, his quiverful of children and Mrs. Kpeglo patiently holding the candle which gave light to little but her uncovered bosom.

In the course of the next 10 days Dennis made friends with a young aspiring poet called Desewa, whom he coached in the use of his vocabulary and the correct use of metre, and with Mr. Tamakloe, an astonishing old man, blind for the last 15 years, who had never been to school but spent his time thinking about what he had read in his youth. Desewa was reading Laurence Binyon's translation of Dante's *Inferno* and Mr. Tamakloe, who turned out to be Mr. G's principal opponent in the law courts, had a lengthy discussion with Dennis about Dr. Johnson's letter to Lord Chesterfield. He was so delighted with Dennis that he decided to send his son back to Achimota (he had previously removed him) and ask that he be put into Livingstone House.

317

Dennis also heard much praise of Achimota-trained teachers and came back buoyed up by his trip, which he pronounced to have been the most interesting ten days he had spent in Africa, though not altogether comfortable.

In July Dennis went on local leave. Things were going well by the time he did write a fortnight into the holiday, but had begun badly because Dennis's obsession with avoiding damp clothes and bedclothes had been exacerbated by days of rain. Then the sun came out and "I fairly draped the house with clothes and dried them all." He and Mr. Joseph, a colleague from Ceylon, were staying at the Rest House at Anum, a place whose beauty he first described in these terms. "You can sit on the verandah on one side of the house and gaze on wooded hills and the junction of the Afram and the Volta, with the Kwaku mountains in the distance, without seeing a house or a road or any other sign of human habitation." Then he bethought himself of how Betty would view this description and, the next day he tried again:

> You will complain that there is nothing for the eye to see in this description of the view, so I will re-write it. On the left is a great hump of a hill completely covered with dark green trees, except for one stretch of steep rock, which looks like the scarred fangs of a leering wolf. This hill slopes down to a great expanse of plain, which is also completely carpeted with trees, except that the Volta cuts across it like a ribbon of steel. A slight ruckle in the ribbon shows the spot at which the Afram river runs into the Volta. Far away in the misty distance is the long line of the Kwahu hills, sometimes indistinguishable from the clouds. Just before sunset, the woods and the hills are covered by a dark blue haze, shot with purple. No sign of human life has ever trespassed on this view, except that one night we watched the solitary lamp of a hunter moving among the trees like a slow fire-fly or will o' the wisp. There is nothing for the ears to hear except the swishing of the wind in the trees, sounding sometimes like heavy rain, and – now and again – the hoot of a bird or the screech of an insect.

Betty's critical faculties were always useful to Dennis, even when they were far apart, and in this letter we also get an insight into their policy on letter-writing, which emphasized quality rather than quantity. Some people would have been continually writing a line to their husband or wife, but "I fancy you would be bored if I told you which day we had sausages and which sardines; or on which afternoon we walked on the Bosn road and which towards Labolabo; or even if I recounted all the conversations Joe and I have had, and the Lexicon scores we have made." There is a revealing comment too on *Gitanjali*, a collection of poems written & translated by Rabindranath

Tagore with an introduction by W.B. Yeats, which Dennis had been reading. "You would like its style, which is packed with things for the eye to see, but would snort at its matter which is 'holy'." Dennis was undoubtedly a man of faith, but he knew he would not get away with any excess piety as far as Betty was concerned.

The Clarks were never very sound on anniversaries and Betty had apparently forgotten their wedding day so a cable from Dennis had mystified not only her, but more surprisingly his mother, who he had never known to forget a date before. So he wrote pointedly that he had celebrated Nicholas's birthday by reading the latest mail from England. He hoped she had remembered that, at least.

> It must have been excitement that made me wake up at 3.30am on
> Nichol's birthday, and I had a pleasant time thinking about Mardale...
> You, I dare say, prefer to forget Mardale & I don't wonder.

Betty was due to visit the gynaecologist shortly to see whether she was fit enough to go out to the Gold Coast again that year and Dennis had some commissions for her:

> When you come out, or rather if you do (don't forget to tell me what
> the gynaecologist says) bring
>
> Bath towels (I have 3 old usable ones)
>
> Mosquito-net for 2 beds (Lawn & Alder)
>
> Gent's Stockings – 6 pairs, size in boots 81/2
>
> Gent's tie (as your present to me for Christmas 1936)
>
> A travelling clock (as my present to you)
>
> It seems hard that we should have to buy a clock, but I do feel that
> we need one.

Elizabeth McClare Herbert (née Clark) 1910-1979, Lady Hemingford.

*Housemaster of Livingstone House
at work.*

The Colonialist

Rev. A.G.& Mrs. Fraser

*Livingstone House, Prince of
Wales College, Achimota, Gold
Coast.*

Dennis in Masonic regalia

Luggage labels from 1930s.

Livingstone House. Football and hockey champions, 1938

Chapter 33

FROM LONDON TO BEIRUT, DJIBOUTI & BUDO

> It is no use pretending that missionary work does not involve sacrifice. It does. Not of the conspicuous and heroic type. The chances of martyrdom are slender....but you had better face the certainty of loneliness and isolation, of back-breaking work under difficult physical conditions, the possibility of harsh and undeserved criticism, of lack of sympathy, of lack of visible results to faithful work. - *S.C.M. Recruiting pamphlet.*

Early in 1939 Dennis was faced with the momentous decision of whether to leave his beloved Achimota and take on the headmastership of King's College, Budo, the school in Uganda whence Canon Grace had come to the Gold Coast. The proposed move was professionally highly attractive. Budo was, with Achimota and Trinity one of the triumvirate of leading schools in the field and Dennis had now been at Achimota for 13 years; some people said he was in a rut, though only his father (rather more diplomatically) and one Achimota colleague (rather undiplomatically) told him so. Dennis wanted to do it and Elizabeth was keen, partly because, in defiance of the doctors, she was pregnant again and by common consent the climate in Buganda, which though plumb on the Equator was 4,500 feet high, was less severe than "the white man's grave". It was more remote than the Gold Coast and less advanced, but tours longer than nine months were possible, which made family life much easier. Fraser was in favour too and sang Budo's praises. Amazingly beautiful and healthy, it would be a joy to the children; there was a good garden, lots of lawn and some very beautiful trees, a cool breeze off the Great Lake all day and nights that were cool and pleasant. He had chosen the site 38 years before as the most healthy and beautiful in all Uganda. Significantly he added:

> No European then believed that we could get it for a school, for it was the sacred cradle of the race. But the Lukiko (Council of Chiefs) and King decided they could put such ground to no better, nobler purpose. They kept a section of the ancient monuments and rites, and gave us the better half, so Dennis goes to a 'National' school as no other is in all Africa, or Europe to my knowledge.

Fraser seemed to think that that was that. If so events were to prove him dramatically wrong. In July, five years to the day after Dennis Nicholas had been born, Celia McClare arrived safely to universal delight. Betty had come through what might have been a severe ordeal unscathed.

Financially, the move was not straightforward. At Achimota the staff were on government pay and conditions; at Budo he would be employed by the Church Missionary Society. In the Gold Coast he subscribed to the government pension fund and, since the salary he was being offered at Budo was half what he was getting at Achimota, even Dennis, with his biblical belief in taking no thought for the morrow, knew he could not afford to pass up continued membership of the pension scheme, but how was this to be secured? As the nation drifted towards, and then into, war there ensued an extraordinary bureaucratic gavotte involving the Colonial Office, the Gold Coast Government, the Uganda Government and the C.M.S. Three of the four wanted to secure Dennis's move; the Gold Coast Government was indifferent. Yet it took six months, endless bickering and the intervention of the Secretary of State for the Colonies, Malcolm Macdonald to work out that Dennis could be seconded to Uganda and thus preserve his pension. Even so, when he left on the boat-train from London before dawn on November 14 in the blackout, one of the most dismal experiences of his life, he still had no certainty that this vital arrangement would be put in place. He had put his trust in God and man. Macdonald said it was gallant of him to take the risk. Elizabeth might have used a different adjective. Rev. Handley Hooper, from the C.M.S., who had been a tenacious supporter of Dennis through the summer, also wrote:

> I deeply admired the determination with which your son met all these most harassing delays and finally took his decision to sail. I found it easy to form a deep regard for him and I think Uganda is very fortunate to secure him, while there are men out there who will welcome him generously into their fellowship and into their vision of the Uganda of another generation.

Dennis was bound for Marseilles en route to Mombasa, but once again he had been forced to leave the family behind, it being considered too hazardous for them to sail because of the danger of magnetic mines. When, in February, Elizabeth did set off in pursuit, hindsight suggests that she went too soon. We now know that a specimen mine had been recovered at Shoeburyness on November 23rd, 1939, a couple of weeks after Dennis's departure, and countermeasures were under way, but the tonnage of shipping lost to mines in February, 1940, was almost identical to the number lost in the previous November. It was not until March that the figure fell by half.

When he heard they were coming, he dare not build up his hopes too much because he knew that wives and families did not have priority. The loyal Hooper, however, was on the case and soon Betty received from the C.M.S. Shipping Department her marching instructions:

> Dear Mrs Herbert,
> I am sending you herewith the following in connexion with your departure from Victoria Station on Sunday evening next:-
>
> A cheque for £10. to cover the incidental voyage expenses on the journey including cost of dispatching baggage, tips on the voyage and other monies to be spent whilst en-route to Mombasa. From Mombasa to the Mission Station tickets and reservation will be made by our agents, Messrs. Sutherland & Co., who have been advised and will arrange to meet you on arrival there. I also enclose passage ticket between Marseilles and Mombasa, 2nd Class rail ticket between Victoria, Folkestone, Calais, Paris and Marseilles, and coupon to cover the reservation of a two-berth cabin on the cross Channel steamer. A supply of baggage labels I am sending you together with the account for the excess amount involved for reservation of cabin, and interpreter to meet you at Paris and Marseilles.

The parents-in-law rallied round, bags were packed, farewells said and, at the last minute Sir Dennis pressed into Betty's hand a note saying:

> To any British Consul
>
> 　　　　　　　　　　　　3rd, February 1940
> Dear Sir,
>
> The Bearer of this letter (whose signature will be set at the foot hereof for verification purposes) is my daughter-in-law Mrs. Elizabeth McClare Herbert, who is about to start from here via Marseilles & Mombasa to join her husband, my son Mr. Dennis George Ruddock Herbert at Budo, near Kampala Uganda, where he is Principal of The King's College: she will travel with her two children aged respectively 5 ½ years & about 6 months.
>
> Should she require any assistance I shall be grateful for any help given to her, and I accept liability for any expense reasonably incurred on her behalf to a limit of (say) One Hundred Pounds.
>
> 　　　　　　　　Yours faithfully,
>
> 　　　　　　　　Dennis Herbert

Armed with little more than these pieces of paper and jammed into the parental Morris 10, its headlights dimmed with blue paint, the family set off from Watford, driven through the blacked-out streets by the inexperienced Oliver. Similarly unlit vehicles loomed suddenly ahead in the dark, necessitating sudden jerks on the steering wheel, but eventually they reached Victoria, where kind Mr. Hooper had taken the trouble to come and say goodbye. He reported to Dennis that Elizabeth was looking remarkably well and "ready for her adventure" and was travelling with other missionary women who he was sure would give her help.

At Folkestone embarkation on the ferry was straightforward, but Celia was upset and, once installed in the cabin, began to shriek. Nothing would calm her and soon a queue of irate women had formed itself outside and people were knocking on the door to complain. One woman said: "Can't you keep that baby quiet?" to which Elizabeth, drawing on all the hauteur she could muster, replied. "No. If you'd ever had one, you would know that you can't." The hapless spinster retreated and the put-down entered the family history. Next morning, expecting to be in Calais, they found that the ship had not sailed because of fog, and was still at the quayside in Folkestone.

They therefore sailed on February 4th, two days before Messrs Chamberlain and Churchill sailed from Dover for a meeting in Paris. On their way back on February 6th the two leaders saw a floating mine in the Channel, which Churchill ordered destroyed by gunfire. Crossing the Channel was still a risky business. In France things were in flux. The German blitzkrieg was still 12 or 13 weeks away, but Elizabeth was convinced that Thomas Cook's agent in Marseilles was a fifth columnist. He announced that all the hotels were full; she told him to take us to the nearest and she would sleep on the floor, but when we got there there were rooms aplenty. This was fortunate as there was a three-day delay at Marseilles.

It was while crossing France that Elizabeth developed a scheme for putting the Hooper/Herbert papers to good use. Confronted by customs or other officials, she would produce a great wedge of paperwork and declare: "I can't find the right paper, would you mind holding the baby while I just ruffle through and find it?" This worked wonderfully, and she was invariably waved through uninspected. On board the Messageries Maritime boat, she found that she and the two children were sharing the two-berth cabin with five other adults, two of whom were fortunately going as missionaries to the Jews and so disembarked at Haifa. But it remained crowded.

Recording her memories of this voyage almost thirty years later, Elizabeth recalled that one day, at sunset in the western Mediterranean the water really looked like the "wine-dark sea" described in the *Odyssey*, and she saw a very beautiful snow-capped mountain in southern Greece. Her narrative continued:

> Because we were on a French boat, we were heading straight for Beirut, which was their port for the war in Syria, and on the Second Class Deck (and we were travelling Second Class) were rows and rows of enormous French army lorries. When we got to Beirut these were run off and I was delighted that we at last had some space to play on the deck. Also a great many French soldiers left the ship so we weren't so congested. But all this took time so we were two or three days in Beirut, so one day, greatly daring, I thought I would take a taxi and go and look and see what the countryside was like. It was rather delightful. We drove out towards the Lebanon mountains. We did not attempt to go up them, but it was a lovely change after quite a long time at sea, to see this beautiful country. Spring was just beginning, and there were lovely pale leaves and little cyclamen and other plants just beginning to peep through.

> We kept passing things which looked like parsnips, but were bright red and I asked the driver what they were. "Oh," he said "they are radishes – very good for the belching!"

In Beirut harbour the ship's screw hit a submerged log and broke a propeller blade, which slowed progress down the eastern Mediterranean. Elizabeth was glad that she had taken the advice of Dennis's fellow-passengers and was still breastfeeding Celia as things were in short supply. However, the stewardess did bring her every morning what she called "Un pot d'eau chaud," a large ewer of hot water. Finally they reached Port Said, where the Gully Gully Man came on board.

> He really was the most amazing conjurer I have ever seen. He looked a bit like Mahatma Gandhi and was dressed in flowing robes, which no doubt did help him with some of his tricks – but not to the eye of the beholder. His only patter was the phrase "Gully, gully, gully, gully". He squatted down on the deck with a crowd of us around, and picked something out of Nico's pocket. It turned out to be a day-old chick. He pulled the head off – "Gully, Gully" – and two chickens were running on the deck. Then he took one of them and pulled off its head and another chicken was running on the deck. Then he put two close together and turned them back into one chicken – three chickens on the deck. Then he quickly pulled the heads off the three and there were six on the deck. Then he pulled something out of other people's pockets, more chickens, more chickens, more heads pulled off until at last there were about twenty chickens all running

and cheeping about the deck. Then he squeezed two together, two together, two together until at last there were no chickens left at all. How did he do it? I simply cannot imagine. It really did seem like magic.

As the ship passed through the Suez Canal, Nicholas developed gastric flu but the French doctor on board soon got him on his feet again. He prescribed bland food – mashed potato, macaroni, rice pudding – but they were sharing a table with a French mother, who seemed to think that Elizabeth wanted to take all the food from her daughter's mouth. She would sit the child down, pile all the bland stuff she could find on to her plate and say: "Mange José, Mange José". So a race developed to see who could get to the suitable food first.

> At Suez, because of our broken propeller, we had to go into dry dock, which is a rather extraordinary feeling. You have forks of wood pressed up against the side of the boat and they gradually let all the water out of the dock. It was boiling hot, of course, but the worst snag of all was we couldn't go to the loo on board. Every time we needed that, we had to go on shore, which meant quite a journey down the companionway and across planks, round corners and then into a not very salubrious place. What with Nico wanting to go one minute and Celia another and me another, I lost a good deal of weight in Suez!

Elizabeth would have preferred to call at Aden, where she hoped to examine the marine life in a glass-bottomed boat, but the next port of call was Djibouti. When Dennis had gone ashore there three months before, his heart had leapt with joy at setting foot again in Africa and seeing the familiar arid vegetation; to Elizabeth it was "the nearest thing to my imagination of hell". Here, when they were returning to the boat after a shore trip, Nicholas spotted a man carrying away the silver christening mug given him by his Grandfather Clark. He piped up loudly in his squeaky voice "Mummy, look that man's got my mug", whereupon there was a considerable brouhaha, in the course of which the culprit dropped the mug and fled down the gangplank. The weather in the Red Sea was hot and passengers were under instructions to keep the portholes closed since, if the ship were torpedoed it would sink more quickly if they were open. This made life at night very uncomfortable, but the friendly French stewardesses decided that stuffing pillows into the opening would meet both cases. The opposite was almost certainly true - little air penetrated the pillows, which would at once have yielded to any onrush of seawater.

At Mombasa the family embarked on a three-day train journey to Kampala, across the Kenya plains and the Rift Valley. The train was a delight.

Excellent meals in the dining car were heralded by a man in a long flowing white robe banging on a gong as he walked along the corridor. Beds materialised when you lifted up the back of the seat to form an upper bunk and there was brown canvas webbing to stop you falling off in the night. Beside the track galloped all manner of game from wildebeest to giraffe and, for short spells at least, the ostriches could outstrip the train. Dennis had wanted to go to Mombasa to greet the family, but the £5 fare was too much and he had to content himself with joining the train two or three stations before it got to Kampala. The piping voice was in evidence again here when Nicholas spotted Dennis on the platform. He got short shrift from his mother, for suggesting anything so fanciful, but gained much credit when it turned out to be true. At Kampala a deputation had gathered to greet the headmaster's family and, while the introductions were being made a kindly attendant enlivened the proceedings by rushing up brandishing Celia's potty, which had been left behind. The epic journey was over.

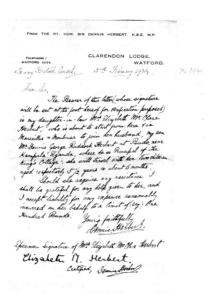

Sir Dennis's "Laisser-Passer" given to Elizabeth for the journey to Uganda

Chapter 34

FROM REFORM TO REVOLUTION

Revolutions most often occur not when bad things are at their worst,
but when they are getting better. - *D.G.R.Herbert*

On November 22, 1939, when Dennis's boat was being buffeted by storms
in the Mediterranean, the Kabaka, or King, of Buganda died and the mantle of
succession fell upon a 15-year-old boy who was a pupil at King's College,
Budo. For the time being three Regents were appointed to rule in his stead,
but the day would come when Edward Mutesa would have to be crowned. The
coronation would have to be, by tradition, on Budo hill and the wisdom of
Fraser's choice of site would be put to the test.

When he arrived at Budo, Dennis was thrilled:

> None of the ecstatic descriptions I have heard from the Graces and
> others is in the least exaggerated. The beauty of the views, of the
> trees, of the gardens gay with flowers, of the buildings of a soft-red
> brick matching the red soil of the paths and beautifully laid out in a
> quad of which Oxford might be proud, took my breath away. The
> staff, European and African, are most attractive: lots of them came
> round the buildings with me, and the Wrights, my most charming
> hosts, had them to coffee after dinner. I am certain that we shall be
> very happy at Budo.

Term, of course, had ended but Dennis was rapidly up to his eyes in
meetings and work. He was hard-pressed to find time to write home, but he
did not fail to send his parents a letter on the 10th anniversary of Robert's
death, in which, summing-up the state of Budo, he identified an issue which
was later to loom very large. This concerned an incredible system of
allowances and perquisites for the African members of staff - bachelors had
allowances for buying food, because they had no wives to cook for them; one
got more than the others because he declared that his stomach was weak;
some got free firewood, others did not; some married men got free milk to put

in their midday cups of coffee. "You won't believe these things, but they are all the solemn truth," Dennis wrote. Within days he had identified changes he would wish to make. In particular he was determined to do away with the rule that only English was to be spoken and that anyone infringing the rule would be given English poetry to learn. He thought there was too much pressure on academic work (shades of his own scholarship-ridden youth) to the exclusion of Canon Grace's excellent arrangements for hobbies. Too many boys, he thought (mindful of Sanderson), had been expelled. He found the climate much less exhausting than the Gold Coast, the pupils much less advanced and the thunderstorms rather terrific. The fact that only two school buildings, the hall and the science block, had electric light was a blow, but in optimistic mood he thought he might become clever with lamps.

Also, he found the pupils delightful and when, in 1941, some of them decided to resume social service by running courses for the school's African employees, his enthusiasm knew no bounds. "This is quite the best thing that has happened since I came to Budo." There was, he thought, a new spirit in the place. He reported with much enthusiasm on Speech Day that July, which had been modelled on Oundle's with every single pupil having a job of work to do. So when it went off successfully - the Governor said he had never been to a better one - everyone was pleased and proud. This was important because "the African schoolchild, like all other school-children, is highly conservative and much distrusts innovations made by new headmasters." One letter, written over a period of about ten days, gives a vivid picture of Dennis's way of life at Budo. Much of it was written while he was having a day of rest in bed because, as he said, over-tiredness was dangerous, especially in the tropics. It was no wonder that he was tired:

> This month, in addition to Speech Day, & ordinary work, I have attended meetings of the following bodies: the Budo Board of Governors, the Education Sub-Committee of C.M.S., the Diocesan Board of Education; the Diocesan Board of Studies; the Standing Committee of C.M.S.; the Governor's Advisory Council on African Education; and the Inter-Diocesan Education Committee. Four of these meetings lasted from breakfast to tea, with only an interval for lunch. All of them met in Kampala. To keep things going up to time at Budo has therefore not been easy. Nevertheless Budo has, in the same 4 weeks, celebrated the Silver Jubilee of Mrs Robinson's arrival in Uganda, won two matches in the great Kabaka's Cup Football Competition, had a lecture from a visitor, staged a concert and a debate, and sent a detachment to a Girl Guide rally in Kampala inspected by Lady Baden Powell.

During the same period Mr Robinson has been removed unconscious to the Hospital, being carried away on a stretcher while the college was having rag-sports in celebration of his wife's Silver Jubilee; the college's female nurse has been all the time in hospital; the college's male nurse has pricked himself with poisoned forceps and been near to death; a girl has splintered a bone in her leg; a senior boy has broken his elbow; the mumps epidemic has gone gently on; and an epidemic of colds has broken out for the second time this term. The College's water-supply has been for several days out of working order; several thefts have taken place, including the syphoning of petrol from the tank of the headmaster's car and the said car has had to undergo repairs.

In the same period I have preached a sermon to the College on Dr. Aggrey, on account of the Chaplain getting fever; conducted a Sunday morning service and a week of daily College Prayers; taken a class with our Confirmation Candidates; presided over five staff meetings and two meetings of the Games Committee; taken two Staff classes in English Pronunciation; re-cast the College time-table because of the absence of Mr. Robinson; drawn up a time-table for the examinations; set eight examination papers; arranged for 23 people to be inoculated against Yellow Fever, and for 48 to be vaccinated and had a tooth stopped. During these eventful 4 weeks we have entertained, as guests staying in our house: a Kenya Chief and his wife; 4 Gold Coast soldiers on leave from the Army; Mr & Mrs Greaves, of Kenya, formerly of the Gold Coast and Mrs Billington, the wife of the doctor who removed Nicho's appendix, and her son who is a few months younger than Celia. All things considered, I think that I deserve a day in bed - or rather part of a day, for I am taking the Evening Service; and I think you will pardon our not having written to you.

He thanked his mother for offering to help them buy a wireless set but did not think they could afford it and did not really need one as the Robinsons were so kind about inviting them to listen to theirs.

We are very happy, and do not worry about money - worry would not increase our income; but Nicho's schooling (not to mention Celia's later on) will be difficult. I don't think we waste money, except that I am afraid I still smoke a lot of cigarettes. Betty is a good manager, in spite of being completely unfussy. Food is cheap here (I fear that must make your mouths water). Servants are cheaper than in the Gold Coast, but one has to employ more of them here as they work on the Indian system, one servant doing only one job. We have to do a good deal of entertaining, for only some of which we get any

> reimbursement from the College or from the guests; but others are
> equally generous to us. I never take alcohol now, but do not feel the
> need of it as I did in the Gold Coast. I find soap can take the place of
> shaving soap quite well. It isn't altogether easy to change one's ways
> of life, but whenever I find myself wishing I had my Achimota
> income I thank God that we are a united family in a peaceful land.
> Betty says I am to assure you that we never stint ourselves "in the
> food line" - but I don't think you need that assurance from us.

In this reflective frame of mind Dennis went on to say how much he would
like to see his parents and tell them of all his joys and difficulties.

> The joys are mostly ones that you would enjoy - the chief being
> Betty & the children. In dealing with the difficulties, I feel very
> much the child of both my parents (with perhaps a spice of Mrs
> Valentine Graeme Bell thrown in!). At the moment I am in great hot
> water with the Bishop, for having voted wrongly (as he thinks) at a
> meeting of the Governor's Advisory Council on Education. I am
> unworried, because I am sure I voted rightly (and so is Turner of
> Makerere) - but the cathedral town of Namirembe is bubbling with
> excitement. It is a splendid thing to have grown up in the house of a
> politician (of the right sort) because you learn not to be incensed by
> opposition - it is true that I have "peppered" the Bishop once, but I
> don't regard him as a leper. He treats me as one at the moment, but
> will fall on my neck next month. Storms in teacups perpetually
> recurred in the climate of the Gold Coast and used to excite me
> greatly 13 years ago - but not now.

> Meanwhile you are facing air-raids & goodness knows what else.
> What surprises life holds! Who would have dreamt when I was
> Nicho's age that you would be a Knight & his Lady sleeping under
> the dining room table, and I would bring up my two children with an
> African King in an African land?

> It is now high time that I went to my comfortable bed: it is after
> midnight (I can hear His Highness's snores) and I hope that you are
> fast asleep under the table.

His Highness was, of course, Mutesa, or to give him his full name Edward
Frederick William David Walugembe Mutebi Luwangula Mutesa II, the 35th
Kabaka in a line stretching back several centuries and his presence at Budo
was about to engulf Dennis in a crisis whose proportions greatly exceeded a
storm in a teacup. The year 1942 was an important one - for Uganda, because
the Allied victory at El Alamein in October removed any chance of Germany
returning to East Africa - for Buganda because it would see the coronation of

the Kabaka in November and - for the Herbert family because a third child, Catherine Grevile, was born on September 9th.

Alamein is outside the scope of this narrative, but people did fear the Germans might advance down the Nile and Dennis, a man of limited military pretensions, was recruited into the Legion of Frontiersmen, which was to guard against invasion. He probably only wore his uniform twice, once when it was fitted and secondly to show his admiring family. When an Italian bomber dropped bombs on the beach at Mombasa, 800 miles away, people rushed out and bought black-out curtains.

In Buganda the situation was hugely complex. In retrospect one can see that the paternalism of the British authorities was just beginning to crack under the strain of the war, of rising African ambitions and of all the technological advances of the 20th century. The Anglican church was divided by a growing movement of "born again" evangelicals with a zealous certainty that God was on their side. Buganda was making the difficult transition from a system of institutional savagery to something less bloody and the situation at Budo was a microcosm of all this. Dennis's task was rather like the old parlour game of Spillikins, in which competitors try to lift a single stick from a tangled mass without moving any of the others. Change was going to be difficult, but Dennis felt that the school was too complacent, too resistant to new ideas and too focused on academic work alone.

It was hardly surprising that there should be strains. When Dennis arrived in Uganda it was less than three-quarters of a century since the first white man, the explorer, John Hanning Speke, had reached it. There were still senior missionaries who had walked the 800 miles from Mombasa and, as a Boy Scout, Nico had recently paraded to mark the 50th anniversary of the establishment of the Uganda Protectorate. Only a century earlier the Kabakas ruled what was, though politically quite sophisticated, one of the most murderous states in the history of mankind. Royal events were customarily marked by human sacrifice and the Kabaka's power to execute courtiers, or anyone else, was frequently exercised by law, ritual or whim. Mutesa's grandfather, Mwanga, had horrified the early Christian missionaries and their African converts by running a court in which homosexuality played a large part. When one of the newly-converted remonstrated with Mwanga, he had him, and many of his associates, put to death. These Christian martyrs were commemorated in stained glass in the Budo chapel and their memorial stood beside the road between Budo and the capital, Kampala. (Echoes of their fate were still reverberating in the Anglican church at the first Lambeth conference of the 21st century when homosexuality was on the agenda.) Mwanga had also to contend with an extension of European politics in the form of three strands of external influences, Protestant, Roman Catholic and Muslim, vying with each other in an unedifying, and at times violent, struggle for supremacy. Vestiges of this were still evident in 1942 - the "White Fathers" had a rival school to Budo on another hilltop. All these events were well within an elderly person's memory. When the Kabaka had been called upon the previous year, to rule on whether his mother, widow of the recently-deceased Daudi Chwa, should be allowed to remarry, it was a tricky decision. In defiance of all tradition, but in accordance with Christian practice, he decreed that her remarriage should be allowed, so there was trouble. Traditionally-minded chiefs were so upset that they forced the resignation of the Prime Minister, who had supported the Queen Mother. Now, with the coronation approaching and workmen in the main quadrangle erecting large ceremonial pavilions made of reeds bound together, there was inevitable excitement and a degree of unrest in the school.

Dennis was well into his programme of reform at Budo which was designed to focus more on the current pupils than on traditions, staff preferences and the prestige of a school which he felt was unduly self-satisfied. But, despite his optimism, he had formidable obstacles. Among them were complacency induced by Julian Huxley, who on a visit to Uganda in the 1930s, had described Budo as the best African school he had seen; opposition from traditional church leaders because he was the first lay headmaster; his inability to understand Luganda and the shortage of European staff who did; the absence on active service of many European staff; a belief among long-serving African members of staff that they could dictate to the headmaster; a faction of evangelical "born again" Christians among the pupils; the practice of homosexuality, involving Europeans and Africans, and the presence in the school of 13 half-brothers of the Kabaka, who had no prospects in life as it was thought to be unsafe to employ or befriend them. In previous generations they would have been put to death.

Some, but certainly not all of this, was clear to Dennis when, on the morning of November 2nd he was told that a European member of staff, Margaret Hamand, had had stones thrown at her the previous evening when she found boys approaching the girls' house. Dennis summoned the Head Prefect to discuss the state of discipline, which they both considered unsatisfactory. The Head Prefect said Dennis had made a mistake in not automatically expelling any boy found to have been drinking - "mwenge", a type of beer made from fermented bananas, was the favoured brew. He went on to outline a more alarming problem:

> In his opinion, he said, the root of a lot of the trouble was that
> homosexuality was going on, and that some prefects were believed
> to be indulging in it, and that it was commonly believed that some
> members of staff were doing so also, and that there was consequently
> little respect for the staff or the prefects. I did not think it fitting that
> I should ask a pupil, even the Head Prefect, for names of staff
> offenders; so I merely thanked him for telling me and said that I
> would make investigations.

A reliable Old Boy confirmed the Head Prefect's report, and named as the
principal offender the Kabaka's European tutor, who was a good friend of
Dennis's. When confronted he admitted that his offences had gone on for
several years and that, in the last four months "he had corrupted six Budo
boys". The Bishop, the Resident, and other authorities, agreed on a cover-up
and the man, with his wife and children, was spirited out of the country on the
pretence of military call-up. An African member of staff admitted that he had
been guilty of the offence ten or twelve years ago, but not since. He was
required to resign at the end of the year. The episode was exceptionally
painful for Dennis and it preoccupied him almost exclusively for the next
three days, but on Friday, November 6 there was an event billed as "College
Farewell to E. Mutesa", the name by which the Kabaka was known at Budo to
emphasise that his position was the same as any other pupil's. A feast for the
whole school and the staff with their wives was followed at about 8.30pm by
a concert in the Big School. According to Dennis this event, which became
engulfed in controversy, was similar to concerts frequently staged on Saturday
evenings, for which:

> Three years ago I made a rule that a concert was not to go on for
> more than a quarter of an hour after the usual time for lights-out, and
> that rule had been enforced. On this night it soon became apparent
> that the programme was, as usual, far too long; and I therefore
> insisted on certain items being cut out; and when the concert had
> dragged on for forty minutes too long, I stopped it. I have no doubt
> that I was right to do this, but I must admit that, being dead-tired, I
> did it tactlessly.

Next day as he was walking to Big School for a Debate, in which Mutesa,
and the Resident were billed to speak, a sub-prefect named Tondo told Dennis
that some boys were gathering to throw stones on the playing fields. He
dispatched an African member of staff with Tondo and another sub-prefect to
deal with this, but he noticed that the debate was less well attended than usual,

particularly by the Baganda. The posse sent to deal with stone-throwing reported that they had met such a hail of stones that they felt bound to retreat. On Sunday, Dennis, trying to deal with the deep anger over his abbreviation of the concert, was unable to reach an accord. The prefects thought the longer the concert, the greater the honour done, whereas he valued quality above length. He accepted that he had not understood their depth of feeling but insisted that he should have been asked for any extension of normal practice.

That night things took a more violent turn. At 8.00 pm the roof of the carpentry building was seen to be on fire and, though pupils did great work in removing equipment, the building was completely destroyed. Next morning a picture of King George VI was found to have been removed from the wall, stamped upon and left on the games field. Dennis convened a meeting of senior staff as a result of which an ultimatum was issued to the school to name the culprits by 4.00pm the following day or suffer unspecified consequences. That evening a boy, whose identity has never been revealed, came to our house and told Dennis of plans for more attacks. To avoid detection they sat on the floor in the passage, the only part of the house without an outside window. Meanwhile something like a riot was taking place in the quadrangle with a large crowd of students trying to stone Tondo. One of the European women on the staff was endangered by the crossfire but not injured. Dennis sent Ellis Hillier, a European master of a rather nervous disposition, to deal with the situation but he decided that nothing could be done. In the light of the secret information, the riotous assembly and his responsibility for the safety of the Kabaka, Dennis decided to take the fateful step of calling in the police, a move which profoundly shocked those who believed in Budo's honour, but it did succeed in restoring order. The Regents of Buganda, concerned about the approaching coronation, the Department of Education, the Archdeacon (vice the Bishop) and the British authorities all became involved. A meeting between the Regents and the staff was held in Luganda, which meant that the Finance Minister had to translate for Dennis's benefit. Initially the ministers refused to meet pupils because they did not want to give the impression they were willing to listen to complaints from them, but they later departed from this wise stance. Some pupils were expelled for beer-drinking but no reply was received to the ultimatum and the decision was made to close the school. Most of he pupils were bussed away on November 12 and the following day 18 of the African staff wrote to the Bishop saying that, unless a new headmaster was appointed, they would resign. A Board of Enquiry was set up and sat from November 28 to December 22, producing an Interim Report which backed Dennis on the key points of his authority vis-a-vis the staff, and acceptance of the 18 resignations and said it would be fatal to accept the view of the African staff that their view should prevail over those of the Headmaster, and even the Bishop, as Chairman of the Governors. The Report said this view, which was represented as truly democratic, was a travesty of the relationship between an African chief and his tribe, upon which it was supposed to be based. It also said that if Dennis had known all the obstacles and difficulty he would face at Budo, he would probably never have accepted the job. However, the report was also critical of Dennis for failing to respond adequately to a memorandum addressed to him a year earlier by the staff expressing concern about discipline and other issues and for introducing a well-intentioned but too liberal educational system. He had failed to appreciate the weakness of his staff, the poor calibre of his prefects and the extent of the undesirable and subversive elements present in the school. To his fury they also suggested that the school's chaplain, Rev. K. Edmunds, who Dennis had told them he thought unsuitable, should be appointed Second Master. When they realised the extent of his resistance to this idea, they dropped it. At the end of the Enquiry the members were required to destroy all their personal papers and notes.

Dennis saw the Interim Report, the existence of which was kept secret, but, though Hooper thought that he ought to see it, he was never shown the final report, equally unpublicised, which was sent to London months later. He assumed, and accepted, that this was because criticism of him by colleagues critical of him might make relationships difficult in the future. However, since there was no such testimony, it is difficult to escape the conclusion that the authorities realised that if Dennis were to see all the much more serious criticisms of him in the full report, he would insist on the resignation which he offered in January, 1943, being accepted. The Governors fearful that, unless Dennis carried on, the forces of insubordination would feel that they had triumphed, passed a resolution backing him and expressing the hope that he would carry on. So he did and the school reopened, with a substantially new staff and a smaller number of pupils, all of whom had to reapply for their positions. By ill-luck a few weeks after it had restarted it had to close again because of food shortages, but that was only a minor setback. It was, though, touch and go whether Dennis would be allowed to continue for when the full report reached London it caused serious misgivings. Though it listed 15 contributory causes for which Dennis could not be held responsible, it went on to accuse him of lack of judgement in selecting staff and prefects, failure to spot danger signals, occasional lack of tact, a tendency to resent criticism however well-meant, over-leniency in disciplinary control, failure to control the "Balangira" or Kabaka's half-brothers and to suppress the so-called Kabaka's Party, a group of 40 cronies with special access to the ruler. It went on to say:

> Incredible as it may seem, and innocent as many held it to be, the school also possessed a "Nazi Party", with officers bearing the names of Hitler, Goering and Goebbels......The average comment regarding this party was to the effect that its members were harmless fools who went in for boxing and guitar playing. Other evidence suggested that the boxing typified the strength of the Nazis; that they also indulged in beer-drinking, smoking, defiance of authority and bravado, and that it was believed they had made swastika badges.

The head of the group was a Kikuyu from Kenya and some of the "Balangira" were members. When Dennis questioned the name of the party, he was told that in Swahili it meant coconut. Dennis decreed that the name must be changed, but then, following normal procedure, registered the party. He told the Enquiry that in doing so he had made a mistake. The report also, by implication, suggested that Dennis had been cowardly in sending Ellis Hillier to deal with the riot and not going himself.

In London, with the Blitz as recent memory and the "Nazi jackboot" still pressing on their neck, officials saw the activities of what in Uganda may have looked liked silly students, in a much more sinister light and used the matter as a weapon to try and procure Dennis's dismissal. One wrote that Dennis was "spineless and incompetent" adding: "This man seems ludicrously out of place as Headmaster in a school of unruly over-sexed adolescents with a love of beer-swilling and stone-throwing." Some of the more judicious turned for advice to Grace, who was still an influential voice in missionary circles and was naturally regarded as an expert on Budo and Uganda. He, however, had appointed most of the 18 dissident members of staff, refused to take seriously their claim to have the final say and was rather less than robust about Dennis, who he felt was too self-justificatory. He proposed that Dennis and a leading dissident, as men working in the Church of Christ, should meet and confess to one another their faults and failings and even hold a public service at which they should take communion together. The loyal Hooper was steadfast ("I believe him capable of great things."), but even he thought Dennis's position "very precarious" and he was handicapped by the fact that a long account of the affair which Dennis had sent him suffered the accidents of war and never reached London. It was almost a year later that this was realised and a second copy was sent. In Uganda Dennis had important supporters. Tim Greaves, MC, Educational Adviser to the Protestant Missions

339

of Kenya and Uganda, who had been a member of the Board of Enquiry, was one of them. He lamented the isolation to which Dennis had been subjected by the language problem and the conspiracy of silence and, though a bit worried that Dennis seemed to think he was entirely right, he reported to London his belief that Dennis would pull Budo together again and thus answer his critics. Everyone agreed that since the crash Dennis had behaved with great dignity, wisdom and firmness. The Bishop too, while accepting that Dennis was not perfect and had made mistakes, urged that he be supported:

> We hope he has learnt valuable lessons: he is unquestionably a fine educationalist; he has courage and "guts". It may well be that in the future he will be remembered as one of the finest of the fine row of Budo headmasters.

In the end this view prevailed and Dennis began the difficult task of excluding some of the alleged malefactors without being able to explain why to their parents. This was because the Enquiry had not heard witnesses on oath and could not, therefore, defend its findings in a court of law. Besides, its findings had not been made public. Dennis was upset that the Board of Enquiry, had not spontaneously asked him to carry on, but Greaves thought that would have smacked of whitewash. Summing up his own reasons for carrying on once he had elicited that the Board of Enquiry wanted him to do so, Dennis wrote:

> As for my own feelings; my pugnacity had been aroused, and I wanted to prove that I could run the school, though I was naturally more home-sick for Achimota than ever; also I knew that if I went, Budo or any other school in Uganda would think that it could get rid of a Head whenever it felt like it; but my main feeling was the certain knowledge that God had sent me to Budo and the strong belief that the work He meant me to do there was not finished. If I had not gone to Budo with a sure conviction of a call, I doubt whether I should have stuck it. My conscience is clear, though I can see that I have made certain mistakes – the chief being that I trusted staff and pupils as I would have trusted Gold Coasters - and that I gave some punishments which would have been effective with Gold Coasters but seemed far too lenient to Baganda.

Dennis suspected that his reputation in London would never be restored and Margaret Hamand, on leave in December 1943, reported that "there is still a bit of uphill before the repercussions die down and you'll need all we can give of thought & prayer & all you can give of yourself". But he felt he could remedy his errors without abandoning his conviction that trust was, in the end, the only effective way to rule a school and he felt a strong obligation to those who had stood by him, his Old Boys now at Makerere, the African staff who had refused to resign, a number of prominent individuals and "my good wife, who has been a rock". So ended an episode which had been, not only an immense personal drama for Dennis, his family, the dissidents and the Church Missionary Society's officers, but also a significant event in the evolution of Buganda and an instructive, if very minor, bellwether in the story of the British Empire. For Elizabeth, nursing a small baby after a difficult pregnancy, it was traumatic, though she tended to thrive on crises. To her friend Betty Parsons she reported breezily:

> I started to miscarry of Catherine whom I subsequently produced in September last, since when we have had a revolution and a famine... My hair is going grey but, what with rats and fleas and family holidays and food shortages it's no wonder.

She might have added that she had also been poisoned and close to death because of what was assumed to be a plot to kill the Kabaka before the coronation, she and he having changed places at the dinner table at the last minute. In between these excitements Elizabeth was busy with other things. She played a large part in a production of *Murder in the Cathedral*, which took place in Kampala, she made flags and scarves for the Boy Scouts, she entertained a stream of house guests and taught English literature to a class of School Certificate candidates, though she was infuriated to discover that, in a land devoid of both horses and foxes, the set book was *Memoirs of a Foxhunting Man*. There was plenty of other wildlife. Lion hunts, accompanied by much ululation, were not uncommon and the fact that puff adders were considered sacred on Budo hill meant that when a snake slithered out from under the sofa, Elizabeth had to dispatch it herself. Termites would devour anything left unwittingly about and safari ants, moving in long, irresistible columns once got into Celia's hair and had to be pulled out one by one. Bright yellow and black weaver birds built long-necked nests of palm leaves and technicolour hornbills dropped fruit stones from the trees. The weather could also be exotic. In one letter home Elizabeth wrote:

> The rainy season has just begun and we are having tremendous storms each day. This morning for the first time since we came out here we lit the fire, as we all felt so cold. Mud lies everywhere inches deep and it is impossible to keep the house anything like clean.

Elizabeth had also to bear the main burden of the poverty which Dennis's reduced salary imposed. In one sense it was relative in that she had a cook, Yokhana, a houseboy, Lutaya, and a "slasher", who coped with the garden.

But these were effectively necessities, given that cooking was done on an open fire and there was no electricity or running water. Apart from hurricane lamps, there were two Tilly lamps with mantles which were supposed to give a superior light. They were known as Nungi and Si-Nungi - Luganda for good and bad to reflect their performance. Bath water, heated in empty ghee cans and poured into zinc bathtubs had to be emptied by hand and the latrine, about 20 yards from the house, consisted of two 20-ft holes in the ground surmounted by a wooden box, which had to be moved from one to the other at monthly intervals. But there was very little spare cash; when Celia lost her sandals, her mother had a hard time assembling the five shillings required to replace them.

On the other hand for most of the time food was plentiful and appetising – no rationing of tea, coffee, meat, sugar, flour, eggs, fruit and vegetables. Moreover, riots and strikes excepted, life was peaceful, and the war, as pinned out on Mr. Robinson's map according to the radio bulletins, seemed curiously remote. Communications from home were also slow and intermittent Sir Dennis sent *The Times*, the *Spectator* and the *Sunday Times*, which arrived weeks late in batches when there was a boat. Life was punctuated by occasional holidays in the highlands of Kenya, where some exotic individuals played host. A community of British Israelites, who according to Elizabeth spent their time measuring the pyramids, come to mind and there was an eccentric lady who fuelled her car with whisky bottles of petrol she begged or borrowed from her neighbours.

When the war ended, the family were fortunate in being able to travel back on leave to Britain together, on a troopship bringing men back from the Far East. In the event only Dennis was to return and then only for a short tour. At his final Speech Day, in July, 1947, there was evidence that Dennis might be going to take a high place, as the Bishop had forecast only four short years before, in the list of headmasters of Budo. The Bishop himself began with an aside, recalling that he had taught Dennis to drive 21 years before at Achimota and adding, to laughter "and Mr Herbert is the world's worst driver". He then said that, though Dennis had had his troubles at Budo, as they all had, he had overcome them and all the pupils and staff would be genuinely sorry to see him go. The Prime Minister, in Luganda, said they would all have wished to keep him longer and the Governor said Dennis had provided inspiration and example to staff and students alike and his departure would be sad for Budo, for Buganda and for the Protectorate as a whole. Dennis's own valedictory was challenging as ever:

> You all love Budo: see that your love for the Budo of today does not

check the growth of the Budo of tomorrow. You all want progress but you all hate change. Remember that you cannot have progress without change. Look always to the future, and never forget Budo's great motto, Gakyali Mabaga – we are only at the beginning.

How delighted he would have been if he had known that, 35 years later at his Memorial Service in Namirembe Cathedral, the Chairman of the Old Budonian Club, would have echoed a comment made about Aggrey when he said:

The years that Lord Hemingford was at Budo will be remembered as the Golden Age of the School. Headmasters may come, and Headmasters may go, but the footprints left by him will never fade, and we shall always try to tread in them.

The Headmaster's House at Budo

Kabaka Mutesa II of Bugand

*Elizabeth, Dennis , Cassie, Nico and
Celia at Budo*

344

The Quad and Chapel, King's College, Budo.

Mutesa's house in the Herberts' garden, where the "Balangira" congregated. At other times it was the Herberts' spare room.

345

FROM UGANDA TO GHANA

Just as the boy is father of the man, so the school is the mother of the state. - Lord Hemingford.

Elizabeth was staying with her brother William in London at the end of January 1947 when two letters from Dennis were delivered bearing momentous news – a career move was in the wind. At New Year Tim Greaves had written to Dennis wondering if he would like to become Reader in Education, in charge of teacher-training, at Makerere and adding "alternatively would you be interested in the Principalship of Achimota, a pretty tricky job?" Nowadays one would pick up the telephone and have an immediate conversation, but it took almost a month for Elizabeth to hear what was afoot. She was in no doubt. Achimota would be best, Makerere second and remaining at Budo third. Sensing that Dennis's feelings of obligation might get in the way of common sense, and despite, in that freezing month, being so cold she could hardly think, she hammered home a down-to-earth assessment:

> I do not think you are ever going to have really adequate staff at Budo which means (a) you will never be able to do anything really creative there. I think you have done your job in cleaning it up and putting it straight. Someone less able could now run it. Because you have a fairly good European staff in 1947 is no reason for supposing that you will in any other year. There are not enough to go round so some of yours will always be taken away, (b) you will, if not kill, at least injure, yourself if you go on at Budo working as you have done - and I see no chance of work diminishing. It is all very well talking of a head lasting more than 10 years. But I very much doubt if physically he could stand it.
>
> For another thing, and here you will say I am wrong, I do not much believe in the theory that the Baganda trust you. I think they trust no one. At the moment you are "up" but do something unpopular and you will go "down" and immediately lose any influence you may

have had. Therefore I do not think you should give up everything because you are needed as a man whom the Baganda trust – there is no such man.

She then tackled Dennis's fears that he might not be up to the job:

> That is absurd. You have excellent experience and range of subject does not matter because you will have experts under you – nor will the fact of your being technically untrained. Your time at Achimota was surely better than any theoretical training. Don't be modest.....But I think it is finally YOUR decision – only do remember health of yourself when making it.

> All love, my dear. I wish we could talk it over.

If Dennis was to follow this wise counsel and put behind him his sense of obligation, his false modesty and his conviction that the events of 1942 would be held against him – and on all these points he received reassurance from Greaves as well - there was no doubt as to the outcome. Achimota had been his first love and, though he had grown to love Budo, it was really no contest. When, therefore, he received in April an offer to become Rector of the Achimota Training College at £1,200, probably rising to £1,600 a year, he accepted with enthusiasm, especially as it solved the pension issue, bringing to an end his "absence on leave" - a nice euphemism for the fire and brimstone of life in Uganda – after 104 months, 17 days. To the Bishop in Kampala, he wrote:

> The prospect of returning, at a time of new development, to the work from which I was seconded in 1939 has naturally many attractions for me; but it will be a painful wrench to leave Budo and the C.M.S.

Dennis flew back to Britain on December 20, 1947, a few days too late to see his father again, and flew out to Accra as the new Lord Hemingford with Elizabeth and their youngest child, Catherine, in mid-January, 1948. This was much faster than the old Elder Dempster boats, but the journey still took 48 hours. No sooner had Elizabeth settled Catherine (or Cass, as she was now known since the Luganda version of her name was Cassalina) than the Captain announced that they would be stopping at Malta because of an expected sandstorm. The delay meant that they had to fly over the Sahara in the heat of day, which made it more bumpy and Elizabeth felt sick. Ferocious heat greeted them at Lagos, where they spent the next night and finally their plane ploughed off the runway at Accra and ended up, in a cloud of red dust, with its nose in a ditch. Fortunately the red was no more than the natural colour of the West African earth, but it was a dramatic start to what turned out to be a dramatic tour. The "new developments" Dennis had foreshadowed consisted of the constitutional dissolution of the old Achimota College and its replacement by three autonomous institutions; Achimota School, Achimota Teacher-Training College, and the University of the Gold Coast. The Gold Coast itself was also operating under a new constitution, which had produced an African majority on the Legislative Council, and many of his former pupils had advanced too. Emily, who used to sort out the knitting tangles for him, was now an Inspector of Schools, and the clever Seth, having won a Military Cross in the Burma campaign, was a Major – the first African to pass through Sandhurst. Though the savage heat somewhat dampened Elizabeth's pleasure, they happily renewed old contacts. Then, as Dennis wrote:

> Suddenly the skies fell: I had to drive my wife and daughter to a camp where they could have military protection. Rioting had broken out in Accra, and there was doubt whether white women and children would be safe, even in the place dedicated to the keys of the piano. Among the supposed ring-leaders of the riots were my old friends, Francis (who now called himself Kwame) Nkrumah and Robert Baden-Powell (who now called himself Kojo) Botsio. I passed through a period of severe disillusionment. It seemed to me that all the things we had been working for had failed. However, order was restored, private friendships remained intact and work went on.

In the concentration camp, dubbed rather piquantly "consolation camp" by Cass, the women and children slept together in a huge dormitory and had to queue for everything in the heat and the boredom. Eventually things settled down and as Christmas, 1948 approached, Elizabeth sat down to write to Betty Parsons:

> I suppose really I have spent more sweltering than freezing Christmases in the last twenty years, but still I feel no more like writing with Xmas Cheer while sweating dankly into a dressing gown than I did in 1932.....I can't think of any really intelligent news. I don't know if the country is going to blow up again, nor if the world supply of chocolate is likely to be permanently imperilled by their not finding a cure for Swollen Shoot in cocoa trees, nor does Dennis seem to be inaugurating a wholly new system of teaching throughout the Empire.
>
> On the other hand, I am playing tennis rather well, we have at last found an ayah for Cass (she is reputed to have a glad eye, but I have decided to be broad-minded) and our luggage is at last thought to have left Uganda. As it contains my sewing machine and Dennis's typewriter, this is momentous.

348

All that actually happened that Christmas was that the servants went on strike and Elizabeth had to cook on an oil stove, though she took the turkey round to the domestic science block for more sophisticated treatment once she and Dennis had finished a titanic struggle to draw the sinews from its legs.

Once the causes of the rioting had been investigated, a new, more adventurous constitution was introduced and the garrulous Francis/Kwame emerged in due course as Prime Minister. He belied his early slogan of "Away with the white man" and soon began recruiting white experts in London and elsewhere. Dennis cheered up – the Gold Coast was making busy, peaceful progress. So much so that the campus at Achimota could no longer accommodate all three institutions and it was decided to move the Teacher-Training College to Kumasi, 75 miles north of Accra, where it would form part of a new Kumasi College of Technology. Dennis decided that he should make the move and, once things were settled, he would retire. In August the Principal-elect of the new College told Dennis that, in addition to heading the Teacher-Training department, he would be appointed Vice Principal of the College

By then Elizabeth and Cass had flown home to be with the elder children during the school holidays and Dennis got down to the task of transporting his whole establishment. Preparations were hectic and Dennis said he had had to work harder than ever before in the Gold Coast. As usual he was sustained by the conviction that God had given him the necessary strength. He gave some idea of the magnitude of the task in a letter home:

> Every package was crated and had the Kumasi address stencilled on it, with a particular colour showing to which department it belonged. The crates, some of which were mountainous, were loaded on lorries and taken to the Accra Goods Yard, where Mr. Wentum checked each one as it was put into the special vans that the Railway had allotted to us. The vans were packed one day and travelled to Kumasi on the following day. We had four vans every day for seven days. I have not yet heard what the total number of crates was but know that the Housecraft Department alone had over a hundred. The largest package of all was Mr. Amu's grand piano, which has arrived without damage. One of the next largest, I imagine, was my steward Goodluck's gigantic wooden bed. Everything went almost like clockwork, mainly because of the magnificent work of our Bursar, Mr. Barnor. He is an African and is more efficient than any of his three European predecessors.

Soon Dennis, with Goodluck's assistance, was personally packing china and glass, wrapping each item carefully and submerging it in sawdust and wood-shavings. They were so pleased with themselves when everything arrived unbroken that they spoke of starting a packing firm, Hemingford & Goodluck. Anything unwanted was presented to the long-serving cook, Tom, who "chuckled with amusement when, as most often happened, he was presented with something utterly useless". At Kumasi, reunited with his 14 packing cases, Dennis found conditions reminded him of Uganda:

> At my bungalow we found pressure lamps lit, which looked as if they had just been carried by a sub-lamper from the Big School at Budo.....Next morning we woke up to a fresh Kumasi morning, and it was delightful to see the luscious green and tall queer-shaped trees of the forest around us. Already I love this place. It is very quiet, especially after Achimota, though there is a good deal of loud talk from the gangs of Northern Territories labourers, who are clearing the bush, and of wild-animal noises by night.

The bath leaked, resisting for 10 days all plumbers' efforts to cure it, and the house gradually filled up with black mud, brought in by carpenters, foremen, washmen, some ducks which waddled in from next door and finally the corps of carriers bringing the packing cases. It was all, Dennis said, "great fun". On September 29 he celebrated the 25th anniversary of his arrival in Africa and, counting his blessings, decided that, given his time again he would unhesitatingly repeat it all.

> I remembered that one of the first things I unpacked on 29 September, 1926, was a photo of the Clarks, including Betty Clark in her school uniform, which led to a battery of questions from Sandy and Andrew Fraser, with whom I shared a room that night. And I thanked God for her, and for my parents, and for my children.

He threw off a long-lasting attack of malaria and the arrival of the dry Harmattan wind helped his rheumatism so he was in sparkling form for an exhausting, but uplifting visit from Alec and Mrs. Fraser; he pleased himself – and he said others – by referring to Fraser in a welcoming speech as "an irrepressibly naughty saint". At the St. Andrew's night dinner, when to his delight "bashed neeps" were on the menu, he replied to the toast of the guests:

> The President said that "the Scots had never been defeated in the field," so, when I said that I was a vassal of the Scots, I added "and my wife, though detribalised, has never been defeated in the field". I went on to say that I was a ruler of Scots as well as a vassal, for I was father to three semi-Scots and, though they were displaced persons, I hoped they would contribute to the greatness of their race.

Things looked quite bright, but the £259 per-term cost of the semi-Scots' school fees was beginning to be a strain on the parlous finances. Dennis's salary for December had been only £52 after deductions and he was overdrawn in both Kumasi and London, the incidental cost of the move had been £50, car insurance was up from £17 to £34 and he had had to buy a new tyre. After this melancholy recital, he wrote to Elizabeth:

> Don't worry unduly, my dear, but let me know what you think. I don't think we need to contemplate leaving the Old Rectory, or taking N. from Oundle earlier than desirable, or putting the girls to a day school, or my resigning at once in order to get part of my pension commuted into a gratuity. Each of these expedients would, I think, be a false economy.

This meant, of course, that he had contemplated all of them, but on the brighter side Dennis was expecting a pay increase as the Principal's deputy once the new College council got round to fixing salaries, the loyal Miss Maguire had offered financial help, his brother Val might also assist and William Clark was ready to pay some more Oundle fees. Moreover, against the day when he would retire, he had made arrangements with the publishing company Longmans Green, to obtain a part-time consultancy as their expert on West Africa. He had postponed this when he decided to stay for the move to Kumasi, but they had agreed to keep it open for a limited time. Alas, the New Year was to prove much worse than expected. The first sign of trouble came in a letter from the newly-appointed Principal of the Kumasi College of Technology, Jim Andrews, whom Dennis had consulted at a distance about engaging a well-recommended artist. The response was "Don't you think he might be too good for teacher-training?" When the Principal finally arrived , Dennis was horrified by some of his ideas and found that he did not like Andrews's choice of Registrar, Mr. Harper, who "pours out flattery on me in trowel-fulls that are too large". Nevertheless he acknowledged that Andrews had preached very well at a memorial service for King George VI and that the Admission Ceremony, which had been the Principal's idea, was a great success. After one early disagreement, the Principal even wrote to say:

> I never seem to learn. It is an old weakness of mine that, after a period of stress, I get some slight grievance, which by this time I ought to be able to remember has invariably proved in the past to be quite unjustified. I am very glad, at any rate, that I came to you and Miss Maguire at once, and I know you are charitable, particularly to Principals who tend to be a poor type.

He was soon to make the same mistake again. The crisis came in March when Andrews told Dennis that he was going to Britain for three weeks but no one would be appointed to act as Principal while he was away. Dennis said he thought this a mistake and later wrote to the Principal as follows:

> My dear Principal,
>
> I have become increasingly doubtful as to whether I retain the confidence which you showed in me in the early days of our association. You marked that confidence in August or thereabouts, by writing to ask me if you might propose to the first meeting of the Council my appointment as Vice Principal. In November you told me that, on second thoughts, you had come to the conclusion that you wanted not a Vice-Principal but a Deputy Principal, who would act for you in your absence; and you assured me that "of course" I should be your deputy.
>
> Today you tell me that the Council considered it unnecessary that there should be any Deputy Principal during your forthcoming visit to Britain. I realise that Council may have come to their decision in opposition to your wishes; but I did not get the impression in our conversation today that this was so, and consequently I feel that your confidence in me has lessened. That being so, it would seem better for the College and for you, as well as for my family and me, that I should go; and I write to notify you of my desire to retire on pension in the near future.

When they met next day Andrews said he had instantly taken a liking to Dennis and retained that, but he had three concerns – the finances of a certain department, severe criticisms of the teacher training department from responsible people and a cleavage in the staff. Dennis replied that the finances had been duly accounted for within a month of the ending of the Achimota Training College and, if there had been any over-expenditure since then, the responsibility was unlikely to be his; he could not comment on the criticisms because he had not heard them and, though he could say a great deal on the staff, he had wanted to allow Andrews time to form his own judgements without prejudicing him. He was reinforced in his decision to resign and all he now asked was that the Principal would issue a notice saying how the college was to be run in his absence. Andrews replied that a notice would be difficult to compose and he thought it unnecessary, but agreed, in debate, that he would have been unhappy if his Principal had left no one in charge at Ibadan when he, Andrews, was Acting Principal and there had been trouble.

> I asked him why he had not told me previously of his anxieties. He said that, when personalities were involved, such matters were not

352

easy to speak about. I agreed that that was so, but thought it hard that because he had anxieties – mostly about other people – which he had not liked to tell me about, I had been condemned unheard & was now to be publicly humiliated. He said he did not wish to quarrel with me. Could we break off for an hour?

When he returned with a draft saying that Lord Hemingford would deputise in all matters of discipline, Dennis said it was an improvement from the College's point of view, but he must not think that it satisfied him – it would be a public announcement that he considered Lord Hemingford unfit to deal with anything except discipline. The following exchange then took place:

Andrews: You think that you ought to be Acting Principal?

Hemingford: Yes, nothing less than that is fair to me, since everyone knows I have previously been Acting Principal. Were you dissatisfied with the way I acted from September to December?

Andrews: No, not in anything important. And you must understand that there is nothing personal in this. We all like you – but there are now things in this College – the Commercial Department & soon the Engineering – which you know nothing about.

Hemingford: But I am accustomed to running places that have activities about which I have no technical knowledge. I have been running Colleges in Africa since 1939.

Andrews: Yes, but there are staff troubles, and in view of them I am not sure that you would run the College as I should wish it run.

Hemingford: It is very nice of you to be so frank. But can you wonder that I think I had better leave?

Andrews: No, I see your point; but I did very seriously think of appointing the Registrar, and I refrained from doing so. Still there are things that the Registrar is doing, which I think he can do better than you – engaging an Accountant, finding a legal adviser.

Hemingford: No doubt he would deal with the correspondence better than I; but I don't know why you should trust his judgement more than mine. I should be happy to pass correspondence to him.

Andrews: Well, you see there are certain things which I have told him he would be responsible for.

Hemingford: Then clearly you cannot go back on your word to him. I understand that..

Andrews: The best thing then is for me to notify the College & the

Chairman, that you will act as Principal.

Hemingford: All right. Then you must tell me what limitations you put upon me.

Andrews: I don't see that I can put any if you are acting as Principal. But would you mind my writing direct to the Registrar on certain matters?

Hemingford: No, I can wear that – provided you ask the Registrar to inform me about matters which a man acting as Principal for 3 weeks ought to be informed of.

Andrews: I will. I think I've made a bad mistake in not talking with you earlier. But will you mind if, later on, when I have looked into things, I make suggestions about your Department?

Hemingford: Not at all. I should welcome them.

Andrews: I'm afraid, in sorting many things out, I <u>have</u> made a bad mistake in not talking with you before.

Hemingford: Well, I've taken over institutions myself & have made mistakes, and bad ones.

Andrews then went and had a notice typed which said that Dennis would act for the Principal in his absence and Dennis reflected that, whatever his weaknesses Andrews was a good man to argue with because he remained cool and reasonable. Then, as he told Elizabeth, he asked himself the question which perhaps underlay many of the controversies and difficulties which he had experienced in a long career:

> I wondered why my amiability leads people to think, at first, that I am a spineless nonentity. I was glad that the Principal would never again think so, & decided that it was the best day's work that I had done for many a day. Then I thought with glee that you would approve of my having stood up for myself.

Did he also remember the advice which Mr. Higham, one of the Directors of Longmans Green, had given him three years earlier?

> Is it really wise for you to consider moving the College and serving for a year at Kumasi? I should have thought that it was for serious consideration whether it would not be better for the man who will eventually carry on under the new regime at Kumasi himself to establish the College there and build it up from the beginning.

When news of this dramatic end to his career in Africa reached Elizabeth, she wrote at once expressing disgust and incredulity that it should all have happened so suddenly but looking typically on the bright side. It would be an advantage for Dennis to start life in England in the summer and perhaps, as the break with Africa was always going to be difficult, it was a good thing that it should come suddenly and even that it should be in anger. She agreed that they would not be able to afford to run a car in England, especially as the budget had just raised the cost of petrol. Besides the price obtained for the car would pay some school fees. Meanwhile he had better have a suit made in Accra; it would cost him £40 in London. In Kumasi financial considerations were soon dominating Dennis's thinking. He had decided that, as he would be marginally better off in retirement than in work, he should try to bring the car to England, where they were difficult to come by, but the problem was that, as he had owned it for four months short of two years, it would be liable to purchase tax of 66.6%, which might amount to £600, well beyond their means. He wrote to the authorities, without much optimism, seeking exemption or reduction and he even contemplated returning to the Gold Coast for a four-month temporary job, after which he could bring the car tax free. On April 26, a month before he left, he wrote Elizabeth a seven-page letter, five pages of which were devoted to finance. For example:

> Our need of money is great. I am hoping to pay the Oundle fees by arranging for a small overdraft with the Kumasi bank, & I have written to Mrs Butler [Headmistress of St. Michael's, Limpsfield] to ask if she will permit me to postpone payment of the St. M. fees until June, when I could arrange an overdraft with my London bank on the security of the gratuity that will come to me through the commutation of a quarter of my pension. .....The only financial comfort is that Peter Rendall & I calculated that, if the Longmans job brings in £700 a year (& I shall ask for more), I ought to be better off on pension than I am at present – certainly we shall save per year £150 rent and £150 wages and (after next March when I am 49) £60 contribution to the West Africa Widows & Orphans Fund, not to mention savings on food & drinks & entertainment.

Elizabeth used to complain that Dennis's financial planning was based on the biblical notion that the Lord would provide and it was unchristian to take thought for the morrow. Here, when he was really up against it, we see that he could be rather more pragmatic, but it was cold comfort for Elizabeth, who had caught mumps from Nicholas and was extremely unwell. When he heard this Dennis had to restrain himself, on financial grounds, from sending her a telegram of sympathy. Instead he attempted a cheerful letter, but there was not much to be cheerful about. True, he was writing from Christiansborg Castle, where he was staying, with his two colleagues, Paddy Maguire and Dorothy Wilkinson as the Governor's guest, and true the Principal had suggested that they have a College driver and car to take them there, but otherwise things back in Kumasi were dire. All arrangements made for Vernacular Teaching in July were to be suspended on the grounds that they were troublesome, expensive and without compensating advantages and, far worse, the Principal had refused to sanction Dennis's best-beloved Social Service programme, which he said "was no part of the function of this College". Nothing could have pained Dennis more. To Elizabeth he wrote:

> It seems as though everything that I have worked for is now in jeopardy & I almost powerless to preserve it. You will understand the turmoil of spirit through which I have been passing & how difficult it is to write or think coherently about it, or indeed anything else.

It was almost over. On May 28 Dennis sailed on Elder Dempster's M.V. Appapa leaving the Gold Coast, as he thought, for ever.

Dennis listens to Kwame Nkrumah

Dennis with Goodluck at Kumasi. Sept. 1951

At Achimota. c. 1950. Paddy McGuire behind.

Dennis favoured drumming.

Elizabeth & Cass: Achimota

AN ADDRESS
TO LORD HEMINGFORD
ON THE OCCASION OF HIS RETIREMENT.

LORD Hemingford had an innate desire to help the country, so whether as a method master at Akropong or as an Assistant master at Achimota he displayed that rare talent and resourcefulness which are the very foundations of success.

A firm believer in co-education, he has contributed in no small measure to its furtherance both as one of its outstanding pioneers and later as its chief champion after the departure of Rev. A.G. Frazer.

Unlike many School-masters, Lord Hemingford believes in giving "privileges" to Students — privileges which must not be confused with law and order, respect for tradition and acquiescence in culture. These, indeed, are the hall-marks of Budo, Achimota and now Kumasi College of Technology.

When Lord Hemingford has left our shores he, like the veteran 'Old Soldier', can look back with pride and satisfaction on the difficult work now accomplished and can re-echo the words of W.S. Landor:—

I strove with none, for none was worth my strife
Nature I loved, and next to Nature, Art;
I warmed both hands before the fire of life,
It sinks, and I am ready to depart.

Presented
By
The Education Society
Kumasi College of Technology

An "illuminated address" presented to Dennis on his retirement, summing up his work in Africa.

Chapter 36

FROM AFRICA TO HUNTINGDONSHIRE

The arras rich with horseman, hawk and hound,
Fluttered in the besieging wind's uproar,
And the long carpets rose along the gusty floor. - *John Keats.*

When Dennis returned to Budo in 1946 Elizabeth remained at home to settle the children. She was, in effect, of no fixed address, but one half of the cottage at Hallbankhead, which had been built for her grandfather, was empty. So that was where she and the children endured the exceptionally cold winter of 1947 with 18-foot drifts of snow which lasted until well into April, by which time incidentally double summer time had been in place for several weeks. The following year Elizabeth spent much time with her brother Ken at Staindrop, comforting him after the loss of his fiancée and it was at about this time, with Dennis preparing to return to Achimota that he was contacted by the Rector of Hemingford Abbots, Rev. Herbert Denison, who told him that the church was going to sell the Rectory. Since he was going to retire in two or three years' time, its purchase had to be considered and somehow the enormous sum of £5,000 was assembled. Elizabeth wrote to Betty Parsons in May:

> We are trying to buy Hemingford Rectory where Dennis's grandfather lived in Trollopean serenity for 40 years, whence the late Lord took his title etc. It seems to rest with the Church Commissioners to decide and they are money grubbers. On the other hand the Bishop and incumbent are on our side as we are known to be sober and godfearing, whereas any casual member of the Great British Public who might buy it in an auction, either might or might not be.
>
> The last incumbent had a theory (based on battleships on the sky line) that if you painted things grey you couldn't see them and orange seems to have been his other favourite colour – but the river Ouse runs through the garden, there is a tennis court, wash basins in every room, Gothic revival windows and a memorial-stained-glass in the church to old Herbert – very feudal.
>
> I shall sell my diamond brooch and two cottages (slum) in Musselburgh to furnish it (probably only beds and chests of drawers)

thereby ceasing to be a capitalist - if you can call it Capital – and safe when your Revolution comes. I hope it won't turn Dennis puritan – Oliver Cromwell, John Bunyan and William Cowper seem to be the local patron saints, but perhaps we'll discover some one more lively if we get there.

She did have other reservations. It was rather too "fenny" and near the wrong university. At Oxford there would, at least, be some hills and a whiff of the Cotswolds, which were her real love. Though it took months the deal was finally done, however, and in December they found themselves the owners of a substantial house and two and a half acres of land, though the donkey field next door – another three acres or so – was considered beyond their reach for another £500. The house lacked heating except open fires, cooking was on a black-leaded range and the wind blew in through the front door and under the linoleum in the long passage so that it floated on many days an inch or so above the floorboards. The kitchen was soon wreathed in the black smoke from burning pans and piled high with washing up waiting to be dealt with because Elizabeth, though she had a genius for producing delicious meals without apparent effort, actually found cooking less interesting than conversation and dishwashing less interesting than either. She had no refrigerator, but the meat safe and the larder allowed for the keeping of food until, as she used to say, "it is bad enough to throw away". The two older children at least, acclimatised by boarding schools, and Elizabeth as a Clark, could cope with the Arctic conditions, despite the fearsome contrast with West African heat, but Dennis soon took to wearing a hat and coat when moving from room to room and frequently otherwise. After a lecture tour which he undertook to the United States in 1954, he progressed to a bright red check woolly hunting jacket complete with cap, astonishing callers to whom he opened the door. The river was real enough but the tennis court existed more in theory than fact until Uncle Teddie's gift of posts, a net and a machine for drawing white lines arrived via St. Ives, Cornwall, to which it had been misdirected. Then Elizabeth, whose form on the hard courts of the Gold Coast had been good, had to adapt to what she called "marsh-tennis", which required a scooping technique to counter the low bounce. Nor was the godfearing sobriety always in evidence when her Clark siblings or William and his *Observer* colleagues descended for a weekend. Croquet out of doors, was one thing, but a lacrosse match in the drawing room caused Dennis some anxiety. Otherwise the lacrosse sticks were used for frequent, but unsuccessful, attempts to hunt the many bats emerging from the trunking round the bathroom plumbing, where they could be heard squeaking during ablutions.

Early in 1953 Dennis received the following communication from the Earl Marshal, the Duke of Norfolk, given at Her Majesty's Command:

> Right Trusty and Wellbeloved
> > We greet you well.
> > Whereas the second day of June next is appointed for the Solemnity of Our Royal Coronation.
> > These are to Will and Command you and the Lady your Wife (all excuses set apart) to make your personal attendance on Us at the time above mentioned furnished and appointed as to your Rank and Quality appertaineth, there to do and perform all such Services as shall be required and belong unto you respectively.
> > Whereof you and she are not to fail. And so we bid you most heartily farewell.

That was all very well, but the bit about being furnished according to rank and quality gave concern. Elizabeth had a set of coronation robes bequeathed to the Dowager by a friend who had two sets, but Dennis was not equipped. Then it was discovered that William Clark, as soon as he heard that the King had died, had rung the appropriate outfitters and reserved in Dennis's name, one of only two available sets of robes. It was a great event and, true to form, Elizabeth described it for Betty Parsons:

> The Coronation was worth it but cold. In spite of ermine, miniver and velvet I don't remember ever feeling colder and had to pin the tail of my train round my neck. Sitting still for hours was utter bliss to me, I wouldn't have minded another five and did, I think, go to sleep between the Princess Royal and the Queen Mother (not their persons – their entrances). I sat next to Lady Keys, very beautiful and statuesque with correct little tales of her obviously well-born children, Lady Moran (Winston's doctor's wife), very discreet and motherly, and buddies with all around. Lady Citrine behind, whose "corns were poppin' somethink crool," didn't know when she'd enjoyed a nice bit of colour on a day out so much before.

> But when the service began it really was very moving; that grave young figure turning humbly to us all as our 'undoubted Queen'; and later the glory of supertunica and crown. We enjoyed shouting "Long live the Queen, May the Queen live for Ever" and were so surprised that what we had thought of as a purely Peeress assembly apparently had male voices. However, it appears the House of Commons were above us.

> On David's advice I drank nothing from lunchtime before (he having lined streets on previous Royal occasions) and was unaffected by

Natural Desires. Everyone else stumbled up & down narrow stairs & passages, much impeded by kirtles, mantles and coronets, but that must have been nothing to the impediment of them when they arrived. My coronet, though supremely uncomfortable as I tipped my tiara too far forward & gave myself a headache, did stay in place – 3 or 4 around me actually fell to the ground in spite of elaborate wire cages, combs etc. I had horsehair and hat pins.......

Dennis regaled fellow-peers with Horlicks tablets and acid drops. When I found that my H. tablets were wrapped in waxed paper, and I in long white kid gloves to the shoulder, I gave up trying and ate nothing from 5.30am till 3.00pm so positively enjoyed the plebeian meal provided in the House of Lords, which consisted mainly of pyramids of hard boiled eggs. Some of the more delicately nurtured peers protested.

Back in Huntingdon Elizabeth had been instrumental in a Coronation Pageant at Hinchingbrooke House, which was fortunately staged on the only four fine days of the summer and was, she thought, a cultural, if not financial, success. Her episode, a highway robbery, which required five horses, two carriages, a blunderbuss, two pistols and some humans went well except that she suspected one of her handmaidens of being seduced by a boy from the local open prison brought in to make up the male numbers.

When he got back from Kumasi, Dennis had still to earn a living. His negotiations with Longmans succeeded in raising his retainer to £900 a year and he had his pension, but he would need more – Nicholas left Oundle at the end of the year, but was destined for Cambridge, and school fees for the girls might be required for another decade. It was not long before Alec Fraser came back upon the scene. On hearing of Dennis's retirement, he had written supportively that the Principal must be a fool and Dennis would be a loss to the Gold Coast. Then he added:

For you it is but a change of work. You lost the Gold Coast for a time & a great & growing circle of friends. Later you will have a great platform for your work on Africa.

Now, having himself been involved in Gordonstoun School in Scotland, he introduced Dennis to Kurt Hahn, its inspirational founder. Hahn, who was trying to persuade his board to appoint a Principal, was very taken with Dennis. He came to stay at Hemingford in one of its rare warm moments and, because he had a metal plate in his head, had to be kept relatively cool, so meals were taken in semi-darkness with the curtains drawn, but he was a remarkable talker. He arranged for Elizabeth and Dennis to travel up by First

Class Sleeper to Aberdeen and later, writing from Salem in Southern Germany, sent Dennis a detailed memorandum setting out his ideas of the Principal's role and a warm invitation to them both to visit Salem. He added, in a a postscript:

> I can imagine the conflict in your and Lady Hemingford's mind as to the renewed call to Africa. I hesitated very much of (sic) expressing my own view. But.......I feel strongly that your warning voice is needed at the centre. There are not many people in England or Scotland who can bear witness on the various issues now to be decided in Africa – and there are very few Tories who could so naturally join forces with true Liberals like Gilbert Murray when a grave international injustice is to be righted.

There is no doubt that Hahn impressed Dennis and their ideas about schoolmastering were similar, but his pursuit of Dennis for Gordonstoun came to nothing, for reasons that are obscure. Dennis's residence at Hemingford and involvement in local government (He had stood unopposed for the Huntingdonshire County Council as representative of the two Hemingford villages) probably had much to do with it. Had he gone there he might have been responsible for the education of the Prince of Wales, whom he was to get to know later in their lives.

What the renewed call to Africa may have been is not known, but, encouraged perhaps by both Hahn and Fraser, Dennis was soon at work on the larger stage. With a number of like-minded individuals, including Mary Benson, Arthur Creech Jones, Dingle Foot, QC, Lady Pakenham and David Astor (who supplied the initial funding), Dennis now became involved with the Africa Bureau, which was set up in 1952 under his chairmanship to keep British people informed and help African people to fight against discrimination. It rapidly became a leading opponent of the British Government's Central African Federation, which united Northern and Southern Rhodesia with Nyasaland. Dennis used every opportunity, including debates in the House of Lords, to make his point that the rationale of the Federation, which was economic rather than political, was unworkable and he was proud of the fact that he was the only Conservative in either House to vote against it. The Africa Bureau, and in particular its Director, Rev. Michael Scott, had an uneasy relationship with Christian Aid, run by the fiery Canon John Collins, which caused Dennis some headaches. Scott was a remarkable man, who seemed to live mainly on air as he had had many of his internal organs removed, but was a relentless lobbyist. He startled the congregation at Hemingford Abbots one morning when he prayed for the soul of "our late lamented friend, Edward". There was much whispering in the pews as to the identity of the deceased, which turned out to be the head of the Herero tribe of South West Africa, who were fighting to avoid incorporation into South Africa. Scott had his finger in so many pies that it was sometimes difficult to keep him focussed on the Africa Bureau's work, but when the Federation collapsed after about 10 years of existence, the Bureau deserved much of the credit.

This was all work very much to Dennis's liking – and he was quite proud of having been sentenced *in absentia* to forty lashes by the apartheid regime in South Africa - but neither it nor his local government labours, brought in any income so Dennis resorted to writing and lecturing. He made epic train journeys to remote venues and gave a series of broadcasts on the B.B.C.'s *Lift up Your Hearts* series which were published under the titles *The Seamless Robe* and *Yesterday, Today and Forever.* He also produced two more in the series of *Overseas Poetry Books*, the first two of which had originally cemented his relationship with Longmans in the 1930s. His abridgement of Trollope's *The Warden*, which had originally been published in 1950, was re-issued seven times between 1952 and 1963 and he followed it with an abridged version of *Ayala's Angel* by the same author in 1964. He also became an examiner for the Examinations Syndicate in Cambridge, marking papers in English Language, a task which he much enjoyed but which frustrated his family because it always produced a surge of work at Christmas. He was fascinated by the process of ensuring fairness on the part of examiners, though he accepted that it was like chasing a will o' the wisp. In a memorandum on the subject he wrote:

> Revision should be planned not to find out whether certain candidates should get 41, 42 or 43 marks; but whether Mr X and Mrs Y are usually within 2,3 or 4 marks of "the beam", and, if not, where they go wrong

Dennis was also recruited on to the London Government Staff Commission, 1963-65, but it was not long before local obligations began to grow more onerous. In 1960 he became a Justice of the Peace and in the following year Chairman of the Huntingdonshire County Council. This soon involved him in the complex process of merging with the Soke of Peterborough, a move which was accomplished in 1965 and of which he was proud, not because it saved any money, which it did not, nor because it was popular, which it was not particularly, but because it was accomplished with civility.

Although governmental assurances were given that there would be no further change for 15 years, within less than a decade, as Chairman of Huntingdon & Peterborough County Council, he was plunged into another merger, this time with Cambridgeshire, which had itself merged with the Isle of Ely. In May, 1968, a letter from 10 Downing Street, signed by Harold Wilson as Prime Minister, arrived. It asked whether Dennis would allow the the Queen to be asked to approve his appointment as Lord Lieutenant of the County of Huntingdon & Peterborough. A number of interesting consequences arose from this appointment. A large flagpole was erected in the flower bed outside the drawing room of the Old Rectory and a small one on the bonnet of Dennis and Elizabeth's battered old Triumph car. Moreover Dennis was required fairly regularly to clamber into the uniform of a Major General in the Army, which he had inherited from a previous holder of the office. The boots, which did not fit too well, were a problem and passengers in the Triumph, once they had got over their surprise that the Lord Lieutenant's car was so full of rust holes, were alarmed to discover that when the driver's spurs got caught under the accelerator, it was touch and go how quickly the vehicle could be brought to a halt. The Bishop of Uganda's description of Dennis as the worst driver in the world may have been a slight exaggeration, but this new hazard did not do anything to improve his performance behind the wheel. The family already knew, from the Coronation, that Dennis was not very handy with a sword – the question was should it be hung from the belt before trying to pass through the eye of the car door or left loose to be hurriedly attached on arrival at some formal ceremony? On one occasion, when he was due to take part in a military parade in Peterborough, Dennis found that he was ahead of schedule so he parked the car in a lay-by only to find that, when the time came to move on, it would not start. Seeing a farm house in the distance he clambered out, sword attached, and began toiling across a ploughed field to ask for help. As he approached he found himself looking down the barrel of a shotgun wielded by the owner who thought that the police had finally caught up with him. One of Dennis's duties, as *Custos Rotulorum* may have been to call out the militia, but this was no time for such legal niceties and a quick disavowal of any attempt at law enforcement produced the desired assistance. Dennis was proud of – and took seriously - his role as the Sovereign's representative, but he remained engagingly ready to laugh at himself.

This was just as well because the job of Lord Lieutenant's helpmeet was emphatically not Elizabeth's cup of tea. She tended to see the whole business as a lot of unnecessary flummery and stood ready to puncture at once any sign of pomposity in her husband. She could be forthright with courtiers or clerics alike. Dennis once overheard her saying to the Bishop of Ely at dinner "Do you think you keep a close enough eye on your lay readers, Bishop?" The Bishop replied that he did his best but he wondered what she had in mind. "Dennis." she replied, "He has to preach a sermon in three weeks' time and all he is doing is ransack his study to find out the year in which we last had a twenty-sixth Sunday after Trinity. What spiritual benefit will the poor people of Kimbolton get from that?" As William Clark said, in a tribute years later, Dennis and Elizabeth were two very different independent characters, but a shared sense of humour enabled them to manage a harmonious way of life.

Elizabeth had helped to restart the village Women's Institute in 1952 because she perceived a lack of community spirit, and she soon began to rise through the ranks to county and then national levels. Her interest in drama was lifelong, nurtured by those performances in the Haltwhistle Mechanics' Institute, and she was instrumental in proposing that performances of Shakespeare's plays should take place in the Elizabethan courtyard of the George Hotel in Huntingdon, which is now an annual event. She also mobilised the village to take part in the 1957 National W.I. Drama Festival. As a result she joined, and was soon chairing, the County Federation's Music and Drama Committee. She was elected at the first attempt to the County Executive, co-opted on to the National Federation's International Committee in 1956 and the Executive three years later. Elected in her own right in 1961, she became Vice Chairman of the National Federation from 1964 to 1966. She became involved in various campaigns, for example to extend the 30 mph. speed limit to all villages, or remove the turnstiles from ladies' public lavatories and, to her great pleasure, chaired the committee which ran the W.I.'s own Denman College. Emphasising for an interviewer her belief in the importance of a sense of community, she said:

> There is a great deal of loneliness, especially on the new estates.
> When we take the W.I. to them, they welcome it with open arms. It is
> the greatest single thing we do.

When succession to the chairmanship was mooted, she decided, not without a pang of regret, that it would be too much and too difficult to reconcile with her other obligations. Her children were all married and were beginning to produce grandchildren. Nico's wedding to Jenny Bailey at Harrogate in 1958 had been the last time she and her brothers were all together. Cass's wedding to Hal Moggridge had been noted for the modern design of the wedding cake and Celia's to Willie Goodhart had to be transferred to the larger church at Godmanchester because of the press of guests. Besides, Elizabeth's health had, on occasion recently, given cause for concern. When her doctor advised cutting down activities, Betty Parsons remarked:

> At least you will have more time for what you do superbly – running a house. Until last autumn The Old Rectory was my second favourite place to visit. Now a lamented death has moved it to First. Both houses remarkable for (1) unfuss (2) kindness that does not constrain. I so much admire your leisurely meals & the absence of tension at your sink. Dennis is just as good at it as you are, & you have no idea how much I respected you both when he drove you to the train in his dressing gown without an exclamation on either side.

The Old Rectory was, she added, just the place for grandchildren, (for whom like cats places were important) and with just a yard or two of wire netting along the river bank they could be given the run of a paradise. She did concede, however, that it might be more tiring than the W.I.

All these concerns and preoccupations were punctuated by various journeys abroad. In October, 1955, for example, they were invited to accompany Mutesa on his return to Uganda after two years' exile imposed by the Governor because of political disagreements. Landing at Cairo to refuel they were met by President Nasser (who would loom large in their lives the following year). Then they dined – unscathed this time – with Mutesa in the back of the aircraft and later Elizabeth described the enthusiastic crowds which lined the 21 miles of road between the airport and Kampala and filled the Cathedral, where a service of thanksgiving was held. She and Dennis were so engulfed afterwards by Old Budonians and friends that they missed the next event and went gratefully to their hotel. Despite fears of trouble, everyone behaved well and with good humour. Next day, with lawyers in wigs and knee breeches, Mutesa in a crimson robe and the Governor in blue and silver with an Imperial cocked hat, an agreement was signed. "Rather long & boring, but very important," was Elizabeth's verdict. For the two years of the Kabaka's exile, the Baganda had forsworn football – an indication of their strength of feeling – so the quality of the celebratory match was below par and the quantity too great since (shades of the notorious Budo concert in 1942) 10 minutes had been added to each half in honour of the Kabaka. If Dennis still harboured any doubts, though, about his position in the pantheon of Budo headmasters, he must have lost them after this trip. Another journey the following year was equally emotional. This time their host was Kwame Nkrumah and the occasion was the inauguration of Ghana as a fully independent country within the Commonwealth, the first former African colony to achieve such status. William Clark, who was there for the BBC, described what happened after the flag-raising ceremony:

> On a hot and humid tropical midnight, distinguished visitors were presented to the cabinet. As Dennis, carefully muffled as always against any improbable night breezes, went slowly down the line, Kwame Nkrumah first, and then more than half his cabinet, saluted him with the simple words "My teacher".

Dennis was astonished at the building which had gone on in the five years since he left and he could scarcely find his way about Accra. He and Elizabeth both came away proud to have been connected with a country that had made such remarkable progress in so short a time and proud of the contribution made by Achimota. When he was asked what he really taught there that was useful to Africans, apart from the academic curriculum, he used to quote his favourite poet, John Milton: "Let not England forget her precedence of teaching nations how to live." He was therefore profoundly shocked when in 1956 Britain and France, in collusion with Israel and in defiance of the United Nations, invaded Egypt. He resigned his membership of the Huntingdonshire Conservative Association in protest, but could not quite bring himself to abandon the party altogether. When later Celia became a parliamentary candidate for the S.D.P. she used to press him to join her party, but he declared that he remained a committed Thatcherite.

Difficult years were to follow in both Ghana and Uganda, but Dennis never lost his faith in their future. Young nations, he said, would try on many suits of clothes before they found what fitted them and he believed that when they did it would probably be more on the basis of their pervasive Christian faith, interpreted in their African way, rather than on economic or political ideology. Uganda tried a particularly disastrous suit of clothes in the days of Idi Amin in the 1970s as Dennis and Elizabeth were to see for themselves. Invited by a group of Old Budonians for an anniversary visit in 1971, they actually appeared on television with Amin, who launched at once into a lengthy monologue. Feeling that he perhaps ought to contribute something to the programme, Dennis intervened with a comment. This threw the dictator completely and the cameras had to be stopped and the programme started all over again, the visitors this time maintaining a discreet silence. They did manage, however, to make a tour of the country, visiting many places which, in the bad old days of petrol shortage, had been inaccessible to them. Elizabeth, particularly, enjoyed the wildlife parks and the beauty of the scenery.

Visits to Nico's family in the United States in 1963 (Elizabeth's first to the New World), and Beirut and the Holy Land in 1967 were also fitted in and Elizabeth began to go frequently with the Moggridges to Tuscany, which became a favourite place. In May, 1973, for example, she wrote enthusiastically of having fallen in love with Siena, where at peril of her life from the traffic, she spent a lot of time wandering the streets. This was a recuperative trip after an illness and she pronounced herself cured. "It's no good trying to describe it all – it's just splendid and just what I needed," she wrote to Dennis. After a second trip to Beirut in 1968, Elizabeth picked up a tubercular infection which affected her lymph system. She recovered from this but was thereafter subject to rather unspecific malaise. Dennis's medical encounters were much more specific. On one of his West African lorry journeys he had been bruised by a carcass of meat falling on him and it later transpired that this had damaged a kidney. He had to have it removed, but his recovery was slowed by a swab being left in the wound which was not discovered until about a year later. He recovered well after it had been attended to but in 1970 he fell on the stairs at The Old Rectory and severed the tendons in both knees. Among the papers he left was one listing the various lifting and stretching exercises he was required to do after the tendons had been repaired. They were successful and he returned to mobility sporting a beard, which he had grown in hospital, but which he abandoned under family pressure.

In time the size of The Old Rectory and particularly of its garden began to weigh heavily and so, when Nico proposed that he should buy the house and convert the Coach House into a place for them, they welcomed the idea. They tolerated, with typical patience, many changes and enjoyed the proximity of four of their grandchildren, with the complex management of whose activities they assisted powerfully.

In 1979 Elizabeth was told that she had a virulent form of leukaemia from whose rapid onset she would not recover, though it could be slowed by blood transfusions. She faced death resolutely, firm in her belief that there was no after-life and a few days after a sentimental journey back to the Northumbrian hills she died on September 29, 1979. Patrick O'Donovan, of the *Observer* and the *Catholic Herald*, with whom she had struck up a particular rapport when he stayed with them in the Gold Coast, had sent her his papal medal with a letter of sympathy when he heard the bad news and it was he who wrote the most moving obituary:

> The great comfort about her death is the splendour of her life – even though it was appallingly hard at times........She was a splendid

person who looked a little like Britannia, had bounding energy and a gift of happiness....We were the most unlikely sort of friends. She was strict, at least with herself, but tolerant of me. Her voice was commanding and yet her conversation was kind and witty and interested. I shall miss her vastly; England produces no better sort of person. In some curious way she created happiness as a potter does his pots. She was the least phoney person I ever knew. She would not have liked me writing thus, but I hope Dennis and their now distinguished children will forgive this rather Catholic eulogy.

Dennis bore his loss with typical stoicism – they had had time to make their farewells and he had the comfort of belief in the hereafter. He then - which would have infuriated her - set about reorganising his life along lines which she had been advocating for years. Thus, in the Coach House, where he continued living, he turned his desk round as she wanted, he took to eating fresh fruit, and he no longer required meat and two veg. twice a day on the dot of 1.00pm and 7.30pm. He even began to pay his income tax on time, although frequent Final Demands from the Inland Revenue could still be found lost between books in his library. He even entertained friends from the village to meals extracted entirely from tins and he continued his duties as a lay reader, preaching in the church at Hemingford Abbots only days before he was taken into Addenbrookes Hospital, Cambridge, where he died on June 19, 1982. At his Memorial Service in Huntingdon, his brother-in-law, William Clark, said:

> In giving thanks to God for Dennis's life, I would like to repeat a quotation from Winston Churchill that Dennis used in this church at the Memorial Service for Sir Winston: "We give thanks to God for the noblest of his blessings, the sense that we have done our duty."
>
> That noble blessing was what Dennis, to the last, desired, deserved and received.

*Dennis George Ruddock Herbert, 2nd Baron Hemingford,
(1904-1982)*

371

Elizabeth. and Dennis. "The Coronation was worth it, but cold."

*The Lord Lieutenant, with sword,
welcoming the Prince of Wales*

The W.I. lady

The hunting jacket.

Dennis receiving his portrait by John Ward, RA. Presented by the County of Huntingdon & Peterborough.

Dennis & Elizabeth at The Old Rectory

Elizabeth at the river.

Memorial window to Dennis & Elizabeth in Hemingford Abbots church. Engraved by David Peace.

Acknowledgements

Staff in Archives and Record Offices are invariably cheerful, helpful and knowledgeable. I have had help from far too many to mention individually, but my gratitude is great nevertheless. They know who they are. Likewise staff in the great repositories - The National Archives, the British Library, the Cambridge University Library and the Society of Genealogists – have been unfailingly cooperative. The Bodleian at Rhodes House permitted me to consult my fatherr's papers, which they hold. The Institute of Jamaica in Kingston distinguished itself during our brief visit by enabling us to solve the Mackenzie problem. Nowadays, of course, one cannot do without the many on-line services such as Ancestry and Jamaican Family Search, from which I have benefited.

Some individuals require to be mentioned. I am particularly grateful to Sir David Bell for allowing me to reproduce the portraits of our common ancestors, Hugh and Bethia Bell, and to Andrew Carruth for taking the photographs of them. Sir David also gave me Maud Bell's delightful letter to her great niece. Thanks too to Mrs. Patsy Clark for a copy of the portrait of John Clark. The Royal Society for the Arts has allowed me to use Mary Okes's prize-winning drawing and the Rector, Churchwardens and Parochial Church Council of the Priory and Parish Church of St. Andrew (Hexham Abbey) sanctioned use of the reproduction from their Parish Register for 1810. The National Gallery of Scotland permitted me to use the portraits of Mrs. Kinnear and Dr. Gardiner and the Minet Library gave me access to the painting of Lonesome Lodge. Mr. John Evelyn allowed me to poke about in his rhododendrons at Wotton, where the scant remains of the house can be seen and churchwardens at Wotton and Stockland Bristol were similarly accommodating. A word of thanks, too, to those who tend the many churchyards I have visited up and down the country.

The late Evelyn Ruddock, of Belfast, supplied me with a bewildering flow of information and speculation about her namesakes, among it the transcription from the family Bible, which she had from Rev. Reginald Ruddock, whom I thank at second hand. My nephew Geoffrey Moggridge enabled me to descend to the bowels of King's College Chapel, to see where Dr. Richard Okes lies buried, and into the recesses of the Provost's (then empty) Lodge to see a picture of Thomas Okes. My Jackson relations Faith McNaughtan and Lyn Connell permitted me to copy photographs in their collections and Katherine Bailey kindly helped in the first case.

Joan Stevens, Secretary of the Lauderdale Historical Society helped me to understand the Scottish nonconformists and Ronald Morrison, Chairman of the Borders Family History Society, most generously went and photographed John Clark's birthplace near Duns. Stephen Setchell, on a visit to South Africa, procured for me a copy of the Diocesan College History, which was not available in Britain. Robert Specken, in Holland, assisted in tracking down elusive details about the portrait painter, Herbert Tuer. Irene Cockroft has helped me with Evans Bell and his family, particularly Ernestine, of whom she is a passionate advocate. Dr. F. Henderson, of Oxford, and Dr. T. Underhill, of Cambridge, both tried, kindly but unsuccessfully, to decipher Henry Okes's shorthand.

Finally various of my relations have helped with encouragement information and correction. I am grateful to them all, but particularly to my poor wife, Jenny, who has had to live with a whole host of unexpected ghosts about the house and a husband with a one-track mind.

Sources

Nearly all the unpublished material which I have used is in the Hemingford Archive - my own inherited collection of letters, papers and documents. The origins of some of these, particularly photographs, is not always clear, but I hope I have contacted any copyright holders. My father's papers, of some of which I have copies, were deposited in the Bodleian collection at Rhodes House. The full report of the Budo Enquiry is in the National Archives at Kew and the CMS on-line records. Rev. W. Cole's MSS is at the British Library. Also at Kew are the voluminous records of Valentine Graeme Bell's dispute with Governor Blake and the Portland-Camden correspondence about Arthur O'Connor and the court records of the trial.

Much of the more colourful detail about the Kinnears comes from a letter written by Maud Bell to her great-niece. The House of Lords Record Office yielded documents on Bubb Dodington's change of name and the Haynes divorce.

Family history is notorious for leading one down byways of research and I have indulged in that pleasure to the full. The following are some of the more useful published works upon which I have drawn:

Part I – The Herberts

Anon: *Annals of Cambridge*
Arliss: *Literary Collections*
Brittain, Vera: *Testament of Youth*
Calamy, Edmund: *Continuation*
Carswell, John (Ed.): *The Political Journal of George Bubb Dodington*
Chute, M.: *Two gentle men - George Herbert & Robert Herrick*
Clark, J.W.: *Old Friends in Cambridge*
Cole, William: *The Blecheley Diaries*
Darwin, Charles: *Life of Erasmus Darwin*
Draper, Marie: *Marble Hill House & its Owners*
Fawcett, John: *Account of an 18-month's residence at the Cape of Good Hope*
Francis, A.D.: *Campaign in Portugal, 1762*
Gardener, John: *Bishops 150: A History of the Diocesan College, Rondebosch*
Gray, L. & Hattersley, A: *A Victorian Lady at the Cape*
Kahan, Gerald: *George Alexander Stevens & The Lecture on Heads*
Le Cordeur, Basil: *The War of the Axe, 1847*
Lear: *Life of Robert Gray, Bishop of Cape Town*
Lewes, Charles Lee: *Comic Sketches*
Lewes, Charles Lee: *Memoirs*
McFetrich, David: *Bramston*
Mander, C.H.W.: *A Descriptive & Historical Account of the Cordwainers*
Mariners Mirror Vol 60 p 41
Okes, Holt: *Attempt to determine year & day Jesus died*
Okes, Holt: *Practical Sermons*
Robertson, J.P & W.P: *Letters on Paraguay*
Shuttleworth, J.M. (Ed.): *The Life of Edward, First Lord Herbert of Chirbury*
Snagge, Thomas: *Recollections of Occurrences:Some 18th Century Theatrical Memoirs*

Timbs, John: *A Picturesque Promenade round Dorking in Surrey*
Walton, Izaak: *The Lives of Dr. John Donne......and Mr. George Herbert*
Warwick, Lou: *Theatre un-royal*
Whibley, Charles: *In Cap & Gown 3 Centuries of Cambridge Wit*
Wilson, Walter: *Dissenting Churches & meeting Houses*
Winstanley, D.A.: *Early Victorian Cambridge*
Yogev, Gedalia: *Diamonds and Coral:Anglo-Dutch Jews & 18ᵗʰCentury Trade*

Part II – The Bells

Bell, George William: *Recollections of My Life*
Bell, Mary Hayley: *What Shall we do Tomorrow?*
Besse, Joseph: *Sufferings of Early Quakers (West Indies)*
Bolhouse, Gladys: *Abraham Redwood* (in Redwood Papers)
Caine, R.Hall: *The Cruise of the Port Kingston*
Coigly, James: *Trial of Arthur O'Connor, James O'Coigly & etc*
Collier, M. & Tidey, M.G.S.(Comp): *The Beehive, 1876-1964*
Dunn, Richard S.: *Sugar and Slaves:Rise of the Planter in the W.I.*
Hames, Jane Hayter: *Arthur O'Connor: United Irishman*
Howarth, David: *The Golden Isthmus*
Mackenzie, Alexander: *History of the Clan Mackenzie*
Nugent: *Lady Nugent's Journal*
Oliver, Vere: *History of Antigua*
Ransom, P.J.G.: *The Mt. Cenis Fell Railway*

Part III – The Clarks:

Devine, T.M. (Ed): *Farm Servants & Labour in Lowland Scotland*
Goyder, Roma: *Hayseed to Harvest: Memories of Katherine Cox & Hayes Court School*
James, Richard Forbes: *Lauder: its Kirk & People*
Moffat, Alistair: *The Borders*
Thomson, A.: *Lauder and Lauderdale*

Part IV – The Jacksons

Jennings, David: *Hexham, 1854-1939, Local Government in a Market Town*

Part V – Dennis & Elizabeth

Anon: *Sanderson of Oundle*
McGregor, G.P.: *King's College Budo*
Mutesa, Kabaka of Buganda: *Desecration of My Kingdom*
Summers, Carol: *Subterranean Evil and Tumultuous Riot in Buganda: authority and alienation at King's College, Budo, 1942. in Journal of African History, Vol. 47, (2006)*
Ward, W.E.F.: *Fraser of Trinity & Achimota*

Descendants of Henry and Mary Herbert

Rev. Henry Herbert, b. 1824, d. 1911
+Mary Ruddock, b. 1834, m. 1868, d. 1917
├── Dennis Henry Herbert, First Baron Hemingford, b. 1869, d. 1947
  +Mary Graeme Bell, Lady Hemingford, b. 1883, m. 1903, d. 1966
  ├── Dennis George Ruddock Herbert, Second Baron Hemingford, b. 1904, d. 1982
  │ +Elizabeth McClare Clark, Lady Hemingford, b. 1910, m. 1932, d. 1979
  │ ├── Dennis Nicholas Herbert, 3rd Baron Hemingford, b. 1934
  │ │ +Jennifer Mary Toresen Bailey, Lady Hemingford, OBE, DL, b. 1933, m. 1958
  │ │ ├── Elizabeth Frances Toresen Herbert, b. 1963
  │ │ │ +John Nigel Evered Witt, b. 1962, m. 1994
  │ │ │ ├── Alice Toresen Isabelle Witt, b. 1996
  │ │ │ ├── Harry John Evered Witt, b. 1997
  │ │ │ ├── Joseph William Evered Witt, b. 1999
  │ │ │ └── Martha Elizabeth Bridget Witt, b. 2002
  │ │ ├── Caroline Mary Louise Herbert, b. 1964
  │ │ │ +Andrew Maynard, b. circa 1955
  │ │ │ ├── Jessica Louise Herbert-Maynard, b. 1993
  │ │ │ ├── Thomas Elliot Herbert-Maynard, b. 1995
  │ │ │ └── Oscar James Herbert-Maynard, b. 1997
  │ │ ├── Alice Christine Emma Herbert, chr. 1968
  │ │ │ +Christopher McManus, b. 1957, m. 1992
  │ │ │ ├── James Nicholas McManus, b. 1994
  │ │ │ ├── Jeremy Bailey McManus, b. 1998
  │ │ │ └── Jennifer Grace McManus, b. 2002
  │ │ └── Christopher Dennis Charles Herbert, b. 1973
  │ ├── Celia McClare Herbert, Lady Goodhart, b. 1939
  │ │ +William Howard Goodhart, Lord Goodhart, b. 1933, m. 1966
  │ │ ├── Annabel Frances Goodhart, b. 1967
  │ │ │ +Jim Dallas, m. 1995
  │ │ │ ├── Josephine Juliet Dallas, b. 1997
  │ │ │ ├── Beatrice Dallas, b. 2000
  │ │ │ └── Katharine Claudia Dallas, b. 2004
  │ │ ├── Laura Christabel Goodhart, b. 1970
  │ │ │ +William Watts, b. 1969
  │ │ │ ├── Matthew Urban Watts, b. 2000
  │ │ │ ├── Kenneth Lando Watts, b. 2002
  │ │ │ └── Fletcher Clement (--?--), b. 2005
  │ │ └── Benjamin Herbert Goodhart, b. 1972
  │ │   +Wendy Young
  │ │   └── Alfred William Goodhart, b. 2008
  │ └── Catherine Grevile Herbert, b. 1943
  │   +Harry Traherne Moggridge OBE, b. 1936, m. 1963
  │   ├── Harriet Fearne Moggridge, b. 1965
  │   │ +Nicholas John Lawrence, b. 1943, m. 1992
  │   │ ├── Joseph John Lawrence Moggridge, b. 1993
  │   │ └── Henry Lawrence Moggridge, b. 1995
  │   ├── Geoffrey Dillwyn Moggridge, b. 1967
  │   └── Lawrence Weston Moggridge, b. 1970
  ├── Valentine Henry Okes Herbert T.D, b. 1905, d. 1983
  │ +Winifred Mabel Pearson, b. 1906, m. 1931, d. 1955
  │ ├── Rosemary Anne Herbert, b. 1932
  │ │ +Brigadier William George Rhyll Turner CBE, b. 1933, d. 1989
  │ │ ├── Valerie Jane Turner, b. 1958
  │ │ │ +Nicholas Russell-Pavier
  │ │ │ ├── Kate Russell-Pavier, b. 1987
  │ │ │ └── Frederick Russell-Pavier, b. 1993
  │ │ │ +Tom Harris
  │ │ ├── Penelope May Turner, b. 1960
  │ │ │ +Andrew Wilson, m. 1984
  │ │ │ ├── Jemima Wilson, b. 1988
  │ │ │ ├── Charles Wilson, b. 1989
  │ │ │ └── George Wilson, b. 1995
  │ │ └── Susan Diana Turner, b. 1964
  │ │   +Simon William de Mouchet Baynham, m. 1992
  │ │   ├── Rupert Baynham, b. 1992
  │ │   ├── Olivia Baynham, b. 1994
  │ │   └── Rory Baynham, b. 1997
  │ │   +Dr Giles Parkes

379

```
|   |   ├── Susan Jean Herbert, b. 1934, d. 1940
|   |   ├── Timothy William Okes Herbert, b. 1936
|   |   |  +Erica Anne Odell, b. 1942, m. 1977
|   |   └── Sylvia Valentine Herbert, b. 1948
|   |  +P.Jeremy B. Sayce, b. 1943, d. 1980
|   |   └── Emily Valentine Sayce, b. 1978
|   |  +J.Robin K. Peile, m. 1983
|   |   ├── Maxwell Herbert Peile, b. 1984
|   |   └── Bertram Kitchener Peile, b. 1988
|   |  +Janet Wigram, b. 1916, m. 1956, d. 1982
|   ├── Robert John Grevile Herbert, b. 1909, d. 1930
|   └── Oliver Hayley Dennis Herbert, b. 1919, d. 2004
|  +Rosemary Muriel Bate, b. 1929, m. 1976
├── Edward Grevile Herbert, b. 1870, d. 1951
|  +Olive Una Linton, b. 1873, d. 1904
|   ├── Olive Mary Herbert, b. 1903, d. 1903
|   └── Charles Henry Herbert, b. 1904, d. 1957
|  +Henrietta Dorothea Begg, m. 1934
|   ├── Mary Macdonald Herbert, b. 1938
|   |  +Dieter Doktor, m. 1961
|   └── Caroline Grevile Herbert, b. 1944
├── Lieut-Col. Louis William Herbert D.S.O, b. 1873, d. 1955
|  +Amy Lilian Jarvis, b. 1893, m. before 1930, d. 1976
├── Richard Charles Herbert, b. 1874, d. 1948
|  +Kathleen Emily Reeves, m. before 1929, d. 1938
|   └── Mary Ruddock Herbert, b. before 1929
|  +John Kent
|   ├── Christine Kent, b. 1948
|   └── Bernice Kent, b. 1950
|  +Michael Gay, m. 1970
├── George Herbert, b. 1876, d. 1947
|  +Muriel Fanny Cecil Stewart, b. 1867, d. 1937
└── Rev. Francis Falkner Herbert, b. 1879, d. 1957
+Madeline King, b. 1882, d. 1980
├── Kenneth Falkner Herbert, b. 1910, d. 1993
|  +Kathleen Robertson
|   ├── Anthony James Herbert, b. 1940
|   |  +Mary Macrae
|   |  +Margaret Lowell Pelton, m. 1968
|   |   ├── Dominic James Herbert, b. 1971
|   |   ├── Daniel Mark Herbert, b. 1973
|   |   └── Julia Lowell Herbert, b. 1978
|   ├── Amanda Herbert, b. 1943
|   |  +Fergus Hinds, m. 1969
|   |   ├── Matthew Frank Hinds, b. 1972
|   |   ├── Paul Kenneth Hinds, b. 1975
|   |   └── Catherine Jane Hinds, b. 1978
|   └── Mark Jeremy Herbert, b. 1948
|  +Shiranhika Pullanayagum, m. 1977
└── Henry Myles Herbert, b. 1915
+Patricia Sullivan, d. 1998
├── Julian David Herbert, b. 1952
|  +Pamela Morris, m. 1981
|   ├── Caroline Valerie Herbert
|   └── Rosanna Herbert, b. 1988
└── Robin Clive Herbert, b. 1955
```

Descendants of John and Jane Clark

John Clark, b. 1818, d. 1882
+Jane/Jean McClare, b. 1821, m. 1849, d. 1868
└── John McClare Clark, b. 1854, d. 1937
+Marion Jackson, b. 1877, m. 1899, d. 1917
├── John Clark, b. 1903, d. 1977
│ +Audrey Dorothy Irwin, m. 1928
│ │ ├── Maud Marion Clark, b. 1929
│ │ +Rev. Stanley Prins
│ │ │ ├── Lucinda Jane Prins, b. 1966
│ │ │ +(--?--) Butler
│ │ │ ├── Katherine Emma Prins, b. 1970
│ │ │ +Jonathan Priest
│ │ │ │ ├── Lucas Priest, b. 2000
│ │ │ │ └── Megan Priest, b. 2003
│ │ │ └── Simon Prins, b. 1971
│ │ +Ruth (--?--)
│ │ │ ├── Samuel Prins, b. 2002
│ │ │ ├── Joshua Prins, b. 2005
│ │ │ └── Daniel Oliver Prins, b. 2008
│ │ ├── Ruth Irwin Clark, b. 1931
│ │ +Jon Nightingale
│ │ │ ├── Jeremy Darby Nightingale, b. 1957
│ │ │ ├── Paul Nightingale, b. 1960
│ │ │ └── Guy Nightingale, b. 1964
│ │ ├── Susan Elizabeth Clark, b. 1933
│ │ +Rev. Basil Dakin Hetherington, b. 1923, d. 1978
│ │ │ ├── Rachel de Game Hetherington, b. 1958
│ │ │ +John Waters, m. 1990
│ │ │ │ ├── Connie Waters, b. 1994
│ │ │ │ └── William Michael Waters, b. 1996
│ │ │ ├── Crispin John Dakin Hetherington, b. 1960
│ │ │ ├── Aidan Hugh Clark Hetherington, b. 1962
│ │ │ +Holly MacNish Porter, b. 1966, m. 1996
│ │ │ └── Sarah McClare Hetherington, b. 1965
│ │ +James Robert Lyness, b. 1963, m. 1994, d. 2000
│ │ │ ├── Katharine Rachel Lyness, b. 1995
│ │ │ ├── Daniel Charles Lyness, b. 1998
│ │ │ └── Edward James Lyness, b. 2000
│ │ └── John Malcolm Clark, b. 1937
├── David George Clark, b. 1907, d. 1960
│ +Patricia Hazeldine, m. 1945
│ +Violet Augusta Grant, b. 1906, m. 1953, d. 1997
├── Elizabeth McClare Clark, Lady Hemingford, b. 1910, d. 1979   [See Descendants of Henry & Mary Herbert]
├── Daniel Nicholas Clark-Lowes, b. 1911
│ +Audrey Frances Scarth Dixon, m. 1941
│ ├── Francis Nicholas Clark-Lowes, b. 1944
│ +Annemarie Elizabeth Seifner, b. 1955, m. 1977
│ │ ├── Philip Frederick Clark-Lowes, b. 1979
│ │ └── Julia Christine Clark-Lowes, b. 1982
│ ├── Jeremy William Clark-Lowes, b. 1947
│ +Sally Reeve-Tucker, m. 1981
│ ├── Daniel David Clark-Lowes, b. 1951
│ +Sherry Macliver
│ +Vivienne Elizabeth Adele Hounsell, m. 1984
│ │ ├── William Henry Clark-Lowes, b. 1985
│ │ └── Rupert Daniel Clark-Lowes, b. 1987
│ └── Julian Philip Clark-Lowes, b. 1953
│ +Jane Dempsey
│ └── Nicholas Clark-Lowes, b. 1983
├── Kenneth Allan Clark T.D., F.S.I., F.L.A.S, b. 1911, d. 1986
│ +Patricia Ann Trotter
│ ├── Vanessa Jane Clark, b. 1952
│ +Richard Fry, m. 1980
│ │ └── Joanna Elizabeth Fry, b. 1989
│ ├── Ursula Sarah Clark, b. 1952
│ +Nichos Spiliopolou
│ │ ├── Constantine Spiliopolou, b. 1981
│ │ └── Panyotta Spiliopolou, b. 1982
│ └── Kenneth Nicholas McClare Clark, b. 1954
│ +Amanda Sangan, m. 1984
│ └── Emily Jane Clark, b. 1988
└── William Donaldson Clark, b. 1916, d. 1985

Index

A

Achimota Training College, 347
Acland, Sir Thomas, 66
Act of Settlement, 57
Addenbrooke's Hospital, Cambridge, 33
Africa Bureau, 363
Aga Khan, 128
Aggrey, Dr., 306, 309, **310**, 332
Agricultural Mortgage Corporation, 243
Alice, Duchess of Gloucester, 272
Alston Puffer, 234
American War of Independence, 213
Amin, Idi, President, 368
Amu, Mr., 349
Andrews, Jim, 351, 353p., 362
Anglican Society, 151
Anti-Magenta-Nose Club, 244, 295
Arbuthnot, Mr., 52
Archbishop of Canterbury, 264
Armstrong College, Newcastle, 251
Armstrong, Kitty, 303
Armstrong, Letitia Mary (nee Jackson), 273
Arthur, T., 209
Associate Burgher Congregation, Lauder, 232
Association for the relief of Soldiers' Wives and Children, 177
Astor,
    David, 264p., 363
    Nancy, Lady, 221
Atkins, George Murray, 276
Atkins, Helen (nee Jackson), 273, **276**
Atlee, Clement, MP, 134
Attwood, Mr., 162
Aytoun, Professor William, 183

B

Backhouse, Charles, 4
Baden Powell, Lady, 331
Balangira (King's Party), 339
Baldwin, Stanley, MP, 135
Ball, Col., 104
Balmer Lawrie & Co. Ltd., 143p.
Banfield, Col., 103
Bank of England, 33
Barnard, Lord, 260
Barnor, Mr., 349
Barrett,
    Edward, 210
    Edward, of Wimpole St., 210
    Eleanor (nee Miten), 210
    Elizabeth (nee Wisdom), 210
    Lieutenant Hearcey, 210
    Margery (nee Green), 210
    Richard, 210
    Samuel, 210
    Samuel (1689-1760), 210
Basil or Bassell,
    William, 57
Bate, Canon Roland, 152
Bateman, R.A., 221
Battles,
    Dunkirk, Retreat from, 251, 257
    Fort Beausejour (1755), Siege of, 213
    Indian Mutiny, 170
    Louisbourg (1758), Capture of, 213
    Mons, 104
    North Cape, 253
    Paardeberg,, 102
    Quebec Campaign (1759), 213
    Seringapatam, Siege of, 161
    The Boyne, 57

The Cauldron, Tobruk, 254
Waterloo, 159, 232
Ypres, First, 104
Beaumont & Sons, 122
Beevor,
    Captain Horace Clarke, 31
    Ellen (nee Okes), 31
Behring-Werke, 201
Bell,
    Agnes (nee MacGowan), 177
    Alexander (1715-), 156
    Anna Louisa, 164
    Anna Maria, 161
    Anne (née McQuoid), 156
    Archibald Graeme, 187, 190, 194
    Archibald Hamilton, 164, **178**
    Augusta (nee Ramsbottom), 179
    Bell & Higginson, 161
    Bethia (nee Bell), **161,** 165
    Edith Jane Anita, 187, 190, 194
    Elizabeth (nee Kinnear), 184, 186
    Elizabeth Fearne, 164
    Elizabeth Fearne (nee Kinnear), 3, 163
    Emilie Georgina (nee Lynch), 189, 195, 199, 219, 333
    Emily Ernst (nee Magnus), "Mrs.Fairfax", 172
    Ethel Louisa Graeme, 137, 189, 194, 198, 224
    Francis Hayley, 177
    Frederick Hayley, 164, **177**
    General Robert, 156, 161
    George William, 157, 162, **166,** 175, 182, 190
    Grace Henrietta Hamilton, 163p.
    Henrietta (1793-1844), 162
    Hugh, **155,** 156p., 165
    Hugh Reid, 164
    Isabella Bethia, 164
    Janet (née Allison), 161
    Jemima (née Scott), 162
    Jessie (nee Hawes), 166
    John M., 32
    Katherine (nee Jackson), 273
    Kenneth Frederick Hamilton, D.S.O., 179
    Leonora Georgiana, 164
    Louise, 164
    Margaret, 194
    Margaret (1784-1851), 161
    Mary Caroline, 164
    Mary Hayley (Playwright), 177, 224
    Maud, 176
    Maud Anna, 182
    Mynie, 172
    Octavius Plunket, 164
    Rebecca Dalzell (nee Filson), 186p.
    Robert, 161p.
    Robert, of Dundee, 161
    Samuel, 156
    Sarah (née Sydenham), 161
    Thomas Evans, 164, **169**
    Valentine Graeme, CMG, 164, **186,** 195, 219
    Valentine Hylton Graeme, 189, 194
    William, 161p., 166, 184, 186
    William (-1891), 168
    William (1683-), 156
Bell Brothers & Co., 162, **163**
Benson, Mary, 363
Berkeley, Sir George, 192
Besse, Joseph, 216

Bethune, Admiral Charles, 236
Bevis Marks Synagogue, 76
Bhonslah family, 169
Biddulph, Thos. J., 58
Billington, Dora, 332
Bishop of London, 209
Bishop Stuart, 333, 342
Blake, Florence (nee Trevor), 82
Blake, Sir Henry, 190p.
Blount family, 16
Board of Deputies of British Jews, 76
Board of Enquiry, 337
Boer War, 177
Bonar Law, MP,, 119
Books,
    1066 and All That, 253
    A Covert in the Storm, 18
    A First Book of Geometry, 169
    A Lecture upon Heads, 14
    A Sermon preached at Wynberg on account of the Irruption of Kaffirs into the Colony, 31
    A Warning to Secure Sinners to prepare for Judgement, 19
    Anecdotes of Painting in England, 51
    Apology for the Bible, 156
    Ayala's Angel, 364
    Back-Bencher and Chairman, 118, 126, 137
    Cataclysm, 267
    Catechism relating to the Six Days' Creation, 31
    Collection of the Sufferings of the people called Quakers, 216
    Diamonds and Coral: Anglo-Dutch Jews and Eighteenth Century Trade, 76
    Dictionary of National Biography, 44
    Encyclopaedia Britannica, 168, 263
    Eric, or Little by Little, 244
    Erskine May, 126
    Fare-Ye-Well with Ladies of the Realm, 225
    Fraser of Trinity & Achimota, 310
    From Three Worlds, 262
    Galore Park, 253
    Heaven or Hell upon Earth: a discourse on Conscience, 18
    Hints for Emigrants' Wives, 87
    Hunting of the Snark,, 253
    Memoirs of a Foxhunting Man, 341
    Moor Fires, 316
    Morning Exercise against Popery, 18
    Murder in the Cathedral, 341
    Musae Etonenses, 45
    Overseas Poetry Books, 364
    Parry's Valuation Tables, 243
    Pilgrim's Progress, 163
    Robinson Crusoe, 163
    She Stoops to Conquer, 15
    Tales of the Borders, 235
    Testament of Youth, 124
    The Age of Reason, 155
    The Annexation of the Punjab and the Maharajah Duleep Singh, 171
    The Border Farm Worker, 233
    The Conversion of a Sinner, 18
    The Conversion of the Soul, 18
    The Day of Grace, 18
    The Law as to Solicitors, 128
    The Love of the World Cured, 18

The Seamless Robe, 364
The True Touchstone, 18
The Warden, 364
Verses on the Celestial Sphere, 31
Waverley Novels, 163
What Parliament is and does, 137
Yesterday, Today and Forever, 364
Border Counties Wood Sales, Ltd., 242
Bosanquet, Lucy, 301, 303
Boston, Lucy, 226
Boswell, James, 262, 264
Botsio, Kojo (Robert Baden-Powell),
312, 348
Bowden, Mr., 175
Bravo,
    Alexandre, 198
    Charlotte Frances (nee Hylton),
    210
    Louisa Marianne Steventon (nee
    Lynch), 198
    Stephen John, 198
Bright, John, MP, 172
British Information Services, 263
British Law Insurance Company, 243
Brittain, Vera, 122
Brook, Sir Norman, 265
Brooke, Colonel Henry William, 197
Brooke, Gordon, 197
Brown, Mr., 94
Browning, Elizabeth (nee Barrett), 210
Browning, Miss, 220
Brunlees, Sir James, 186
Bubb,
    Jeremiah, 33
    Mary (nee Dodington), 33
Buccleugh,
    Henry, third Duke of, 272
Buccleugh, Dukes of, 271
Buchanan, Handasyde (Handy), 253, 260
Buchanan, Molly (nee ?), 253
Bulganin, Nikolai, 265
Bunkly, Col. John, Governor of Antigua,
216
Burne-Jones, Edward, 162
Butterfield, Richard, 4, 6, 15, 25
Byrne, Nicholas, 160

C
Cadiz Waterworks Company, 188
Caithness,
    Captain, 31
    Eliza, 31
    Pamela Holt (nee Okes), 31
Calamy, Edmund, 19
Callaghan,Cahir, 57
Cambridge University,
    Caius College, 31
    Emmanuel College, 107
    Examinations, 220
    Girton College, 169
    Homerton College, 112
    King's College, 29, 44, 120
    Public Orator, 50
    Selwyn College, 105
Camden, Earl, 156p.
Campbell, Governor, 196
Campbell, Lord William, Governor of
Nova Scotia, 213
Canadian Pacific Railway, 168
Canning, George, MP, 156
Carlyle, Thomas, 166
Casablanca Conference, 133
Central African Federation, 363
Chamberlain, Neville, MP, 130, 326
Charing Cross Hospital, 168
Chavasse, Christopher, 306
Chisholm,
    Anna Louisa (nee Bell), **168**
    Henry, 168
Chobham, Lord, 33

Christian Aid, 363
Christian martyrs, 334
Church Commissioners, 359
Church Missionary Society, 223, 324,
347
Churchill, Winston, MP, 131, 133, 136,
241, 256, 326, 370
Chute, Marchette, 50
Citrine, Lady, 361
Civil Defence, 136
Clark,
    Agnes, 229, 232, 236
    Alison (nee Wood), 232, 234
    Audrey Dorothy (nee Irwin), 246,
    251, 258, 298
    David George, 241, 251, **252,** 260,
    272, 283, 361
    Euphemia (nee Tosh), 236, 282
    George I, 231, **232**
    George II, 231, **236,** 282
    Isabella (nee Cockburn), 232
    Jane (nee McClare), 229, 236, 303
    John I, **229,** 238, 303
    John II, 241, **250,** 256p., 260p.,
    281, 283, 294
    John Malcolm, 251
    John McClare, 1p., 231, **240,**
    248p., 261p., 281, 294, 299, 314,
    328
    Kenneth Allan, **256,** 283, 294, 359
    Kenneth Nicholas, 260
    Margaret , 232
    Marion (nee Jackson), 2, 240,
    272p., **280**
    Patricia (nee Hazeldine), 253
    Patricia Ann (nee Trotter), 260
    Violet Augusta (nee Grant), 253
    William Donaldson, 3, 240, 246,
    261, 272, 283, 294p., 351, 361,
    366, 368
Clark-Lowes,
    Audrey (nee Dixon), 255
    Daniel Nicholas, 251, **254,** 260,
    283, 294, 302
    Francis, 3, 272
Clarke, Rawlins & Co., 122
Clifton-Brown, Col., MP, 134, 138
Cobb, Joan, 251
Cobbett, William, 160
Cock,
    Anne, 52
    Anne (nee Tuer), 51
Cockroft, Irene, 174
Codrington, Sir Christopher, 217
Coghlan, Mr., 288
Colditz, 258
Cole,
    Catherine, 51
    Catherine (nee Tuer), 51
    Jane, 51
    Mary, 51
    Rev. William, 51
    William, 51
College of Heralds, 76
Collins, Canon John, 363
Colonial Office, 324
Conrad, Joseph, 296
Conservative Political Centre, 149
Cooper, Miss C.R., 276
Coote, Sir Eyre, 161
Cornford, Frances, 296
Corporation of London, 208
Corty,
    Aline Johanna (nee Hofer), 200p.
    Basil Francis, 200
    Ella (nee Lynch), 199, 202
    Enriquetta (nee Hartling), 201
    Ernst Carl, **199**
    Freda , 201

Luis, 201
Cottnam,
    Martha (neé Howe), 214
    William, 214
Court of Arches, Canterbury, 80
Court of Common Pleas, 80
Cox, Katharine A., 295, 302
Creech Jones, Arthur, 363
Cresswell,
    Jane (nee Okes), 37
    Rev Francis, 37
    Rev. W., 39, 42
Cresswell, Rev. W., 42
Croker,
    Edward, 57p.
    Rachel (nee Ruddock), 57p.
Cromwell, Oliver, 55, 76
Cronje, General, 103
Cudjoe, 210
Cumberland, Duke of, 205p.

D
d'Aranyi, Jelly, 296
Dalhousie, Lord, 169, 171
Dalzell,
    Jane, 186
Danvers,
    Sir John, 49
Danvers, Mr., 68
Darien Expedition, 204
Dartmouth, Lord, 213
Darwin,
    Charles, 29
    Erasmus, 29
Daudi Chwa, Kabaka, 330, 335
Dawes, Mr., 70
de Gabay, Isaac Siprut, 75
de la Mare, Walter, 296
Denison, Rev. Herbert, 359
Denman College, 366
Derby, Lord, 44, 170
Diamond trade, 76
Dickson, Rev. R.B., 92, 220
Disraeli, Benjamin, MP, 75, 166
Dixon, William Scarth, 255, 262
Dodington,
    George, 33
    George Bubb, Lord Melcombe
    Regis, 32
    Mary (nee Beaghan), 33
Doktor,
    Dieter, 102
    Mary Macdonald (nee Herbert),
    102
Donne, John, 49p.
Doodle-Bugs, 136
Dows,
    Jane (nee Strachan), 233, 245, **246,**
    253, 295, 303
Duleep Singh, 171
Duncombe, T.,MP, 22
Dunn, Isabella (nee Jackson), 273

E
East Eureka Mining Company, 188
East India Company, 76
East, Mrs. Anne, 33
Ebsworth, Ernest, 106
Eden, Sir Anthony, MP, 264
Edgeworth, Maria, 163
Edmunds, Rev. K., 338
Elder Dempster & Co., 300
Eldon, Lord, 158
Elgiva, Princess, 208
Eliot, Thomas Stearns, 264
Ellaby, Miss, 106
Ely Diocesan Board of Finance, 109
Equity & Law Life Assurance Co., 128,
132
Estcourt, Sotheron, MP, 22

Evans, Canon, 109
Evelyn, John, 79
Evered,
    John, 67
    Mr., 67
    The Misses, 67
    W.H., 68
Exeter Cathedral, 30
Eyre, Governor, of Jamaica, 205
Eyres-Monsell, MP, 118

F

Fairbairn, Walter, 232
Fairs, John, 43
Fausset, Capt., 103
Fell, J.B., 187
Fellows, Mr., MP, 22
Fellowship of St Alban and St. Sergius, 152
Filson,
    Dr Alexander Bell, 186
    Mary (nee Bell), 186
Fisher, Kenneth, 307, 310
Fitz-Clarence, Capt.Lord Augustus,RN, 39
Fitzgerald, Lord Edward, 156
Fitzroy, Capt., MP, 128p., 134
Flying Scotsman, 260
Folk Museum, Cambridge, 35
Foot, Dingle, 363
Forbes,
    Fearne (nee Kinnear), Mrs. Aytoun, 183
    James, 183
Forester Friendly Society, 274
Fox, Charles James, 159
Francia, Dr., Dictator of Paraguay, 40, 44
Franco,
    Abraham (1681-1777), 76, 82
    Abraham II, 75p.
    David, 77
    Jacob, 75p.
    Joseph, 76
    Leah (nee d'Aguilar), 77
    Moses (1700-), 76
    Ralph, 77
    Raphael, 76
    Simha (nee Franco), 76
    Solomon, 76
Fraser, Alexander, 310
Fraser, Andrew, 300
Fraser, Mr & Mrs.A.G., 350
Fraser, P.A., 190
Fraser, Rev. A.G., 306, 308, 310p., 323, 362p.
Free Gardeners, 274
Fry, Roger, 296
Fry, Vanessa (nee Clark), 260
Fudge, John, 68

G

Galant, Mary, 231
Gardiner, Dr. John, 183
Garibaldi, 187
Garrick Club, 168
Garrick, David, 14
Gebrüder Volkart, 202
Gibbons, Grinling, 78
Gillum,
    Leonora Georgiana (nee Bell), **174**
    William James, 174
Gold Coast Government, 324
Gold Standard, 117
Goldsmith, Oliver, 15
Goldwyer, Mr., 65
Goodhart,
    Celia McClare (nee Herbert), Lady, 226, 267, 324, 329, 341, 366, 368
    William Howard, Lord, 366
Goodluck, 349

Gordon,
    Elizabeth (nee Mackenzie), 206
    Larchin, 206
Gordon, George W., 205
Gough, Dr., 314
Gourlay, James, 246
Governor's Advisory Council on Education, 333
Grace, Canon Myers, 315, 330p., 339
Gray,
    Anne (nee Cock), 52
    Joseph, 37, 52
Greaves, "Tim" & Mrs., 332
Greaves, L.B. ("Tim"), 339, 346p.
Grevile,
    Anne (nee Whippin), 61, 65
    Edward, 61
    Elizabeth, 61, 68
    Mary, 61
    Rev. Edward Colston, 60p., 68
    Sally, 61
Grey, Bishop Robert, 88
Grout,
    William, 7
Gully Gully Man, 327

H

Hahn, Kurt, 362p.
Halbert family, 252
Halifax, Lord, 263
Hall, Gertrude Octavia (nee Jackson), 273
Haltwhistle Mechanics' Institute, 235, 366
Haltwhistle Rural District Council, 252
Hamand, Margaret, 224, 335, 340
Harbottle,
    Bridget, 6
    Christopher, 6
    Cornelius, 7
    Dennis I, (Cordwainer), 6
    Edward, 5
    Edward (1619-), 6
    Henry, 6
    Joan (nee ?), 5
    John, 7
    Martha (nee Smith), 5p.
    Mary, 6
    Mary (-1695), 15
    Name change, 8
    Ralph, 5p.
    Robert, 6
    Valentine, 6
    William, 7
    Zachary, 5
    Zachary (1621-), 6
Hardwicke, Lord, 21
Harewood, Lord, 316
Harmonists' Glee Club, 162
Harper, Mr., 351
Hart,
    Frances Alicia (nee Okes), 31
    Major Henry George, 31
    Sir Reginald Clare, VC, 32
Hartling, Mr., 201
Harvey, David, 267
Hawtrey, Dr., 45
Haydon Foxhounds, 242
Haynes,
    Catherine (nee Franco), 79
    Daniel, 79
    Daniel Franco, 79
    David Franco, 79
    Edward, 80
    Elizabeth (Betsey), 82
    Elizabeth (née Marshall), 82
    Flora, 80
    Mary, 80
    Rev. David, 82
    William Richard, 79

Heesom, Dudley, 262
Herbert,
    Admiral, 8
    Amy (nee Jarvis), 104, 137
    Anna (nee Vincent, 8
    Anna (nee Vincent), 19
    Anne (nee Pateman), 20
    Caroline, 26, 90, 97, 107, 144
    Caroline, of Toronto, 102
    Charles Henry, 100
    Cornelius Pateman, 15, 25
    Coronation Picture, 372
    Dennis (of Huntingdon), 22, 24, 28, 86, 90p.
    Dennis George Ruddock, 2, 112, 122, 127, 133, 138, 147, 194, 220, 226, 245, 251, **287**, 294, 297, 370p., 374
    Dennis Henry, 1pp., 45, 48, 67, 84, 94, 107, **117**, 198, 220, 251, 288, 299, 306, 315, 342
    Dennis I (Cordwainer), 9
    Dennis II, 8, 19
    Dennis III (Actor-Manager), 8, 19, 24
    Dennis IV, 9, 15, 20, 25
    Dennis Nicholas, 313, 366, 369
    Edward Grevile, 93, **99**, 108, 121, 360
    Elizabeth (1728-), 10
    Elizabeth McClare (nee Clark), 2, 241, 245, 251, 272, 283, **294**, 369
    Emma, 90
    General Dennis (1771-1861), 25
    George, 93, **105**, 115p.
    George (1766-1806), 25
    George, the poet, 48, 50
    Hemingford, Lord, 134
    Henrietta Dorothea (nee Begg), 102
    Henry Myles, 102, 107, 109
    Henry, Master of the King's Revels, 50
    Herbert of Chirbury, Lord, 48, 50
    Jane (nee Anstruther), 25
    Janet (nee Wigram), 147p.
    Jennifer Mary Toresen (nee Bailey), 366
    Kathleen (nee Robertson), 111
    Kathleen Emily (nee Reeves), 105
    Kenneth Falkner, 107
    Louis William, 93, **102**, 107, 137, 222
    Madeline (nee King), **107**, 108, 110
    Magdalen (nee Newport), **49**, 50, 54
    Mary (nee Fisher), 10
    Mary (nee Okes), 22, 28, 37, 46, 52, 90
    Mary (nee Perkins), 21, 26
    Mary (nee Ruddock), 71, 82, 89, 95, 97p., 220, 289, 315
    Mary Graeme (nee Bell), 2p., 97, 122, 143, 148p., 189, 198, 204, 208, **219**, 227p., 287, 298, 303, 313
    Muriel Fanny C. (nee Stewart), 106
    Name change, 8
    Nathaniel, 10
    Nathaniel (1726-), 10, 13
    Nathaniel Vincent (1780-1844), 25
    Olive Una (nee Linton), 99
    Oliver Hayley Dennis, 143, 145, **148,** 221, 303, 326
    Philip, 4th Earl of Pembroke, 48
    Rev. Francis Falkner, 93, 100, **106**, 115
    Rev. Henry, 22, 24, 67, 82, 84, 86, 98, 107, 147, 175, 220, 229, 288
    Richard, 49p., 93

Richard Charles, 93, **105**
Robert John Grevile, 122, 148, 221, **222**, 298, 309, 330
Rosemary (nee Bate), 152
Rosemary Anne (nee Herbert), 144
Sir Richard, of Colebrook, 50
Susan Jean, 144
Sylvia Valentine (nee Herbert), 146
Thomas, 50
Timothy William Okes, 144
Valentine Henry Okes, 122, 135, 138, **142**, 194, 220, 287, 302, 351
William, 21, 50, 52, 86
William (-1833), 31, 86
William, 3rd Earl of Pembroke, 48
Winifred Mabel (nee Pearson), 133, 143, 146, 149p., **224**, 226, 302
Hetherington, Susan Elizabeth (nee Clark), 251
Hexham Board of Health, 271
Hicks,
    Sarah (nee Herbert), 26
Higginson, Joseph, 161
Higgs-Walker, J.A., 307
Higham, C.S.S., 354
Hillier, Ellis, 337, 339
Hindenburg Line, 240
Hitler, Adolph, 130
Hoffer, Mrs., 267
Hogarth Club, 174
Holkar, Maharajah of, 171
Hollyman, Justinian, 215
Holyoake, George Jacob, 173
Honourable East India Company, 156, 161, 169
Hooper, Rev. Handley, 324, 338p.
Hope , James, MP, 128
Hope-Wallace,
    family, 229
    James, 234
    John George Frederick, 234
    Mary, 236
Hopetoun, Earl of, 229, 233
Hopkins,
    Ann (1784-) (nee Okes), 37
Houses,
    15, Langley Way, Watford, 149, 225
    36, Woburn Place, London, 166
    Abbey View, Hexham, 275
    Allens Green, Hexham, 254
    Ardmore, Watford, 287
    Ashcroft, Haltwhistle, 243, 245, 249
    Bellister Castle, Haltwhistle, 240, 243, 256, 258, 274, **275**
    Bramston House, 250, 254, 261, 290
    Cargilfield, Edinburgh, 182, 184
    Carntyne, Hexham, 275
    Christiansborg Castle, 355
    Cinnamon Hill, Jamaica, 210
    Clarendon Lodge, Watford, 127, 136, 223, 313
    Coach House, Hemingford Abbots, 369
    Cumberland Union Bank, Haltwhistle, 234
    Dovenby Estate, Cockermouth, 236, 281
    Edens Lawn, Haltwhistle, 235
    Farenough, 206
    Featherstone Castle, Haltwhistle, 229p., 233, 239
    Hallbankhead, 229, 233, **252**, 359
    Highford Farm, Hexham, 274
    Hinchingbrooke, 362
    Hylton Castle, 207, 211
    Kelmscott Manor, 177

Laundimer House, 251, 290
Little Marble Hill, 77
Littlecote, 226
Livingstone House, Achimota, 311
Lonesome Lodge, **77**, 83
Manderston, Duns, 234
Muckross Abbey, Killarney, 26
Netherton, Hexham, 275
No 1 Pembridge Place, Kensington, 177
No 36, Lower Tewin, Herts., 152
No. 16 Scarsdale Villas, Kensington, 122, 287
Rock House, Washington, Sussex, 246
Sheepbrook, Watlington, 265
St. Audrey's, Hatfield, 153
The Old Rectory, Hemingford Abbots, 96, 226, 367, 369
The Paragon, Blackheath, 254
The Tyddyn, Mold, 144, 146
Wimpole Hall, 21
Withywood, Carlisle Bay, Jamaica, 210
Howard,
    Caprt. Edward Henry, 198
    Midshipman Edward John, 198
    Sophia Caroline Lucille (nee Lynch), 198, 219
Hughes, Prof., 45
Hunnybun, Mr., 45
Huntingdon Brewery, 21, 91
Huntingdonshire Conservative Association, 368
Huntingdonshire County Council, 363p.
Huxley, Aldous, 296
Huxley, Julian, 335
Hylton,
    Charlotte Frances, 197
    Henry, 207p.
    Margaret (nee Campbell), 210
    Mary Pool (nee Johnson), 197, 209
    Mehitabel (nee Lawrence), 208, 218
    Nathaniel, 208
    Ralph, 208
    Samuel Barrett, 197, 209
    William, 197, 207p.
Hylton-Hylton,
    Gladys (nee Bravo), 194, 198
    Muriel (nee Bravo), 194, 198

I

Inland Revenue, 370
Inns of Court,
    Lincoln's Inn, 17
Institute of Civil Engineers, 188
Institution of Chartered Surveyors, 242
International Institute for Environment and Development, 266
Ireton, General Henry, 56
Isle of Ely County Council, 112
Isle of Ely Society for the Blind, 112

J

J.M.Clark & Sons, 237, 251, 260, 300
Jackson,
    Charles Strathnairn, 273, **277**
    Daniel, 4, 241, **270**, 281
    Daniel Noel, 247, 273, **277**, 282
    Donaldson Bell, 273, 276, **277**
    Edythe, 273
    George Scott, 273, **277**
    Isabella (nee Scott), 3p., **271**, 281
    James, 271
    Jane, 241, 273
    John, 271
    John Archibald, 273, 275, **277**, 282
    Robert, 273
Jackson, Adeline, 120

Jackson, F.S., Governor of Bengal, 128
Jackson, Mr., 52
Jacobites, 7
Jacobsen, Theodore, 78
James, Henry, 296
James, William, 296
Janojeeh, 169
Jenkins, Sir Leoline, 51
Jensen, Maria (nee Corty), 201
Jodl, General Alfred, 258
John Summers & Sons, 144
Johnson,
    Christian (nee Barrett), 209p.
    Jacob, 209
Johnson, Dr. Samuel, 262, 264
Joseph, Mr., 318

K

Kabaka's Party, 339
Kaffir Wars, 87
Kahan, Gerald, 14
Kayneth, Christopher, Governor of Antigua, 215
Kent,
    Kent, John, 105
    Mary Ruddock (nee Herbert), 105
Kent, Duke & Duchess of, 316
Keregan's Company, 11
Keynes, Maynard, 263
Keys, Lady, 361
Khruschev, Nikita, 265
Kinder, Ellen, 222
King's College, London, 168
King's College Hospital, 167p.
Kinnear,
    Alexander Smith, 183
    David, 184
    Elizabeth Fearne, 162
    Fearne (nee Gardiner), 182
    Fearne (nee Kinnear), 184
    George, 162, 183p.
    James, 183
    John Gardiner, 183p.
    Thomas, 184
Kipling, Rudyard, 162, 244
Kitchener, Lord, 103
Knight,
    John, 67
Knox, General John, 157
Koch, Robert, 273
Kpeglo, Mr., 317
Kumasi College of Technology, 349

L

Land Agents' Society, 252
Landowska, Wanda, 296
Langford,
    Anne (nee?), 217
    Jonas, **215**
    Mehitabel, 217
Lattman, Frau, 281
Laufen P.O.W. camp, 258
Law Fire Insurance Office, 167
Law Society, 128
Lawrence,
    Daniel, 218
    Mary (nee Redwood), 218
Lea, Governor of Antigua, 216
Legge, Francis, Governor of Nova Scotia, 213
Lennox, Nancy, 226
Lewes,
    Charles Lee, 12, 15
Linton, Rev. George, 99
Livery Companies,
    Bricklayers, 7
    Clockmakers, 7
    Cordwainers, 7
    Feltmakers, 7
    Grocers, 251

Haberdashers, 7
Lloyd George, David, MP, 119
Local Government Board, 274
Lockhart,
    Marion (nee Kinnear), 183
Lockhart, Robert, 183
London,
    Great Fire, 8
London Government Staff Commission,
    1963-65, 364
Longmans Green & Co., 351, 354
Lopes, Sir Massey, 77
Lords Cricket Ground, 120
Lucas, F.L., 262
Ludlum, Mr., 43
Lukiko (Council of Chiefs), 323
Lukin, Henry, 10
Lumpkin,
    Antony, 15
    John, 15
Lynch,
    Eliza (nee Turner), 197, 199
    Francis George Mackinnon, 199
    Francis Robertson, 189, 197, 199,
        210
    Georgina Johnson (nee Hylton),
        197
    John, 197
    Larchin, 197
    Mark, **196**, 219
    Mary Larchin (nee Gordon), 196,
        206
    Maud (nee Isaacs), 199
    Nora, 122, 198
    Robert B., 199
    William, 198

M

Macdonald, Malcolm, 324
Macdonald, Ramsey, MP, 117, 194
Mackenzie,
    Alexander, of Darien, Bt., 204p.
    Arthur, 206
    George, 205
    George, Bt., 206
    Janet (nee Linen), 205
    John, 205
    Mackenzie of Gairloch, Bt., 205
    Mackenzie of Scatwell, Bt., 205
    Mary (nee Jenners), 206
    Sir James Dixon, 206
Maddison, Pamela, 224, 303
Magnetic mines, 324
Magnus, George Eugene, 172
Maguire, Paddy, 351, 356
Maharaja Gaikwar of Baroda, 128
Makerere College, 346
Malcolm, Sir Ian, 45
Mallet, Major, 216
Marshall, James, 91
Marshalsea Prison, 16
Mary, Princess, 316
Maurice, F.D., 167
Maurice, Prince of Orange, 208
Mawdsley & Daking, cheesemongers, 52
McClare,
    Agnes (nee Gourlay), 229, 233
McNamara, Robert S., 266
Mercantile Marine Service Association,
    105
Messrs. Wren and Hopkinson,
    Manchester, 186
Military Units,
    14th Indian Jungle Training
        Division, 148
    1st Hertfordshire Regiment, 142
    1st Punjab Regiment, 148
    23rd L.A.A. Regiment, Royal
        Artillery, 145
    23rd Parachute L.A.A., Anti-Tank

Regiment, 135
2nd Flotilla Motor Torpedo Boats,,
    252
2nd Madras Europeans, 169
45th Foot,, 213
4th Battalion, Royal
    Northumberland Fusiliers, 242,
    251, 254, 256
69th East Anglian Division, 107
7th Battalion, Royal
    Northumberland Fusiliers, 277
83rd Regiment of Foot, 29
British Expeditionary Force, 256
Calcutta Light Horse, 143
Cape Mounted Rifles, 88
Egyptian Coastguard Service, 95,
    106
Eighth Army, 254
Indian Airborne Division, 145
Legion of Frontiersmen, 334
Madras Artillery, 161
Natal Carbineers, 177
Observer Corps, 112
Queen's Regiment, 148
Rifle Brigade, 95
Royal Artillery, 179
Royal Flying Corps, 95
Royal Welch Fusiliers, 145
South Lancashire Regiment, 95,
    104
Territorial Army, 142
Wynberg & Simon's Town
    Volunteers, 88
Mills,
    Dr. Herbert, 174
    Dr. Hermia, 174
    Ernestine (nee Bell), 174
Mills, Sir John, 177, 224
Milton, John, 368
Ministry of Agriculture, 264
Moggridge,
    Catherine Grevile (nee Herbert),
        152, 334, 341, 347, 366
    Harry Traherne, 366
    Moggridge family, 369
Monarchs,
    Charles I, 51
    Charles II, 271
    Elizabeth II, 361
    Ethelread, 208
    George III, 64, 156
    George IV, 64, 81, 162
    George V, 261
    George VI, 45, 337, 351
    James I, 7
    James II, 18, 57
    Queen of Norway, 316
    Queen Victoria, 162, 200, 220
    Tsar Nicholas II, 240
    William and Mary, 8
    William III, 57
    William IV, 38, 162, 179
Montague, Donald, 4
Montgomery, General Bernard, 256
Montgomery, James, 233
Moran, Lady, 361
Morris, 251, 256
Morris, J., 158
Morris, William, 174
Mountayne, Arthur, 7
Mt. Cenis Railway, 186
Munro, Bullock & Lynch, 197
Murray, Gilbert, 363
Mutesa, Kabaka Edward, 330, 333, 336,
    367
Mwanga, Kabaka, 334
Mysore, Maharajah of, 173

N

Nagle,

Family, 56
Sir Richard, 57
Napoleonic Wars, 242
Nasser, Gamel Abdel, President, 367
National Portrait Gallery, 51
Naval Knights of Windsor, 37p.
Naworth Coal Company, **243**
Nene & Welland Fisheries Board, 112
Newcastle and Gateshead Water
    Company, 242
Newspapers,
    Africa Bureau, 364
    Cambridge Chronicle, 52
    Cambridge Independent Press and
        Chronicle, 21
    Carlisle Patriot, 235
    Catholic Herald, 369
    Cork Reporter, 163
    Daily Gleaner, 193
    Dumfries & Galloway Advertiser,
        143
    Estates Gazette, 237
    Gentleman's Magazine, 15
    Haltwhistle Echo, 2, 237, 247, 258
    Hexham Courant, 235, 274
    Hexham Herald, 234
    Hunts Post, 94p.
    Indian Spectator, 173
    Morning Post, 159p.
    Norwich Mercury, 11
    Notes and Queries, 23
    Observer, 263, 266, 369
    Pastime, 276
    Sheffield Iris, 233
    Spectator, 151
    St. Jago Gazette, 209
    The Policy-Holder, 129
    The Statesman of India, 171, 173
    The Times, 147
    Time and Tide, 124
    Time Magazine, 178
    Tribune, 173
    Watford Observer, 138
    West Herts Post, 124
Nicholson, Dr. John, 273
Nicholson, Isaac, 184
Nightingale, Florence, 174
Nightingale, Ruth Irwin (nee Clark), 251
Nkrumah, Kwame (Francis), 312, 348p.,
    367p.
Noblett, Joan Aileen, 260
Noblett, Miss, 56
Norfolk, Duke of, 79, 159, 233, 361
Norman, Sir Henry, 189
Northern Rock Building Society, 261
Norwich Union, 261

O

O'Brien, Capt., 43
O'Coigly, or Quigley, James, 157
O'Connor, Arthur, 156, 159, 162
O'Donovan, Patrick, 369
Oddfellows, 274
Okes,
    Ann (nee Gray), 3, 37, 48, 52, 86
    Ann Otto (nee Bayer), 31
    Augusta (nee Butcher), 31
    Caroline, 38
    Charles, 44
    Dr. Richard, DD, 44, 46
    Elizabeth (1785-1787), 37
    Elizabeth (nee Scott), 31
    Ellen (nee Short), 31
    Francis, 39, 43
    Francis (1786), 37
    George (1780-), 37
    Henry, 37, 39
    Henry Matson Robert, 32
    Holt, 32
    Holt, Rev., 86p., 90

John, 29, 38
John Thomas, 31
Lieut. Charles, RN, 37
Lieut. William, RN, 37
Margaret, 90
Margaret (1806-1854), 31
Mary (nee Sibthorpe), 45
Mary (nee Verney), 32
Mary Anne, 37
Nancy (nee ?), 32
Pamela Holt, 31
Patricia (nee Busby), 31, 87, 90
Persis, 38
Peter Thomas Walter (1792-1793), 38
Portia Victoria Pamela, 32
Rebecca Lydia (nee Butcher), 30, 87
Richard, 38, 86, 90, 120
Robert, 87
Robert Frederick, 31
Robert John, 30
Sarah (1791- 1793), 37
Sarah (nee Lloyd), 29
Thomas, 29
Thomas (1781-), 37
Thomas (1782-), 37
Thomas Holt Edward, 31
Thomas Verney, 22, **33**, 48, 52
William, 31
William Samuel, 31
Oliver,
    Anne (nee Ruddock), 68
    William, 67
Oskenonton, 296
Overseas Development Institute, 266
Oxford Group, 254
Oxford University,
    Balliol College, 254, 302
    Christchurch, 17
    Corpus Christi, 17
    Oriel College, 261, 267
    St. John's College, 69
    Trinity College, 60, 71
    Wadham College, 85, 120, 148
    Worcester College, 85
    Wycliffe College, 254
Oxford University Missionary Campaign, 306
Oyer and Terminer, Court of, 158

P

Painters,
    Brown, Ford Madox, 174, 177
    Gainsborough, 77
    Harcourt, George, R.A., 129, 136
    Herkomer,Sir Hubert von, 45
    Porter, Robert Ker, 161
    Raeburn, Henry, 182
    Rosetti, Dante Gabriel, 174
    Shields, Frederic, 174
    Solomon, Simeon, 173
Pakenham, Lady, 363
Parishes,
    All Saints, Huntingdon, 21
    Billingshurst, Sussex, 208
    Dodington, 60
    Easton-in-Gordano, 60
    Farthing Alley, Southwark, 17
    Fugglestone and Bemerton, Wilts., 50
    Great Waldingfield, Suffolk, 39
    Harkstead and Erwarton, 90
    Hartford, Huntingdon, 37
    Holy Cross, Haltwhistle, 241, 247
    Knaresdale, 231
    Langley Marsh, 16
    Lavenham, Suffolk, 31
    Leighton Bromswold, Huntingdonshire, 50

Lilbourne, Northants, 199
Marlow, Bucks, 107
Mutford and Barnby, Suffolk, 31
Oakwood chapelry, 79
Sedgefield, Co.Durham, 17
Seer Green, Bucks., 90
St Bartholomew the Great, 26
St Mary Abbots, Kensington, 220
St Mary, the Virgin, Primrose Hill, 152
St Mary's, Huntingdon, 21
St Mary's, Reading, 91
St Paul's Cathedral, 163
St Peter's Droitwich, 10
St Stephen's, Bristol, 64, 66
St Thomas the Apostle, Exeter, 31
St. Andrew's, Half Way Tree, 189
St. Botolph, Lincoln, 15
St. Giles, Camberwell, 8
St. John's, Watford, 134
St. Margaret of Scotland, New Galloway, 143
St. Margaret's, Hemingford Abbots, 22, 91, 113, 226
St. Mary's, Swansea, 197
St. Michael's, Cambridge, 38
St. Nicholas, Bristol, 57
St. Olave's , Southwark, 6
St. Paul's, Quarndon, 147
St. Stephen's, Bristol, 60
Stockland Gaunts als. Stockland Bristol, 60
Waldingfield, Suffolk, 37
West Wratting, Cambs., 37
Westbury-cum-Priddy, 71
Wheatacre, Norfolk, 31
Withcall, Lincs., 10
Wotton, Surrey, 79
Wynberg, South Africa, 30
Parsons, Betty, **297**, 341, 348, 359, 361, 367
Pattle,
    Col. W., CB, 32
    Isabella Clara (nee Okes), 32
Patton, General, 259
Pearson,
    Jack, 143
    Pearson, Lady, 143
    Sir Herbert, 143
Peel,
    General, 22
    Sir Robert, 22
Pembroke & Tenby Railway, 186
Pembroke, Earls of, 23
Penn, Admiral, 210
Perkins, John, 21
Pimlico Enamelled Slate Works, 172
Player, Sister, 314
Plowden, George, 170
Ponsonby, Lord, 171
Pooler, Louie, 241, 243, **244**, 245, 252
Portland, Duke of, 156p.
Powley, Edward, 4
Poynter,
    Louisa (nee Bell), 162
    Sir Edward, 162
Praed, William Mackworth, 44
Prince Consort, 172
Prince of Wales, 316
Prins, Maud Marion (nee Clark), 251
Privy Council of Great Britain, 129
Psychical Research Society, 255
Public Houses,
    George Hotel, Huntingdon,, 366
    Ramsholt Arms, 55
    Red Lyon, Godmanchester, 21
    Rose & Crown, Godmanchester, 21
    The Jolly Waterman, Cambridge, 46

Wallace Arms, 252
White Horse Inn, Baldock, 14
Wootton Hatch, 78
Pusey, 44

Q

Queen Caroline, 64

R

Raghuji III, Rajah of Nagpore, 169
Ranjitsinhji, 128
Rankin, Sir George, 144
Redwood,
    Abraham, 217
    Abraham, Jr., 218
    Jonas Langford, 218
Redwood Library, Newport, R.I.,, 218
Relief of Kimberley, 103
Rendell, Peter, 355
Rhondda, Lady, 122
Richards, Rev. M., 62
Richardson, Celia, 303
Rijksmuseum, Holland, 51
Ripon, Lord, 191
Roach, John, 78
Roberts, Lord, 103
Roberts, Mona, 226
Robertson,
    John Parish, 39, 41, 43
    William Parish, 40
Robertson, James Shaftoe, 13
Robinson, Elsie, 331
Robinson, Mr. "Robbie", 332, 342
Roborough, Lord, 77
Robson, Michael, 233
Rockett, Mrs., 63
Rodriguez,General, 41
Roman Catholics,
    Irish Roman Catholics, 156
    Papal Gold Medal, 126
    Pope Pius XI, 126
    Roman Catholic Relief Bill, 126
Romanis, Rev., 91, 96
Romsey, Jane, 78
Royal College of Music, 143
Royal College of Physicians, Edinburgh, 183
Royal College of Surgeons, 30
Royal Humane Society, 35
Royal Institution of Chartered Surveyors, 252
Royal Naval College, Greenwich, 254
Royal Society for the Arts, 46
Ruddock,
    Abigail (nee Barry), 57
    Andrew, 56, 63
    Andrew II, 56
    Andrew III, 57
    Andrew IV, 58
    Ann, 58
    Ann (nee Wharton), 57
    Anne (nee Grevile), 59
    Arthur Edward Vyvyan (1833-), 71
    Captain Andrew, 55, 210
    Catherine 1817-), 65
    Catherine (nee Creagh), 57
    Catherine (nee Stawell), 57
    Charles, 63
    Charles Edward (1850), 71
    Dorothy (nee Hardwick), 72
    Edward Grevile, 60, 71
    Edward Noblett (1847-), 71
    Edward Stanley Colston Grevile (1852-), 71
    Elizabeth Mary Gertrude (1844-), 71
    Emma (nee Haynes), 71, 82
    Emma Mary (1840-), 71
    Evelyn (nee ?), 72
    Evelyne (nee ?), 72

Fanny Mary (1843-), 71
Grevile, 70
Hannah Wall, 57
Hester "Hettie" (nee Yeld), 72
John, 62p., 69
John (1773-1773), 58
John, "of Ballylunger", 57
Kathleen Gertrude (nee Fry), 72
Lucy Mary (1837-), 71
Mary Ann, 68
Mary Anne (1815-), 60
Mary Emily (1842-), 71
Montague Alleyne Grevile, 72
Montague Grevile (1839-), 71
Noblett (1804-1823), 59
Noblett I, 57
Noblett II, 58p.
Reginald Colston Grevile (1848-), 71
Rev. Edward Grevile, 82
Rev. N.H.C., 220
Rev. Reginald, 72
Richard, 65
Sarah Amy (nee Hay), 72
Wall family, 57
William, 66
William, injured in fire, 69
Russell, Lord John, 159
Russian Revolution, 240
Rysbrack, 78

S
Saltmarsh, John, 45
Sampson, C.H., 307
Sanderson, F.W., 250, 289p., 306, 331
Sandwich, Lord, 22, 27
Schools,
    Collegiate School, Cape Town, 89
    Dartmouth College, 252
    Durham School, 260
    Eton College, 86
    Gartlet School, 223
    Gordonstoun, 362p.
    Haberdashers' Aske, 255
    Hayes Court, Bromley, 295, 301
    Industrial Home for Destitute Boys, 174
    King's College, Budo, 315, 323, 330, 346
    King's School, Ely, 84, 105, 120
    Montrose Academy, 231
    Oundle, 137, 142, 148, 254, 261, 288, 290, 307, 351, 355, 362
    Prince of Wales, Achimota, 306, 323, 340, 346
    Radley College, 89
    Revd. M.P. Richards's, Tiverton, 62
    Seafield, Bexhill-on-Sea, 288
    Sevenoaks, 307
    Shirley House, Watford, 288
    Shrewsbury, 255
    St. Michael's, Limpsfield, 355
    The Beehive School, Windsor, 219
    The Boys' Farm Home, 175
    Trinity College, Kandy, 323
Scott,
    Ann (nee Heads), 272
    Francis, 271p.
    George, 271, **272**
    Jane (nee Bell), 271
    Margaret, 272
Scott, Rev. Michael, 363
Scott, Sir Walter, 163, 183
Scottish National Gallery, 182
Segovia, 296
Seven Years War, 29, 213
Shelley,
    Harriet (nee ?), 80
    Mary, 80
    Mary (nee Wollstonecraft), 80

Percy Bysshe, 44, 80
Sir Timothy, Bt., 80
Shelley, Lady, 208
Shelton Iron, Steel & Coal Co., 146
Sheridan, Richard Brinsley, 159
Shipley, Beatrice, (nee ?), Mrs. Bell, 194
Shipley, Robert M., 194
Ships,
    City of Poonah, 169
    Gambia, 30
    H.M.S. Conway, 105
    H.M.S. Edinburgh, 252
    H.M.S. King George V, 253
    H.M.S. Raccoon, 198
    H.M.S. Royal Oak, 252
    H.M.S. Royal Sovereign, 253
    H.M.S. Vampire, 245
    Jane Gordon, 43
    Lavinia, 43
    M.V. Appapa, 356
    Scharnhorst, 253
Sibthorpe,
    Allen, 45
    MaryElizabeth (nee Okes), 38
Six Point Group, 122
Smart,
    Mary Ann (nee Okes), 31
    Pamela Holt (nee Okes), 31
Smart, Sir George, 162
Smith,
    Clement, 5
    Elizabeth (nee?), 5
    Jo Mackrill, 177
Smith, James, 94
Smiths Gore, 243
Snowden, Philip, 117
Society of Friends, 218
Soke of Peterborough, 364
Solomon, 296
Sparrow, Lady Olivia, 91
Speke, John Hanning, 334
Spiliopolou, Ursula Sarah (nee Clark), 260
Stawell,
    Rachel (nee Ruddock), 57
Stephenson, General, 103
Sterk, Mr., 32
Stevens,
    Elizabeth (nee Herbert), 14, 25
    George Alexander, 14, 25
Strawbridge, Mrs., 33
Stuart, James, MP, 131
Student Christian Movement, 306
Suez War, 1956, 265
Sutherland, Duke of, 187
Swatman, Mr.A.H., 24
Sweeting,
    Harriet, 67
Swinburne, Algernon, 296
Swinnerton, Lord, 212

T
Tagore, Rabindranath, 319
Tawney, R.H., 263
Taylor, Mrs., 136
Tedder, Air Chief Marshal, 259
Tennyson, Alfred Lord, 166
Test Act (1672), 21
Theatres,
    Drury Lane, 14
    Moot-Hall, Newcastle-on-Tyne, 11
    Sheffield, 13
Thomas Coram Foundation, 78
Three Mullets, 23
Tivoli Gardens, Copenhagen, 223
Tondo, 336
Tonge,
    Caleb, 212
    Captain Winckworth, 212
    Frances (nee Fitzherbert-Richards),

212
    Maria (nee Mackglashan), 214
    Martha (nee Cottnam), 214
    Rebecca, 212
    Rev. Caleb, 212
    William, 212
    William Cottnam , 214
    William Sheriffe, 214
Trades Unions, 135
Travers, Samuel, 38
Tree, Lambert, 8
Trevor,
    Florence (nee Blake), 82
    James O'Hara, 80
    Margaret, 82
Tuer,
    Catherine (nee Vaughan), 51
    Elizabeth (nee van Heymenbergh), 51
    Herbert, 51, 53
    Mary (nee van Gammeren), 51, 53
    Theophilus, 51, 53
Turner,
    Eliza, 194
    Sophia (nee Tonge), 214
Turner, Brig. William,, 147
Turner, George, 333
Tyler, Captain, 188

U
Uganda Government, 324
United Irish Society, 156
United Nations, 368
United Presbyterian Church, 232
University of the Gold Coast, 348

V
van Millingen,
    Evelyn, 277
    Kathleen (nee Jackson), 277
Vane, Willie, Lord Inglewood, 241, 300
Vaughan,
    Margaret (nee Herbert), 48, 51
    Owen, 51
Venables, General, 210
Vernon, Anne (Martha Naish), 3
Victoria & Albert Museum, 79
Victory Services Club, 152
Vincent,
    Anna (nee ?), 16
    John, 17
    Rev. Nathaniel, 8, 16, 19
    Thomas I, 17
    Thomas II, 17
Voltaire, 33

W
Wales, Prince of, 363
Wall,
    James, 57
    Robert, 57
Waller, General, 55
Wallis, J., 158
Walpole, Horace, 51, 77
Walters, Lucy, 271
Walton, Izaak, 49p.
War Agriculture Department, 251
War of Spanish Succession, 76
War of the Axe, 87
Ward, Dame Barbara, Lady Jackson, 266
Ward, W.E.F., 310, 312
Warner,
    Thomas, "India", 216
    Warner, Philip, Governor of Antigua, 216
Water Souchy, 78
Watford Conservative Mixed Choir, 223
Watts, Sybil, 106
Wayte, John, 8
Webb, Philip, 174, 177
Wellingtonia tree, 93

Wells, Samuel, 21
Welsh, Frances (nee Jackson), 273, 281
Wentworth, Sir John, Governor of Novia
Scotia, 214
West Herts. Divisional Conservative
Association, 119
White, Rev. H.M., 89
Whitely, James, 13
Wigram, Rev. Gerrard, 147
Wilde, Cecilia (nee Bell), 179
Wilde, Rev. Oscar Wade, 179
Wilkinson, Dorothy, 356
Will, Mr. & Mrs., 144
Willan, Agnes Nona (nee Jackson), 273

Williamson, Sister, 314
Wimbledon Singles Final, 276
Wisdom, Henry, 210
Witten, Mary, **300**
Wolfe, General, 213
Women's Institute, 366
Women's Voluntary Service, 130, 224
Wood,
    John, 232
    Mary (nee Lidgate), 232
Wood, Col., 256
Woodcock, Elizabeth, 33, 35
Woodhouse, Charles, 303
Woolf, Virginia, 296

World Bank, 266
World War I, 242
World War II, 252
Wright, Stephen, 330

Y

Yeats, W.B., 296, 319
Yogev, Gedalia, 76
York, Duke and Duchess of, 316
Young,
    Frank, 169
    Grace (nee Chisholm), 168
    William, 169
Young, E.H., 316
Young, T.J., 242

Printed in the United Kingdom
by Lightning Source UK Ltd.
134189UK00002BB/7/P